Fo
LEAGUE

POCKET ANNUAL 1998-99

Bruce Smith

1st Year of Publication

Football League Pocket Annual 1998-99

Copyright © Bruce Smith – Author 1998

ISBN: 0-7535-0217-8

The right of Bruce Smith to be identified as the Author of the Work has been asserted by him in accordance with the *Copyright, Designs and Patents Act 1988*.

First published August 1998 by
Virgin Publishing

Virgin Publishing Limited
Thames Wharf Studios
Rainville Road
London, W6 9HT

Typeset by Bruce Smith

All rights reserved. No part of this publication may be reproduced, stored in a retrieval system, or transmitted, in any form or by any means, without prior permission in writing of the publisher, nor be otherwise circulated in any form of binding or cover other than that in which it is published and without a similar condition including this condition being imposed on the subsequent purchaser.

Contact Bruce Smith at:

Bruce Smith,
PO Box 382, St Albans,
Herts, AL2 3JD

email: Bruce-Smith@msn.com

Disclaimer

In a book of this type it is inevitable that some errors will creep in. While every effort has been made to ensure that the details given in this annual are correct at the time of going to press, neither the editor nor the publishers can accept any responsibility for errors within.

We welcome comments, corrections and additions to this annual. Please send them to Bruce Smith at the address opposite or email them direct to him at: Bruce-Smith@msn.com

Printed by: Caledonian International Books, Glasgow, Scotland.

This is not an approved nor an official publication of the Football League.

CONTENTS

Pocket Annual Guide 5
At a Glance 97-98 7
Premier League and Vauxhall Conference Final Tables 1997-98 8

Nationwide League Division 1
Final Table 9
Season Review 11
Play-Offs 1997-98 25
Results Grid 1997-98 26
Top Scorers – All Competitions 28
Top Scorers and Attendances by Club 28
Division Hat-tricks 29
Division Red Cards 29
A-Z Club Directory 1998-99 32
Division 1 All-time Table 80

Nationwide League Division 2
Final Table 83
Season Review 85
Play-Offs 1997-98 101
Results Grid 1997-98 102
Top Scorers – All Competitions 104
Top Scorers and Attendances by Club 104
Division Hat-tricks 105
Division Red Cards 105
A-Z Club Directory 1998-99 108
Division 2 All-time Table 156

Nationwide League Division 3
Final Table 159
Season Review 161
Play-Offs 1997-98 173
Top Scorers – All Competitions 173
Top Scorers and Attendances by Club 174
Division Hat-tricks 174
Division Red Cards 175
Results Grid 1997-98 178
A-Z Club Directory 1998-99 180
Division 3 All-time Table 228

FA Cup, Coca-Cola Cup, Auto Windscreens Shield and Awards
FA Cup 1997-98 1st Round to Final 231
FA Cup Final Results 1872-1998 236
FA Cup Wins by Club 240
Coca-Cola Cup 1997-98 1st Round to Final 241
Football League Cup Final Results 1961-1998 247

Football League Cup Wins by Club 248
FA Charity Shield Winners 1908-1997 249
Auto Windscreens Shield – History and Previous Winners 251
Auto Windscreens Shield Competition Review 252
Auto Windscreens Shield 1997-98 254
FWA Footballer of the Year 255
PFA Awards 1997-98 256

England Internationals
Results 1997-98 257
England Managers' Records/Goalscorers' Summary 1997-98 260
Player Summary 1997-98 261
1997-98 Appearance Chart 262
France '98 264
Euro 2000 Group 5 Fixtures 266

Transfers
Transfers Involving Nationwide Clubs to March 1998 268
Player Loans 280

Record Sequences
Longest Winning Runs 284
Longest Undefeated Runs 284
Most Games Without a Win 285
Most Successive Drawn Games 286
Most Successive Games Without a Draw 286
Longest Losing Run 286
Successive Number of Clean Sheets 287
Successive Number of Games in which Scored a Goal 287
Successive Number of Games in which Did Not Score a Goal 288
Start of Season: Most Games Undefeated 289
Start of Season: Most Games No Win 289
Division 1 Winning Records 290

Ups and Downs
Promotions 293
Relegations 296

Form 'n' Encounter Guide
All the important game dates along with results from previous seasons 302

This is not an approved nor an official publication of the Football League.

Pocket Annual Guide

Welcome to the 100th season of the Football League! The *Virgin Football League Pocket Annual* will help guide you through this monumental landmark in footballing history. The pocket annual has been divided into a number of easy-to-use sections to make it easy for you to navigate and access those vital bits of information. The pocket annual provides you with a complete review of the 1997-98 season and a statistical summary of the state of play for your team and the other 71 in the Nationwide Football League. From this standpoint you will be able to mark the milestones as and when they happen throughout the full season.

Central to the Pocket Annual is the club directory, which is arranged in three sections – the start of each of which is clearly marked. Each section starts with the final table combined with a list showing how far each club reached in the two major cup competitions. Well done to both Sheffield United and Wolverhampton Wanderers for making it to the penultimate stage of the FA Cup Final. Only single goals denied them a chance of becoming the first Football League clubs to walk the hallowed turf of Wembley since the FA Premier League was formed back in 1992. Beyond this comes a comprehensive month-by-month review of the season. Follow pre-season to May glory and heartbreak for all the teams.

Catch up on results via each division's grid and find out who the individual main players were for the season. Want to know the top scorer? Who fired the most hat-tricks and which players saw red? It's there.

Every club is then provided with a two-page home base of information. A season review is followed by a concise club summary which provides both practical details and some record makers. The information relates directly to the Football League unless specified. Under the section 'Managers', only the most recent (normally last five) are listed.

The stats file then supplies the most complete summary of every club's existence, not to be found anywhere else. First comes a complete PWDLFA for every division the club has competed in and then for each of the major cubpcompetitions. The league summaries are given for combined divisions. Thus 'Division 1n/2' relates to the new Division 1 which was also the old Division 2. The values of Yr, B, W are the number of Years (seasons) in that division, and the Best and Worst positions achieved in the division.

This is followed by a list of sequences relating to the Football League. Dates for the start and end of the sequence are given:

Winning Run	The highest number of successive wins
Without Defeat	The highest number of games gone without a defeat
Without Win	The highest number of games gone without a win
Drawn Games	The highest number of successive drawn games
Without Draw	The highest number of games gone without a draw

Losing Run	The highest number of successive defeats
Clean Sheets	The highest number of games gone without conceding a goal
Goals Scored	The highest number of successive games in which a goal has been scored
No Goals For	The highest number of games gone in which a goal has not been scored by the team
SOS Undefeated	SOS = Start of Season. This is the number of games at the start of a season before a defeat (thus games were either won or drawn)
SOS No Wins	Number of games at the start of the season without a win.

There may be several instances of a particular sequence. In such cases the number of times the sequence occurred is listed in brackets and the last two occasions it happened are detailed. Thus:

Clean Sheets (5)

would indicate that the specified number of clean sheets have been maintained on five different occasions.

List of Acknowledgements
Many thanks to everyone who has contributed to this year's annual – not least the following: David Tavener (reviews), Mark Webb, Sarah Smith, Paul Davison and not forgetting editor Ben Dunn at Virgin.

Deadlines
The World Cup dominated throughout the close season – and it seemed there was little early close-season transfer activity. This will have accelerated during the final weeks after the final leading up to the new season's kick-off. Where possible changes are reflected in this annual. However, the copy cut-off date was July 1st 1998. Events occurring after this may not be reflected in this annual.

The Author
Bruce Smith is an award-winning journalist who has written over 150 books on a variety of topics. He now concentrates on sports titles and also edits a bi-monthly magazine *Stadium & Arena Management*. A former BBC Radio commentator, he appeared on *The Big Breakfast* as their 'World Cup Monitor' throughout France '98. He is an Arsenal season ticket holder and a Green Bay Packers fan.

At a Glance
1997-98

Competition	Winners (Promoted)	Losers (Relegated)
FA Carling Premiership	Arsenal (Champions)	Everton (18th)
		Barnsley (19th)
		Crystal Palace (20th)
Nationwide Division 1	N. Forest (Champions)	Manchester City (22nd)
	Middlesbrough (2nd)	Stoke City (23rd)
	Charlton Athletic (P)	Reading (24th)
Nationwide Division 2	Watford (Champions)	Brentford (21st)
	Bristol City (2nd)	Plymouth Argyle (22nd)
	Grimsby Town (P)	Carlisle United (23rd)
		Southend United (24th)
Nationwide Division 3	Notts County (Champions)	Doncaster Rovers (24th)
	Macclesfield Town (2nd)	
	Lincoln City (3rd)	
	Colchester United (P)	
Vauxhall Conference	Halifax Town (Champions)	

FA Cup	Arsenal v Newcastle United	2-0	
Coca-Cola Cup	Chelsea v Middlesbrough	2-0	
Auto Windscreens Shield	Grimsby Town v AFC Bournemouth		

Play-Offs

Nationwide Division 1	Charlton v Sunderland	4-4	7-6 pens
Nationwide Division 2	Grimsby Town v Northampton Town	1-0	
Nationwide Division 3	Colchester United v Torquay United	1-0	

FA Carling Premier League

Psn		P	W	D	L	F	A	Pts	
1	Arsenal	38	23	9	6	68	33	78	Champions
2	Manchester U.	38	23	8	7	73	26	77	
3	Liverpool	38	18	11	9	68	42	65	
4	Chelsea	38	20	3	15	71	43	63	
5	Leeds United	38	17	8	13	57	46	59	
6	Blackburn Rovers	38	16	10	12	57	52	58	
7	Aston Villa	38	17	6	15	49	48	57	
8	West Ham United	38	16	8	14	56	57	56	
9	Derby County	38	16	7	15	52	49	55	
10	Leicester City	38	13	14	11	51	41	53	
11	Coventry City	38	12	16	10	46	44	52	
12	Southampton	38	14	6	18	50	55	48	
13	Newcastle United	38	11	11	16	35	44	44	
14	Tottenham H.	38	11	11	16	44	56	44	
15	Wimbledon	38	10	14	14	34	46	44	
16	Sheffield W.	38	12	8	18	52	67	44	
17	Everton	38	9	13	16	41	56	40	
18	Bolton Wanderers	38	9	13	16	41	61	40	Relegated
19	Barnsley	38	10	5	23	37	82	35	Relegated
20	Crystal Palace	38	8	9	21	37	71	33	Relegated

Vauxhall Conference

Psn		P	W	D	L	F	A	Pts	
1	Halifax Town	42	25	12	5	74	43	87	Promoted
2	Cheltenham Town	42	23	9	10	63	43	78	
3	Woking	42	22	8	12	72	46	74	
4	Rushden & Diamonds	42	23	5	14	79	57	74	
5	Morecambe	42	21	10	11	77	64	73	
6	Hereford United	42	18	13	11	56	49	67	
7	Hednesford Town	42	18	12	12	59	50	66	
8	Slough Town	42	18	10	14	58	49	64	Relegated
9	Northwich Victoria	42	15	15	12	63	59	60	
10	Welling United	42	17	9	16	64	62	60	
11	Yeovil Town	42	17	8	17	73	63	59	
12	Hayes	42	15	10	16	62	52	58	
13	Dover Athletic	42	15	10	17	60	70	55	
14	Kettering Town	42	13	13	16	53	60	52	
15	Stevenage Borough	42	13	12	17	59	63	51	
16	Southport	42	13	11	18	56	58	50	
17	Kidderminster Harriers	42	11	14	17	56	63	47	
18	Farnborough Town	42	12	8	22	56	70	44	
19	Leek Town	42	10	14	18	52	67	44	
20	Telford United	42	10	12	20	53	76	42	
21	Gateshead	42	8	11	23	51	87	35	Relegated
22	Stalybridge Celtic	42	7	8	27	48	93	29	Relegated

NATIONWIDE LEAGUE DIVISION 1

Final Table 1997-98

Pn	Team	P	W	D	L	F	A	Pts		FA	LC
1	Nottingham Forest	46	28	10	8	82	42	94	P	3	2
2	Middlesbrough	46	27	10	9	77	41	91	P	4	F
3	Sunderland	46	26	12	8	86	50	90		4	3
4	Charlton Athletic	46	26	10	10	80	49	88	P	4	1
5	Ipswich Town	46	23	14	9	77	43	83		4	5
6	Sheffield United	46	19	17	10	69	54	74		SF	3
7	Birmingham City	46	19	17	10	60	35	74		5	3
8	Stockport County	46	19	8	19	71	69	65		4	2
9	Wolverhampton W.	46	18	11	17	57	53	65		SF	2
10	WBA	46	16	13	17	50	56	61		4	3
11	Crewe Alexandra	46	18	5	23	58	65	59		3	1
12	Oxford United	46	16	10	20	60	64	58		3	4
13	Bradford City	46	14	15	17	46	59	57		3	1
14	Tranmere Rovers	46	14	14	18	54	57	56		5	3
15	Norwich City	46	14	13	19	52	69	55		3	1
16	Huddersfield Town	46	14	11	21	50	72	53		4	2
17	Bury	46	11	19	16	42	58	52		3	2
18	Swindon Town	46	14	10	22	42	73	52		3	1
19	Port Vale	46	13	10	23	56	66	49		3	1
20	Portsmouth	46	13	10	23	51	63	49		3	1
21	QPR	46	10	19	17	51	63	49		3	1
22	Manchester City	46	12	12	22	56	57	48		4	1
23	Stoke City	46	11	13	22	44	74	46	R	3	3
24	Reading	46	11	9	26	39	78	42	R	5	5

Play-Off Semi-Finals
Ipswich Town v Charlton Athletic	0-1	0-1	0-2 on aggregate
Sheffield United v Sunderland	2-1	0-2	2-3 on aggregate

Final
Charlton Athletic v Sunderland	4-4	7-6 on penalties

Full Table 1997-98

		P	HOME					AWAY					Pts
			W	D	L	F	A	W	D	L	F	A	
1	Nottingham Forest	46	18	2	3	52	20	10	8	5	30	22	94
2	Middlesbrough	46	17	4	2	51	12	10	6	7	26	29	91
3	Sunderland	46	14	7	2	49	22	12	5	6	37	28	90
4	Charlton Athletic	46	17	5	1	48	17	9	5	9	32	32	88
5	Ipswich Town	46	14	5	4	47	20	9	9	5	30	23	83
6	Sheffield United	46	16	5	2	44	20	3	12	8	25	34	74
7	Birmingham City	46	10	8	5	27	15	9	9	5	33	20	74
8	Stockport County	46	14	6	3	46	21	5	2	16	25	48	65
9	Wolverhampton W.	46	13	6	4	42	25	5	5	13	15	28	65
10	WBA	46	9	8	6	27	26	7	5	11	23	30	61
11	Crewe Alexandra	46	10	2	11	30	34	8	3	12	28	31	59
12	Oxford United	46	12	6	5	36	20	4	4	15	24	44	58
13	Bradford City	46	10	9	4	26	23	4	6	13	20	36	57
14	Tranmere Rovers	46	9	8	6	34	26	5	6	12	20	31	56
15	Norwich City	46	9	8	6	32	27	5	5	13	20	42	55
16	Huddersfield Town	46	9	5	9	28	28	5	6	12	22	44	53
17	Bury	46	7	10	6	22	22	4	9	10	20	36	52
18	Swindon Town	46	9	6	8	28	25	5	4	14	14	48	52
19	Port Vale	46	7	6	10	25	24	6	4	13	31	42	49
20	Portsmouth	46	8	6	9	28	30	5	4	14	23	33	49
21	QPR	46	8	9	6	28	21	2	10	11	23	42	49
22	Manchester City	46	6	6	11	28	26	6	6	11	28	31	48
23	Stoke City	46	8	5	10	30	40	3	8	12	14	34	46
24	Reading	46	8	4	11	27	31	3	5	15	12	47	42

Season Review

August

Two of the three clubs relegated from the Premiership enjoy a winning start to life in the Nationwide League. Nottingham Forest win with a Kevin Campbell goal at Port Vale and Middlesbrough come from a goal down to win at the Riverside thanks to Ravanelli's last-minute strike. But Sunderland, on the Sunday, are beaten 2-0 at Sheffield United, who are one of five teams to be joint top by virtue of such scorelines. Birmingham City start well, with Peter Ndlovu scoring on his debut against Stoke City.

Forest make a mockery of being forced to play in the Coca-Cola Cup 1st Round with an 8-0 thumping of Division Three side Doncaster Rovers at Belle Vue on the 11th. The following night Manchester City concede a 1st Leg advantage to Blackpool and, in an all Division One clash at Loftus Road, Queens Park Rangers go down 2-0 to Wolverhampton Wanderers. Stockport County, newly promoted to Division One and Coca-Cola Cup semi finalists the previous season, suffer a 4-2 reversal at Mansfield Town. Portsmouth draw 2-2 for the second time in four days, this time at Peterborough United, in a match marred by a 21 man free-for-all which ends in the dismissal of two players.

Four matches on the first Friday of the season underline two points. Firstly that Manchester City have made a poor start, as exemplified by a 3-1 defeat at Sunderland and, secondly, that Forest are aiming for a quick return to the Premiership when they hammer home the point with a 4-1 win over Norwich City. West Bromwich Albion and Swindon Town join Forest on six points with respective wins at Crewe Alexandra and Reading. Portsmouth also score three, at the expense of pointless Port Vale but face a setback with two players, Paul Hall and Fitzroy Simpson, set to miss three weeks whilst on international duty with Jamaica. Birmingham make it two out of two with a 3-0 success over Reading and West Brom stay level with Forest courtesy of a 1-0 Sunday victory over Wolves. Swindon slip up for the first time when held at home by Huddersfield, who celebrate their first point of the season. Only Norwich are still looking for a point after three games while Bury are the only side to have drawn all three games.

Eight Division One sides bow out of the Coca-Cola Cup midweek – five of them to lower league opposition. Manchester City's decline continues with a penalty shoot-out defeat by Blackpool while Norwich and Portsmouth are defeated by Division Three sides Barnet and Peterborough. Two late goals carry Stockport County to a thrilling 8-7 aggregate victory over Mansfield.

The final weekend of the month sees Norwich, at Sunderland, pick up their first points of the season while Forest retain the last 100 per cent winning record with Van Hooijdonk scoring a hat-trick during a 4-0 thrashing of QPR. Bradford, West Brom and Swindon are just two points behind the leaders but Manchester City are still without a win.

September

Goals by Brazilian Endinho and Robbie Blake clinch victory for Bradford at Yorkshire neighbours Huddersfield on the 2nd, and with it comes pole position. Sunderland kick into gear with a 3-1 win over Oxford United and Birmingham also score three times at Tranmere. Frank Clark has reasons to be cheerful as his Manchester City side win their first game of the season, somewhat surprisingly at the home of his former club Nottingham Forest. West Brom stay close to the top with a goalless draw which leaves Stoke City still looking for their first success at the new £15m Britannia Stadium. Bradford's stay at the top is put into doubt on the 5th by Sunderland who win 4-0 at the Pulse Stadium with the scoring completed by the 37th minute. An Andy Hunt goal on the Sunday leaves Reading rooted to the foot of the table and takes West Brom to the top, a situation which is aided by Swindon and Forest sharing the spoils at the County Ground. Midlands sides occupy the top three places as Birmingham move behind WBA and Forest on the back of a 1-0 win at Huddersfield. Stockport are still without a win after going down 2-1 at Port Vale, for whom Lee Mills scores inside 32 seconds. Birmingham strengthen their squad with the £1.5m signing of Vale midfielder Jon McCarthy. Wolves splash out £200,000 on Vauxhall Conference striker Jason Roberts of Hayes.

In the Friday match Georgi Kinkladze misses a penalty as Manchester City draw 1-1 at Bury. The 13th is an unlucky day for the top sides as West Brom go down to their first defeat, at QPR, Forest suffer their first away loss, at Sheffield United, and Bradford drop more points at home in a 2-2 draw with improving Middlesbrough. Swindon are the main benefactors to go second as goals from veteran Mark Walters and the on-loan Chris Casper see off lowly Tranmere. Reading are off the bottom with victory over Oxford United at Elm Park. Terry Fenwick's Portsmouth are heading for trouble with the FA when Adrian Whitbread becomes the third Pompey player to be dismissed this season as the south coast side lose 3-2 at home to Crewe.

While most attention is focused on the 2nd Round of the Coca-Cola Cup, Port Vale condemn Crewe to a third successive home defeat. In the cup the outstanding result is achieved by Huddersfield, who grab a 1st Leg lead against West Ham through Hammers' supporter Alex Dyer. A last-minute Mick Stockwell goal saves Ipswich from an embarrassing home defeat by Torquay United. Convincing wins for Stoke, Tranmere and Oxford United put them within touching distance of the next round.

The following night sees Norwich's brief recovery emphatically repelled by Charlton who win 4-0 in the league at Carrow Road, with record signing Clive Mendonca scoring a hat-trick inside 21 first-half minutes. Stockport seem unlikely to repeat last season's thrilling Coca-Cola Cup run and face an early elimination after going down 4-1 at Birmingham. Nottingham Forest, down to seventh in the table, slip up 1-0 at home to Division Two side Walsall, having put ten past Doncaster in the previous round.

On the penultimate Saturday of the month a Van Hooijdonk goal is sufficient to take Forest back to the summit, at the expense of struggling Portsmouth. Overseas stars Kinder, Beck and Emerson get the goals which give Middlesbrough a 3-1 win over Birmingham in front of 30,125 spectators at the Riverside. The biggest gate of the day is at the Stadium of Light where 30,682 see Sunderland and Wolves finish all square. Five different players get on the scoresheet as Tranmere chalk up the division's biggest win to date with a 6-0 thrashing of lowly Reading – the two sides started the day on equal points. Huddersfield remain below Reading following a 3-0 reversal which sees Stockport clinch their first win of the season. Sheffield United and QPR edge closer to the top with good away wins at Oxford United 4-2 and Crewe 3-2 respectively. In the Sunday match Mendonca is again amongst the goals with a brace as Charlton this time put four past Bradford.

Division One sides fare well in the 2nd Leg matches of the Coca-Cola Cup with beaten finalists Middlesbrough, Sunderland, Reading, Sheffield United, Birmingham, Ipswich, Tranmere and WBA all making progress. Birmingham's success is at the cost of Stockport. Reading's cause at Peterborough is aided by the first-minute dismissal of Posh midfielder Derek Payne. The following night sees Stoke and Wolves reach Round Three but Nottingham Forest draw 2-2 at Walsall after extra time to go out on aggregate. John Spencer's third goal in four games – all of which QPR have won – disposes of Portsmouth at Loftus Road and lifts Rangers into second place. Rangers also pick up £1.3m from the sale of Andy Impey to West Ham while Middlesbrough part company with Ravanelli who signs for Marseille. Forest return to the top of the table on the final Saturday of the month with a Kevin Campbell goal securing all three points at home to Stoke and West Brom move into second place with a hat-trick by the transfer-listed Paul Peschisolido handing Bury only their second defeat of the season. QPR slip up 2-0 at Port Vale – boss Stuart Houston still wins the Manager of the Month Award – but Bradford halt their slide with a goalless draw at Oxford United. Having conceded just five goals from their opening eight games, Swindon Town are knocked for six at Maine Road with Paul Dickov grabbing two of Manchester City's goals. The biggest crowd of the weekend is on the Sunday at Sunderland to see visitors Middlesbrough win the north-east derby and move within five points of leaders Forest, with two games in hand.

On the last day of the month Huddersfield are put out of the Coca-Cola Cup by West Ham with an aggregate 3-1 defeat. A poor week for the winless Yorkshire club concludes on the Friday as goals by Colin Cooper and Dean Saunders take Forest four points clear at the opposite end of the table.

October

The first Saturday of the new month kicks off with West Brom failing to peg Forest back as Oxford United grab their first away success of the season at the Hawthorns. Bradford return to winning ways with a good 2-0 home win over Wolves and they, along with West Brom, are joined on 18 points by Swindon, who beat Port Vale 4-2 with Chris Hay scoring the first hat-trick of his career. Reading, having scored just six goals in their opening nine league games, crush Sunderland 4-0 at Elm Park and Charlton also hit four, with their 4-2 victory at Loftus Road taking them above the home side. Crewe, beaten in four of their five home games, make it three wins out of four away from home with a Mark Rivers goal seeing off Birmingham. Mixed fortunes for the East Anglian sides as Ipswich record only their second win of the season, 1-0 at home to Manchester City, who they join on just nine points, but Norwich have Rob Newman and Mike Milligan dismissed during a 2-0 defeat at Tranmere which takes the Merseysiders out of the bottom three. On the Sunday, Sheffield United safely protect the last unbeaten record in Division One and become the fourth club ganging up on 18 points, courtesy of a 2-1 win at the Riverside to end Middlesbrough's eight-match unbeaten run.

Portsmouth are fined £12,500 by the FA, £10,000 suspended, following their on-pitch Coca-Cola Cup bust up with Peterborough.

Crewe, winners of three of their five away games to date, take a 3-0 lead at Reading but have to cling on for a draw as the Royals pull level by the hour. Oxford United also strike late, two goals in the final ten minutes, but lose 3-2 at Stockport. Brett Angell scores the 100th league goal of his career as Stockport chalk up a fifth successive win. Swindon move into second place with a 2-1 win over Bury.

In the 3rd Round of the Coca-Cola Cup on the 14th, Ipswich take advantage of a self-weakened Manchester United side to chalk up their first ever cup success at Portman Road over the Reds. In all Division One clashes, Oxford United defeat Tranmere on penalties following a 1-1 draw and Reading hand Wolves a third consecutive defeat, 4-2 at Elm Park. Birmingham City take the lead at Highbury before going down 4-1 in extra time while Sheffield United, unbeaten in the league, are humbled 2-1 at Division Two Walsall. Back in the league, Charlton cruise to a 3-0 win at Huddersfield to go third in the table. Three more Division One sides are sent packing from the Coca-Cola Cup the following day as Stoke, after extra time, and West Brom lose at home to Leeds and Liverpool respectively while another north-east derby sees Middlesbrough comfortably on top in a 2-0 win over Sunderland. On its way from the stadium after the game, the Sunderland players' coach is vandalised by idiots throwing bricks and concrete.

Forest surrender two points in a home draw with Tranmere but Swindon fail to cash in as new signing Dougie Freedman puts Wolves on the path to a 3-1 win at Molineux. Wolves have Steve Bull dismissed and he is joined by Swindon pair Lee Collins and Chris Casper. West Brom move within two points of the leaders with a flattering 3-2 victory at Portsmouth and Ipswich come down to earth with a bump with a 1-0 defeat at Oxford. Huddersfield, under new manager Peter Jackson, complete an 11th league match without a win and a missed Kinkladze penalty costs Manchester City two points in a goalless draw with Reading.

A Kevin Campbell goal takes Forest four points clear and drops ten-man West Brom down to fourth by the 21st as Sheffield United climb to second on the strength of a Flitcroft hat-trick in a 6-1 thrashing of Stockport. Middlesbrough rise to seventh and protect their unbeaten away record with a 4-1 trouncing of Oxford United. Twenty-four hours later Charlton lose ground after a home draw with Birmingham but Stoke close to within a point of second place by virtue of success at Maine Road. On the last Friday of October, Forest move five points clear with a 3-3 draw at Reading who take their unbeaten run to eight games. Forest lead 2-0 at one stage before having on-loan keeper Dave Beasant controversially sent off. Swindon, West Brom and early leaders Bradford keep the heat on Forest with home wins but Charlton are held at Tranmere and Sheffield United lose their ten match unbeaten start to the season at the Hawthorns. Bottom dogs Huddersfield and Portsmouth share the spoils at the McAlpine Stadium and Manchester City, having dropped into the bottom three on the Saturday, have their position cemented with a 2-0 defeat at QPR the following day.

Middlesbrough, boosted by a Mikkel Beck double, climb four places to third with a 3-0 win over Huddersfield on the 29th. Over 27,000 spectators are at Maine Road on the 29th to see the debut-making teenager Chris Greenacre score City's winning goal against Crewe. It is the home side's first goal in 414 minutes. In the final match of the month Chris Hay's winning goal at Portsmouth takes Swindon to the top of the table.

November

Nottingham Forest reclaim pole position with a 3-1 victory over Crewe at the City Ground but the side with most to celebrate are Huddersfield who, at the 15th attempt, become the last side in the division to win a league match. Fellow strugglers Oxford United and Manchester City draw 0-0. City are without Kinkladze who is recovering after injuring himself in a midweek crash in his Ferrari. Tranmere concede two late goals at Bramall Lane to lose 2-1 as Sheffield United jump into fourth place, above Bradford and West Brom who hold each other to a goalless draw and Middlesbrough who go down 1-0 to Wolves for their first away defeat of the season. An almost full midweek programme closes with Forest's position coming under threat as they crash 1-0 to an impressive Bury display, while Sheffield United win at Reading and West Brom beat Norwich with a late goal. Charlton, at Sunderland, take home a point but fail to score for only the second time this season. Port Vale twice come from behind to add to Frank Clark's problems at Maine Road. Police on horseback are used to disburse aggrieved home fans after the game. The following night, Bonfire Night, Swindon make light of being forced to play injured goalkeeper Perry Digweed to beat QPR 3-1 and move above Forest for a second time. Middlesbrough's push is slowed by a late Portsmouth equaliser at the Riverside. Oxford United announce that chairman Robin Herd is to stand down in favour of Keith Cox. Manchester City will be without record signing Lee Bradbury, through injury, until after Christmas. On the first Friday in November a Rob Edwards goal gives Huddersfield their first away win of the season to plunge City's season into deeper turmoil.

As Forest drop two points at Sunderland, in front of over 33,000 fans, Swindon – despite a crippling injury list and having sold their top scorer for the previous season, Wayne Allison – move four points clear with Steve Cowe netting the winner at the County Ground against Bradford, who include new signing from Bolton, John McGinlay. West Brom and Middlesbrough keep up the pressure with home wins over Charlton and QPR. Rangers' chairman Chris Wright sacks manager Stewart Houston and his assistant Bruce Rioch, the latter learning of his departure through Ceefax. West Brom boss Ray Harford is unlikely to be the new Rangers manager after agreeing to sign a contract at the Hawthorns.

Portsmouth make the position at the foot of the table more compact with victory at Bury and Ipswich move out of the bottom three on the Sunday by drawing with Sheffield United. Recent acquisition Paul Cook has a sparkling debut for Stockport as his new side topple Swindon from pole position on the 15th with a 4-2 victory at Edgeley Park. Forest reclaim the summit with Campbell's goal accounting for Birmingham, who have won just once in 13 games. Middlesbrough, West Brom and Sunderland all look to be heading for surprise defeats before turning the tables at Norwich, Port Vale and Portsmouth respectively. The Baggies' win puts them level on points with table-topping Forest. Peter Jackson continues to breathe new life into Huddersfield as a Paul Dalton goal gives the Yorkshire side their third win in four outings and only a last-minute Kevin Horlock equaliser saves Manchester City from slipping to bottom place. Early season leaders Bradford drop out of the top ten as a John Aldridge goal clinches Tranmere's first away success of the season.

While Bradford and Sheffield United share the spoils in the league, two Division One sides, Reading and Middlesbrough, cover themselves in Coca-Cola Cup glory. Reading, having won just once and scored three times away from home in the league, astound Leeds with a 3-2 4th Round victory at Elland Road thanks to veteran Trevor Morley's late winner. Boro come from behind to beat one of the sides who replaced them in the Premiership, Bolton, with Craig Hignett's extra-time strike. Ipswich, without an away win in the Nationwide League, progress to the quarter-finals with an extra-time victory over Oxford United at the Manor Ground. Oxford, already £10m in debt and reeling from the resignation of chairman Robin Herd, place their full squad on the transfer list.

On the 22nd, Paul Merson's seventh goal in nine games condemns Swindon to an unjust home defeat as Middlesbrough edge into second place above the Wiltshire club, but Sunderland's surge stutters with a draw at Bury. Forest contribute to Charlton's fading challenge with a Hooijdonk hat-trick confirming Forest's position as top scorers at home during a 5-2 success. Stockport's rise gathers momentum with victory at Crewe but Sheffield United's challenge stalls with a fourth consecutive draw. Ipswich complete a fine week with a 4-0 destruction of Reading in Berkshire. Manchester City again leave it late before Tony Vaughan's last-minute penalty eases Frank Clark's strugglers out of the bottom three. A Midlands derby at the Hawthorns ends with West Brom and Birmingham continuing to head in opposite directions as Richard Sneekes' first goal in three months secures the points for the Baggies. An entertaining midweek showdown at the Riverside ends goalless between third-placed Boro and leaders Forest.

The final weekend of the month kicks off with an emphatic Friday night victory for Charlton, 3-0 over Swindon, whose stay at the top looks a distant memory as Clive Mendonca takes his tally to 12 in 18 games. Stockport, Sunderland and Wolves also score three times on the Saturday but solitary strikes by Campbell for Forest and Beck for Middlesbrough are enough for both to move a step closer to the Premiership. Boro's victory is significant as it lifts them over their victims West Brom. Sheffield United return to winning ways with a victory which leaves visitors Crewe floundering in the bottom three after just one win from 11 games. Huddersfield are off the bottom courtesy of victory over Bury and Portsmouth's defeat at St Andrews as Birmingham win at last.

December

Middlesbrough and West Brom squander games in hand on Forest on the 2nd. Boro draw at Ipswich while the Baggies surprisingly lose at home to Manchester City. Sheffield United overturn a deficit to beat Stoke 3-2 at Bramall Lane and move into third place. Peace breaks out at Portsmouth as the players receive their delayed November wages. Just for good measure Pompey have their £2.5m Fratton End stand closed after the council withdraw a safety certificate. Portsmouth fans are aghast to learn that Venables has received a £300,000 bonus from the club.

Having decided against signing a contract offered to him by West Brom the previous month, manager Ray Harford quits and, after compensation is agreed, joins QPR. Charlton suspend Jamie Stuart after he becomes the fourth Athletic player to fail a drugs test. A week later he is sacked by the club.

Having had a let-off midweek, Forest surrender the number one position to Middlesbrough on the 6th. Forest are held at home by Bradford despite leading 2-0 at one stage while Boro win at Bury. West Brom close the gap on second place to just two points with a 3-2 win which slows Stockport's upturn in fortunes. Swindon stay in the hunt with a 4-1 thrashing of Oxford United and it is a good day for old stagers as Tony Cottee scores Birmingham's winner at Port Vale and Niall Quinn does likewise for Sunderland, who spoil Harford's first day at Loftus Road. Crewe's slump continues as Huddersfield rattle in five at Gresty Road and fellow strugglers Portsmouth and Reading are also celebrating with wins over Stoke and Charlton. Sheffield United have Dutchman Michel Vonk dismissed when suffering only their second defeat of the season, 2-1 at Norwich. The Blades lose again in the middle of the week as another brace from Mendonca gives Charlton victory at the Valley. Wolves suffer a setback at Fratton Park where they have Steve Sedgley sent off and captain Keith Curle misses a penalty during a 3-2 defeat which lifts Portsmouth out of the bottom three.

The second weekend of the month kicks off on the Friday with Oxford United accounting for QPR 3-1. Rangers announce that John Hollins is their new assistant manager. Middlesbrough, on the Saturday, put daylight between themselves and the pack with Craig Hignett and Mikkel Beck scoring twice each during the final 13 minutes as Reading are overwhelmed at the Riverside. A good day for the north-east is assured as Sunderland dent West Brom's hopes with a 2-0 home win thanks in no small part to French goalkeeper Lionel Perez. Charlton and Bradford stay in contention with home wins while Sheffield United reclaim third place with Dean Saunders scoring his first goal for the club. Stockport come from a goal down against Tranmere to preserve their unbeaten home record with a 3-1 win but the comeback of the day is at St Andrews as Birmingham, having fallen behind in the 88th minute against Manchester City, grab all three points with two goals during seven minutes of injury time. The bottom six of Huddersfield, Portsmouth, Bury, Manchester City, Crewe and Tranmere all lose. The promotion pack tightens on the 14th with Wolves beating Forest 2-1 at Molineux.

On the final Saturday before Christmas, Middlesbrough have their title credentials damaged by a 2-0 defeat in front of more than 28,000 spectators at Maine Road as two first-half goals lift the home side to a dizzy 19th. Sunderland move to within six points of their neighbours with a commanding 3-0 success at lowly Crewe and Forest move level with Boro as two late goals hand Stockport their eighth away defeat. Charlton stay very much in the frame with a 2-0 win which sends Portsmouth back to the bottom, while a Brian Deane equaliser at Bury keeps Sheffield United in third place. West Brom lose ground with a 2-0 home defeat which allows Huddersfield to clamber out of the bottom three. Oxford are also on the up with their third win in four games, this time 2-0 at Tranmere. Two sides on the fringes of the promotion race, Swindon and Birmingham, battle out a 1-1 draw with Town midfielder Darren Bullock being dismissed. Also off early are Wolves' Paul Simpson and Reading's Paul Bodin during a stormy clash at Elm Park – both for the first time in their careers.

Two days before Christmas, West Brom unveil Oxford boss Denis Smith as their new manager. His reign starts in unusual fashion with Andy McDermott scoring an own goal inside 34 seconds as the Baggies go down to a fifth defeat in six games on Boxing Day, 2-1 at Reading. Another own goal steers Middlesbrough to victory at Huddersfield after they are outplayed. Forest are more assertive as they go three up by the interval at home to Swindon. Charlton move closer to the top two with a home win over Norwich which takes them above Sheffield United who rescue a point with a last-minute equaliser at troubled Stoke. Although still down in tenth position, Birmingham are fast becoming serious promotion candidates and their cause is aided by a Jason Cundy own goal which clinches victory at Ipswich. A remarkable crowd of 40,055 witnesses Kevin Phillips' fifth goal in six games as Sunderland march to a fifth straight win, this time 2-0 over Bradford. Stockport's impressive home form continues with Simon Travis netting his first two goals for the club in a 3-0 win over out-of-form Port Vale. Wins for Crewe and Portsmouth, at home to Manchester City and QPR respectively, mean that just five points separate the bottom eleven sides.

On the last Saturday of the year the top two sides, Middlesbrough and Forest, play and win in front of gates in excess of 30,000. Boro see off Stockport 3-1 at the Riverside and Forest, boosted by two Hooijdonk penalties, take a three-goal lead at Maine Road before coming away with a 3-2 triumph. Charlton, on a run of four successive wins, are crushed 4-1 at Bramall Lane as Sheffield United move back into the top three, but of the remaining sides looking for a play-off position only Wolves, at Port Vale, collect all three points. Vale's sixth consecutive defeat is their worst run for 15 years. QPR's Danny Maddix and Reading's Carl Asaba are both dismissed during a 1-1 draw at Loftus Road. West Brom pick up their first point under Denis Smith while his replacement at Oxford, Malcolm Crosby, is delighted as his new side takes a point off one of his former clubs, Sunderland. Portsmouth are set to end the year as the division's bottom club following a 2-0 defeat at Norwich on the 30th. League leaders Middlesbrough agree to part company with unpredictable Brazilian Emerson after a delayed return from his homeland over the holiday period.

January

There are mixed fortunes for Division One sides in the 3rd Round of the FA Cup on the 3rd. Port Vale gain a surprise draw at Arsenal and Portsmouth, having briefly led 2-0, draw at home to Aston Villa. Charlton, beaten 5-2 at home by Forest in the league, return the compliment with a 4-1 win over Dave Bassett's side in the cup. The most emphatic win though is achieved by Sunderland, for whom Kevin Phillips helps to celebrate Peter Reid's December Manager of the Month Award by scoring four times in a 5-1 win at Rotherham. Also through are Birmingham, Manchester City and Stockport. There are humiliating casualties though as Swindon are beaten 2-1 at home by non-leaguers Stevenage, and Norwich are turned over 3-0 at Grimsby. Oxford suffer a less surprising defeat at Leeds, 4-0, while QPR against Middlesbrough, Sheffield United against Bury and Ipswich at Bristol Rovers finish all square. Brett Angell confirms his position as the second highest scorer in the division with the two goals which give Stockport victory at Preston.

Cup action again takes centre stage midweek as an injury-time Craig Hignett goal takes

Middlesbrough through to the Coca-Cola semi-finals at the expense of Reading. Chris Kamara pays the price for Bradford's slide down the table as he is sacked. Returning to the league on the Friday night, out-of-form sides Tranmere and West Brom draw 0-0 at Prenton Park; the Merseyside club have gone close on seven hours without a goal. The following day sees five sides score three or more but the most astonishing scoreline is at Stoke's new Britannia Stadium where Trevor Francis's Birmingham go on a seven-goal rampage. Sadly, a good number of Stoke fans do likewise after the final whistle as the club suffers its third pitch invasion of the season. Star of the show is Paul Furlong who bags a hat-trick. Another hat-trick hero is Dougie Freedman as he leads Wolves' 5-0 rout of Norwich. Also hitting the target five times are Huddersfield, who overcome Oxford 5-1, yet remain behind their victims in 20th place. Charlton's biggest crowd since returning to the Valley in 1992 sees Middlesbrough's good week come to a crushing end as the Addicks, helped by a Shaun Newton brace, romp home 3-0 to stay third. Nottingham Forest cash in on Boro's off day and with two goals from the division's leading scorer, van Hooijdonk, beat Port Vale to reopen a three-point lead. Sunderland stay just a point behind Charlton and move above Sheffield United with a 4-2 win over United which includes two more goals for Phillips. Manchester City join the list of big winners with a 3-0 success at Portsmouth which saves the visitors from the humiliation of dropping to the foot of the table. Bradford put their managerial problems behind them to hand Stockport their first home defeat for almost a year. Swindon's misery shows no sign of easing on the Sunday as Crewe give manager Dario Gradi good cause to celebrate his 800th match in charge with a welcome 2-0 victory at Gresty Road.

Division One sides, generally, have a good night in the FA Cup on the 13th. In delayed 3rd Round ties, Huddersfield survive heavy pressure to see off Bournemouth, and Tranmere's goal drought ends with a three-goal salvo at Conference side Hereford. Reading do less well against non-league opposition but salvage a draw at Cheltenham. Stoke's fortunes show little sign of improving as at West Brom as the Baggies go through 3-1 with Richard Sneekes scoring twice. Five sides are involved in replays; Ipswich go through 1-0 at home to Bristol Rovers and in all Division One ties Sheffield United win at Bury and QPR go down 2-0 at Middlesbrough. Not only do Boro make cup progress but their coffers are swollen by £4m following the prolonged departure of Emerson to Tenerife.

With Terry Venables' future at Portsmouth in some doubt, the man he brought to Fratton Park as manager two years earlier, Terry Fenwick, is dismissed by Martin Gregory. On the 14th Portsmouth's interest in the FA Cup ends at Villa Park as they lose 1-0 in a replay. Port Vale go even closer to causing an upset as Wayne Corden equalises during extra-time against Arsenal but England keeper David Seaman carries the Gunners to a penalty shoot-out victory. Wolves are again amongst the goals as they put four past Darlington, but it is a flattering 4-0 final score.

Failure on the pitch is matched by humiliating defeat in court for Portsmouth chairman Venables as he is found guilty on 19 charges of serious misconduct. He is banned from holding the position of company director for seven years following a three-year investigation by the Department of Trade and Industry.

The violent atmosphere present at home Stoke matches forces chairman Peter Coates to stand down after 12 years in charge. Sheffield United's promotion push receives a setback as leading scorer Brian Deane signs for Benfica in a £1m deal and Jan Aage Fjortoft signs for Barnsley for £800,000. United do very nicely without the pair of them though at the weekend as Brazilian Marcello strikes to take all three points off Wolves. Sunderland stay just above the Blades as Phillips scores for the seventh successive match to account for Manchester City at Maine Road. Charlton cling on to third place with two goals in the last nine minutes clinching victory at Oxford, whose manager Malcolm Crosby stands down after just five winless games in charge. Middlesbrough, who have Gianluca Festa sent off, drop two points when held at home by Ipswich but it proves to be a point gained as Forest slip to a 1-0 defeat at Norwich. It is a day of few goals as only Charlton, Port Vale, 2-1 winners at home to Portsmouth, and Reading, 2-0 victors at Swindon, find the net more than once.

Chris Kamara makes a swift reappearance in the Nationwide League with his appointment as manager of Stoke, whose 2-1 win over Bradford last Friday ended a run of 11 games without a win. Portsmouth are also under new management as Alan Ball returns to Fratton Park for his second spell. A last-minute goal by Oxford's Joey Beauchamp on the 25th condemns Ball to a losing start. Swindon salvage a point with an injury-time Chris Hay goal at Bradford and a late headed Colin Cooper goal at Loftus Road gives Forest a five-point lead at the top of the table. Port Vale's slide continues with a 3-2 home defeat by Crewe who have now taken 13 points from the last 15. On the same day Division One sides have a disappointing time in the FA Cup although Birmingham, 2-1 winners over Stockport, and Tranmere, surprising 1-0 victors over Sunderland, progress to Round Five. Stockport's hopes of ending Birmingham's nine-match unbeaten run are dashed by red cards for Brett Angell and Martin McIntosh. Charlton's aim of an eighth successive home win ends with a 1-1 draw with Wolves. Reading live to fight again with a fortuitous draw at Cardiff, and Ipswich and Sheffield United must do battle again after drawing at Portman Road. But it is the end of the road for Middlesbrough, Huddersfield and West Brom, beaten by Arsenal, Wimbledon and Aston Villa respectively, and Manchester City whose exit at home to West Ham owes much to a penalty miss by Rosler when the scores are level.

QPR's failure to be amongst the promotion pack leads to the transfer of Trevor Sinclair to West Ham for £3m. Rangers pick up Iain Dowie and Keith Rowland as part of the deal. Bradford name Paul Jewell as boss until the end of the season and he celebrates his appointment with a 4-1 home win over Reading on the 27th. Birmingham are also knocking in the goals with another Paul Furlong hat-trick seeing the Blues to a 4-1 success over Stockport. Wolves strengthen their position in the play-off places with a 3-1 win at Bury who have now gone 14 games without a win. Sheffield United slip up when held at Bramall Lane by Huddersfield in a Yorkshire derby. Middlesbrough, despite taking the lead through Paul Merson, go down to a second cup defeat in three days, this time 2-1 at Liverpool in the 1st Leg of their Coca-Cola Cup semi-final encounter.

Sunderland miss out on second place with a 2-1 defeat at Norwich which ends the Wearsiders' 16-match unbeaten run. Manchester City and Charlton both strike late to draw at Maine Road; Charlton lose keeper Mike Salmon through injury at half-time while City have Shelia dismissed. On the final day of the month Nottingham Forest crash 3-1 at home to Oxford but few of the chasing sides cash in. Birmingham have Furlong and Chris Marsden sent off during a 2-0 reversal at Reading, Wolves go down 1-0 at home to West Brom whose victory is their first under Denis Smith, Sheffield United are held at Portsmouth as are Charlton at home to Bury. Those results make for a good day for Sunderland as Phillips is amongst their scorers in a 4-2 win over Port Vale which lifts them into third place.

February

Stoke's poor run continues on the 1st as Middlesbrough cement their title push with a 2-1 victory at the Britannia Stadium. Three Division One sides make FA Cup progress on the 3rd in fluctuating circumstances. Wolves win an error-strewn encounter with Charlton at Molineux, 3-0, while Reading have keeper Nicky Hammond to thank for a penalty shoot-out triumph over Cardiff. A successful penalty in normal time by Sheffield United's Don Hutchison and a missed one by David Johnson of Ipswich takes United through to the 5th Round. Paul Merson scores twice against Tranmere in the one league game played on the 4th to take Middlesbrough above Forest into pole position.

Boro are quickly deposed when drawing at Birmingham on the 7th, a result which allows Forest to go top again through Steve Chettle's winner at Portsmouth – only his eighth league goal in 12 years. Sunderland leave it late before edging above Charlton into third place with an important win at Wolves; Charlton lose at Bradford. Sheffield United add to Charlton's misery with a home success over Oxford while West Brom increase Swindon's problems with a 2-0 victory at the County Ground. Manchester City collect a point at Norwich but are joined on 30 points by two off the bottom Tranmere, who win 3-1 at Reading. Norwich have teenager Craig Bellamy dismissed for spitting at Kinkladze.

Tranmere hit three more during the week as the Swindon slump rolls on. Sheffield United, at the expense of Reading, are through to the 6th Round of the FA Cup on Friday 13th thanks to Lee Sandford's late goal against the club he was on loan to earlier in the season. The Blades may have to fly the Division One flag alone in the last eight as Birmingham and Tranmere bow out at Leeds 3-2 and Newcastle 1-0 respectively. Wolves come from behind to hold Wimbledon at Selhurst Park. With Forest not in action, Middlesbrough move top with a home victory over Bradford but the league story of the day is at Maine Road where Bury end a 17-match winless run to drag City into the bottom three. Ipswich striker David Johnson takes his season's total of goals to 20 with two during a 5-1 thrashing of Huddersfield. QPR boss Ray Harford endures a traumatic reception on his first return to West Brom but it is Rangers who have most to celebrate from the 1-1 draw, achieved through Iain Dowie's first league goal for almost two years.

Eight league games on the 17th lead once again to the switching of the top two when Van Hooijdonk scores twice as Forest cruise to a 3-0 win over Huddersfield. Sunderland's first league gate in excess of 40,000 at the Stadium of Light witness another two goals for Kevin Phillips as Reading are seen off 4-1. Charlton's challenge dips with a home draw against QPR and West Brom stumble to a 2-1 defeat at Oxford. Birmingham edge closer to the leading pack with victory at Crewe. Portsmouth start the day by announcing debts of £5.6m and end it with Steve Claridge's winner against Stockport. Swindon halt their decline with three points at relegation-threatened Port Vale. Bury draw with Stoke to rise above Manchester City, who sink further into trouble with a home defeat the following night by Ipswich. City's reputation is further tarnished earlier in the day as Frank Clark learns via a radio that he is no longer manager at Maine Road. City's new manager, their 11th in 12 years, is their one-time player Joe Royle. Elsewhere, Steve Bull returns after three months out through injury to score his 300th goal for Wolves during a 2-1 win over Bradford. Tranmere take another step towards safety with a 2-0 success at Norwich.

On the penultimate Saturday of February, Forest grab a late equaliser at Stoke but Middlesbrough, with two goals from new signing Marco Branca, win the north-east derby with Sunderland 3-1 to return to the summit. The East Anglian derby also goes the way of the home side as Alex Mathie scores a hat-trick during Ipswich's 5-0 destruction of Norwich. But it is a poor day for many of the play-off hopefuls. West Brom drop two points at home to lowly Bury, Wolves go down to a last-minute defeat at Huddersfield and Charlton are trounced 3-0 by Stockport, who climb to seventh. Sheffield United suffer their fifth defeat of the season on the Sunday as Birmingham, helped by Michael Johnson's first goal in 250 league games, win 2-0 at St Andrews. A sequence of unlikely results sees three of the bottom four sides – Portsmouth, Manchester City and Port Vale – all win away from home. Portsmouth keep the momentum going midweek with a 3-0 success at the Hawthorns but Manchester City return to reality with a 3-0 defeat at fellow strugglers

Reading. Mathie is on target again for Ipswich but this time it is David Johnson, against Oxford, who strikes three times as Town hit five for the third successive home game. Allan Johnston also claims a treble as Sunderland get their promotion bid back on course with a testing 3-2 win at Huddersfield. Forest drop more points in a goalless draw at Tranmere. Charlton end a run of seven games without a win to collect all three points at Stoke but Birmingham's charge is slowed by Bury's 3-1 away win. Neil Maddison's winning goal ten minutes from time against Crewe takes Middlesbrough three points clear at the top. Wolves grab the FA Cup spotlight when coming from behind to beat Wimbledon at Molineux.

On the final day of the month, Wolves are brushed aside by visitors Birmingham while Sheffield United and Charlton boost their play-off aspirations with home wins. Sunderland come from two down against in-form Ipswich to salvage a home point while Bury, Manchester City and Portsmouth all win again to plunge Huddersfield into the bottom three.

March

Nottingham Forest wipe out Middlesbrough's three-point lead on the opening day of the month with a blistering 4-0 win at the City Ground against their main title rivals. Van Hooijdonk scores twice. In the bottom of the table Potteries derby, Port Vale and Stoke are goalless at Vale Park. Of their combined last 40 games the two sides have won just three.

Sheffield United are rocked by the resignation of manager Nigel Spackman and one day later lose their unbeaten home record to fast-rising Ipswich. Senior club officials are blamed for Spackman's departure. Two sides aiming for the play-offs, Charlton and Stockport, both hit five as West Brom and Reading are sent packing – Clive Mendonca, Brett Angell and Chris Byrne all hit doubles. With a 3-1 win at Huddersfield, Manchester City put seven teams between themselves and the foot of the table.

Bryan Robson's February Manager of the Month celebrations go flat as Andy Townsend is sent off and Boro are hammered again, this time 5-0 at struggling QPR. Worse still for Boro is that Sunderland trounce Forest 3-0 at the City Ground with Phillips notching his 23rd goal of the season. Port Vale plunge deeper into trouble with a 1-0 defeat which lifts visitors Tranmere four places to 17th.

Forest make light of their midweek blip to trounce Crewe 4-1 at Gresty Road with Kevin Campbell scoring a 15-minute hat-trick. Another hat-trick hero is Sunderland's Niall Quinn as Stockport are banished 4-1 at the Stadium of Light. Ipswich recover from a goal down to chalk up a 3-1 victory at Portman Road over Charlton and move to a season's high of fifth. Stoke crash 2-1 at home to fellow strugglers Huddersfield and are sent to the foot of the table by Port Vale's 3-0 success at Reading. Oxford move closer to safety with an important 2-0 win at Manchester City while Bury also improve their survival hopes with a home win over Norwich. Birmingham stay on course for the play-offs with victory over QPR but are stunned after the game to learn of Trevor Francis's resignation, stating that his family had been abused. Wolves are the toast of the Nationwide League as a late Don Goodman goal knocks Leeds out of the FA Cup at Elland Road. Sheffield United, under the guidance of caretaker manager Steve Thompson, also continue to fly the flag, with Brazilian born Marcello grabbing their equaliser at Coventry.

Two days after announcing his departure, Francis, following a meeting with club chairman David Gold, withdraws his resignation. The Blues look set to celebrate Francis's return with victory at Sunderland on the 10th but Allan Johnston's last-minute goal rescues a point for the second-placed Wearsiders. Middlesbrough, needing six goals to replace Forest at the summit, do just that with Branca, Neil Maddison and Alun Armstrong scoring two each in a 6-0 destruction of Swindon.

Forest waste no time in returning to the top with three second half goals disposing of Bury on the 14th. **Middlesbrough** fall two points behind after failing to win at Portsmouth. Ipswich's surge continues unabated at Stockport where they win 1-0 and Sheffield United have four different scorers in a 4-0 win over Reading, which keeps them in the play-off places. **Manchester City**'s fortunes dip again as Port Vale record a useful 2-1 win at Vale Park and Oxford United put five past desperate Stoke. Huddersfield dent Tranmere's recovery **with a 3-0 win**, during which Rovers' striker Graham Branch is sent off. Swindon have keeper Fraser Digby harshly dismissed at QPR but Town still manage to pick up just their **third win in 19 games**. Peter Reid, gaining national headlines for his colourful use of the English language in a documentary about Sunderland, risks confrontation with the FA on the Sunday after being pulled away from referee Clive Wilkes following his side's 1-1 draw **at Charlton**; Sunderland have Alex Rae dismissed but will appeal against the dismissal.

Francis Lee finally bows to the tirade of abuse from supporters and quits as Manchester City **chairman on the 16th**. He is replaced by David Bernstein. Sheffield United come within a minute of going out of the FA Cup in a 6th Round replay at Bramall Lane but an 89th-minute David Holdsworth equaliser takes the game into extra-time and, ultimately, a penalty shoot-out victory for the Blades, thanks to keeper Alan Kelly. A 3-0 defeat for Reading at Oxford paves the way for the resignation of Royals' boss Terry Bullivant after just nine months in charge.

Birmingham's promotion hopes suffer a setback on the 21st as Forest come from behind at St Andrews to clinch a win which, briefly, takes them four points clear of the pack. Sunderland grab a late winner against Portsmouth to move above Middlesbrough, and two other sides inside the top six, Charlton and Ipswich, both complete excellent 3-0 wins. Sheffield United move three points clear of seventh-placed Birmingham with a draw at Maine Road. Stoke notch a rare win, their first in almost eight weeks under Kamara's leadership, to dump Reading to bottom place. On the Sunday, Middlesbrough keep the leapfrog game going as a 3-0 win over Norwich takes them back above Sunderland.

Three days before appearing in the Coca-Cola Cup Final, Middlesbrough sign Paul Gascoigne from Rangers for £3.45m. Charlton boost their play-off ambitions with a thrilling 4-2 win over Forest at the Valley on the 28th and Sunderland move to within a point of the leaders with victory over Bury. Birmingham grab a last-minute Midlands derby win over West Brom but cannot shift Sheffield United from the top six as they beat Port Vale 2-1. Ipswich stay five points clear of Birmingham with a single goal success over Reading. Of the sides in the bottom eight at the start of the day only Tranmere win. The trend continues on the Sunday with Portsmouth going down at Wolves.

April

Sheffield United may have one eye on their FA Cup semi-final next weekend but Forest are clearly focused on the league on April Fool's Day as they hand United their heaviest defeat of the season, 3-0, to reopen a four-point lead, with van Hooijdonk taking his season's tally to 30. QPR move a point closer to safety after drawing with Wolves.

Portsmouth chairman Martin Gregory withdraws from talks to sell the club and looks to invest £10m and build a 30,000 all-seater stadium close to Fratton Park.

Sunderland's hopes of an automatic promotion place are boosted by a 2-1 defeat for **Middlesbrough at West Brom**. For Baggies manager Denis Smith it is his first success in 11 attempts. Gascoigne is booked on his league debut. Charlton cement their play-off position with a single goal triumph at Swindon. Birmingham's top six aspirations appear tentative as Portsmouth grab a potentially vital last-minute equaliser on the south coast. Reading move level with Pompey after a 2-0 victory over Stoke, who slump back to the bottom of the table. Bury are held at home by Huddersfield but Norwich slip to just three points above the relegation zone with a 3-2 home defeat by Bradford while the biggest winners of the day are Manchester City, whose 4-1 win over nearby Stockport takes them out of the bottom three. Port Vale grab a lifeline with a comfortable 3-0 victory over Oxford. Forest reassert their authority on the Sunday when coming from behind to end Ipswich's 16-match unbeaten run with a 2-1 success at the City Ground. The result sours George Burley's March Manager of the Month celebrations. Hopes of the first all-Nationwide League FA Cup Final are shattered as Sheffield United fall to Alan Shearer and Arsenal silence the Wolves.

Just two days after the cup defeat Sheffield United leapfrog Ipswich with a 1-0 win over out-of-sorts Middlesbrough, who also miss a penalty through Paul Merson. Wolves, though, cannot shake off their cup disappointment and are beaten at Charlton who move above Boro to third. Portsmouth again leave it late before salvaging another point at Tranmere. Chris Kamara parts company with Stoke on the 8th after just 14 games. City legend Alan Durban is back in charge after 17 years away.

Bradford, beaten only twice at Valley Parade all season, are hammered 3-0 by Forest on the 11th. On the back of a hat-trick by Marco Branca, Middlesbrough trounce Bury 4-0 but a number of the promotion-chasing sides stutter. Birmingham, Ipswich, Sheffield United and Wolves are all held at home by Port Vale, Tranmere, Norwich and Manchester City respectively. Portsmouth look to be heading out of the bottom three after taking the lead at Stoke but goals in the final 12 minutes by Ally Pickering and Kyle Lightbourne get Durban's second stint off to a winning start.

Forest's seventh win in eight games on Easter Monday just about ends Wolves' play-off hopes and leaves Dave Bassett's side on the verge of an instant return to the Premiership. Sunderland's hopes of joining them are jolted at West Brom where two Niall Quinn goals only secure a 3-3 draw; Lee Hughes scores twice for West Brom. Charlton and Middlesbrough join Sunderland on 81 points with 1-0 wins at Port Vale and Reading while Ipswich, 1-0 winners at Portsmouth, climb to fifth at the expense of Sheffield United who draw at Swindon. Dele Adebola's last-minute goal keeps alive Birmingham's play-off dreams and condemns Manchester City to an 11th home defeat. Norwich ease their growing relegation fears with a 5-0 win over Huddersfield; it is the Canaries' biggest win for over ten years. QPR's slow progress towards safety continues with a home draw against Oxford.

Middlesbrough move three points clear of the pack to claim second place on the Friday with an eighth successive home win, this time at Manchester City's cost, but Boro have Steve Vickers dismissed. Sixth-placed Sheffield United, on the 18th, retain a three-point advantage over seventh-placed Birmingham with both sides winning 3-0 at home. Brum see off Swindon with Paul Furlong scoring twice in his first game for two months and Dean Saunders bags a brace to account for Bury. Ipswich are also amongst the goals, with David Johnson taking his season's tally to 29 during a 5-1 thrashing of Port Vale. Portsmouth have just two games in which to get out of the bottom three following a 1-0 reversal at Charlton. Sunderland join Charlton on 84 points with a 2-1 win over Crewe. Bottom dogs Reading are almost down following a 3-1 defeat at Wolves but Stoke clamber above Manchester City and out of the bottom three after a 2-0 success over Norwich. Huddersfield make certain of their salvation with victory over West Brom. Despite being held 2-2 at Stockport, Forest are still six points clear at the top.

Portsmouth manager Alan Ball signs a five-year contract and Pompey's cause is aided by Middlesbrough on the 24th as they win at Port Vale through Merson's early strike. A maximum four points from their last two games will gain Boro automatic promotion.

Two goals from Clive Mendonca on the last Saturday of April give Charlton a 2-0 win over Tranmere and a club record eighth successive victory. Sunderland join Charlton and Boro on 87 points, three behind Forest, with two Kevin Phillips goals in a 3-0 win over almost doomed Stoke taking his tally for the season to 31. Birmingham move level on points with Sheffield United following a 2-0 win at Oxford but United stay above Francis's side on goals scored despite a 4-2 home defeat by West Brom. Stockport also score four on their travels with two late goals clinching a 4-3 success at Molineux. But the highest scorers of the day are Norwich and Crewe with five each. Ipswich are definitely into the play-offs through Mick Stockwell's match-winning strike at Bury. Forest have to wait until the Sunday for the three points successfully gleaned off Reading which all but mathematically ensures a return of Premiership football to the City Ground. But for Reading, Chris Bart-Williams' goal spells relegation.

Sheffield United's nervous stumble towards the play-offs continues as they trail 3-1 at Tranmere on the 28th before rescuing a valuable point. Ipswich dent Sunderland's desire to claim the second automatic promotion slot with a 2-0 victory over their promotion rivals at Portman Road. That result also confirms Nottingham Forest's promotion. By only drawing with Wolves the following night, Boro hand the Championship to Forest but know that victory on the final day will guarantee their own promotion. On the last day of the month Sheffield United fall again, with Crewe taking all the points from a thrilling encounter at Gresty Road.

May

There are goals galore on the final day of the 46-match league programme with some astounding results for many of the struggling clubs. Forest celebrate the Championship with a 1-1 draw at West Brom while Middlesbrough, after a tense first-half, slam four past Oxford United in front of a record crowd at the Riverside of 30,228. Alun Armstrong and Craig Hignett both score twice. Phillips bags two more as the Wearsiders end with a 2-1 win at Swindon. Charlton are fourth with a goalless draw at Birmingham which serves to carry Sheffield United into the play-offs despite them losing 1-0 at Stockport. Ipswich finish in fifth place with an entertaining 3-2 win over Crewe.

The real drama is at the other end of the table where Manchester City storm to a 5-2 victory at Stoke's Britannia Stadium with deadline-day signing Shaun Goater grabbing two. But, remarkably, Port Vale hammer Huddersfield 4-0 at the McAlpine Stadium and Portsmouth beat Bradford 3-1 at Valley Parade to confirm City's relegation to Division Two for the first time in the club's history. Reading, the only side down before the final day, lose again, this time to Norwich, who parted company with manager Mike Walker for a second time three days earlier. John Aldridge signs off his playing days by scoring both Tranmere goals during a 2-1 win over Wolves.

Sunderland may have come down with Forest and Middlesbrough, but their hopes of going up again with that duo take a knock on the 10th as Sheffield United win 2-1 at Bramall Lane in the 1st Leg of their play-off semi-final. United come back from one down against the side which earned 16 points more than the Blades during the season. Charlton look to have got themselves into an even stronger position as a Jamie Clapham own goal gives them a 1st Leg success over Ipswich at Portman Road. Charlton have defender Danny Mills harshly dismissed.

Over 40,000 turn up at the Stadium of Light to see Sunderland go ahead on aggregate by half time in the return meeting with Sheffield United. An unfortunate Nicky Marker own goal and an instinctive prod by Kevin Phillips clinch Sunderland's trip to Wembley. Phillips' goal equals Brian Clough's 36-year record of 34 goals in one season for the Rokermen. With an astonishing ninth successive clean sheet, Charlton ensure that they too are heading for Wembley. A spectacular Shaun Newton goal gives the Addicks a 2-0 aggregate victory over Ipswich.

Stoke appoint Brian Little as their new manager. Little tells Chic Bates and Alan Durban they will not be retained for next season.

The play-off final between Charlton and Sunderland is a classic. Charlton take a first-half lead but then have to come from behind three times to take the breathtaking finale to a penalty shoot-out. Goalkeeper Sasa Ilic is the toast of south London as he saves Sunderland's seventh penalty, taken by Michael Gray, to give the Addicks a pulsating 7-6 victory. Earlier in the afternoon Phillips scored his record-breaking 35th goal of the season. Richard Rufus scored his first goal for Charlton, but the brightest star of the lot was Charlton's £700,000 signing from Grimsby, Mendonca – a Sunderland supporter – who notched a hat-trick. Charlton's promotion could be worth £10m to the club; 24 hours after the match Sunderland saw that much wiped off their value on the stock exchange. ■

Play-Offs 1997-98

Nationwide Division 1

Semi-Finals 1st Leg

Ipswich Town	0	Charlton Athletic OG (Clapham 12)	1	21,681
Sheffield United Marcello (57); Borbokis (76)	2	Sunderland Ball (17)	1	23,900

Semi-Finals 2nd Leg

Charlton Athletic Newton (36)	1	Ipswich Town	0	15,585
Charlton Athletic win 2-0 on aggregate				
Sunderland OG (Marker 21); Phillips (38)	2	Sheffield United	0	40,092
Sunderland win 3-2 on aggregate				

Final – *at Wembley Stadium*

Charlton Athletic Mendonca (23, 71, 103); Rufus (85)	4	Sunderland Quinn (50, 73); Phillips (58) Summerbee (99)	4	77,739
		aet. Charlton Athletic win 7-6 on penalties		

NATIONWIDE LEAGUE 1

	Birmingham City	Bradford City	Bury	Charlton Athletic	Crewe Alexandra	Huddersfield Tn	Ipswich Town	Manchester City	Middlesbrough	Norwich City	Nottingham Fst	Oxford United
Birmingham City	—	0-0	1-3	0-0	0-1	0-0	1-1	2-1	1-1	1-2	1-2	0-0
Bradford City	0-0	—	1-0	1-0	1-0	1-1	2-1	2-1	1-2	2-1	0-3	0-0
Bury	2-1	1-0	—	0-0	1-0	2-2	2-0	1-1	0-1	1-0	2-0	1-0
Charlton Athletic	1-1	4-1	0-0	—	3-2	0-0	0-0	1-0	3-0	2-1	4-2	3-2
Crewe Alex.	0-2	5-0	1-2	0-3	—	2-5	0-0	1-3	0-1	1-2	1-4	2-1
Huddersfield Town	0-1	1-2	2-0	0-3	2-0	—	2-2	0-1	1-1	0-2	0-2	5-1
Ipswich Town	0-1	2-0	2-0	3-1	3-2	5-1	—	1-0	1-0	5-0	0-1	5-2
Manchester City	0-1	1-0	4-0	2-2	1-0	0-1	1-2	—	2-0	0-1	1-1	0-2
Middlesbrough	3-1	1-0	2-2	0-4	2-3	3-0	1-0	1-0	—	2-3	2-3	4-1
Norwich City	3-3	2-3	3-0	5-2	0-2	5-0	2-1	4-0	1-3	—	0-1	2-1
Nottingham Forest	1-0	2-2	1-1	1-2	3-1	3-0	1-3	1-3	4-0	4-1	—	1-3
Oxford United	0-2	3-0	1-1	1-2	1-0	3-0	0-1	2-0	1-4	2-0	1-0	—
Port Vale	0-1	0-0	0-1	0-1	2-3	0-0	1-0	2-1	3-0	2-2	0-1	3-0
Portsmouth	1-1	1-1	1-1	0-2	3-2	2-1	0-4	0-3	5-0	2-2	0-1	1-1
QPR	1-1	1-0	3-0	2-4	3-3	4-1	0-1	3-0	0-0	1-1	1-1	3-3
Reading	2-0	0-3	0-0	4-1	3-2	3-0	0-1	1-1	1-1	1-1	3-3	1-1
Sheffield United	1-1	1-2	3-2	2-0	0-1	0-2	2-1	2-5	0-1	2-2	1-1	2-1
Stockport County	2-2	0-0	2-1	0-1	0-2	1-0	0-2	3-1	1-2	2-2	2-2	1-0
Stoke City	0-7	3-2	3-1	1-2	1-2	2-1	2-2	2-5	1-2	1-1	2-1	3-2
Sunderland	1-1	2-1	0-0	0-1	1-2	3-1	0-2	3-1	1-1	1-0	1-1	0-0
Swindon Town	1-1	2-0	1-1	0-1	2-0	3-1	0-1	1-3	2-1	0-1	1-1	3-1
Tranmere Rovers	0-3	3-1	3-1	2-2	0-3	2-1	1-1	0-0	1-2	0-1	0-0	4-1
WBA	1-0	1-1	1-0	1-0	1-0	0-1	1-1	0-1	2-1	5-0	1-1	0-1
Wolverhampton W.	1-3	2-1	4-2	3-1	1-0	1-1	1-1	2-2	1-0	0-1	2-1	1-0

RESULTS 1997-98

	Port Vale	Portsmouth	QPR	Reading	Sheffield United	Stockport County	Stoke City	Sunderland	Swindon Town	Tranmere Rovers	WBA	Wolverhampton W.
Birmingham City	1-1	2-1	1-0	3-0	2-0	4-1	2-0	0-1	3-0	0-0	1-0	1-0
Bradford City	2-1	1-3	1-1	4-1	1-1	2-1	0-0	0-4	1-1	0-1	0-0	2-0
Bury	2-2	0-2	1-1	1-1	1-1	2-1	0-0	1-1	1-1	1-0	1-3	1-3
Charlton Athletic	1-0	1-0	2-3	3-0	2-1	1-3	1-1	1-1	3-0	2-0	5-0	1-0
Crewe Alex.	0-1	3-1	1-1	1-0	0-0	1-0	2-0	0-3	2-0	3-0	1-1	0-2
Huddersfield Town	0-4	1-1	1-1	1-0	0-0	1-0	1-2	2-0	0-0	1-1	1-0	1-0
Ipswich Town	5-1	2-0	0-0	1-0	2-0	0-2	2-3	3-0	6-0	1-0	3-0	3-0
Manchester City	2-3	2-2	2-2	0-0	1-2	4-1	0-1	0-1	5-0	3-0	1-1	0-1
Middlesbrough	1-0	2-1	3-0	4-0	0-0	3-1	1-0	0-1	3-0	0-2	1-0	1-1
Norwich City	2-1	1-0	4-0	1-0	3-0	1-1	0-0	2-1	0-1	2-2	2-1	3-0
Nottingham Forest	2-0	1-0	3-1	3-0	2-4	3-0	5-1	0-3	0-1	1-1	0-1	3-0
Oxford United	2-0	1-0	3-1	3-0	2-4	3-0	5-1	0-3	0-1	1-1	0-1	3-0
Port Vale	—	2-1	2-0	0-2	1-1	2-1	0-0	1-4	0-1	0-0	2-0	3-2
Portsmouth	3-1	—	3-1	0-2	1-1	2-1	1-1	0-1	0-1	0-1	2-0	0-0
QPR	0-1	1-0	—	—	1-0	2-1	2-0	4-0	0-1	0-1	2-1	0-0
Reading	0-3	2-1	2-2	—	2-2	1-0	3-2	4-0	2-1	1-3	2-3	1-0
Sheffield United	3-0	3-1	3-1	4-0	—	5-1	1-0	5-1	2-1	2-1	2-1	0-0
Stockport County	2-1	2-1	2-2	5-1	1-0	—	3-0	1-1	4-2	3-1	2-4	1-0
Stoke City	4-2	3-1	2-2	4-1	2-2	4-1	—	1-2	2-3	0-3	2-1	0-0
Sunderland	4-2	2-1	3-1	6-0	4-2	1-1	3-0	—	0-1	3-0	0-0	1-1
Swindon Town	1-2	0-1	3-1	0-2	0-2	3-2	1-0	1-2	—	3-0	2-0	0-0
Tranmere Rovers	2-2	0-3	1-1	1-0	1-1	3-2	3-1	0-2	—	—	0-0	2-1
WBA	2-2	0-3	1-1	1-0	3-3	3-2	1-1	0-2	—	2-1	—	2-1
Wolverhampton W.	1-1	2-0	3-2	3-1	0-0	3-4	1-1	0-1	3-1	2-1	0-1	—

SCORERS

Top Scorers – All Competitions

Player	Club	L	F	C	Total
Pierre VAN HOOIJDONK	N. Forest	31	1	4	36
Kevin PHILLIPS •	Sunderland	30	4	0	34
David JOHNSON *	Ipswich Town	26	2	3	31
Clive MENDONCA	Charlton Athletic	23	1	1	25
Kevin CAMPBELL	N. Forest	23	0	0	23
Brett ANGELL	Stockport County	18	2	3	23
Paul FURLONG	Birmingham City	15	2	2	19
Alun ARMSTRONG †	Middlesbrough	19	1	2	22
Shaun GOATER ††	Manchester City	19	0	1	20

L=League, F=FA Cup, C=Coca-Cola Cup.
• Total of 30 includes goals in play-offs.
* includes 5 for Bury; † includes 12 for Stockport County; †† includes 17 for Bristol City.

Top Scorers and Attendances 1997-98

Team	Psn	Top Scorer	Agg Att	Ave Att
Birmingham City	7	Furlong (15)	405,400	18,427
Bradford City	13	Steinder, Edhino (10)	342,087	15,549
Bury	17	Ellis (7)	142,110	6,178
Charlton Athletic	4	Medonca (23)	305,244	13,271
Crewe Alexandra	11	Little (13)	120,597	5,243
Huddersfield Town	16	Stewart (17)	263,735	11,987
Ipswich Town	5	Johnson (20)	323,440	14,701
Manchester City	22	Dickov (8)	648,533	28,197
Middlesbrough	2	Beck (14)	659,710	29,986
Norwich City	15	Bellamy (12)	332,229	14,444
Nottingham Forest	1	van Hooijdonk (31)	472,497	20,543
Oxford United	12	Beauchamp (13)	172,213	7,487
Port Vale	19	Mills (13)	193,930	8,431
Portsmouth	20	Aloisi (12)	256,421	11,148
QPR	21	Sheron (11)	285,695	12,986
Reading	24	Asaba (8)	207,723	9,441
Sheffield United	6	Taylor, Saunders, Deane (10)	412,526	17,935
Stockport County	8	Angell (18)	181,744	8,261
Stoke City	23	Thorne (10)	317,064	14,412
Sunderland	3	Phillips (30)•	789,194	34,312

Swindon Town 18	Hay (14)	203,739	9,260
Tranmere Rovers... 14	Kelly (12)	172,860	7,857
WBA 10	Hughes, Hunt (13)	359,622	16,346
Wolverhampton W. 9	Keane (11)	534,822	23,253

Division 1 Hat-tricks

Player	Gls	Match (result)	Date
VAN HOOIJDONK	3	N. FOREST v QPR (4-0)	30-Aug-97
MENDONCA	3	Norwich C. v CHARLTON A. (0-4)	17-Sep-97
HAY	3	SWINDON T. v Port Vale (4-2)	04-Oct-97
FJORTOFT	3	SHEFFIELD U. v Stockport Co. (5-1)	21-Oct-97
VAN HOOIJDONK	3	N. FOREST v Charlton A. (5-2)	22-Nov-97
FURLONG	3	Stoke City v BIRMINGHAM C. (0-7)	10-Jan-98
MATHIE	3	IPSWICH T. v Norwich C. (5-0)	21-Feb-98
CAMPBELL	3	Crewe Alex. v N. FOREST (1-4)	07-Mar-98
QUINN	3	SUNDERLAND v Stockport Co. (4-1)	07-Mar-98
BRANCA	3	MIDDLESBROUGH v Bury (4-0)	11-Apr-98
LITTLE	3	CREWE ALEX. v Bradford C. (5-0)	25-Apr-98

Division 1 Red Cards

Players	Opponents	Venue	Date	Official
Birmingham City				
Wassal	Sheffield U.	A	27-Sep-97	Heilbron
Furlong	Reading	A	31-Jan-98	Rejer
Marsden	Reading	A	31-Jan-98	Rejer
Johnson	N. Forest	H	21-Mar-98	Mathieson
Bradford City				
Beagrie	Charlton A.	A	21-Sep-97	Leake
Pepper	Portsmouth	A	21-Oct-97	Bennnett
Kulcsar	Portsmouth	A	21-Oct-97	Bennnett
O'Kane	Sheffield U.	H	18-Nov-97	Wolstenholme
Edinho	Bury	H	13-Dec-97	Frankland
Youds	Ipswich T.	A	31-Jan-98	Styles
Peppper	Ipswich T.	A	31-Jan-98	Styles
Blake	Portsmouth	H	03-May-98	Cain
Bury				
Jepson	Reading	A	10-Jan-97	Pierce
Hughes	Ipswich T.	A	25-Oct-97	D'Urso
Gray	Ipswich T.	A	25-Oct-97	D'Urso
Swan	Bradford C.	A	13-Dec-97	Frankland
Charlton Athletic				
Newton	Bury	A	23-Aug-97	Frankland
Mills	Ipswich T. (PO)	A	10-May-98	Fletcher

Players	Opponents	Venue	Date	Official
Ipswich Town				
Festa	Middlesbrough	A	17-Jan-97	Dean
Swailes	Stoke C.	H	20-Sep-97	Knight
Scowcroft	Middlesbrough	H	2-Dec-97	Fletcher
Harrison	Middlesbrough	A	2-Dec-97	Fletcher
Manchester City				
Kernaghan	Sunderland	A	15-Aug-97	Wolstenholme
Shelia	Charlton A.	H	28-Jan-98	Richards
Whitley Jeff	Bradford C.	A	28-Mar-98	Wolstenholme
Middlesbrough				
Festa	Tranmere R.	A	30-Aug-97	Richards
Townsend	QPR	A	4-Mar-98	D'Urso
Hignett	Reading	A	13-Apr-98	Knight
Vickers	Manchester City	H	17-Apr-98	Wiley
Norwich City				
Newman	Tranmere R.	A	4-Oct-97	Wolstenholme
Milligan	Tranmere R.	A	4-Oct-97	Wolstenholme
Milligan	Charlton A.	A	26-Dec-97	Danson
Nottingham Forest				
Beasant	Reading	A	24-Oct-97	Brandwood
Oldham Athletic				
Hodgson	Bristol City	H	31-Mar-98	Pugh
Oxford United				
Purse	Portsmouth	A	30-Aug-97	Mathieson
Ford R.	Sheffield U.	H	20-Sep-97	Brandwood
Portsmouth				
Allen	Norwich C.	H	2-Sep-97	Knight
Whitbread	Crewe Alex.	H	13-Sep-97	Taylor
Thomson	Bradford C.	H	21-Oct-97	Bennnett
Thomson	Port Vale	A	17-Jan-98	Bailey
QPR				
Maddix	Swindon T.	A	5-Nov-97	Pugh
Brazier	Norwich C.	H	3-Dec-97	Rejer
Maddix	Reading	H	28-Dec-97	Knight
Quashie	Manchester C.	A	25-Apr-98	Leach
Reading				
Bernal	Birmingham C.	A	23-Aug-97	Lomas
Bodin	Wolverhampton	H	20-Dec-97	Bennett
Asaba	QPR	A	28-Dec-97	Knight
Legg	Ipswich T.	A	28-Mar-98	Coddington
Bernal	Ipswich T.	A	28-Mar-98	Coddington

Players	Opponents	Venue	Date	Official
Sheffield United				
Vonk	Norwich C.	A	6-Dec-97	Bennnett
Tracey	Portsmouth	A	31-Jan-98	Halsey
Southend United				
Jones, N.	Bristol C.	A	28-Feb-98	Styles
Stoke City				
Whittle	QPR	H	21-Mar-98	Leake
Sunderland				
Williams	Reading	A	4-Oct-97	Brandwood
Rae	Charlton A.	A	15-Mar-98	Wilkes
Gray	WBA	A	13-Apr-98	Lomas
Swindon Town				
Collins	Wolverhampton	A	18-Oct-97	Foy
Bullock	Birmingham C.	H	20-Dec-97	Styles
Digby	QPR	A	14-Mar-98	Butler
Tranmere Rovers				
Jones, G.	Sheffield U.	A	1-Nov-97	Leake
Branch	Huddersfield T.	A	14-Mar-98	Laws
WBA				
Burgess	N. Forest	A	21-Oct-97	Pugh
Wolverhampton Wanderers				
Bull	Swindon T.	H	18-Oct-97	Foy
Casper	Swindon T.	A	18-Oct-97	Foy
Sedgley	Portsmouth	A	9-Dec-97	Orr
Simpson	Reading	A	20-Dec-97	Bennett
Osborn	Ipswich T.	A	21-Mar-98	Knight
Sedgley	Manchester C.	H	11-Apr-98	Halsey

Barnsley

Tyketanic Season

Starting their first ever season in the top flight of English football as just about the hottest favourites ever for relegation, Barnsley were considered as little more than cannon fodder for the big guns. Indeed, defeats of 5-0, 6-0 and 7-0 were suffered, but Barnsley gained the nation's affection for their endearing spirit and the magnificent support of their fans.

The Tykes got off to a dream start by going ahead against West Ham at Oakwell on the first day of the season but the game ended in defeat. The writing was very much on the wall following a 6-0 home defeat by Chelsea. With just two wins from the next 16 games Barnsley were anchored to the foot of the table. That run included eight games when three or more goals were conceded – amazingly one of the two wins was at Anfield where Ward's goal ensured the biggest shock league result of the season.

Five successive home matches without defeat including three wins raised hopes in late February, but the Yorkshire club failed to score in their final three games as the bookies were ultimately proved right. Barnsley's demise was generally greeted with great disappointment.

In the FA Cup there was glory including a 5th Round win over Manchester United while Southampton proved too tough an obstacle in the Coca-Cola Cup.

Formed:	1887
Ground:	Oakwell Ground, Barnsley, South Yorkshire, S71 1ET
Phone:	01226 211211 **Box Office:** 01226 211211
Info:	0891 12 11 52
Internet:	http://www.yorkshire-web.co.uk/bfc/BFC.HTML
Capacity:	19,101
Colours:	Red, White, Red
Nickname:	The Tykes or Reds
Manager:	John Hendrie
Honours:	FA Cup Winners 1911-12; Runners-up 1909-10; Division 1 Runners-up 1996-97; Division 3N Champions 1933-34, 1938-39, 1954-55; Runners-up 1953-54; Division 3 Runners-up 1980-81; Division 4 Runners-up 1967-68; Promoted 1978-79.
Managers:	Bobby Collins 1984-85, Allan Clarke 1985-89, Mel Machin 1989-93, Viv Anderson 1993-94, Danny Wilson 1994-1998
Previous Names:	Barnsley St Peters
Record League Win:	9-0 v Loughborough Town, D2, 28/1/1899 9-0 v Accrington Stanley, D3N, 3/2/34
Record League Defeat:	0-9 v Notts County, D2, 19/11/27
Most GF in Season:	118 – Division 3N, 1933-34

All-time League Apps:	564 – Barry Murphy, 1962-78
All-time League Goals:	130 – Ernie Hine, 1921-26 and 1934-38
Most Goals in a Season:	34 – Cecil McCormack, 1950-51
Most Goals in a Match:	5 – F. Eaton v South Shields, D3N, 9/4/27
	5 – P. Cunningham v Darlington, D3N, 4/2/33
	5 – B. Asquith v Darlington, D3N, 12/11/38
	5 – C. McCormack v Luton, D2, 9/9/50
Record Fee Received:	£1.5m from N. Forest for Carl Tiler, 5/91
	£1.5m from Bolton W. for Gerry Taggart, 8/95
Record Fee Paid:	£1.5m to Partizan Belgrade for Giorgi Hristov, 6/97
Record Attendance:	40,255 v Stoke City, FA Cup 5th Round, 15/2/36

Stats File

Division	P	W	D	L	F	A	Pts	Yr	B	W
Premier/1:	38	10	5	23	37	82	35	1	19	19
Division 1n/2:	2504	871	622	1011	3474	3905	2626	61	2	22
Division 2n/3:	552	183	159	210	736	838	525	12	2	24
Division 3n/4:	460	177	127	156	628	555	481	10	2	16

Cup Records	P	W	D	L	F	A
FA Cup:	238	89	62	87	318	320
League Cup:	103	31	25	47	129	146
A/F Members Cup:	9	2	3	4	17	18

Sequence	Games	Start		End
Winning Run:	10	5-Mar-55	to	23-Apr-55
Without Defeat:	21	1-Jan-34	to	5-May-34
Without Win:	26	13-Dec-52	to	26-Aug-53
Drawn Games:	7	28-Mar-11	to	22-Apr-11
Without Draw:	22	14-Nov-14	to	2-Apr-15
Losing Run:	9	14-Mar-53	to	25-Apr-53
Clean Sheets:	8	5-Mar-55	to	12-Apr-55
Goal Scored:	44	2-Oct-26	to	8-Oct-27
No. Goals For:	6	7-Oct-1899	to	2-Dec-1899
	6	27-Nov-71	to	7-Jan-72
SOS Undefeated:	10	1946-47		
SOS No Wins:	23	1952-53		

5-Year Record

	Div	P	W	D	L	F	A	Pts	Psn	
1993-94	1n	46	16	7	23	55	67	55	18	
1994-95	1n	46	20	12	14	63	52	72	6	
1995-96	1n	46	14	18	14	60	66	60	10	
1996-97	1n	46	22	14	10	76	55	80	2	Promoted
1997-98	P	38	10	5	23	37	82	35	19	Relegated

Birmingham City

Fringe Players

For a club which missed out on a play-off position only by failing to win its last match of the season – a crucial showdown with Charlton – Birmingham went through several traumatic moments. A poor spell led to speculation concerning the future of manager Trevor Francis who did actually resign in March after yobs had insulted members of his family. Francis was persuaded to return but there appeared to be an uneasy truce.

Britain's first £1m player, Francis was very active in the transfer market during the close season with 15 players moving in or out of St Andrews. Another four players joined for six-figure fees during the season and in February Dele Adebola stepped up from Crewe in a £1m deal.

Birmingham were forever on the fringe of the leading group but that they failed to beat any of the promoted sides suggests that they are not quite there just yet. In the FA Cup, two Paul Furlong goals took Birmingham past Crewe and two strikes by Bryan Hughes put paid to Stockport before a thrilling 5th Round tie at Leeds was lost 3-2. Gillingham and Stockport were competently despatched from the Coca-Cola Cup before Arsenal, in extra-time, ended the run in the 4th Round.

Formed:	1875
Ground:	St Andrews, Birmingham, B9 4NH
Phone:	0121 772 0101 **Box Office:** 0121 772 0101
Info:	0891 121188
Capacity:	25,812
Colours:	Royal blue and white shirts, white shorts with blue trim, red socks
Nickname:	The Blues
Manager:	Trevor Francis
Honours:	Division 2 Champions 1892-3; 1920-21, 1947-48, 1954-55, 1994-95; FA Cup Runners-up 1930-31, 1955-56; Football League Cup Winners 1962-63; Leyland Daf Cup Winners 1990-91; Auto Windscreens Shield Winners 1994-95.
Managers:	Garry Pendrey 1987-89, Dave Mackay 1989-91, Lou Macari 1991, Terry Cooper 1991-93, Barry Fry 1993-96.
Previous Names:	Small Heath Alliance 1875-88, Small Heath 1888, Birmingham 1905-1944
Record League Win:	12-0 v Walsall Town Swifts, D2, 17/12/1892 12-0 v Doncaster Rovers, D2, 1/4/1903
Record League Defeat:	1-9 v Sheff Wednesday, D1, 13/12/1930 1-9 v Blackburn Rovers, D1, 5/1/1895
Most GF in Season:	103 – Division 2, 1893-94

All-time League Apps:	551 – Gil Merrick, 1945-60	
All-time League Goals:	267 – Joe Bradford, 1920-35	
Most Goals in a Season:	42 – Walter Abbott, 1898-99	
Most Goals in a Match:	5 (4 times):	
	Ben Green v Middlesbrough, D1, 26/12/1905 (7-0);	
	Jimmy Windridge v Glossop, D2, 23/1/15 (11-1);	
Record Fee Received:	£2.5m from Coventry C. for Gary Breen, 1/97	
Record Fee Paid:	£1.85m for Jon McCarthy from Port Vale, 9/97	
Record Attendance:	66,844 v Everton, FA Cup 5th Round, 11/2/1939	

Stats File

Division	P	W	D	L	F	A	Pts	Yr	B	W
Premier/1:	2040	651	501	888	2776	3296	1845	50	6	22
Division 1n/2:	1630	709	393	528	2621	2106	1943	41	1	23
Division 2n/3:	184	82	55	47	258	197	301	4	1	12

Cup Records	P	W	D	L	F	A
FA Cup:	272	117	54	101	429	375
League Cup:	135	54	35	46	200	188
A/F Members Cup:	24	17	1	6	44	31

Sequence	Games	Start		End
Winning Run:	13	17/12/1892	to	16/9/1893
Without Defeat:	20	3-Sep-94	to	2-Jan-95
Without Win:	17	28-Sep-85	to	18-Jan-86
Drawn Games:	8	18-Sep-90	to	23-Oct-90
Without Draw:	43	10/12/1892	to	22/09/1894
Losing Run (3):	8	2-Dec-78	to	13-Feb-79
	8	28-Sep-85	to	23-Nov-85
Clean Sheets:	7	29-Oct-94	to	17-Dec-94
Goal Scored:	24	24/9/1892	to	23/9/1893
No. Goals For:	6	1-Oct-49	to	5-Nov-49
	6	26-Oct-85	to	30-Nov-85
	6	11-Feb-89	to	11-Mar-89
SOS Undefeated:	15	1900-01		
SOS No Wins:	13	1978-79		

5-Year Record

	Div	P	W	D	L	F	A	Pts	Psn	
1993-94	1n	46	13	12	21	52	69	51	22	Relegated
1994-95	2n	46	25	14	7	84	37	89	1	Promoted
1995-96	1n	46	15	13	18	61	64	58	15	
1996-97	1n	46	17	15	14	52	48	66	10	
1997-98	1n	46	19	17	10	60	35	74	7	

Bolton Wanderers

New Stadium – Old Story
Promotion to the Premiership, a move to the new Reebok Stadium, victory at Southampton on the opening day of the season. Everything seemed to be going Bolton Wanderers' way late in the summer of 1997 but it was not long before the harsh reality of the Premiership came home and Bolton were back into the Football League. Money was spent and players were added to bolster the side but they failed to ignite the run of points that would mean safety. Crucially, Bolton failed to take maximum points at home to the other struggling clubs. Barnsley, Everton and Tottenham all achieved draws at the Reebok and a 12-match winless run provided a bleak outlook in the bottom three.

However, as the season neared completion, a win at Villa and a home victory over Palace meant that a point at Chelsea on the final day would have spelled survival. Bolton could not raise themselves sufficiently and returned to the Nationwide League following a 2-0 defeat at Stamford Bridge.

For the fourth year Bolton made little headway in the FA Cup, bowing out of the competition at the first hurdle following a trip to Barnsley, while interest in the Coca-Cola Cup was ended by Middlesbrough.

Formed:	1874
Ground:	The Reebok Stadium, Mansell Way, Horwich, Bolton
Phone:	01204-698800 **Box Office:** 01204-389200
Info:	0891-12 11 64
Internet:	http://www.boltonwfc.co.uk
Capacity:	25,000
Colours:	White, Navy Blue, Navy Blue
Nickname:	The Trotters
Manager:	Colin Todd
Honours:	FA Cup Winners 1922-23, 1925-26, 1928-29, 1957-58; Runners-up 1883-84, 1903-04, 1952-53; Division One Champions 1996-97; Division Two Champions 1908-09, 1977-78; Division Three Champions 1972-73; League Cup Runners-up 1994-95; FA Charity Shield Winners 1958; Sherpa Van Trophy Winners 1988-89; Freight Rover Trophy Runners-up 1985-86.
Managers:	George Mulhall 1981-82, John McGovern 1982-85, Charlie Wright 1985, Phil Neal 1985-92, Bruce Rioch 1992-95, Roy McFarland 1995-96.
Record League Win:	8-0 v Barnsley, D2, 6/10/34
Record League Defeat:	0-7 v Burnley, D1, 1/3/1890
	0-7 v Sheffield Wednesday, D1, 1/3/15

	0-7 v Manchester City, D1, 21/3/1936
Most GF in Season:	96 – Divison 2, 1934-35
All-time League Apps:	519 – Eddie Hopkinson, 1956-70
All-time League Goals:	285 – Nat Lofthouse, 1945-61
Most Goals in a Season:	38 – Joe Smith, 1920-21
Most Goals in a Match:	5 – J. Cassidy v Sheffield Utd, FAC, 1/2/1890 (13-0)
	5 – T. Caldwell v Walsall, D3, 10/9/1983 (8-1)
Record Fee Received:	£4.5m from Liverpool for Jason McAteer, 9/95
Record Fee Paid:	£1.5m to Partizan Belgrade for Sasa Curcic, 10/95 and
	£1.5m to Barnsley for Gerry Taggart, 8/95
Record Attendance:	69,912 v Manchester City, FA Cup 5th Round,
	18/2/33 (Burnden Park)

Stats File

Division	P	W	D	L	F	A	Pts	Yr	B	W
Premier/1:	2384	885	531	968	3661	3854	2318	62	3	22
Division 1n/2:	1030	443	255	332	1601	1265	1229	25	1	22
Division 2n/3:	506	200	134	172	667	590	692	11	1	21
Division 3n/4:	46	22	12	12	66	42	78	1	3	3

Cup Records	P	W	D	L	F	A
FA Cup:	336	155	80	101	581	447
League Cup:	129	51	33	45	211	209
A/F Members Cup:	42	24	6	12	58	43

Sequence	Games	Start		End
Winning Run:	11	5-Nov-04	to	2-Jan-05
Without Defeat:	23	13-Oct-90	to	9-Mar-91
Without Win:	26	7-Apr-02	to	10-Jan-03
Drawn Games:	6	25-Jan-13	to	8-Mar-13
Without Draw:	27	4-Nov-11	to	20-Apr-12
Losing Run:	11	7-Apr-02	to	18-Oct-02
Clean Sheets:	7	24-Feb-00	to	14-Apr-00
Goal Scored:	24	22-Nov-96	to	12-Apr-97
No. Goals For:	5	3/1/1898	to	22/2/1898
	5	16-Mar-90	to	31-Mar-90
SOS Undefeated (3):	7	1896-97		
	7	1906-07		
SOS No Wins:	22	1902-03		

5-Year Record

	Div	P	W	D	L	F	A	Pts	Psn	
1993-94	1	46	15	14	17	63	64	59	14	
1994-95	1	46	21	14	11	67	45	77	3	
1995-96	P	38	8	5	25	39	71	29	20	Relegated
1996-97	1	46	28	14	4	100	53	98	1	Promoted
1997-98	P	38	9	13	16	41	61	40	18	Relegated

Bradford City

Slip Sliding Away

Following a season in which Bradford City only avoided relegation by two points and won just two away games all season, manager Chris Kamara made ten signings before the start of the season, including club record signing Robert Steiner from Norrkopping for £600,000. The changes appeared to work with Bradford topping the table during the early weeks of the season and even at the end of October the Bantams were still in the top four. But a run of just four wins in 21 league and cup matches saw Bradford slip into a mid-table position and, although there was never a threat of relegation, the poor run led to the sacking of Kamara in January. Prior to his dismissal Kamara had fallen out with chairman Geoffrey Richmond. Paul Jewell, in his tenth season with the club, took charge until the end of the season. Despite the upheavals Bradford finished eight places higher than the previous season.

Kamara's final match as manager was a 2-0 3rd Round FA Cup defeat at Manchester City and Bradford's Coca-Cola Cup exploits were equally brief with a 1st Round 1st Leg 2-1 defeat at neighbours Huddersfield being followed by a 1-1 draw at the Pulse Stadium.

Formed:	1903
Ground:	Valley Parade Ground, Bradford, West Yorkshire, BD8 7DY
Phone:	01274 773355 **Box Office:** 01274 770022
Capacity:	18,018
Colours:	Amber/claret stripes, claret shorts, amber socks
Nickname:	The Bantams
Manager	Paul Jewell
Honours:	Division 2 Champions 1907-08; Division 3 Champions 1984-85; Division 3N Champions 1928-29; FA Cup Winners 1910-11.
Managers:	Terry Yorath 1989-90, John Docherty 1990-91, Frank Stapleton 1991-94, Lennie Lawrence 1994-95, Chris Kamara 1995-1998.
Previous Names:	–
Record League Win:	11-1 v Rotherham United, D3N, 25/8/29
Record League Defeat:	0-8 v Manchester City, D2, 7/5/27
	1-9 v Colchester United, D4, 30/12/61
Most GF in Season:	128 – Division 3N, 1928-29
All-time League Apps:	502 – Cyril Podd, 1970-84
All-time League Goals:	285 – Nat Lofthouse, 1945-61
Most Goals in a Season:	38 – Joe Smith, 1920-21
Most Goals in a Match:	5 – J. Cassidy v Sheffield United, FAC, 1/2/1890 (13-0)
	5 – T. Caldwell v Walsall, D3, 10/9/83 (8-1)

Record Fee Received: £2m from Newcastle U. for Des Hamilton 3/97
Record Fee Paid: £625,000 to Bolton for John McGinlay, 11/97
Record Attendance: 39,146 v Burnley, FA Cup 4th Round, 11/3/11

Stats File

Division	P	W	D	L	F	A	Pts	Yr	B	W
Premier/1:	392	138	106	148	516	533	382	10	5	21
Division 1n/2:	1040	354	265	421	1380	1553	1074	25	1	23
Division 2n/3:	736	269	192	275	1022	1059	902	16	1	24
Division 3n/4:	780	307	205	268	1174	1089	845	17	2	23

Cup Records	P	W	D	L	F	A
FA Cup:	223	93	48	82	369	306
League Cup:	120	44	29	47	183	202
A/F Members Cup:	32	13	6	13	62	56

Sequence	Games	Start		End
Winning Run:	10	26-Nov-83	to	3-Feb-84
Without Defeat:	21	11-Jan-69	to	2-May-69
Without Win:	16	28-Aug-48	to	20-Nov-48
Drawn Games:	6	30-Jan-76	to	13-Mar-76
Without Draw:	24	7-Oct-63	to	7-Mar-64
Losing Run:	8	21-Jan-33	to	11-Mar-33
Clean Sheets (6):	5	29-Aug-53	to	12-Sep-53
	5	16-Jan-54	to	20-Feb-54
Goal Scored:	30	26-Dec-61	to	15-Sep-62
No. Goals For:	7	18-Apr-25	to	5-Sep-25
SOS Undefeated:	8	1979-80		
SOS No Wins:	9	1926-27		

5-Year Record

	Div	P	W	D	L	F	A	Pts	Psn	
1993-94	2	46	19	13	14	61	53	70	7	
1994-95	2	46	16	12	18	57	64	60	14	
1995-96	2	46	22	7	17	71	69	73	6	Promoted PO
1996-97	1	46	12	12	22	47	72	48	21	
1997-98	1	46	14	15	17	46	59	57	13	

Bristol City

Snatch Champs

Starting the season as joint favourites for promotion was a burden Bristol City carried with great ease as they, along with Watford, dominated the Division Two Championship race. City seemingly had the trophy in the bag as the final round of matches began but defeat at Preston allowed Watford to sneak in and deny their first title success in 43 years.

Bristol started relatively slowly and languished in 19th place after seven games but by the time they drew at manager John Ward's old club Watford in mid December they were 12 points clear of the third-placed club and even a six-match winless run in late winter never seriously threatened their promotion push. Leading City's surge was Shaun Goater whose 18 goals tempted Manchester City to splash out £500,000 on him on transfer deadline day.

City's FA Cup run kicked off with victory over Millwall but was then terminated at Bournemouth. The Robins enjoyed complete supremacy over rivals Bristol Rovers in the league and also put them out of the Coca-Cola Cup with an away 2nd Leg success. City also showed their quality with a 2nd Round 2nd Leg victory at home to Leeds but still went out 4-3 on aggregate.

Formed:	1894
Ground:	Ashton Gate, Bristol, BS3 2EJ
Phone:	0117 9632812 **Box Office:** 0117 9666666
Info:	0891 12 11 76
Capacity:	21,479
Colours:	Red shirts, white shorts, red and white socks
Nickname:	The Robins
Manager:	John Ward
Honours:	Division 1 Runners-up 1906-7; Division 2 Champions 1905-06; Division 3S Champions 1922-23, 1926-27, 1954-55; FA Cup Runners-up 1926-27; Welsh Cup Winners 1934; Anglo-Scottish Cup Winners 1978; Freight Rover Trophy Winners 1986.
Managers:	Joe Jordan 1988-90, Jimmy Lumsden 1990-92, Denis Smith 1992-93, Russell Osman 1993-94, Joe Jordan 1994-97.
Previous Names:	Bristol South End 1894-97
Record League Win:	9-0 v Aldershot, D3S, 28/12/46
Record League Defeat:	0-9 v Coventry City, D3S, 28/4/34
Most GF in Season:	104, D3S, 1926-27
All-time League Apps:	597 – John Atyeo, 1951-66
All-time League Goals:	314 – John Atyeo, 1951-66
Most Goals in a Season:	36 – Don Clark, 1946-47
Most Goals in a Match:	6 – T.Walsh v Gillingham, D3S, 15/1/27 (9-4)

Record Fee Received: £1.75m from Newcastle Utd for Andy Cole, 3/93
Record Fee Paid: £500,000 to Arsenal for Andy Cole, 7/92
Record Attendance: 43,335 v Preston NE, FA Cup 5th Round, 16/2/35

Stats File

Division	P	W	D	L	F	A	Pts	Yr	B	W
Premier/1:	358	114	94	150	428	510	322	9	2	20
Division 1n/2:	1648	590	421	637	2217	2346	1675	40	1	23
Division 2n/3:	690	301	173	216	1085	866	976	15	2	23
Division 3n/4:	92	37	27	28	129	114	138	2	4	14

Cup Records	P	W	D	L	F	A
FA Cup:	243	98	57	88	383	336
League Cup:	112	39	29	44	135	163
A/F Members Cup:	38	19	7	12	51	36

Sequence	Games	Start		End
Winning Run:	14	9-Sep-05	to	2-Dec-05
Without Defeat:	24	9-Sep-05	to	10-Feb-06
Without Win:	15	29-Apr-33	to	4-Nov-33
Drawn Games (6):	4	30-Oct-82	to	13-Nov-82
	4	17-Apr-93	to	1-May-93
Without Draw:	35	30-Jan-04	to	31-Dec-04
Losing Run:	7	5-Sep-31	to	3-Oct-31
	7	3-Oct-70	to	7-Nov-70
Clean Sheets:	5	11-Oct-96	to	29-Oct-96
Goal Scored:	25	26-Dec-05	to	22-Sep-06
No. Goals For:	6	10-Sep-10	to	15-Oct-10
	6	20-Dec-80	to	31-Jan-81
SOS Undefeated:	13	1954-55		
SOS No Wins:	13	1933-34		

5-Year Record

	Div	P	W	D	L	F	A	Pts	Psn	
1993-94	1	46	16	16	14	47	50	64	13	
1994-95	1	46	11	12	23	42	63	45	23	Relegated
1995-96	2	46	15	15	16	55	60	60	13	
1996-97	2	46	21	10	15	69	51	73	5	
1997-98	2	46	25	10	11	69	39	85	2	Promoted

Bury

Ternent's Extra

Stan Ternent, manager of Bury, will not have got a mention when the Manager of the Year Awards were dished out but the achievements of the Gigg Lane club since his appointment in September 1995 are outstanding. Playing at their highest level for almost 30 years, courtesy of two consecutive promotions, Bury were a strong tip to go down, especially considering the number of 'big' clubs in Division One, but they held their own to finish four points above the drop positions and even chalked up historic wins over both Nottingham Forest and Manchester City.

Ternent worked well in the transfer market with the sale of David Johnson to Ipswich for £800,000 in November funding the arrival of several players, including Tony Ellis who finished the season as the Shakers' top scorer.
Bury's FA Cup journey was ended in the 3rd Round by Sheffield United who won a replay at Gigg Lane. Three goals in 19 minutes set up a 3-2 win at Crewe in the 1st

Round of the Coca-Cola Cup but Bury needed an extra-time equaliser in the 2nd meeting to clinch a dramatic 6-5 aggregate victory. It was another Division One side, Sunderland, who curtailed the run in the 2nd Round. As for Ternent, he was replaced by Neil Warnock in the close season!

Formed:	1885
Ground:	Gigg Lane, Bury, Lancs, BL9 9HR
Phone:	0161 764 4881
Info:	0930 190003
Capacity:	11,841
Colours::	White shirts, navy blue shorts, navy blue socks
Nickname:	Shakers
Manager:	Neil Warnock
Honours:	Division 2 Champions 1894-95; Division 3 Champions 1960-61; FA Cup Winners 1900, 1903.
Managers:	Jim Iley 1980-84, Martin Dobson 1984-89, Sam Ellis 1989-90, Mike Walsh 1990-95, Stan Ternent 1995-98.
Record League Win:	8-0 v Tranmere Rovers, D3, 10/1/1970 (Bury have scored eight goals four times in the League)
Record League Defeat:	0-8 v Sheffield United, D1, 6/4/1896
	0-8 v Swindon Town, D3, 8/12/79
Most GF in a Season:	108 – Division 3, 1960-61
All-time League Apps:	506 – Norman Bullock, 1920-35
All-time League Goals:	129 – Craig Madden, 1977-86
Most Goals in a Season:	35 – Craig Madden, 1981-82
Most Goals in a Match:	5 – Ray Pointer v Rotherham United, D2, 2/10/65 (6-1)
	5 – Eddie Quigley v Millwall, D2, 15/2/47 (5-2)

Record Fee Received: £800,000 from Ipswich for David Johnson 11/97
Record Fee Paid: £200,000 to Ipswich for Chris Swailes, 11/97
Record Attendance: 35,000 v Bolton Wanderers, FA Cup 3rd Round, 9/1/60

Stats File

Division	P	W	D	L	F	A	Pts	Yr	B	W
Premier/1:	804	279	180	345	1176	1340	738	22	4	21
Division 1n/2:	1576	591	335	650	2361	2512	1528	38	1	22
Division 2n/3:	920	347	246	327	1277	1163	1075	20	1	22
Division 3n/4:	540	230	151	159	830	635	767	12	3	15

Cup Records	P	W	D	L	F	A
FA Cup:	236	87	57	92	366	366
League Cup:	120	48	24	48	169	188
A/F Members Cup:	43	17	6	20	58	63

Sequence	Games	Start		End
Winning Run:	9	26-Sep-60	to	19-Nov-60
Without Defeat:	18	4-Feb-61	to	29-Apr-61
Without Win:	19	1-Apr-11	to	2-Dec-11
Drawn Games (12):	4	5-Apr-94	to	23-Apr-94
	4	20-Dec-97	to	10-Jan-98
Without Draw:	27	27-Dec-30	to	14-Sep-31
Losing Run (4):	6	3-Oct-53	to	7-Nov-53
	6	14-Jan-67	to	4-Mar-67
Clean Sheets:	8	9-Feb-24	to	22-Mar-24
Goal Scored:	24	1/9/1894	to	2/3/1895
No. Goals For:	6	11-Jan-69	to	1-Mar-69
SOS Undefeated:	10	1975-76		
SOS No Wins:	13	1905-06		
	13	1911-12		

5-Year Record

	Div	P	W	D	L	F	A	Pts	Psn	
1993-94	3	42	14	11	17	55	56	53	13	
1994-95	3	42	23	11	8	73	36	80	4	
1995-96	3	46	22	13	11	66	48	79	3	Promoted
1996-97	2	46	24	12	10	62	38	84	1	Promoted
1997-98	1	46	11	19	16	42	58	52	17	

Crewe Alexandra

No Change at Crewe

The magic wand which manager Dario Gradi has been waving at Gresty Road for the past 15 years was again very much in evidence during the 1997/98 season as Crewe Alexandra not only defied the bookmakers by avoiding relegation but went on to finish 11th in Division One, their highest ever placing.

Gradi's reputation for bringing on young players and selling them on was further enhanced when former Crewe trainee Dele Adebola was transferred to Birmingham for £1m in February. That one sale more than covered the amount Gradi had invested on making four signings during the season.

The Railwaymen can reflect on their first season at this level this century with no shortage of pride as they defeated Manchester City at home, drew with Middlesbrough and won away at the likes of Birmingham and West Brom. Crewe's record of five draws was the least of any club in the Nationwide League.

Birmingham, though, took revenge with a 2-1 victory at Gresty Road in the 3rd Round of the FA Cup. Crewe's Coca-Cola Cup ambitions proved to be equally brief with Bury winning 3-2 at Gresty Road before clinching an extra-time 3-3 draw at Gigg Lane to progress to the 2nd Round.

Formed:	1877
Ground:	Gresty Road, Crewe, Cheshire, CW2 6EB
Phone:	01270 213014 **Box Office:** 01270 252610
Info:	0898 12 16 47
Capacity:	6,000
Colours:	Red shirts, white shorts, red socks
Nickname:	The Railwaymen
Manager:	Dario Gradi
Honours:	Promoted from Division 2 1996-97 (play-offs); Welsh Cup Winners 1936, 1937.
Managers:	Harry Gregg 1975-78, Warwick Rimmer 1978-79, Tony Waddington 1979-81, Arfon Griffiths 1981-82, Peter Morris 1982-83.
Record League Victory:	8-0 v Rotherham United, D3N, 1/10/32
Record League Defeat:	1-11 v Lincoln City, D3N, 29/9/51
Most GF in Season:	95 – Division 3N, 1931-32
All-time League Apps:	436 – Tommy Lowry, 1966-78
All-time League Goals:	126 – Bert Swindells, 1928-37
Most Goals in a Season:	35 – Terry Harkin, 1964-65
Most Goals in a Match:	5 – Tony Naylor v Colchester Utd, D3, 24/4/93

Record Fee Received: £1m from Birmingham City for Dele Adebola, 2/98
Record Fee Paid: £750,000 to Shrewsbury for David Walton, 10/97
Record Attendance: 20,000 v Tottenham Hotspur, FA Cup 4th Round, 30/1/60

Stats File

Division	P	W	D	L	F	A	Pts	Yr	B	W
Division 1n/2:	156	38	22	96	198	405	116	5	10	16
Division 2n/3:	322	119	71	132	433	461	404	7	3	23
Division 3n/4:	1458	505	377	576	1907	2086	1565	32	3	24

Cup Records	P	W	D	L	F	A
FA Cup:	203	75	48	80	314	344
League Cup:	96	29	23	44	131	173
A/F Members Cup:	43	12	17	14	64	53

Sequence	Games	Start		End
Winning Run (3):	7	4-Mar-86	to	29-Mar-86
	7	30-Apr-94	to	3-Sep-94
Without Defeat:	17	25-Mar-95	to	16-Sep-95
Without Win:	30	22-Sep-56	to	6-Apr-57
Drawn Games (3):	5	16-Mar-68	to	1-Apr-68
	5	31-Aug-87	to	18-Sep-87
Without Draw:	27	19-Apr-30	to	3-Jan-31
Losing Run (3):	10	26-Dec-57	to	1-Mar-58
	10	16-Apr-79	to	22-Aug-79
Clean Sheets:	5	4-Apr-59	to	25-Apr-59
Goal Scored:	26	7-Apr-34	to	26-Dec-34
No. Goals For:	9	6-Nov-74	to	28-Dec-74
SOS Undefeated:	10	1953-54		
SOS No Wins:	10	1936-37		

5-Year Record

	Div	P	W	D	L	F	A	Pts	Psn	
1993-94	3	42	21	10	11	80	61	73	3	Promoted
1994-95	2	46	25	8	13	80	68	83	3	
1995-96	2	46	22	7	17	77	60	73	5	
1996-97	2	46	22	7	17	56	47	73	6	Promoted
1997-98	1	46	18	5	23	58	65	59	11	

Crystal Palace

Too Many Cooks

With both of their two previous ventures in the Premiership having lasted for the duration of one season, Crystal Palace manager Steve Coppell sought to build on their return to the top flight with the purchase of some experienced players. Close on £8m was spent prior to the start of the season and the players continued to arrive at an alarming rate during the course of the year.

It seemed to work. When Neil Shipperley scored the winning goal at Tottenham on 24 November, it took Palace into the top ten and they had still yet to win a home match! In fact, they only achieved two home wins all season – the first coming against Derby in mid-April.

The results fell away though and Coppell stepped down, to be replaced by Atillio Lombardo, whose lack of command of the English language did little to help Palace's cause. When relegation was confirmed, the Italian wasted no time in declaring that management was not for him. Ray Lewington filled the gap before Terry Venables finally agreed to take charge in the close season.

On 13 occasions Palace conceded three or more goals in the league while no player could muster more than a single goal in a Premiership game.

In the FA Cup Palace had a good run before losing to eventual winners Arsenal after a 5th Round replay. The Coca-Cola Cup brought nothing but humiliation when Hartlepool won over the two legged 2nd Round tie.

Formed:	1905
Ground:	Selhurst Park, South Norwood, London SE25 6PU
Phone:	0181 768 6000 **Box Office:** 0181 771 8841
Info:	0891 400 333
Capacity:	26,995
Colours:	Red/Blue, Red, Red
Nickname:	The Eagles
Manager:	Terry Venables
Honours:	Division 1 Champions 1993-94; Division 2 Champions 1978-79; Runners-up 1968-69; Play-off Winners 1996-97; Division 3 Runners-up 1963-64; Division 3S Champions 1920-21; Runners-up 1928-29, 1930-31, 1938-39; Division 4 Runners-up 1960-61; FA Cup Runners-up 1989-90; Zenith Data System Cup Winners 1991.
Managers:	Alan Smith 1993-95, Steve Coppell 1995-96, Dave Bassett 1996-97, Steve Coppell 1997-Apr 98, Atillio Lombardo Apr 98, Ray Lewington May 98.

Record League Win:	9-0 v Barrow, D4, 10/10/59
Record League Defeat:	0-9 v Liverpool, D1, 12/9/89
Most GF in Season:	110 – Division 4, 1960-61
All-time League Apps:	660 – Jim Cannon, 1972-86
All-time League Goals:	166 – Peter Simpson, 1929-34
Most Goals in a Season:	46 – Peter Simpson, 1930-31.
Most Goals in a Match:	6 – Peter Simpson v Exeter, D3S, 4/10/30
Record Fee Received:	£4.5m from Tottenham for Chris Armstrong, 6/95
Record Fee Paid:	£2.25m to Millwall for Andy Roberts, 7/95
Record Attendance:	51,482 v Burnley, D2, 5/5/79

Stats File

Division	P	W	D	L	F	A	Pts	Yr	B	W
Premier/1:	492	130	144	218	505	730	481	12	3	22
Division 1n/2:	984	377	269	338	1271	1189	1221	23	1	21
Division 2n/3:	276	113	86	77	419	332	312	6	2	15
Division 3n/4:	138	68	30	40	284	204	166	3	2	8

Cup Records	P	W	D	L	F	A
FA Cup:	229	84	62	83	315	325
League Cup:	129	53	30	46	193	158
A/F Members Cup:	23	14	1	8	44	33

Sequence	Games	Start		End
Winning Run:	8	9-Feb-21	to	26-Mar-21
Without Defeat:	18	22-Feb-69	to	13-Aug-69
Without Win:	20	3-Mar-62	to	8-Sep-62
Drawn Games:	5	28-Mar-21	to	16-Apr-21
	5	30-Dec-78	to	24-Feb-79
Without Draw:	24	31-Dec-60	to	26-Aug-61
Losing Run:	8	18-Apr-25	to	19-Sep-25
	8	10-Jan-98	to	14-Mar-98
Clean Sheets:	6	1-Sep-20	to	25-Sep-20
Goal Scored:	24	27-Apr-29	to	21-Dec-29
No. Goals For:	9	19-Nov-94	to	2-Jan-95
SOS Undefeated:	11	1978-79		
SOS No Wins:	15	1973-74		

5-Year Record

	Div	P	W	D	L	F	A	Pts	Psn	
1993-94	1	46	27	9	10	73	46	90	1	Promoted
1994-95	P	42	11	12	19	34	49	45	19	Relegated
1995-96	1	46	20	15	11	67	48	75	3	
1996-97	1	46	19	14	13	78	48	71	6	Promoted
1997-98	P	38	8	9	21	37	71	33	20	Relegated

Grimsby Town

Buckley's Winners
Following their relegation from Division One, Grimsby Town turned to Alan Buckley to revive their fortunes and the transformation was simply staggering. Grimsby finished third in Division Two, two points clear of those who just failed to make the play-offs, and booked their ticket to Wembley with a fully deserved two-legged victory over Fulham. Kevin Donovan's 21st goal of the season accounted for Northampton in the final in front of a record attendance for the Division Two final.

Grimsby became accustomed to Wembley a month earlier when Wayne Burnett's 'golden goal' clinched a 2-1 Auto Windscreens Shield victory over Bournemouth in a game witnessed by the third highest attendance in that competition's 15-year history.

Replays were required to dismiss Shrewsbury and Chesterfield from the FA Cup before Norwich were emphatically beaten 3-0 but in the 4th Round Grimsby met their match against Leeds at Elland Road. The Mariners' Coca-Cola Cup journey started with defeat at Oldham but a Jack Lester hat-trick contributed to a 5-1 aggregate victory. A bigger scalp was claimed in the 2nd Round with Sheffield Wednesday going down 3-2 on aggregate. Next to go were holders Leicester who were cut down 3-1, but Liverpool ended the dream in the 4th Round.

Formed:	1878
Ground:	Blundell Park, Cleethorpes, South Humberside, DN35 7PY
Phone:	01472 697111　　　　**Box Office:** 01472 697111
Info:	0891 555 855
Capacity:	8,870
Colours:	Black and white striped shirts, black shorts and white stockings
Nickname:	The Mariners
Manager:	Alan Buckley
Honours:	Division 2 Champions 1900-01, 1933-34; Division 3N Champions 1925-26; Division 3 Champions 1979-80; Division 3 Play-Off Winners 1997-98; Division 4 Champions 1971-72; Auto Windscreens Shield Winners 1997-98.
Managers:	Mick Lyons 1985-87, Bobby Roberts 1987-88, Alan Buckley 1988-94, Brian Laws 1994-95, Kenny Swain 1997.
Previous Names:	Grimsby Pelham
Record League Win:	9-2 v Darwen, D2, 15/4/1899 7-0 v Bristol Rovers (a), D2, 1957-58
Record League Defeat:	1-9 v Arsenal, D1, 28/1/31
Most GF in Season:	103 – Division 2, 1933-34

All-time League Goals: 197 – Pat Glover, 1930-39
Most Goals in a Season: 42 – Pat Glover, 1933-34
Most Goals in a Match: 6 – Tommy McCairns v Leicester Fosse, D2, 11/4/1896
Record Fee Received: £1m from Blackburn Rovers for Gary Croft, 3/96
Record Fee Paid: £300,000 to Southampton for Tommy Widdrington, 7/96
Record Attendance: 31,657 v Wolverhampton W., FA Cup 5th Round, 20/2/37

Stats File

Division	P	W	D	L	F	A	Pts	Yr	B	W
Premier/1:	488	167	97	224	756	940	431	12	5	22
Division 1n/2:	1840	676	413	751	2763	2933	1937	47	1	22
Division 2n/3:	736	291	185	260	1031	950	822	16	1	23
Division 3n/4:	368	155	92	121	520	460	441	8	1	23

Cup Records	P	W	D	L	F	A
FA Cup:	236	88	48	100	358	412
League Cup:	117	45	27	45	152	155
A/F Members Cup:	22	10	3	9	28	33

Sequence	Games	Start		End
Winning Run:	11	19-Jan-52	to	29-Mar-52
Without Defeat:	19	16-Feb-80	to	30-Aug-80
Without Win:	18	10-Oct-81	to	16-Mar-82
Drawn Games:	5	25-Dec-20	to	22-Jan-21
	5	6-Feb-65	to	6-Mar-65
Without Draw:	30	29-Apr-33	to	10-Feb-34
Losing Run:	9	30-Nov-07	to	18-Jan-08
Clean Sheets:	8	2-Apr-56	to	30-Apr-56
Goal Scored:	33	6-Oct-28	to	27-Apr-29
	33	31-Jan-33	to	25-Nov-33
No. Goals For:	5	8-Apr-83	to	2-May-83
	5	21-Mar-87	to	18-Apr-87
SOS Undefeated:	10	1960-61		
SOS No Wins:	9	1937-38		
	9	1927-28		

5-Year Record

	Div	P	W	D	L	F	A	Pts	Psn	
1993-94	1	46	13	20	13	52	47	59	16	
1994-95	1	46	17	14	15	62	56	65	10	
1995-96	1	46	14	14	18	55	69	56	17	
1996-97	1	46	11	13	22	60	81	46	22	Relegated
1997-98	2	46	19	15	12	55	37	72	3	Promoted PO

Huddersfield Town

Late Win Sets Tone

Each year since winning promotion in 1995 Huddersfield Town have seen their points total fall, but that will not unduly worry manager Peter Jackson as the Terriers were winless after 14 games, of which nine had been lost. Jackson, then manager of Halifax, was called in to replace Brian Horton who was dismissed when Town had just four points from nine games. Under Horton, Town made no new signings during the summer. Huddersfield, the last side in the top two divisions of the Nationwide League to win a game, broke their duck on 1st November with a 3-1 success over Stoke at the McAlpine Stadium. By the time Huddersfield were beaten 4-0 at home by Stoke's neighbours Port Vale on the last day of the season, the Terriers had secured their own future.

    Huddersfield's improved form came just in time for the FA Cup but after a 1-0 victory at Bournemouth the Yorkshire side lost by the same score at home to Wimbledon. Some relief from their early season problems was to be found in the Coca-Cola Cup where a 1st Round success against Bradford was followed by a home win over West Ham – but the Premiership club took the tie 3-1.

Formed:	1908
Ground:	McAlpine Stadium, Huddersfield, West Yorks, HD1 6PX
Capacity:	19,600
Phone:	01484 420335 **Box Office:** 01484 424444
Info:	0891 12 16 35
Nickname:	The Terriers
Manager:	Peter Jackson
Colours:	Blue & white striped shirts, blue shorts, blue with red & white socks
Honours:	Division 1 Champions 1923-24, 1924-25, 1925-26;
	Division 2 Champions 1969-70; Division 4 Champions 1979-80;
	FA Cup Winners 1922.
Managers:	Malcolm Macdonald 1987-88, Eion Hand 1988-92, I. Ross 1992-93,
	Neil Warnock 1993-95, Brian Horton 1995-Oct 98.
Record League Win:	10-1 v Blackpool, D1, 13/12/30
Record League Defeat:	1-10 v Manchester City, D2, 7/11/87
Most GF in a Season:	101 – Division 4, 1979-80
All-time League Apps:	521 – W. H. Smith, 1913-34
All-time League Goals:	142 – George Brown, 1921-29
Most Goals in a Season:	35 – Sam Taylor, D2, 1919-20
	35 – George Brown, D1, 1925-26
Most Goals in a Match:	5 – D. Mangnall v Derby County (h), D1, 21/11/31
	5 – A. P. Lythgoe v Blackburn R. (h), D1, 13/4/35
Record Fee Received:	£275,000 from Southampton for Simon Charlton, 6/93
Record Fee Paid:	£800,000 to Swindon for Wayne Allison, 11/97

Record Attendance: 18,775 v Birmingham City, D2, 6/5/95
(at McAlpine Stadium);
67,037 v Arsenal, FA Cup 6th Round, 27/2/32

Stats File

Division	P	W	D	L	F	A	Pts	Yr	B	W
Premier/1:	1260	480	317	463	1874	1854	1277	30	1	22
Division 1n/2:	1254	477	321	456	1766	1684	1381	30	1	23
Division 2n/3:	552	217	148	187	753	674	750	12	3	24
Division 3n/4:	230	100	64	66	337	246	264	5	1	11

Cup Records	P	W	D	L	F	A
FA Cup:	224	100	48	76	343	273
League Cup:	115	41	29	45	156	173
A/F Members Cup:	33	14	9	10	53	43

Sequence	Games	Start		End
Winning Run:	11	5-Apr-20	to	4-Sep-20
Without Defeat:	27	24-Jan-25	to	17-Oct-25
Without Win:	22	4-Dec-71	to	29-Apr-72
Drawn Games:	6	3-Mar-87	to	3-Apr-87
Without Draw:	23	3-Feb-12	to	5-Oct-12
Losing Run:	7	6-Dec-13	to	1-Jan-14
	7	8-Oct-55	to	19-Nov-55
Clean Sheets:	8	13-Mar-65	to	19-Apr-65
Goal Scored:	21	5-Dec-31	to	9-Apr-32
No. Goals For:	7	22-Jan-72	to	21-Mar-72
SOS Undefeated:	13	1962-63		
SOS No Wins:	14	1997-98		
	14	1987-88		

5-Year Record

	Div	P	W	D	L	F	A	Pts	Psn	
1993-94	2	46	17	14	15	58	61	65	11	
1994-95	2	46	22	15	9	79	49	81	5	Promoted PO
1995-96	1	46	17	12	17	61	58	63	8	
1996-97	1	46	13	15	18	48	61	54	20	
1997-98	1	46	14	11	21	50	72	53	16	

Ipswich Town

Play-off Misery Again

Having missed out on a return to the Premiership in 1997 after a two-year break through an unsuccessful appearance in the play-offs, Ipswich Town manager George Burley strengthened his squad with the £800,000 signing of Matt Holland from Bournemouth and Mark Venus and Lee Bracey. In November Burley forked out a further £800,000 on Bury striker David Johnson, who proved an excellent acquisition with 24 league goals to his credit by the end of the season.

After a poor start Ipswich switched into top gear after Christmas when a 16 match unbeaten run carried them into the top six. But as with a year earlier, the play-off was to be the end of their promotion drive with Charlton winning both semi-final encounters 1-0.

Ipswich went out of the FA Cup to Sheffield United, having beaten Bristol Rovers in Round Three. But the Blues enjoyed a lengthy run in the Coca-Cola Cup. Torquay proved tricky opposition before Ipswich pulled off a stunning 2-0 win over Manchester United at Portman Road. Extra time was needed to win at Oxford United but Ipswich put in a tremendous performance against Chelsea in the 5th Round, only to bow out in a penalty shoot-out.

Formed:	1878
Ground:	Portman Road, Ipswich, Suffolk, IP1 2DA
Phone:	01473 400500 **Box Office:** 01473 400555
Info:	0839 66 44 88
Capacity:	22,500
Colours::	Royal blue shirts with white collars and sleeves, white and blue trim shorts, blue socks
Nickname:	Blues or Town
Manager:	George Burley
Honours:	Division 1 Champions 1961-62; Runners-up 1980-81; Division 2 Champions 1960-61, 1967-68, 1991-92; Division 3S Champions 1953-54, 1956-57; FA Cup Winners 1978.
Managers:	Bill McGarry 1964-48, Bobby Robson 1968-82, Bobby Ferguson 1982-87, John Duncan 1987-90, John Lyall 1990-94.
Record League Win:	7-0 v Portsmouth, D2, 7/11/64
	7-0 v Southampton, D1, 2/2/74
	7-0 v West Bromwich Albion, D1, 6/11/76
Record League Defeat:	1-10 v Fulham, D1, 16/12/83
Most GF in Season	106 – Division 3S, 1955-56
All-time League Apps:	741 – Mick Mills, 1966-82
All-time League Goals:	227 – Ray Crawford, 1958-69
Most Goals in a Season:	41 – Ted Phillips 1956-57

Most Goals in a Match:	5 – Ray Crawford v Floriana, European Cup, 25/9/62 (10-0)	
	5 – Alan Brazil v Southampton, D1, 16/2/82 (5-2)	
Record Fee Received:	£1.9m from Tottenham for Jason Dozzell, 8/93	
Record Fee Paid:	£1m to Tottenham for Steve Sedgley, 6/94	
Record Attendance:	38,000 v Leeds Utd, FA Cup 6th Round, 8/3/75	

Stats File

Division	P	W	D	L	F	A	Pts	Yr	B	W
Premier/1:	1008	373	250	385	1344	1394	1104	24	1	22
Division 1n/2:	786	334	205	247	1258	1094	1049	18	1	21

Cup Records	P	W	D	L	F	A
FA Cup:	174	76	42	56	284	233
League Cup:	124	58	25	41	206	163
A/F Members Cup:	22	15	2	5	42	29

Sequence	Games	Start		End
Winning Run:	8	23-Sep-53	to	31-Oct-53
Without Defeat:	23	8-Dec-79	to	26-Apr-80
Without Win:	21	28-Aug-63	to	14-Dec-63
Drawn Games:	7	10-Nov-90	to	21-Dec-90
Without Draw:	26	10-Sep-47	to	20-Mar-48
	26	14-Oct-50	to	26-Mar-51
Losing Run:	10	4-Sep-54	to	16-Oct-54
Clean Sheets:	5	5-Apr-97	to	25-Apr-97
Goal Scored:	28	1-May-53	to	16-Jan-54
No. Goals For:	7	28-Feb-95	to	11-Apr-95
SOS Undefeated:	14	1980-81		
SOS No Wins:	8	1964-65		

5-Year Record

	Div	P	W	D	L	F	A	Pts	Psn	
1993-94	P	42	9	16	17	35	58	43	19	
1994-95	P	42	7	6	29	36	93	27	22	Relegated
1995-96	1	46	19	12	15	79	69	69	7	
1996-97	1	46	20	14	12	68	50	74	4	
1997-98	1	46	23	14	9	77	43	83	5	

Norwich City

Despondant Canaries

Since their relegation from the Premiership in 1995 – two years after finishing third in the top flight – Norwich have made little impact in the Nationwide League despite going through four managers in that time. In June 1996 the Canaries turned to Mike Walker, who guided the club through a very successful spell earlier in the decade. But just as his second season at the helm was drawing to its conclusion Norwich issued a statement declaring that Walker was leaving the club by mutual consent. Although Norwich had not had a good season, the timing of Walker's departure was curious coming shortly after two 5-0 home wins which had at least ensured that the club would not be dropping into Division Two. This was a distinct possibility as they were just two points clear of the relegation places with five games to go.

The two cup competitions did nothing other than add to the air of despondency around Carrow Road as the Canaries crashed out of both competitions at the first hurdle to lower league opposition. Grimsby did the damage in the FA Cup while Barnet did likewise in the Coca-Cola Cup, despite Norwich having won the 1st Leg.

Formed:	1902
Ground:	Carrow Road, Norwich, NR1 1JE
Phone:	06103 760760 **Box Office:** 01603 761661
Info:	0839 664477
Capacity:	21,994
Internet:	–
Colours:	Yellow shirts with green splashes, green shorts, yellow stockings
Nickname:	The Canaries
Manager:	Bruce Rioch
Honours:	Division 2 Champions 1971-72, 1985-86; Division 3S Champions 1933-34; Football League Cup Winners 1962.
Managers:	Mike Walker 1992-94, John Deehan 1994-95, Martin O'Neill 1995, Gary Megson 1995-96, Mike Walker 1996-98.
Record League Win:	10-2 v Coventry City, D3S, 15/3/30 8-0 v Walsall, D3S, 29/12/51
Record League Defeat:	0-7 v Walsall, D3S, 13/9/30 0-7 v Sheffield Wednesday, D2, 19/11/38
Most GF in Season:	99 – Division 3S, 1952-53
All-time League Apps:	680 – Kevin Keelan, 1963-80
All-time League Goals:	132 – John Gavin, 1949-58
Most Goals in a Season:	31 – Ralph Hunt, D3S, 1955-56
Most Goals in a Match:	5 – Roy Hollis v Walsall, D3S, 29/12/51 5 – T. Hunt v Coventry City, D3S, 15/3/30 (10-2)

Record Fee Received: £5m from Blackburn Rovers for Chris Sutton, 7/94
Record Fee Paid: £1m to Leeds Utd for Jon Newsome, 6/94
Record Attendance: 43,984 v Leicester City, FA Cup 6th Round, 30/3/63

Stats File

Division	P	W	D	L	F	A	Pts	Yr	B	W
Premier/1:	826	257	251	318	970	1177	930	20	3	22
Division 1n/2:	978	374	249	355	1405	1380	1089	23	1	21
Division 2n/3:	92	46	24	22	171	116	116	2	2	4

Cup Records	P	W	D	L	F	A
FA Cup:	224	89	52	83	337	327
League Cup:	159	83	36	40	279	173
A/F Members Cup:	16	8	2	6	26	22

Sequence	Games	Start		End
Winning Run:	10	23-Nov-85	to	25-Jan-86
Without Defeat:	20	31-Aug-50	to	30-Dec-50
Without Win:	25	22-Sep-56	to	23-Feb-57
Drawn Games:	7	9-Dec-78	to	10-Feb-79
Drawn Games:	7	15-Jan-94	to	26-Feb-94
Without Draw:	23	22-Dec-23	to	28-Apr-24
Losing Run (3):	7	12-Jan-57	to	23-Feb-57
	7	1-Apr-95	to	6-May-95
Clean Sheets (10):	4	19-Oct-91	to	16-Nov-91
	4	24-Aug-94	to	10-Sep-94
Goal Scored:	25	31-Aug-63	to	18-Jan-64
No. Goals For (3):	5	12-Mar-27	to	9-Apr-27
	5	12-Dec-92	to	10-Jan-93
SOS Undefeated:	13	1971-72		
SOS No Wins:	13	1920-21		

5-Year Record

	Div	P	W	D	L	F	A	Pts	Psn	
1993-94	P	42	12	17	13	65	61	53	12	
1994-95	P	42	10	13	19	37	54	43	20	Relegated
1995-96	1	46	14	15	17	59	55	57	16	
1996-97	1	46	17	12	17	63	68	63	13	
1997-98	1	46	14	13	19	52	69	55	15	

Oxford United

Turbulent Manor

Oxford United's second season back in Division One proved to be turbulent, after an opening which saw seven defeats in 11 games, and after 19 games the Us were in the bottom three. Against a background of concern over the club's financial status, a large number of the squad was placed on the transfer list and manager Denis Smith departed after more than four years at the Manor Ground. Malcolm Crosby replaced Smith but decided it was not for him after five winless games. Next into the hot seat was former United player Malcolm Shotton. Oxford, boosted by a good home record, ended the season five places higher than a year earlier despite their points total only improving by one.

Oxford were swiftly removed from the FA Cup by Leeds, 4-0, but embarked on a fruitful Coca-Cola Cup run. Taking a two-goal lead to Plymouth for the 2nd Leg of a 1st Round tie, Oxford were three down after 46 minutes but stormed back to win 5-3 (7-3) before crushing York 6-2 over two legs. In the 3rd Round a penalty shoot-out was needed to beat Tranmere, but the run ended with a home defeat by Ipswich.

Formed:	1893
Ground:	Manor Ground, London Road, Headington, Oxford, OX3 7RS
Capacity:	9,572
Phone:	01865 761503 **Box Office:** 01865 761503
Info:	0891 440055
Colours:	Yellow shirts with navy sleeves and white trim, navy blue shorts, yellow and blue socks
Nickname:	The Us
Manager:	Malcolm Shotton
Honours:	Division 2 Champions 1984-85; Division 3 Champions 1967-68, 1983-84; Football League Cup Winners 1986.
Managers:	Ian Greaves 1980-82, Jim Smith 1982-85, M. Evans 1985-86, Mark Lawrenson 1988, Brian Horton 1988-93, Denis Smith 1993-98, Malcolm Crosby Dec-Jan 1998.
Previous Names:	Headington United
Record League Win:	7-0 v Barrow, D4, 19/12/64
Record League Defeat:	0-6 v Liverpool, D1, 22/3/86
Most GF in Season:	91 – Division 3, 1983-84
All-time League Apps:	534 – John Shuker, 1962-77
All-time League Goals:	77 – Graham Atkinson, 1962-73
Most Goals in a Season:	30 – John Aldridge, 1984-85
Most Goals in a Match:	4 (6 times) 4 – Richard Hill v Walsall (a), D2, 26/12/88 (5-1) 4 – John Durnin v Luton Tn (h), D1, 14/11/92 (4-0)

Record Fee Received: £1.6m from Leicester City for Matt Elliott, 1/97
Record Fee Paid: £285,000 to Gillingham for Colin Greenall, 2/88
Record Attendance: 22,750 v Preston North End, FA Cup 6th Round, 29/2/64

Stats File

Division	P	W	D	L	F	A	Pts	Yr	B	W
Premier/1:	124	27	38	59	150	229	119	3	18	21
Division 1n/2:	746	245	201	300	889	973	831	17	1	23
Division 2n/3:	598	236	171	191	826	721	757	13	1	18
Division 3n/4:	138	50	43	45	216	178	143	3	4	18

Cup Records	P	W	D	L	F	A
FA Cup:	104	39	24	41	163	173
League Cup:	135	60	34	41	205	169
A/F Members Cup:	22	9	4	9	36	34

Sequence	Games	Start		End
Winning Run:	6	6-Apr-85	to	24-Apr-85
Without Defeat:	20	17-Mar-84	to	29-Sep-84
Without Win:	27	14-Nov-87	to	27-Aug-88
Drawn Games (4):	5	24-Nov-67	to	26-Dec-67
	5	7-Oct-78	to	28-Oct-78
Without Draw:	14	26-Dec-96	to	18-Mar-97
Losing Run:	7	4-May-91	to	7-Sep-91
Clean Sheets:	5	21-Dec-63	to	18-Jan-64
Goal Scored:	17	4-Oct-67	to	20-Jan-68
	17	10-Sep-83	to	26-Dec-83
No. Goals For:	6	26-Mar-88	to	13-Apr-88
SOS Undefeated:	9	1994-95		
	9	1983-84		
SOS No Wins:	6	1991-92		
	6	1978-79		

5-Year Record

	Div	P	W	D	L	F	A	Pts	Psn	
1993-94	1	46	13	10	23	54	75	49	23	Relegated
1994-95	2	46	21	12	13	66	52	75	7	
1995-96	2	46	24	11	11	76	39	83	2	Promoted
1996-97	1	46	16	9	21	64	68	57	17	
1997-98	1	46	16	10	20	60	64	58	12	

Portsmouth

All Change at Pompey

Surely no club had as troubled a season as Portsmouth. The Fratton Park club found a battle against relegation just one of numerous irritations during a unique campaign. During the season the club changed ownership, manager and chairman, had trouble paying its players and experienced problems in obtaining safety notices to keep the whole ground open.

Given Terry Venables' connections in Australia perhaps it was not surprising to see a number of players from Down Under lining up on the south coast but it was not a successful partnership and Venables left the club in January shortly before being banned by the Department of Trade and Industry from holding a company director position for seven years. Manager Terry Fenwick was sacked at the same time as control of the club passed over to Martin Gregory.

Alan Ball was appointed manager for his third spell at Fratton Park. Pompey were bottom at the time of Ball's arrival but against expectations he masterminded their survival, with a 3-1 win at Bradford on the final day condemning Manchester City to relegation.

Portsmouth's cup fortunes went as per the form book with Aston Villa and Peterborough removing them from the FA Cup and the Coca-Cola Cup at the first hurdle.

Formed:	1898
Ground:	Fratton Park, Frogmore Road, Portsmouth, PO4 8RA
Phone:	01705 731204 **Box Office:** 01705 618777
Info:	0891 121182
Capacity:	16,061
Colours:	Royal blue shirts, white shorts, red socks
Nickname:	The Pompey
Manager:	Alan Ball
Honours:	Division 1 Champions 1948-49, 1949-50; Division 3 Champions 1961-62, 1982-83; FA Cup Winners 1939.
Managers:	Alan Ball 1984-89, John Gregory 1989-90, Frank Burrows 1990-91, Jim Smith 1991-95, Terry Fenwick 1995-98.
Record League Win:	9-0 v Notts County, D2, 9/4/27
Record League Defeat:	0-10 v Leicester City, D1, 20/10/28
Most GF in Season:	91 – Division 4, 1979-80
All-time League Apps:	829 – Jimmy Dickenson, 1946-65
All-time League Goals:	208 – Peter Harris, 1946-60
Most Goals in a Season:	47 – Guy Whittingham, 1992-93
Most Goals in a Match:	5 – Alf Strange v Gillingham, D3, 27/1/23
	5 – Peter Harris v Aston Villa, D1, 3/9/58

Record Fee Received: £1.7m from Tottenham H. for Darren Anderton, 6/92
Record Fee Paid: £450,000 to QPR for Colin Clarke, 5/90
Record Attendance: 51,385 v Derby County, FA Cup 6th Round, 20/2/49

Stats File

Division	P	W	D	L	F	A	Pts	Yr	B	W
Premier/1:	1090	405	257	428	1729	1828	1074	26	1	22
Division 1n/2:	1426	500	373	553	1996	2056	1615	33	2	22
Division 2n/3:	276	108	80	88	366	331	337	6	1	24
Division 3n/4:	92	44	24	24	153	97	112	2	4	7

Cup Records	P	W	D	L	F	A
FA Cup:	228	85	57	86	332	331
League Cup:	121	48	27	46	172	165
A/F Members Cup:	12	5	0	7	16	18

Sequence	Games	Start		End
Winning Run:	7	19-Apr-80	to	30-Aug-80
	7	22-Jan-83	to	26-Feb-83
Without Defeat:	15	16-Apr-21	to	15-Oct-21
	15	18-Apr-24	to	18-Oct-24
Without Win:	25	29-Nov-58	to	22-Aug-59
Drawn Games:	5	28-Sep-77	to	15-Oct-77
Without Draw:	38	17-Mar-28	to	9-Feb-29
Losing Run (4):	9	2-Mar-63	to	16-Apr-63
	9	21-Oct-75	to	6-Dec-75
Clean Sheets:	8	26-Aug-22	to	30-Sep-22
Goal Scored:	23	30-Aug-30	to	27-Dec-30
No. Goals For (3):	6	12-Oct-74	to	9-Nov-74
	6	27-Dec-93	to	5-Feb-94
SOS Undefeated:	13	1948-49		
SOS No Wins:	15	1937-38		

5-Year Record

	Div	P	W	D	L	F	A	Pts	Psn
1993-94	1	46	15	13	18	52	58	58	17
1994-95	1	46	15	13	18	53	63	58	18
1995-96	1	46	13	13	20	61	69	52	21
1996-97	1	46	20	8	18	59	53	68	7
1997-98	1	46	13	10	23	51	63	49	20

Port Vale

Last Gasp Survival

A season which began with two successive defeats, saw Port Vale spend practically the entire campaign in mid-table but it almost ended in disaster for long-serving manager John Rudge and his side when relegation to Division Two was only avoided in their 46th and final league game of the season.

Vale's problems began in December when they embarked on a dreadful run which saw them pick up one point from nine games. Victory over Portsmouth halted the slide and it was wins over a number of the struggling sides, including the double over Manchester City, which led to their survival. Needing to win on the last day to be certain of staying up, Vale did so in style with a 4-0 success at Huddersfield which included a brace for Jan Jansson. Jansson joined Vale for £200,000 in August and a month later Rudge spent a club record £500,000 on Lincoln's Gary Ainsworth.

Vale came close to adding another FA Cup scalp to an impressive list of giant cup killings with Arsenal only going through in the 3rd Round courtesy of a penalty shoot-out. But in the Coca-Cola Cup it was the Valiants who were humbled when Division Two side York put them out in the 1st Round.

Formed:	1876
Ground:	Vale Park, Burslem, Stoke-on-Trent, ST6 1AW
Capacity:	22,356
Phone:	01782 814134 **Box Office:** 01782 814134
Info:	0891 121636
Colours:	White shirts with black flashes, black shorts, black and white socks
Nickname:	The Valiants
Manager:	John Rudge
Honours:	Division 3N Champions 1929-30, 1953-54;
	Division 4 Champions 1958-59; Autoglass Trophy Winners 1992-93.
Managers:	C. Harper 1977, R. Smith 1977-78, D. Butler 1978-79,
	A. Bloor 1979, J. McGrath 1979-83.
Previous Names:	Burslem Port Vale 1884-1909
Record League Win:	9-1 v Chesterfield, D2, 24/9/32
	8-0 v Gateshead, D4, 1958-59
Record League Defeat:	0-10 v Sheffield United, D2, 10/12/1892
	0-10 v Notts County, D2, 26/2/1895
Most GF in Season:	154 – Wilf Kirkham, 1923-29 & 1931-33
All-time League Apps:	760 – Roy Sproson 1950-72.
Most Goals in a Season:	38 – Wilf Kirkham, D2, 1926-27
Most Goals in a Match:	6 – Stewart Littlewood v Chesterfield, D2, 24/9/32
Record Fee Received:	£1.85m from Birmingham for Jon McCarthy, 9/97

Record Fee Paid: £500,000 to Lincoln City for Garry Ainsworth, 9/97
Record Attendance: 49,768 v Aston Villa, FA Cup 5th Round, 20/2/60

Stats File

Division	P	W	D	L	F	A	Pts	Yr	B	W
Division 1n/2:	1544	521	347	676	2134	2572	1489	39	5	24
Division 2n/3:	920	336	255	329	1240	1237	1047	20	2	23
Division 3n/4:	598	220	185	193	802	715	704	13	1	20

Cup Records	P	W	D	L	F	A
FA Cup:	222	93	53	76	340	315
League Cup:	90	24	17	49	99	137
A/F Members Cup:	33	14	8	11	45	47

Sequence	Games	Start		End
Winning Run:	8	8/4/1893	to	30/9/1893
Without Defeat:	19	5-May-69	to	8-Nov-69
Without Win:	17	7-Dec-91	to	21-Mar-92
Drawn Games:	6	26-Apr-81	to	12-Sep-81
Without Draw:	20	10-Sep-06	to	19-Jan-07
Losing Run:	9	9-Mar-57	to	20-Apr-57
Clean Sheets:	7	11-Feb-22	to	18-Mar-22
Goal Scored:	22	12-Sep-92	to	13-Feb-93
No. Goals For (12):	4	26-Nov-83	to	26-Dec-83
	4	22-Nov-97	to	13-Dec-97
SOS Undefeated:	18	1969-70		
SOS No Wins:	8	1904-05		

5-Year Record

	Div	P	W	D	L	F	A	Pts	Psn	
1993-94	2	46	26	10	10	79	46	88	2	Promoted
1994-95	1	46	15	13	18	58	64	58	17	
1995-96	1	46	15	15	16	59	66	60	12	
1996-97	1	46	17	16	13	58	55	67	8	
1997-98	1	46	13	10	23	56	66	49	19	

QPR

Underachievers

Queens Park Rangers remain one of the most ambitious clubs in the Nationwide League but this season was one of great disappointment with the club disappearing from both major cups in the opening round, and in the league just one point separated them from the relegation zone.

Having missed the play-offs by five points the previous season, manager Stewart Houston forked out £3.25m on Mike Sheron and Matthew Rose but in November paid the price for Rangers failing to offer a serious promotion challenge by getting the chop along with his assistant Bruce Rioch.

Houston's replacement was West Brom boss Ray Harford, who oversaw the sale of Trevor Sinclair to West Ham. Rangers got Iain Dowie and Keith Rowland in exchange plus £2.3m, but results did not improve and on the last day of the season a 1-0 win for Bury at Loftus Road left the Rs just one point above relegated Manchester City.

Rangers failed to move beyond the 3rd Round of the FA Cup for the first time in four years with a replay defeat at Middlesbrough. An early exit was also made from the Coca-Cola Cup with Wolves winning 3-2 over two matches, despite Houston's side winning 2-1 at Molineux.

Formed:	1885
Ground:	Rangers Stadium, South Africa Road, London, S12 7PA
Phone:	0181 743 0262 **Box Office:** 0181 743 0262
Info:	0891 12 11 62
Capacity:	19,148
Colours:	Blue and white hoop shirts, white shorts, white with blue hooped socks
Nickname:	The Rangers, The Rs
Manager:	Ray Harford
Honours:	Division 1 Runners-up 1975-76; Division 2 Champions 1982-83; Division 3S Champions 1947-48; Football League Cup Winners 1967.
Managers:	Trevor Francis 1989-90, Don Howe 1990-91, Gerry Francis 1991-94, Ray Wilkins 1994-96, Stewart Houston 1996-98.
Previous Names:	St Judes, 1885-87
Record League Win:	8-0 v Merthyr, D3S, 9/3/29
Record League Defeat:	1-8 v Mansfield, D3, 15/3/65
	1-8 v Manchester United, D1, 19/3/69
	(Also lost 0-7 on three occasions)
Most GF in Season:	111 – Division 3, 1961-62
All-time League Apps:	548 – Tony Ingham, 1950-63
All-time League Goals:	186 – George Goddard, 1926-33

Most Goals in a Season: 37 – George Goddard, D3S, 1929-30
Most Goals in a Match: 5 – Alan Wilks v Oxford United, LC R3, 10/10/67
Record Fee Received: £6m from Newcastle U. for Les Ferdinand, 6/95
Record Fee Paid: £2.35m to Chelsea for John Spencer, 11/96

Stats File

Division	P	W	D	L	F	A	Pts	Yr	B	W
Premier/1:	822	277	223	322	1028	1111	969	20	2	22
Division 1n/2:	638	261	172	205	924	794	769	15	1	22
Division 2n/3:	414	188	98	128	782	601	474	9	1	15

Cup Records	P	W	D	L	F	A
FA Cup:	239	96	60	83	398	326
League Cup:	133	68	26	39	254	169
A/F Members Cup:	7	2	1	4	7	13

Sequence	Games	Start		End
Winning Run:	8	7-Nov-31	to	28-Dec-31
Without Defeat:	20	3-Dec-66	to	8-Apr-67
	20	11-Mar-72	to	23-Sep-72
	20	7-Dec-68	to	7-Apr-69
Drawn Games:	6	14-Dec-57	to	11-Jan-58
	6	28-Mar-98	to	25-Apr-98
Without Draw:	25	9-Mar-85	to	12-Oct-85
Losing Run:	9	25-Feb-69	to	5-Apr-69
Clean Sheets:	7	7-Sep-46	to	5-Oct-46
	7	7-Mar-67	to	1-Apr-67
Goal Scored:	33	9-Dec-61	to	8-Sep-62
No. Goals For:	6	14-Mar-25	to	11-Apr-25
	6	18-Mar-39	to	10-Apr-39
SOS Undefeated:	12	1947-48		
SOS No Wins:	12	1968-69		

5-Year Record

	Div	P	W	D	L	F	A	Pts	Psn	
1993-94	P	42	16	12	14	62	61	60	9	
1994-95	P	42	17	9	16	61	59	60	8	
1995-96	P	38	9	6	23	38	57	33	19	Relegated
1996-97	1	46	18	12	16	64	60	66	9	
1997-98	1	46	10	19	17	51	63	49	21	

Sheffield United

Blade Drama

This was surely one of the most dramatic seasons in Sheffield United's history. United reached the last four of the FA Cup, were in the play-offs for a second successive year but had problems off the field with the departure of their manager, chairman and chief executive.

United's successful league campaign was based on dominant form at Bramall Lane where they remained unbeaten until a day after manager Nigel Spackman resigned in early March. He was replaced by Steve Thompson. The Blades' away form was less impressive although their ten-match unbeaten start to the season was the best of any club in the Nationwide League. Thirty-six matches later United just pipped Birmingham to a play-off place on goals scored. Sheffield beat Sunderland 2-1 in the 1st Leg of the play-off but fell 2-0 in the return.

In the FA Cup both Bury and Ipswich took United to replays while a late Lee Sandford goal disposed of Reading. In the 6th Round a late David Holdsworth equaliser took Coventry to a penalty shoot-out which the Division One side won, only to be beaten by Newcastle in the semi-final. Some success was also to be had in the Coca-Cola Cup with Wrexham and Watford defeated before United surprisingly lost to Walsall.

Formed:	1889		
Ground:	Bramall Lane Ground, Sheffield, S2 4SU		
Phone:	0114 221 5757	**Box Office:**	0114 221 1889
Info:	0891 888650		
Capacity:	30,370		
Colours:	Red/white striped shirts, white shorts, red/white socks		
Nickname:	The Blades		
Manager:	Steve Bruce		
Honours:	Division 1 Champions 1897-98; Division 2 Champions 1981-82; FA Cup Winners 1899, 1902, 1915, 1925.		
Managers:	Martin Peters 1981, Ian Porterfield 1981-86, B. McEwan 1986-88, Dave Bassett 1988-95, Howard Kendall 1995-97, Nigel Spackman 1978-Mar 98, Steve Thompson Mar 98-Jul-98.		
Record League Win:	10-0 v Port Vale (a), D2, 10/12/1892		
	10-0 v Burnley, D1, 19/1/29		
Record League Defeat:	3-10 v Middlesbrough, D1, 18/11/33		
	1-8 v Arsenal, D1, 12/4/30		
	0-7 v Arsenal, D1, 24/12/32		
	0-7 v Tottenham H., D2, 12/11/49		
Most GF in Season:	102 – Division 1, 1925-26		
All-time League Apps:	689 – Joe Shaw, 1948-66		

All-time League Goals: 223 – H. Johnson, 1919-31
Most Goals in a Season: 41 – Jimmy Dunne, 1930-31
Most Goals in a Match: 5 – Harry Hammond v Bootle, D2, 26/11/1892 (8-3)
5 – Harry Johnson v West Ham Utd, D1, 26/12/27 (6-2)
Record Fee Received: £2.7m from Leeds United for Brian Deane, 7/93
Record Fee Paid: £700,000 to Ipswich Town for Brian Gayle, 9/91
Record Attendance: 68,287 v Leeds United, FA Cup 5th Round, 15/1/36

Stats File

Division	P	W	D	L	F	A	Pts	Yr	B	W
Premier/1:	2318	861	552	905	3499	3707	2325	59	1	22
Division 1n/2:	1262	549	322	391	2089	1665	1571	30	1	21
Division 2n/3:	230	100	49	81	366	300	317	5	2	21
Division 3n/4:	46	27	15	4	94	41	96	1	1	1

Cup Records	P	W	D	L	F	A
FA Cup:	306	133	78	95	446	371
League Cup:	110	43	24	43	165	161
A/F Members Cup:	17	6	4	7	27	27

Sequence	Games	Start		End
Winning Run (4):	8	1-Feb-58	to	5-Apr-58
	8	14-Sep-60	to	22-Oct-60
Without Defeat:	22	2-Sep-1899	to	13-Jan-00
Without Win:	19	27-Sep-75	to	7-Feb-76
Drawn Games (4):	5	5-Mar-94	to	26-Mar-94
	5	16-Dec-95	to	20-Jan-96
Without Draw:	38	22-Oct-04	to	18-Nov-05
Losing Run:	7	19-Aug-75	to	20-Sep-75
Clean Sheets:	7	20-Mar-71	to	17-Apr-71
Goal Scored:	34	30-Mar-56	to	1-Jan-57
No. Goals For:	6	20-Oct-90	to	24-Nov-90
	6	4-Dec-93	to	29-Dec-93
SOS Undefeated:	22	1899-00		
SOS No Wins:	16	1990-91		

5-Year Record

	Div	P	W	D	L	F	A	Pts	Psn	
1993-94	P	42	8	18	16	42	60	42	20	Relegated
1994-95	1	46	17	17	12	74	55	68	8	
1995-96	1	46	16	14	16	57	54	62	9	
1996-97	1	46	20	13	13	75	52	73	5	
1997-98	1	46	19	17	10	69	54	74	6	

Stockport County

County's Division Best
How to successfully follow their magnificent season of 1996/97 was always going to be a tall order for Stockport County, especially in view of manager Dave Jones's departure to Southampton. But under new boss Gary Megson, County did a good job by claiming their highest placing in Division One of eighth.

Such a good finish seemed unlikely during the early weeks of the season as Megson had to wait eight games for his first taste of victory. That came when Huddersfield were defeated 3-0 with top scorers Brett Angell and Alun Armstrong doing the damage. Angell finished the season with 23 goals while Armstrong was transferred to Middlesbrough for a club record of £1.5m in February.

Despite their poor start Stockport pushed hard for a play-off place but ultimately fell ten points short of their target. It was, none-the-less, a fine first season for the new manager.

FA Cup progress was made at the expense of Preston before Birmingham beat them in Round 4. Looking to repeat their memorable run to the Coca-Cola Cup semi-final of a year earlier, County had an extraordinary 8-7 aggregate victory over Mansfield in the 1st Round only to again lose to Birmingham in the 2nd Round.

Formed:	1883
Ground:	Edgeley Park, Hardcastle Road, Edgeley, Stockport, Cheshire, SK3 9DD
Phone:	0161 286 8888 **Box Office:** 0161 286 8888
Info:	0891 12 16 38
Capacity:	12,086
Colours:	Royal blue shirts with white and red bands, blue shorts, white socks
Nickname:	The Hatters
Manager:	Gary Megson
Honours:	Division 3N Champions 1921-22 1936-37; Division 4 Champions 1966-67; Division 3N Cup Winners 1934-35; Autoglass Trophy Runners-up 1991-92, 1992-93.
Managers:	Jimmy Melia 1986 , Colin Murphy 1986-87, Asa Hartford 1987-79, Danny Bergara 1989-95, Dave Jones 1995-97.
Previous Names:	Heaton Norris Rovers 1883-88; Heaton Norris 1888-90
Record League Win:	13-0 v Halifax Town, D2N, 6/1/34
Record League Defeat:	1-8 v Chesterfield, D2, 19/4/1902
	0-7 (5 times) v Aldershot, D4, 22/2/64
	0-7 v Hull City, D4, 29/1/83
Most GF in Season:	115 – Division 3N, 1933-34
All-time League Apps:	489 – Andy Thorpe, 1978-86 & 1987-92
All-time League Goals:	132 – Jack Connor, 1951-56

Most Goals in a Season: 46 – Alf Lythgoe, 1933-34
Most Goals in a Match: 5 (7 times):
    Jack Connor 5 v Workington (h), D3N, 8/11/52 (6-0)
    Jack Connor 5 v Carlisle U. (h), D3N, 7/4/56 (8-1)
Record Fee Received: £1.5m from Middlesbrough for Alan Armstrong, 2/98
Record Fee Paid: £250,000 to Tranmere for Paul Cook, 10/97
Record Attendance: 27,833 v Liverpool, FA Cup 5th Round, 11/2/50

Stats File

Division	P	W	D	L	F	A	Pts	Yr	B	W
Division 1n/2:	856	257	194	405	1017	1446	727	22	8	22
Division 2n/3:	460	180	116	164	642	592	602	10	2	24
Division 3n/4:	1332	438	352	542	1600	1896	1380	29	1	24

Cup Records	P	W	D	L	F	A
FA Cup:	181	71	31	79	265	276
League Cup:	109	36	29	44	131	172
A/F Members Cup:	49	22	8	19	75	70

Sequence	Games	Start		End
Winning Run:	8	26-Dec-27	to	28-Jan-28
Without Defeat:	18	28-Jan-33	to	28-Aug-33
Without Win:	15	17-Mar-89	to	1-Sep-89
Drawn Games:	7	4-May-73	to	19-Sep-73
	7	17-Mar-89	to	14-Apr-89
Without Draw:	36	12-Oct-46	to	25-Aug-47
Losing Run:	9	19-Dec-08	to	13-Feb-09
Clean Sheets:	8	2-May-21	to	1-Oct-21
Goal Scored:	24	8-Sep-28	to	2-Feb-29
	24	28-Jan-39	to	16-Sep-46
No. Goals For:	7	10-Mar-23	to	7-Apr-23
SOS Undefeated (3):	7	1980-81		
	7	1929-30		
SOS No Wins:	12	1988-89		
	12	1964-65		

5-Year Record

	Div	P	W	D	L	F	A	Pts	Psn	
1993-94	2	46	24	13	9	74	44	85	4	
1994-95	2	46	19	8	19	63	60	65	11	
1995-96	2	46	19	13	14	61	47	70	9	
1996-97	2	46	23	13	10	59	41	82	2	Promoted
1997-98	1	46	19	8	19	71	69	65	8	

Sunderland

Light Blows in Shoot-out
With the Nationwide League Division One being home for a number of large clubs, there was always the likelihood that one of the big guns would miss out on promotion. Sadly for Wearsiders it was Sunderland, who at least had the consolation of taking part in one of the greatest matches ever staged at Wembley as they lost out in a penalty shoot-out with Charlton for the right to play in the Premiership.

Manager Peter Reid brought in five players at a cost of almost £4.5m but Sunderland made a disappointing start with five defeats inside the first ten games. Then a 16-match unbeaten run, built around the goalscoring exploits of Kevin Phillips, put the Wearsiders in the promotion picture. Automatic promotion was a distinct possibility but despite victory at Swindon on the final day, a win for Middlesbrough over Oxford condemned Reid's side to the play-offs. After a tense semi-final success over Sheffield United, Sunderland fought out an extraordinary 4-4 draw with Charlton, during which Phillips scored his 35th goal of the season.

Cup success was muted with an FA Cup victory over Rotherham being followed by defeat against Tranmere while a Coca-Cola Cup win over Bury precipitated a 2-0 defeat at Middlesbrough.

Formed:	1879
Ground:	Sunderland Stadium of Light, Stadium Park, Sunderland, Tyne and Wear, SR5 1SU
Phone:	0191 551 5000
Box Office:	0191 551 5000
Info:	0898 12 11 40
Colours:	Red and white striped shirts, black shorts, red shocks with white band
Nickname:	The Rokerites
Capacity:	42,000
Manager:	Peter Reid
Honours:	Division 1 Champions 1891-92, 1892-93, 1894-95, 1901-02, 1912-13, 1935-36, 1995-96; Division 2 Champions 1975-76; Division 3 Champions 1987-88; FA Cup Winners 1937, 1973.
Managers:	Lawrie McMenemy 1985-87, Denis Smith 1987-91, Malcolm Crosby 1991-93, Terry Butcher 1993, Mick Buxton 1993-95.
Previous Names:	Sunderland and Teachers AFC 1879-80
Record League Win:	9-1 v Newcastle, D1, 5/12/08 8-0 v Derby County, D1, 1/9/1894
Record League Defeat:	0-8 v Sheffield Wednesday, D1, 26/12/11 0-8 v West Ham United, D1, 19/10/68 0-8 v Watford, D1, 25/9/82
Most GF in Season:	109 – Division 1, 1935-36

All-time League Apps: 537 – Jim Montgomery, 1961-77
All-time League Goals: 209 – Charlie Buchan, 1911-25
Most Goals in a Season: 43 – Dave Halliday, 1928-29
Most Goals in a Match: 5 – C. Buchan v Liverpool, 7/12/19 (7-0)
5 – R. Gurney v Bolton W, 7/12/35 (7-2)
5 – D. Sharkey v Norwich, 20/2/62 (7-1)
Record Fee Received: £1.8m from Crystal Palace for Marco Gabbiadini, 9/91
Record Fee Paid: £1m to Manchester City for Nicky Summerbee, 11/97
Record Attendance: 75,118 v Derby County, FA Cup 6th Round Replay, 8/3/33 (at Roker Park)

Stats File

Division	P	W	D	L	F	A	Pts	Yr	B	W
Premier/1:	2770	1117	631	1022	4566	4270	2927	71	1	21
Division 1n/2:	1082	447	303	332	1592	1320	1364	25	1	21
Division 2n/3:	46	27	12	7	92	48	93	1	1	1

Cup Records	P	W	D	L	F	A
FA Cup:	299	125	73	101	498	409
League Cup:	113	42	29	42	170	169
A/F Members Cup:	14	5	3	6	24	20

Sequence	Games	Start		End
Winning Run:	13	14/11/1891	to	2/4/1892
Without Defeat:	18	10-Feb-96	to	27-Apr-96
Without Win:	14	16-Apr-85	to	14-Sep-85
Drawn Games:	6	26-Mar-49	to	19-Apr-49
Without Draw:	46	26-Dec-07	to	13-Mar-09
Losing Run:	9	23-Nov-76	to	15-Jan-77
Clean Sheets (5):	6	18-Dec-82	to	15-Jan-83
	6	6-Apr-96	to	27-Apr-96
Goal Scored:	29	8-Nov-97	to	25-Apr-98
No. Goals For:	10	27-Nov-76	to	5-Feb-77
SOS Undefeated:	14	1910-11		
SOS No Wins:	10	1969-70		
	10	1976-77		

5-Year Record

	Div	P	W	D	L	F	A	Pts	Psn	
1993-94	1	46	19	8	19	54	57	65	12	
1994-95	1	46	12	18	16	41	45	54	20	
1995-96	1	46	22	17	7	59	33	83	1	Promoted
1996-97	P	38	10	10	18	35	53	40	18	Relegated
1997-98	1	46	26	12	8	86	50	90	3	

Swindon Town

A Season of Two Halves

The end of the 1996/97 season could not come quickly enough for Swindon Town as they collected just two points and scored only one goal in their last eight games. Manager Steve McMahon, approaching his third full season in charge, attempted to arrest the decline with four summer signings, including £330,000 striker Chris Hay from Celtic and veteran defender Alan McDonald from QPR. Later in the campaign he added George Ndah and Ifem Onuora to his squad while the previous season's top scorer Wayne Allison was sold for £800,000 as Swindon swept to the top of the table.

The Robins made an excellent, if unexpected, start to the season and after 17 games were three points clear at the summit, but with a spell of only one win in 11 games Swindon drifted away from the promotion pack. The poor run extended to just three wins in 19 games and by the time they lost on the final day of the season the relegation zone was just four points away.

McMahon suffered one of the most humbling moments of his career in the FA Cup when his side were beaten at the County Ground by Stevenage and in the Coca-Cola Cup they succumbed to Division Two Watford.

Formed:	1881
Ground:	County Ground, Swindon, SN1 2ED
Phone:	01793 430430 **Box Office:** 01793 529000
Info:	0891 12 16 40
Colours:	Red shirts, red shorts, red socks with white and green trim
Nickname:	The Robins
Capacity:	15,728
Manager:	Steve McMahon
Honours:	Division 2 Champions 1995-96; Division 4 Champions 1985-86; Football League Cup Winners 1969; Anglo Italian Cup Winners 1970.
Managers:	Ken Beamish 1983-84, Lou Macari 1984-89, Osvaldo Ardiles 1989-91, Glenn Hoddle 1991-93, John Gorman 1993-94.
Record League Win:	9-1 v Luton Town, D3S, 28/4/21 8-0 v Newport County, D3S, 26/12/38 8-0 v Bury, D3, 8/12/79
Record League Defeat:	0-9 v Torquay United, D3S, 8/3/52
Most GF in Season:	100 – Division 3S, 1926-27
All-time League Apps:	889 – John Trollope, 1960-81
All-time League Goals:	230 – Harry Morris, 1926-33
Most Goals in a Season:	47 – Harry Morris, 1926-27

Most Goals in a Match:	5 – Harry Morris v QPR, D3S, 18/12/27 (6-2)
	5 – v Norwich City, D3S, 26/4/30 (5-1)
	5 – Keith East v Mansfield, D3, 20/11/65 (6-2)
Record Fee Received:	£1.5m from Manchester City for Kevin Horlock, 1/97
Record Fee Paid:	£800,000 to West Ham Utd for Joey Beauchamp, 8/94
Record Attendance:	32,000 v Arsenal, FA Cup 3rd Round, 15/1/72
	29,106 v Watford, D3, 29/3/69

Stats File

Division	P	W	D	L	F	A	Pts	Yr	B	W
Premier/1:	42	5	15	22	47	100	30	1	22	22
Division 1n/2:	706	240	196	270	943	1003	824	16	4	22
Division 2n/3:	874	358	237	279	1315	1101	1016	19	1	22
Division 3n/4:	184	87	39	58	263	211	300	4	1	17

Cup Records	P	W	D	L	F	A
FA Cup:	252	124	44	84	454	344
League Cup:	146	65	32	49	245	217
A/F Members Cup:	27	11	6	10	47	35

Sequence	Games	Start		End
Winning Run:	8	6-Nov-26	to	28-Dec-26
	8	12-Jan-86	to	15-Mar-86
Without Defeat:	22	12-Jan-86	to	23-Aug-86
Without Win:	19	17-Apr-93	to	20-Nov-93
Drawn Games:	6	22-Nov-91	to	28-Dec-91
Without Draw:	29	6-Sep-85	to	15-Mar-86
Losing Run (4):	6	3-May-80	to	6-Sep-80
	6	2-May-93	to	25-Aug-93
Clean Sheets:	6	17-Aug-68	to	14-Sep-68
Goal Scored:	31	17-Apr-26	to	5-Feb-27
No. Goals For (3):	5	26-Apr-66	to	10-May-66
	5	5-Apr-97	to	4-May-97
SOS Undefeated:	9	1995-96		
	9	1963-64		
SOS No Wins:	15	1993-94		

5-Year Record

	Div	P	W	D	L	F	A	Pts	Psn	
1993-94	P	42	5	15	22	47	100	30	22	Relegated
1994-95	1	46	12	12	22	54	73	48	21	Relegated
1995-96	2	46	25	17	4	71	34	92	1	Promoted
1996-97	1	46	15	9	22	52	71	54	19	
1997-98	1	46	14	10	22	42	73	52	18	

Tranmere Rovers

Aldridge Bows Out

Tranmere Rovers' player/manager John Aldridge took his final bow in a playing capacity and marked the ending of his glorious 20-year career with a brace of goals to clinch victory over Wolves. It was the 18th season in which he has taken his goals' tally into double figures.

Unfortunately for Aldridge his goals and the dozen scored by £350,000 strike partner David Kelly were just about the high points of a disappointing league campaign for Rovers, who accumulated nine points less than the previous season. After a slow start to the season, Tranmere recovered but could not put a good enough winning run together to get into the top half of the table. Certainly there appeared to be money in the bank to strengthen the side following the £2m sale of Alan Rogers during the close season.

Rovers made promising progress in the FA Cup with a 3-0 win at Hereford being followed by a home victory over Sunderland, courtesy of a goal from local-born Andrew Parkinson, but Newcastle blocked further success in the 5th Round. Division Three sides Hartlepool and Notts County were both overcome in the Coca-Cola Cup and Tranmere drew at Oxford United in the 3rd Round but lost a penalty shoot-out 6-5.

Formed:	1885
Ground:	Prenton Park, Prenton Road West, Birkenhead, Merseyside, L42 9PN
Phone:	0151 609 1824
Box Office:	0151 608 4194
Info:	0891 12 16 46
Internet:	–
Colours:	White shirts, shorts and socks with green and blue trim
Capacity:	16,789
Nickname:	The Rovers
Manager:	John Aldridge
Honours:	Division 3N Champions 1937-38; Welsh Cup Winners 1934-35; Leyland Daf Cup Winners 1990.
Managers:	John King 1975-80, Bryan Hamilton 1980-85, Frank Worthington 1985-87, Ronnie Moore 1987, John King 1987-96.
Previous Names:	Belmont, 1884-85
Record League Win:	11-1 v Durham City, D3N, 7/1/28 13-4 v Oldham, D3N, 26/12/35
Record League Defeat:	2-9 v QPR, D3, 3/12/60 0-8 (4 times) 0-8 v Lincoln City, D3N, 21/4/30 0-8 v Bury, D3, 10/1/70
Most GF in Season:	111 – Division 3N, 1930-31

All-time League Goals: 161 – Ian Muir, 1985-93
All-time League Apps: 636 – Ray Mathias, 1967-84
Most Goals in a Match: 9 – Robert Bell v Oldham Athletic, 26/12/35
Most Goals in a Season: 35 – Robert Bell, 1933-34
Record Fee Received: £1.5m from Sheffield Wednesday for Ian Nolan, 8/94
Record Fee Paid: £450,000 to Aston Villa for Shaun Teale, 8/95
Record Attendance: 24,424 v Stoke City, FA Cup 4th Round, 5/2/72

Stats File

Division	P	W	D	L	F	A	Pts	Yr	B	W
Division 1n/2:	364	131	98	135	484	495	485	8	4	22
Division 2n/3:	736	242	213	281	980	1028	743	16	4	23
Division 3n/4:	780	318	185	277	1179	1057	953	17	2	21

Cup Records	P	W	D	L	F	A
FA Cup:	180	68	45	67	311	270
League Cup:	125	48	33	44	180	187
A/F Members Cup:	39	21	6	12	73	48

Sequence	Games	Start		End
Winning Run:	9	26-Oct-64	to	28-Dec-64
	9	9-Feb-90	to	19-Mar-90
Without Defeat:	18	16-Mar-70	to	4-Sep-70
Without Win:	16	8-Nov-69	to	14-Mar-70
Drawn Games:	5	25-Oct-76	to	13-Nov-76
	5	26-Dec-97	to	31-Jan-98
Without Draw:	31	21-Jan-53	to	26-Sep-53
Losing Run:	8	29-Oct-38	to	17-Dec-38
Clean Sheets:	6	25-Aug-73	to	19-Sep-73
Goal Scored:	32	24-Feb-34	to	15-Dec-34
No. Goals For:	7	20-Dec-97	to	4-Feb-98
SOS Undefeated:	9	1923-24		
	9	1935-36		
SOS No Wins:	7	1978-79		

5-Year Record

	Div	P	W	D	L	F	A	Pts	Psn
1993-94	1	46	21	9	16	69	53	72	5
1994-95	1	46	22	10	14	67	58	76	5
1995-96	1	46	14	17	15	64	60	59	13
1996-97	1	46	17	14	15	63	56	65	11
1997-98	1	46	14	14	18	54	57	56	14

Watford

Taylor Made Champions

After a season as general manager at Watford, former England manager Graham Taylor resurrected his managerial career in time for the 1997/98 season with spectacular results. A phenomenal success in his first spell at Vicarage Road, Taylor has got the Hornets going again with the Division Two Championship being won at the first attempt.

Watford lost the exciting talent of David Connolly on a free transfer to Feyenoord but received over £1.5m for Kevin Miller and Kevin Phillips. Micah Hyde was Taylor's most expensive capture at £250,000 while striker Jason Lee successfully rebuilt his career.

The Hornets won eight and drew two of the opening 11 games and had little trouble in taking full advantage of that great start as they, and Bristol City, monopolised the division. The Championship, though, looked to be heading away from Hertfordshire when Watford wobbled during early spring but a final-day win at Fulham – Watford were the only side to win ten or more away games – clinched the title.

Barnet and Torquay were beaten in the FA Cup before Watford lost a 3rd Round penalty shoot-out at Premiership Sheffield Wednesday. And it was also in Sheffield, at United, where Watford's Coca-Cola Cup exploits finished, having earlier beaten Swindon.

Formed:	1891
Ground:	Vicarage Road Stadium, Watford, WD1 8ER
Phone:	01923 49600 **Box Office:** 01923 496010
Info:	0891 104104
Capacity:	20,000
Colours:	Yellow shirts with black/red trim, black shorts with yellow trim, black socks with yellow tops
Nickname:	The Hornets
Manager:	Graham Taylor
Honours:	Division 1 Runners-up 1982-83; Division 3 Champions 1968-69; Division 4 Champions 1977-78; FA Cup Runners-up 1983-84.
Managers:	Steve Harrison 1988-90, Colin Lee 1990, Steve Perryman 1990-93, Glenn Roeder 1993-96, Kenny Jackett 1996-97.
Previous Names:	Watford Rovers until 1891
Record League Win:	8-0 v Sunderland, D1, 25/9/82
Record League Defeat:	1-8 v Crystal Palace, D4, 23/9/59
Most GF in Season:	92 – Division 4, 1959-60
All-time League Apps:	495 – Luther Blissett, 1975-92 (in three periods)
All-time League Goals:	180 – Luther Blissett, 1975-92 (in three periods)
Most Goals in a Season:	42 – Cliff Holton, 1959-60

Most Goals in a Match: 5 – Eddie Mummery v Newport Co., D3S, 5/1/24 (8-2)
Record Fee Received: £2.3m from Chelsea for Paul Furlong, 5/94
Record Fee Paid: £550,000 to AC Milan for Luther Blissett, 8/94
Record Attendance: 34,099 v Manchester United, FA Cup Round 4th Round Replay, 3/2/69

Stats File

Division	P	W	D	L	F	A	Pts	Yr	B	W
Premier/1:	250	93	58	99	386	372	337	6	2	20
Division 1n/2:	620	199	176	245	736	807	721	14	2	23
Division 2n/3:	690	281	199	210	998	845	801	15	1	23
Division 3n/4:	230	110	51	69	387	296	271	5	1	15

Cup Records	P	W	D	L	F	A
FA Cup:	249	111	59	79	399	323
League Cup:	122	47	29	46	199	187
A/F Members Cup:	13	4	2	7	14	20

Sequence	Games	Start		End
Winning Run:	7	17-Nov-34	to	29-Dec-34
Without Defeat:	22	1-Oct-96	to	1-Mar-97
Without Win:	19	27-Nov-71	to	8-Apr-72
Drawn Games:	7	30-Nov-96	to	27-Jan-97
Without Draw:	19	29-Apr-78	to	18-Nov-78
Losing Run:	9	18-Dec-71	to	26-Feb-72
	9	26-Dec-72	to	27-Feb-73
Clean Sheets:	8	24-Sep-49	to	12-Nov-49
Goal Scored:	22	20-Aug-85	to	28-Dec-85
No. Goals For:	7	18-Dec-71	to	12-Feb-72
SOS Undefeated:	7	1923-24		
SOS No Wins:	9	1990-91		
	9	1984-85		

5-Year Record

	Div	P	W	D	L	F	A	Pts	Psn	
1993-94	1	46	15	9	22	66	80	54	19	
1994-95	1	46	19	13	14	52	46	70	7	
1995-96	1	46	10	18	18	62	70	48	23	Relegated
1996-97	2	46	16	19	11	45	38	67	13	
1997-98	2	46	24	16	6	67	41	88	1	Promoted

WBA

Firepower Problems

What at one stage looked as though it could be a season of great excitement for West Bromwich Albion petered out into one of consolidation for the Baggies following the departure of manager Ray Harford in December. At the time of Harford's sudden exit from the Hawthorns, the Baggies were third in the table, but fell away and new manager Denis Smith was left to hope that the undoubted potential within the squad would be fulfilled.

After 18 games West Brom were level on points with leaders Nottingham Forest but a lack of goals, just 22, thwarted further progress. By the end of the season the Baggies were down to 10th with a poor run-in leaving them a distant 13 points from a play-off place. On the plus side, Andy Hunt took his goals tally into double figures for a fifth consecutive year while Lee Hughes, a £200,000 signing (rising to double that) from Kidderminster, scored 12 times in his first season.

A four-year run without an FA Cup victory ended with a 3-1 success over Stoke but it was followed by a hefty 4-0 defeat at Aston Villa. Cambridge and Luton were beaten in the Coca-Cola Cup prior to a 2-0 defeat at home to Liverpool.

Formed: 1878-79
Ground: The Hawthorns, West Bromwich, B71 4LF
Phone: 0121 525 6664　　　　**Box Office:** 0121 553 5472
Info: 0898 12 11 93
Capacity: 25,296
Colours: Navy blue/white striped shirts, white shorts, white socks
Nickname: The Throstles, Baggies, Albion
Manager: Denis Smith
Managers: Bobby Gould 1991-92, Ossie Ardiles 1992-93,
Keith Burkinshaw 1993-94, Alan Buckley 1994-97,
Ray Harford 1997-Dec 97.
Previous Names: West Bromwich Strollers 1878-80
Record League Win: 12-0 v Darwen, D1, 4/4/1892
Record League Defeat: 3-10 v Stoke City, D1, 4/2/37
Most GF in Season: 105 – Division 2, 1929-30
All-time League Apps: 574 – Tony Brown, 1963-80
All-time League Goals: 218 – Tony Brown, 1963-79
Most Goals in a Season: 39 – William Richardson, 1935-36
Most Goals in a Match: 6 – Jimmy Cookson v Blackpool, D2, 17/9/27
Record Fee Received: £1.5m from Manchester U. for Bryan Robson, 10/81
Record Fee Paid: £1.25m to Preston NE for Kevin Kilbane, 6/97
Record Attendance: 64,815 v Arsenal, FA Cup 6th Round, 6/3/1937

Stats File

Division	P	W	D	L	F	A	Pts	Yr	B	W
Premier/1:	2652	988	637	1027	4134	4224	2673	68	1	22
Division 1n/2:	1212	508	301	403	1935	1569	1457	29	1	23
Division 2n/3:	92	44	24	24	152	103	156	2	4	7

Cup Records	P	W	D	L	F	A
FA Cup:	341	170	71	100	605	397
League Cup:	122	52	33	37	189	160
A/F Members Cup:	16	8	1	7	29	28

Sequence	Games	Start		End
Winning Run:	11	5-Apr-30	to	8-Sep-30
Without Defeat:	17	7-Dec-01	to	22-Mar-02
	17	7-Sep-57	to	7-Dec-57
Without Win:	14	28-Oct-95	to	3-Feb-96
Drawn Games (5):	5	5-Feb-83	to	5-Mar-83
	5	20-Apr-91	to	11-May-91
Without Draw:	35	3-Apr-15	to	25-Feb-20
Losing Run:	11	28-Oct-95	to	26-Dec-95
Clean Sheets:	6	8-Apr-50	to	29-Apr-50
Goal Scored:	36	26-Apr-58	to	31-Mar-59
No. Goals For (16):	4	12-Feb-83	to	5-Mar-83
	4	12-Jan-85	to	23-Feb-85
SOS Undefeated:	9	1953-54		
SOS No Wins:	12	1985-86		

5-Year Record

	Div	P	W	D	L	F	A	Pts	Psn
1993-94	1	46	13	12	21	60	69	51	21
1994-95	1	46	16	10	20	51	57	58	19
1995-96	1	46	16	12	18	60	68	60	11
1996-97	1	46	14	15	17	68	72	57	16
1997-98	1	46	16	13	17	50	56	61	10

Wolverhampton W.

Wembley Out Both Ways

Although Mark McGhee took his side to the last four of the FA Cup for the first time in 17 years, this was another season of underachievement at Molineux as Wolverhampton Wanderers once again failed to win promotion.

After a mediocre start to the season Wolves soon climbed the table and by midway through the campaign had risen into the top six. But as their cup run took over, McGhee's side fell off the pace and by the time they went out of the cup Wolves were five points short of the play-off places with just six games to go. An indifferent spell ensured that they would not match the previous season's appearance in the play-offs.

Wolves' charge to the FA Cup semi-final kicked off with wins over Darlington and Charlton before a late Dougie Freedman winner accounted for Wimbledon after a replay. Wolves' greatest moment came at Leeds in the 6th Round with Don Goodman grabbing a sensational winner but in the semi-final Arsenal proved just too strong. Wolves saw off London sides QPR and Fulham in the Coca-Cola Cup before going down 4-2 at Reading.

Steve Bull's legendary status at Molineux was further enhanced by his 300th goal for the club.

Formed:	1877
Ground:	Molineux Ground, Waterloo Road, Wolverhampton, WV1 4QR
Phone:	01902 655000
Box Office:	01902 653653
Info:	0898 12 11 03
Colours:	Gold shirts, black shorts, gold socks
Capacity:	28,525
Nickname:	The Wolves
Manager	Mark McGhee
Honours:	Division 1 Champions 1953-54, 1957-58, 1958-59; Division 2 Champions 1931-32, 1976-77; Division 3N Champions 1923-24; Division 3 Champions 1988-89; Division 4 Champions 1987-88; FA Cup Winners 1893, 1908, 1949, 1960; Football League Cup Winners 1974, 1980; Texaco Cup Winners 1971; Sherpa Van Trophy Winners 1988; UEFA Cup Runners-up 1971-72.
Managers:	Bill McGarry 1985, Sammy Chapman 1985-86, Brian Little 1986, Graham Turner 1986-94, Graham Taylor 1994-95.
Record League Win:	10-1 v Leicester City, D1, 15/4/38 9-0 v Fulham, D1, 16/9/59
Record League Defeat:	1-10 v Newton Heath, D1, 15/10/1892

Most GF in Season:	115 – Division 2, 1931-32
All-time League Apps:	501 – Derek Parkin, 1967-82
All-time League Goals:	279 – Steve Bull, 1986-98
Most Goals in a Season:	38 – D. Westcott, 1946-47
Most Goals in a Match:	5 (5 times): W. Hartill v Notts Co., D2, 12/10/29 (5-1)
	5 – W Hartill v Aston Villa, D1, 3/9/34 (5-2)
Record Fee Received:	£2m from Crystal Palace for Neil Emblen, 8/97
Record Fee Paid:	£1.85m to Bradford City for Dean Richards, 5/95
Record Attendance:	63,315 v Liverpool, FA Cup 5th Round, 11/2/39

Stats File

Division	P	W	D	L	F	A	Pts	Yr	B	W
Premier/1:	2270	911	506	853	3874	3671	2344	59	1	22
Division 1n/2:	1470	588	343	539	2276	2061	1703	35	1	22
Division 2n/3:	92	37	24	31	153	147	135	2	1	23
Division 3n/4:	92	51	16	25	151	93	169	2	1	4

Cup Records	P	W	D	L	F	A
FA Cup:	331	154	76	101	606	425
League Cup:	95	42	17	36	139	124
A/F Members Cup:	24	14	5	5	45	20

Sequence	Games	Start		End
Winning Run (4):	8	14-Mar-87	to	20-Apr-87
	8	15-Oct-88	to	26-Nov-88
Without Defeat:	20	24-Nov-23	to	5-Apr-24
Without Win:	19	1-Dec-84	to	6-Apr-85
Drawn Games:	6	22-Apr-95	to	20-Aug-95
Without Draw:	37	3-May-30	to	4-Apr-31
Losing Run:	8	5-Dec-81	to	13-Feb-82
Clean Sheets:	8	31-Aug-82	to	9-Oct-82
Goal Scored:	41	20-Dec-58	to	5-Dec-59
No. Goals For:	7	2-Feb-85	to	16-Mar-85
SOS Undefeated:	12	1992-93		
	12	1949-50		
SOS No Wins:	14	1983-84		

5-Year Record

	Div	P	W	D	L	F	A	Pts	Psn
1993-94	1	46	17	17	12	60	47	68	8
1994-95	1	46	21	13	12	77	61	76	4
1995-96	1	46	13	16	17	56	62	55	20
1996-97	1	46	22	10	14	68	51	76	3
1997-98	1	46	18	11	17	57	53	65	9

Division 1 All-Time Table

The table lists the total record of all clubs who have played in what is now Division 1. It incorporates the records of the former Division 2. Yrs=Number of years (seasons) in the division. H=Highest position achieved. L=Lowest position.

Team	P	W	D	L	F	A	Pts	Yrs	H	L
Barnsley	2504	871	622	1011	3474	3905	2626	61	2	22
Leicester C.	2074	854	514	706	3212	2933	2401	52	1	22
Hull C.	2074	723	547	804	2818	3017	2072	50	3	24
Fulham	1984	752	472	760	2917	2799	2040	48	1	22
Birmingham C.	1630	709	393	528	2621	2106	1943	41	1	23
Grimsby T.	1840	676	413	751	2763	2933	1937	47	1	22
Middlesbrough	1556	651	377	528	2466	2094	1870	37	1	21
Charlton A.	1628	576	425	627	2395	2583	1795	38	2	22
Oldham A.	1526	561	396	569	2160	2195	1727	36	1	23
Blackburn R.	1446	583	364	499	2134	1981	1723	34	1	22
Derby Co.	1466	598	357	511	2293	2062	1712	35	1	22
Blackpool	1694	650	409	635	2460	2436	1709	43	1	20
Wolverhampton	1470	588	343	539	2276	2061	1703	35	1	22
Stoke C.	1496	580	384	532	2104	1984	1695	35	1	24
Bristol C.	1648	590	421	637	2217	2346	1675	40	1	23
N. Forest	1584	599	394	591	2414	2353	1643	38	1	21
Portsmouth	1426	500	373	553	1996	2056	1615	33	2	22
Sheffield U.	1262	549	322	391	2089	1665	1571	30	1	21
Notts Co.	1516	549	378	589	2224	2325	1550	37	1	24
Leyton O.	1682	540	447	695	1970	2380	1537	41	2	22
Bury	1576	591	335	650	2361	2512	1528	38	1	22
Port Vale	1544	521	347	676	2134	2572	1489	39	5	24
Southampton	1428	559	353	516	2221	2140	1471	34	2	21
WBA	1212	508	301	403	1935	1569	1457	29	1	23
West Ham U.	1230	537	300	393	1958	1622	1444	29	1	20
Millwall	1286	464	348	474	1702	1766	1435	30	1	22
Leeds U.	1144	483	309	352	1731	1451	1417	27	1	19
Plymouth Arg.	1446	474	373	599	2066	2337	1406	34	4	22
Luton T.	1332	488	343	501	1997	1945	1394	32	1	24
Huddersfield T.	1254	477	321	456	1766	1684	1381	30	1	23
Sunderland	1082	447	303	332	1592	1320	1364	25	1	21

Team										
Cardiff C.	1344	480	340	524	1838	1994	1336	32	2	22
Swansea	1428	497	321	610	2156	2489	1322	34	3	22
Newcastle U.	1046	481	218	347	1798	1438	1318	26	1	20
Preston NE	1270	485	340	445	1953	1843	1309	31	1	22
Burnley	1264	488	306	470	1836	1830	1305	32	1	22
Sheffield Wed.	1088	460	281	347	1693	1401	1285	26	1	22
Bolton W.	1030	443	255	332	1601	1265	1229	25	1	22
Crystal Palace	984	377	269	338	1271	1189	1221	23	1	21
Manchester City	878	431	195	252	1727	1189	1169	23	1	22
Norwich C.	978	374	249	355	1405	1380	1089	23	1	21
Bradford C.	1040	354	265	421	1380	1553	1074	25	1	23
Ipswich T.	786	334	205	247	1258	1094	1049	18	1	21
Chelsea	786	383	202	201	1323	887	1048	19	1	18
Lincoln C.	1258	376	260	622	1740	2399	1012	34	5	22
Manchester U.	816	406	168	242	1433	966	980	22	1	20
Rotherham U.	966	344	219	403	1435	1614	937	23	3	21
Bradford PA	900	345	187	368	1448	1471	877	22	2	22
Oxford U.	746	245	201	300	889	973	831	17	1	23
Swindon T.	706	240	196	270	943	1003	824	16	4	22
Bristol R.	810	272	209	329	1164	1317	794	19	6	24
Tottenham H.	668	311	172	185	1253	851	794	16	1	12
QPR	638	261	172	205	924	794	769	15	1	22
Coventry C.	756	279	186	291	1050	1099	744	18	1	22
Brighton & HA	646	229	155	262	881	983	737	15	2	23
Stockport Co.	856	257	194	405	1017	1446	727	22	8	22
Watford	620	199	176	245	736	807	721	14	2	23
Chesterfield	776	263	190	323	1070	1237	716	20	4	21
Carlisle U.	630	229	158	243	837	857	670	15	3	20
Liverpool	428	243	82	103	977	571	568	11	1	11
Glossop	584	193	126	265	798	952	512	16	2	20
Reading	480	152	118	210	611	777	508	11	2	22
Arsenal	428	216	73	139	824	550	505	13	2	10
Shrewsbury T.	426	138	119	169	481	549	504	10	8	22
Aston Villa	422	179	111	132	617	487	491	10	1	21
Tranmere R.	364	131	98	135	484	495	485	8	4	22
Gainsborough	564	175	118	271	718	1029	468	16	6	20
Doncaster R.	564	160	136	268	724	1043	456	14	7	22
Brentford	424	156	109	159	588	625	434	10	1	22
Burton U.	484	147	80	257	657	994	374	15	6	20
Cambridge U.	344	103	104	137	389	476	370	8	5	23
Gateshead	378	129	99	150	489	536	357	9	6	22
Leeds C.	380	140	77	163	575	616	357	10	4	19
Southend U.	276	88	69	119	328	414	333	6	12	24

Walsall	372	112	84	176	580	746	313	11	6	24
Scunthorpe U.	252	86	63	103	376	431	235	6	4	22
Everton	168	77	45	46	348	257	199	4	1	16
Bournemouth	136	43	30	63	166	206	159	3	12	22
Wrexham	168	51	45	72	168	192	158	4	15	21
Darwen	176	64	19	93	326	424	147	6	3	18
Wimbledon	84	37	23	24	129	112	134	2	3	12
Northampton T.	126	48	31	47	171	194	127	3	2	21
New Brighton	102	48	24	30	194	148	120	3	4	10
Crewe Alex.	156	38	22	96	198	405	116	5	10	16
Peterborough U.	92	24	27	41	103	139	99	2	10	24
Burton W.	90	42	13	35	167	146	97	3	4	15
Loughborough	158	34	20	104	170	409	88	5	12	18
Darlington	84	26	16	42	151	175	68	2	15	21
York C.	84	24	18	42	90	126	66	2	15	21
Rotherham T.	88	24	8	56	133	250	56	3	12	15
Nelson	42	10	13	19	40	74	33	1	21	21
Hereford U.	42	8	15	19	57	78	31	1	22	22
Mansfield T.	42	10	11	21	49	69	31	1	21	21
Northwich V.	50	12	5	33	72	156	29	2	7	15
Newport Co.	42	10	3	29	61	133	23	1	22	22
Middlesbro' Irn	28	8	4	16	37	72	20	1	11	11
Bootle	22	8	3	11	49	63	19	1	8	8

NATIONWIDE LEAGUE DIVISION 2

Final Table 1997-98

Pn	Team	P	W	D	L	F	A	Pts		FA	LC
1	Watford	46	24	16	6	67	41	88	P	3	2
2	Bristol City	46	25	10	11	69	39	85	P	2	2
3	Grimsby Town	46	19	15	12	55	37	72	P	4	4
4	Northampton Town	46	18	17	11	52	37	71		3	1
5	Bristol Rovers	46	20	10	16	70	64	70		3	1
6	Fulham	46	20	10	16	60	43	70		3	2
7	Wrexham	46	18	16	12	55	51	70		3	1
8	Gillingham	46	19	13	14	52	47	70		1	1
9	Bournemouth	46	18	12	16	57	52	66		3	1
10	Chesterfield	46	16	17	13	46	44	65		2	2
11	Wigan	46	17	11	18	64	66	62		3	1
12	Blackpool	46	17	11	18	59	67	62		2	2
13	Oldham Athletic	46	15	16	15	62	54	61		3	1
14	Wycombe Wanderers	46	14	18	14	51	53	60		1	1
15	Preston NE	46	15	14	17	56	56	59		3	2
16	York City	46	14	17	15	52	58	59		2	2
17	Luton Town	46	14	15	17	60	64	57		1	2
18	Millwall	46	14	13	19	43	54	55		1	2
19	Walsall	46	14	12	20	43	52	54		4	4
20	Burnley	46	13	13	20	55	65	52		1	2
21	Brentford	46	11	17	18	50	71	50	R	1	2
22	Plymouth Argyle	46	12	13	21	55	70	49	R	1	1
23	Carlisle United	46	12	8	26	57	73	44	R	1	2
24	Southend United	46	11	10	25	47	79	43	R	2	2

Play-Off Semi-Finals
Bristol Rovers v Northampton Rovers   3-1   0-3   3-4 on aggregate
Fulham v Grimsby Town   1-1   0-1   1-2 on aggregate

Final
Grimsby Town v Northampton Town   1-0

		P	HOME W	D	L	F	A	AWAY W	D	L	F	A	Pts
1	Watford	46	13	7	3	36	22	11	9	3	31	19	88
2	Bristol City	46	16	5	2	41	17	9	5	9	28	22	85
3	Grimsby Town	46	11	7	5	30	14	8	8	7	25	23	72
4	Northampton Town	46	14	5	4	33	17	4	12	7	19	20	71
5	Bristol Rovers	46	13	2	8	43	33	7	8	8	27	31	70
6	Fulham	46	12	7	4	31	14	8	3	12	29	29	70
7	Wrexham	46	10	10	3	31	23	8	6	9	24	28	70
8	Gillingham	46	13	7	3	30	18	6	6	11	22	29	70
9	Bournemouth	46	11	8	4	28	15	7	4	12	29	37	66
10	Chesterfield	46	13	7	3	31	19	3	10	10	15	25	65
11	Wigan Athletic	46	12	5	6	41	31	5	6	12	23	35	62
12	Blackpool	46	13	6	4	35	24	4	5	14	24	43	62
13	Oldham Athletic	46	13	7	3	43	23	2	9	12	19	31	61
14	Wycombe Wanderers	46	10	10	3	32	20	4	8	11	19	33	60
15	Preston NE	46	10	6	7	29	26	5	8	10	27	30	59
16	York City	46	9	7	7	26	21	5	10	8	26	37	59
17	Luton Town	46	7	7	9	35	38	7	8	8	25	26	57
18	Millwall	46	7	8	8	23	23	7	5	11	20	31	55
19	Walsall	46	10	8	5	26	16	4	4	15	17	36	54
20	Burnley	46	10	9	4	34	23	3	4	16	21	42	52
21	Brentford	46	9	7	7	33	29	2	10	11	17	42	50
22	Plymouth Argyle	46	10	5	8	36	30	2	8	13	19	40	49
23	Carlisle United	46	8	5	10	27	28	4	3	16	30	45	44
24	Southend United	46	8	7	8	29	30	3	3	17	18	49	43

Season Review

August

Quickest off the mark on the opening day of the season is Wigan midfielder Brendan O'Connell who strikes after just five minutes against Wycombe and goes on to complete a hat-trick on his debut as newly promoted Athletic romp to a 5-2 victory; Keith Scott scores both Wycombe goals. Pre-season bookies' favourites for the Championship, Bristol City and Luton Town, make a quiet start. City draw at Grimsby Town, relegated from Division One, and the Hatters lose 1-0 at Blackpool. Much-fancied Watford enjoy a winning start with new signing Jason Lee scoring the deciding goal against Chris Waddle's Burnley in front of the only five-figure gate of the day in Division Two. The other two sides relegated, Oldham Athletic and Southend United, are off the mark; Oldham beat York City 3-1 and United draw with promoted Carlisle United at Roots Hall. The remaining promoted side, Fulham, take maximum points off Wrexham, who have Steve Watkin sent off. Biggest winners are Millwall who, under new boss Billy Bonds, see off managerless London rivals Brentford. John Duncan watches his Chesterfield side put three past Walsall at Saltergate. The sole away winners are Bournemouth who beat Northampton Town with second-half goals from Jamie Vincent and Steve Fletcher. The only goalless match is at Priestfield where Gillingham and Preston North End share the spoils.

Just three days after the start of the league season, Division Two sides are in Coca-Cola Cup action with 1st Round 1st Leg ties on the 12th. The biggest crowd of the night is at Ashton Gate to see the Bristol pair of City and Rovers grind out an entertaining goalless draw. The two outstanding results are achieved by York, 2-1 winners at Port Vale thanks to Gary Bull and Steve Bushell, and Blackpool who overcome Manchester City at Bloomfield Road through Andy Preece's goal. Oldham win again with veteran Andy Ritchie's goal accounting for Grimsby while Chesterfield, Fulham, Carlisle, Luton and Preston also look good for a place in the next round following away wins.

Brentford, in the wake of David Webb's sudden departure on the eve of the season, appoint Eddie May as manager with former Chelsea and Woking winger Clive Walker as his number two. Watford's good start continues on the 13th with a fine 2-0 win at Division One Swindon in the Coca-Cola Cup and the Hornets match that result the following weekend with a successful trip to Carlisle. But top of the table after two games, purely due to alphabetical reasons, are Bournemouth following a last-minute win at Dean Court over Wigan, who have Paul Rogers sent off. No other side has maximum points but quite remarkably, after just two games, only one side is still pointless, York. Burnley and Gillingham end all square at 0-0 and ten men each at Turf Moor after David Eyres and Leo Fortune-West are sent packing in separate incidents, Waddle is also booked on his home debut. Comeback of the day is achieved by Grimsby, who come from two down to hold Plymouth Argyle at Home Park. Bristol City fire out a warning with a 2-0 home win over Blackpool. Luton play their second game of the season on the Monday and, with Stuart Douglas's goal, secure their first points with victory over Southend.

Bournemouth's brief flirtation with life at the summit ends on the 23rd with two goals from Sean McCarthy giving Oldham their second win of the season. Watford attract another five-figure gate as they become the only side with a 100 per cent winning record after three games following a comfortable 3-1 win over Brentford. Bristol Rovers go third with a similar victory over Carlisle but Chesterfield have to sweat when a three-goal lead is whittled down to one as Preston strive, unsuccessfully, to avoid their first defeat of the campaign. Wycombe may have the leakiest defence in the division but they are also joint highest scorers as a goal deficit is overturned during a 4-2 win at Blackpool. Kim Grant scores twice for Millwall but it cannot ruin York's day as they lose the tag of the only pointless club in the division with a 3-2 triumph at the New Den. They are replaced at the foot of the table by Burnley and three other sides on one point.

Division Two sides have a pretty good night in the Coca-Cola Cup on the 26th with pride of place going to Blackpool and Watford, who remove senior opposition from the competition. Watford surrender their winning record but a draw is sufficient to oust Swindon, and Blackpool squeeze through in a penalty shoot-out at Maine Road thanks to keeper Steve Banks. The battle for supremacy in Bristol is won during extra time by visitors City, with Junior Bent's goal two minutes from the end of extra time ending Rovers' unbeaten start to the season. Wycombe fans who travelled to Craven Cottage witnessed another goal feast but the 4-4 draw was enough for Fulham to go through 6-5 on aggregate. Two Second Division sides scored five. Grimsby striker Jack Lester had a hat-trick in the bag inside 11 minutes as the Mariners made light of Oldham's one-goal lead from the first meeting to go through 5-1. Brentford, held at home by Shrewsbury a fortnight earlier, strike five times at Gay Meadow to repel a hat-trick from Town striker Steele. Plymouth sample the highs and lows of football in a fluctuating contest in Devon. Two down from the 1st Leg at Oxford, the Pilgrims take a 3-0 lead by the 46th minute only to see United rattle in five goals to secure a bizarre 7-3 aggregate victory. Victims of an upset are Bournemouth, who draw at Torquay, but a goal deficit from the 1st Leg is enough to end the Cherries' hopes of cup glory. A last-minute goal by John Gayle levels the aggregate scores for Northampton at Millwall but it is the Lions who progress to the 2nd Round courtesy of an unusually low 2-0 penalty shoot-out win.

Bournemouth get back to winning ways in the league when a 2-0 success over Blackpool on the penultimate day of the month takes them back to the top of the table. Watford surrender that position after Kurt Nogan scores twice as Preston maintain their winning home record in front of 11,042 spectators at Deepdale. Going one better than Nogan are Bristol City's Shaun Goater and Walsall's Roger Boli in respective wins over Wigan and Southend. Goater's triple came in 13 first-half minutes. Burnley are still looking for their first league goal but a goalless draw at Bristol Rovers does take them off the foot of the table at the expense of Carlisle, who succumb to two goals by David Seal at Brunton Park. Brentford, at home to Grimsby, secure their first win while Wycombe, goals aplenty on their travels, have yet to concede at Adams Park following a 2-0 win over Fulham.

September

Southend, on the 2nd, have the pleasure of being the first visiting side to score at Adams Park but maybe wish they hadn't as Mark Stallard scores twice in a 4-1 win for Wycombe. Also scoring four, and pulling off an amazing comeback in the process, are Blackpool, who come from three down at Wrexham after 51 minutes to win 4-3 with the aid of a magnificent Tony Ellis hat-trick. Preston again win 2-0 at home, this time against Grimsby, while Northampton, Millwall, Fulham and Brentford also win by two clear goals. Bournemouth, held at home by Bristol Rovers, are knocked off top spot by Watford who end Plymouth's unbeaten home run through 17-year-old Gifton Noel-Williams' second-half goal. Burnley draw another blank at home to Oldham but it is not enough to keep them from sinking to the bottom due to Gareth McAlindon's last-minute winner for Carlisle at home to Wigan.

Chesterfield go second with an Andy Morris goal securing the points at York. Gillingham and Southend both come from behind on the 5th to complete their second home wins at the expense of Bournemouth – who lose the chance to go top – and Brentford. The programme is truncated on the 6th due to the funeral of Diana, Princess of Wales, but a crowd in excess of 12,000 see Watford end Wycombe's good run with a 2-1 win at Vicarage Road. Chesterfield stay a point behind the Hornets with Tony Lormer's early goal seeing off bottom dogs Burnley at Saltergate. Waddle's side have now set a club record of six consecutive games without a goal. Waddle slaps six of his squad on the transfer list. Blackpool climb nine places to seventh on the back of a 2-1 win over lowly Carlisle.

Five games midweek are notable for the fact that none of the away sides can muster a goal. After a losing start to the campaign, Northampton continue to fight back in style and, with a Sean Parrish goal after just 22 seconds, the Cobblers defeat Luton to move into third place. Bristol Rovers beat Walsall to go fourth and Oldham and Fulham also move into the top six with home wins over Preston and Plymouth.

Chesterfield's six-match unbeaten start comes to an end at Watford, who make it four wins out of four at Vicarage Road to open up a four-point lead. Northampton dent Oldham's winning home record with a 2-2 draw at Boundary Park. Wycombe's unbeaten home run comes to a shattering halt as Carlisle, having scored just four times in their opening six games, rattle in four at Adams Park. Carlisle chairman Michael Knighton picked the team having sacked manager Mervyn Day earlier in the week. Grimsby celebrate their first success, 2-0 at Fulham, while Wigan, in stark contrast to their away form, chalk up another convincing home win, this time 3-0 against Blackpool. The total includes a brace for David Lowe, who is just nine goals away from the club record. There is a shock at York as Burnley, after 552 minutes, score their first goal of the season. Little good it does them though as the home side win 3-1. Millwall also come from behind to beat Southend by the same score.

Division Two sides, on the whole, do not fare too favourably in the Coca-Cola Cup 2nd Round on the 16th although Blackpool, through David Linighan, defeat Premiership Coventry. Luton hold West Brom at Kenilworth Road and Watford grab a late equaliser against Sheffield United. Chesterfield come within three minutes of defeating Barnsley but ultimately go down 2-1 at home. Southend go down 1-0 at home to Derby and Fulham's lack of goals rolls on as Wolves win at Craven Cottage. York take the lead at Oxford United but are beaten 4-1; Millwall do even worse as Wimbledon hit five at Selhurst Park.

Knighton again weaves his magic the following night as Carlisle come within an ace of humbling Spurs at White Hart Lane in the Coca-Cola Cup 2nd Round; United eventually go down 3-2. But on a good night for Division Two sides, Grimsby pull off a magnificent 2-0 win over Sheffield Wednesday with goals from Paul Groves and Steve Livingstone while Skinner's second-half goal gives Walsall a stunning victory at Nottingham Forest. Both Brentford and Bristol City, defeated 3-1 at Southampton and Leeds respectively, face an uphill struggle. Preston's task is more of a mountain as they go down 6-0 at Blackburn.

Bristol City, on the 20th, continue to fail to live up to expectations as a 1-1 home draw with Bournemouth keeps them down in 19th place. Rivals Bristol Rovers are having no such problems as a draw at high-flying Chesterfield is sufficient to retain fifth position. With a five-goal salvo at Luton, which includes a hat-trick for Karl Connolly, Wrexham become the joint highest scorers in the division. It is Wrexham's biggest away win in eight years under Brian Flynn but it's misery for Luton who had nine regulars missing at the start and lose striker Dwight Marshall after just eight minutes. Oldham, Plymouth and leaders Watford all come from behind twice to collect away draws at Blackpool, Carlisle and Gillingham. With a late Andy Cooke goal, after David Eyres had missed a penalty, Burnley end their home goal drought but can only draw with Preston. Fulham's slide continues with defeat at Southend while Walsall rise three places with a 2-0 win over York. David Seal's lone strike gives Wigan a fourth successive away defeat and closes the gap on Watford to two points.

Cup glory expires for a number of sides on the 23rd as the bigger guns demonstrate their fire power in 2nd Leg 2nd Round Coca-Cola Cup ties. Watford go down 4-0 at Bramall Lane and Luton lose 4-2 at West Brom. York, as with the first leg, take the lead against Oxford but lose again thanks to two goals inside the final two minutes. Twenty-four hours later, Burnley and Fulham bow out at Stoke and Wolves, and Walsall look to be heading the same way when Forest take an early lead at the Bescot Stadium. The visitors increase their lead early in extra time but two goals from Andy Watson give Walsall a memorable 3-2 aggregate victory.

Mohamed Al Fayed begins to wield his muscle at Fulham with the dismissal of manager Micky Adams and double appointments of Kevin Keegan as chief executive and Ray Wilkins as manager. But the duo get a rude awakening in their first match, at Wigan, as the Latics further boost their impressive home record with a 2-1 victory. York again lose a lead gained this time at Watford but return home happy with a point. Northampton seize the opportunity to move level at the top with a 2-0 win over Millwall at the Sixfields Stadium; the visitors have Paul Sturgess dismissed. Blackpool move upward with a 3-0 win over Southend and Bristol City's season kicks into gear with three first-half goals condemning Luton to another defeat. Oldham look set to climb into the top three when taking a three-goal lead against Bristol Rovers inside 25 minutes but by the interval a brace from Peter Beadle has the sides level by half-time. Both sides score once more after the break to complete a 4-4 draw. Chesterfield stay third with a goalless draw at Wrexham while Paul Groves scores the goal for Grimsby which ends Bournemouth's 11 match unbeaten run at Dean Court. A missed penalty denies Preston an extra two points at Wycombe after the home side have Paul McCarthy sent off for handball.

Midweek Coca-Cola Cup matches see all four Division Two sides in action bow out of the competition but Bristol City refuse to without a fight. Having conceded an early goal, City battle back to win 2-1 against ten-man Leeds but lose 4-3 on aggregate. Brentford and Carlisle lose 2-0 at home to Southampton and Spurs while Chesterfield go down 4-1 at Barnsley.

October

The first day of the month marks the end of the road in the Coca-Cola Cup for Southend and Millwall, who are well beaten by Derby and Wimbledon, but Grimsby, with a positive performance, strike twice in three second-half minutes on their way to an excellent 4-3 aggregate victory over Sheffield Wednesday. Blackpool, having taken the lead at Coventry to double their 1st Leg advantage, bow out 3-2 on aggregate as Scotland captain Gary McAllister converts two penalties, the second coming a minute from time.

Watford reassert their authority at the weekend when completing the scoring of a 4-0 win inside the opening half hour at neighbours Luton. Peter Kennedy scores twice in the Hornets' first win over the Hatters for ten years. Northampton, boasting the meanest defence in the division, drop two points when firing blanks with Southend. Bristol Rovers claim third place, six points adrift of Watford, with a 1-0 win over Wrexham. They are joined on 17 points by Chesterfield who draw 1-1 at home with Bournemouth. A fine week for Grimsby is concluded successfully with two Kevin Donovan penalties extending Wigan's pointless away record to five games despite David Lowe notching the visitors' first away goal of the season. Burnley maintain their record of drawing every home game and score twice in the same match for the first time but are held by Wycombe.

Burnley, five home draws and five away defeats, break the mould on the 11th with a 3-1 home win over Carlisle in front of the day's biggest gate, 10,687. Luton deny Burnley the chance of moving off the foot of the table though, by beating Plymouth 3-0 with Tony Thorpe scoring twice. The only downbeat note for Luton is the dismissal of the debut-making Matthew Spring. Wigan also break their duck with a 3-2 win at injury-hit Chesterfield which ends the Spireites' long unbeaten home record. Northampton also lose their unbeaten away record as the Grimsby revival gathers momentum. Another first is Bristol City's win at Southend which, to keep the sequence going, is the Shrimpers' first home reversal. Bournemouth halt their decline with a victory at Deepdale which ends Preston's undefeated home record. London sides Millwall and Gillingham move into the top four with respective victories over Oldham and Wycombe. The Gills' winning goal is record-signing Ade Akinbiyi's fifth of the season.

Grimsby, with two goals from Steve Livingstone, remove Leicester's hands from the Coca-Cola Cup with a tremendous 3-1 victory at Blundell Park after the holders take a first-half lead. Not far behind in the glory stakes are Walsall, who also come from behind to oust Sheffield United at Bescot Stadium. Andy Watson is again on target but it is an own goal by Carl Tiler which ensures Walsall's safe passage. Returning to the league, Watford move five points clear with a 2-1 victory at Bristol Rovers, who miss out on the chance to go third.

Bristol City leapfrog Rovers with a 2-1 Friday night victory over York and Preston climb into third place with their first away win of the season, 2-0 at Carlisle. Record signing Ade Akinbiyi scores his sixth of the season for Gillingham on the Saturday but he cannot stop Northampton from notching a fifth win in six home games. Better still for Northampton is the news that Paul Shaw's goal for third-placed Millwall inflicts a first home defeat of the season on Watford. Burnley grab their first away point at the home of fellow strugglers Wrexham and Southend go one better with their first away success at lowly Plymouth, courtesy of Sada N'Diaye scoring on his debut. Brentford make hay against poor travellers Walsall with a 3-0 win at Griffin Park while Bournemouth move in front of a season's best attendance of over 7,000 with a 2-1 victory over Fulham. The Cottagers field record £500,000 signing Ian Selley.

A busy midweek programme sees Watford bolster their position with a 2-0 victory at Vicarage Road which leaves Fulham still looking for their first away point under the new management team. Bristol City's rise continues with a late Gregory Goodridge goal clinching a 2-1 win over Preston, and Rovers stay close behind by handing Brentford their first home defeat. Wigan's unbeaten home record is also shattered as Gillingham ram in four goals at Springfield Park. Millwall stay third with a draw at Bournemouth. Luton move out of the bottom three with victory at Carlisle while a Mark Stallard hat-trick for Wycombe hands Walsall a sixth defeat in seven away outings.

Fulham's attempt to buy success steps up a gear with Paul Peschisolido, from Birmingham, being the first £1m signing by a Division Two club.

Watford end the month with a flourish as Ronny Rosenthal scores the winner inside 36 seconds at Grimsby. Northampton take a point at Fulham, for whom Peschisolido scores on his debut. Gillingham rise to third when coming from behind to beat Plymouth. Carlisle's poor run looks to be over as they lead 3-1 at York with eight minutes to go but they slump to a 4-3 defeat, with Paul Stephenson scoring twice for the Minstermen. Carlisle have Andy Couzens sent off. Bristol City's surge is slowed by a goalless draw at Walsall but it is better than Rovers can achieve as they crash 3-0 at home to Blackpool. Chesterfield end a run of ten games without a win with a 1-0 victory over Wycombe, who have keeper Martin Taylor dismissed. A second successive win for Luton eases their worries. The final match of the month, on the 29th, confirms Bristol City's rise as goals from Steve Torpey (against his former club) and Adam Locke lift the visitors above their hosts Millwall.

November

Jason Lee scores twice as Watford move eight points clear on the 1st with a 4-1 win over Blackpool. Bristol Rovers have Brian Gayle dismissed but end a run of three defeats in four games with a draw at Northampton. Bristol City move above Northampton into second place with a home win over Oldham. Millwall bounce back to end Gillingham's unbeaten home record with a 3-1 victory at Priestfield. Goal-shy Grimsby more than double their tally for the season at Blundell Park with a 5-1 hammering of Southend. The visitors' plight is made worse by a draw for Luton at Wycombe, victory for Plymouth – the Pilgrims' first away success since March – at Preston, and a rare home win for Burnley against Walsall. Carlisle are now bottom following a home draw with Wrexham after leading 2-0.

The misery continues midweek for Southend boss Alvin Martin as Peter Kennedy scores all three Watford goals during a 3-0 stroll at Roots Hall. That result sends Southend to bottom place as Carlisle take all the points from fading Brentford. Bristol supremacy is City's as they inflict on Rovers a fourth home defeat, thanks to a couple of Shaun Goater goals. Northampton draw again, this time at Blackpool. London pride is shared at the New Den as Millwall grab a late equaliser against Fulham. Oldham protect one of only two unbeaten home records in the division with a 3-1 success over nearby Wigan. Two Graham Alexander goals cannot maintain Luton's improved run as Burnley complete a rise of six places in two games with a 3-2 victory at Kenilworth Road. Fellow strugglers Plymouth are also amongst the goals as Carlo Corazzin strikes twice in a minute to pave the way for a 4-2 win over Wycombe. Preston's slide continues with a 1-0 defeat at York but off the pitch the club is awarded a £7.5m Lottery grant to help fund a national football museum at Deepdale.

Brentford's decline costs manager Eddie May and assistant Clive Walker their jobs. They are replaced by Micky Adams, who left Swansea after just 13 days in charge. Adams' assistant is Glenn Cockerill.

Walsall again prove difficult to beat at Bescot Stadium on the 8th and a goalless draw with Watford allows Bristol City to close the gap at the top to six points following a 4-1 trouncing of Brentford at Griffin Park. Goater again scores twice whilst the Bees have Adams ordered from the bench. York move into the top three for the first time with a 2-0 success over Wycombe. Plymouth's recovery gathers pace with a 3-0 win over south coast rivals Bournemouth but Luton are downward again as Preston win 3-1 at Kenilworth Road despite Tony Thorpe's 50th goal for the Hatters. Millwall are surprisingly held at home by Carlisle while Northampton also slip up, going down 1-0 at improving Wrexham. Southend, in front of their lowest gate for nine years, beat Wigan 1-0.

Goalkeeper Maik Taylor is the latest big money addition to the Fulham squad as he joins from Southampton for an initial fee of £700,000.

The FA Cup takes centre stage over the third weekend of the month. On the Friday night four goals cannot separate Bristol Rovers and Gillingham and 24 hours later there are few real shocks although Luton lose at home to Torquay United. Wycombe are held at home by Ryman League strugglers Basingstoke Town and Brentford, Oldham and Plymouth fail to progress at home to Division Three opposition. Southend avoid a giant-killing with a 2-0 success at Woking and Watford come from a goal down to see off Barnet at Underhill. Phil Clarkson's late goal spares Blackpool from being held at home by Blyth Spartans. In all Division Two clashes Bristol City beat Millwall and Wigan do likewise at Carlisle. Margate take an early lead on the Sunday against Fulham before the Cottagers pull through 2-1.

A return to the league the following Tuesday means business as usual for Watford and Bristol City with respective wins over Oldham and Plymouth.

Millwall dent Burnley's recovery with a 2-1 success at Turf Moor which takes them into third place and leaves Oldham as the possessors of the only unbeaten home record. Brentford's plight shows little sign of improving as Northampton score all four goals prior to the interval in their 4-0 win at Sixfields. Carlisle are now just one place above bottom-of-the-table Brentford following a 2-0 home defeat by Chesterfield. Division Two interest in the Coca-Cola Cup dwindles as Grimsby go down 3-0 at Liverpool. The interest is completely extinguished the following night due to Walsall's 4-1 defeat at West Ham.

Friday night football is to Fulham's liking as Peschisolido scores twice during a 3-0 win over Gillingham. The following afternoon there are also three-goal victories for Grimsby and Preston but Watford and Bristol City still reign supreme. The Hornets' win at Northampton takes them 13 points clear of third-placed Millwall – held at home by Chesterfield – who trail City by seven points. Walsall's abysmal away run ends at Luton where John Hodge's goal lands the Hatters a fourth successive home defeat.

Division Two sides have a dreadful time in FA Cup 1st Round replays on the 25th. Wycombe go out on penalties at Basingstoke. Brentford go the same way following a goalless night at Colchester. Burnley are trounced 3-0 at home by Rotherham, and Plymouth, after being two up, lose at Cambridge. Better news is provided by Grimsby who beat Shrewsbury Town 4-0, Oldham who win at Mansfield, and Northampton with a 2-1 victory over Exeter City. Gillingham fail to make home advantage count and bow out 2-0 to a Bristol Rovers side which is enjoying good success on its travels.

Out comes the Fulham cheque book again as Derby midfielder Paul Trollope signs for £600,000.

The month ends with neither Watford nor Bristol City showing any signs of fallibility. The Hornets hand lowly Wigan an eighth away defeat in ten games while City cruise to a 3-0 victory at bottom dogs Carlisle; Goater claims two more. Millwall go down 2-1 at Bristol Rovers and are joined in third place on 32 points by Chesterfield, who account for Southend at Saltergate. After 15 unsuccessful attempts, Oldham, at Plymouth, win an away game to move within a point of Chesterfield. The win is all the more pleasing for Latics boss Neil Warnock who was sacked by Plymouth ten months earlier. Northampton lose ground with a defeat at Burnley while Luton and Walsall move away from the relegation zone with useful wins. Wrexham stretch their unbeaten run to 12 games with a draw at Brentford. The Fulham roadshow is humbled at Preston where a Lee Ashcroft hat-trick hands the Cottagers a 3-1 defeat.

December

Fulham continue to perform on a different playing field to the rest of the division as Chris Coleman, after originally rejecting the club's overtures, moves to Craven Cottage from Blackburn for £2.1m. Coleman joins three other débutants on the 2nd but Fulham again underachieve as their former manager, Micky Adams, collects a satisfactory point with his new club Brentford. A last-minute goal by Wrexham's Mark McGregor, the first conceded by Watford in five away games, denies the leaders maximum points and enables Bristol City to close the gap to four points as they retrieve a goal deficit to beat Burnley 3-1. More success for Oldham at Boundary Park, a 3-1 win over Carlisle, lifts them to third. The Latics overtake Northampton and Chesterfield who draw a blank at Sixfields. On a day when seven of the 11 games played end all square, of the strugglers, only Southend and Wigan win.

A midweek defeat for Millwall, at home to Walsall, stops the Lions from rising to third. Five Division Two sides are definitely through to the 3rd Round of the FA Cup following 2nd Round ties on the 6th. Leading the charge are Fulham, Walsall – with a spectacular 7-0 win at Macclesfield – Oldham, Wigan and Bristol Rovers. Basingstoke cause further embarrassment with a 1-1 draw at Northampton while Grimsby, Chesterfield, Preston and Watford also face replays.

The FA grant Wigan permission to ground-share with rugby league club Wigan Warriors next season while construction of a new 25,000-seater stadium gets underway.

Grimsby, on the 12th, close in on the promotion pack with a 4-0 trouncing of Bristol Rovers; Steve Livingstone scores twice. Bristol City fare better than their neighbours, the following day, as 16,072 fans watch the top two sides share the spoils in a 1-1 draw at Vicarage Road. Oldham, beaten at Wycombe, Chesterfield, held at home by Luton, and Millwall and Northampton, beaten at Plymouth and Preston respectively, all fail to close the gap. York have no such problems with a 1-0 home win over Wrexham. It is a great day for many of the lowly sides as Carlisle (at home to Fulham), Brentford, Plymouth, Southend, Wigan and Wycombe all win. Brentford's cause is aided by visitors Blackpool who have Chris Malkin and Ben Dixon dismissed, while Southend score twice in injury time to win at Gillingham.

Grimsby end Chesterfield's hopes of more FA Cup glory on the 16th following the previous season's run to the last four. Jack Lester and Paul Groves get the goals which give Grimsby victory at Saltergate and end the Spireites' 11-match unbeaten run. Watford are taken to extra time before seeing off Torquay, and Northampton have to wait even longer before winning a penalty shoot-out at Basingstoke. Preston pull off the best result of the night with an extra-time success away to Division Three leaders Notts County.

The outstanding match of three games played on the Friday night is at Roots Hall where visitors York take the lead but then have to come from behind three times to deny Southend maximum points. The final weekend matches before the holiday period have a touch of deja vu as Watford and Bristol City both win 1-0. Clubs just above the relegation places breathe a sigh of relief as all five of the bottom sides slither to defeat. Brentford are trounced 4-0 at Wigan, for whom Dutchman Jorg Smeetes scores twice. Luton also concede four at home to Bristol Rovers with all the scoring in Rovers' 4-2 win being completed inside 38 minutes.

Wycombe, one defeat in 12 home games, slow Watford's title charge on Boxing Day with a goalless draw at Adams Park. Bristol City, relishing playing in front of a home gate of 16,128, hammer Millwall 4-1 to extend their unbeaten run to 15 games. Fulham also hit four as Plymouth lose at home to the Cottagers for the first time in 61 years; Paul Moody nets two of the Fulham goals. But the biggest winners of the day are Bournemouth, who take advantage of the early departure of

Gillingham defender Adrian Pennock to win 4-0 at Dean Court with Steve Jones scoring twice. Two sides in the bottom half of the table, Burnley and Preston, both attract gates well over 10,000 but are held to draws by Chesterfield and Oldham respectively.

Late goals are the order of the day on the 27th. Watford, having fallen behind on 86 minutes, equalise against Plymouth four minutes later while neighbours Luton do even better with Steve Davis and Tony Thorpe netting in the dying moments of the Hatters' trip to Millwall. Gareth Owen and Neil Wainwright also score inside the final five minutes to give Wrexham victory at Blackpool, and a Jonathan Greening strike deep into injury time rescues a point for York at Chesterfield. Bristol City are beaten by Moody's goal at Craven Cottage but Bristol Rovers, Northampton and Grimsby all boost their play-off hopes with home wins. Rovers skipper Peter Beadle hits a hat-trick during the 5-3 win over Bournemouth. Carlisle are off the bottom by virtue of a 2-0 win at Wigan. Gillingham sign off the year in style with a 4-1 win over Brentford on the 30th.

January

Gillingham continue to climb on the 3rd with a 2-0 win over Burnley. Luton, with their seventh away match without defeat, win at Southend to jump above the Shrimpers. Grimsby are the toast of Division Two as they add Norwich to their list of giant-killings with a 3-0 3rd Round FA Cup win which stretches their unbeaten run to 12 games. Watford gain a creditable home draw with Sheffield Wednesday and Bristol Rovers, thanks to keeper Andy Collett, hold Ipswich. But it is the end of the road for Wigan, Oldham, Preston and Northampton. Wrexham, playing on the Sunday, record an excellent goalless draw at Wimbledon. The following night sees the end of Fulham's cup dreams as goalkeeper Maik Taylor suffers a nightmare during a 3-1 defeat at Tottenham.

The second weekend of the year throws up two surprising results, the consequence of which is that Bristol City are the new leaders. Colin Cramb scores after just 14 seconds to set City on the path to a 4-1 victory over in-form Grimsby at Ashton Gate. Watford, at Burnley, fall to defeat as Andy Cooke scores twice but the home side remain at the foot of the table. Bristol Rovers, although 15 points in arrears of their city rivals, move to third with a win at Plymouth. They join Northampton – beaten 3-0 at Bournemouth – and Fulham, victors by the same margin at Wrexham, on 40 points. Injury-hit Southend field three YTS players as they are hammered 5-0 at Carlisle. A hat-trick by Tony Thorpe gives Luton victory over Blackpool as the Hatters rise to 18th. Brentford climb out of the bottom three courtesy of a 2-1 win over Millwall. Oldham draw a blank at York and have won just once in 13 away outings.

Delayed 3rd Round FA Cup ties bring disappointment for inconsistent Bournemouth on the 13th as they lose at home to Huddersfield, but Walsall win at Peterborough with two Andy Watson goals. Replays fail to go the way of Division Two sides though as Bristol Rovers lose 1-0 at Ipswich and Wrexham, after taking an early lead, go down 3-2 at home to Wimbledon. In a disappointing tie at Hillsborough, Watford take ten man Sheffield Wednesday to extra time before bowing out in a penalty shoot-out.

Crewe midfielder Wayne Collins becomes a part of the Fulham jigsaw in a £500,000 move.

Watford get their title push back on the rails on the 17th with a 3-1 win over a Preston side now managed by David Moyse. Bristol City stay top due to goals scored following an impressive 3-0 success at Wigan. Of the chasing pack, Bristol Rovers, Northampton and Grimsby stay in the hunt with the latter bouncing back to form with a 4-0 win over a Brentford side still without an away victory after 15 attempts. Luton's revival flounders at Boundary Park where Oldham successfully defend their unbeaten record with a 2-1 win. Watford and Fulham, who are held by Wycombe, both draw five-figure attendances. Walsall warm up for a trip to Manchester United with a fourth successive win, this time at Southend. Chesterfield grab their first win in 12 at the expense of struggling Plymouth.

Northampton, well placed for a shot at the play-offs, help knock Bristol City from pole position with a goalless draw at Ashton Gate on the 24th which allows Watford to reopen a two-point lead following a 2-1 win at bottom but one Brentford. With Oldham held at Bournemouth and Bristol Rovers being cut down by an Ian Stevens hat-trick for lowly Carlisle, Fulham seize the chance to move into third place. Moody scores a treble for Ray Wilkins' side in a 4-1 win at Luton. Burnley move level with Brentford and Southend at the bottom of the table thanks to a 1-0 win over the Essex club and fellow strugglers Plymouth drag Wigan into the mire with a 3-2 success at Home Park, after the visitors led by two goals at the interval.

Reading continue to fly the flag in the FA Cup with a Carl Asaba goal securing a replay with Cardiff. Walsall have the memory of a Roger Boli goal from their trip to Old Trafford but Manchester United move through to the 5th Round with a comfortable 5-1 win.

One midweek match sees Oldham edge closer to a play-off position with a 3-0 win over Wrexham but the Welsh club fight back well at Bristol City on the last Saturday of the month to take a point from Ashton Gate. Watford, with Noel-Williams' late strike at Saltergate, move four points clear and hand Chesterfield their second home defeat of the season. Most of the chasing pack draw but on a day of relatively few goals, Burnley, bottom at the start of the day, rip up the form book and with a hat-trick from Andy Cooke overturn a deficit at Turf Moor to thrash York 7-2. Brentford also ease their load with a 3-1 win over Plymouth.

February

Two goals from Matt Hewlett keep Bristol City on course for promotion with a 2-2 draw at Blackpool on the 3rd. The following weekend's results bring joy for the sides chasing the play-off positions as Bournemouth beat Bristol City at Dean Court with a Steve Fletcher goal and Gillingham, through two Ade Akinbiyi goals, hand Watford their second defeat of the season at Vicarage Road. For Bournemouth, it is the Cherries' third win in two months against City following success in the FA Cup and Auto Windscreen Shield. Oldham slip two places to fifth as Blackpool hand Neil Warnock's side their first home defeat of the season. Fulham and Bristol Rovers leapfrog the Latics. Of the bottom ten sides only Burnley, with a last-minute goal at Preston, are victorious.

Blackpool's surge continues on the 14th with a 3-0 rout of Millwall but it is Gillingham who grab the headlines with another impressive 2-0 away win, this time at Bristol City. Watford are surprisingly held at home by nearby Luton, who had lost their four previous games. Oldham return to winning ways with an important home win over Fulham which allows Northampton to reclaim third place courtesy of a 3-1 home win over bottom dogs Southend – United's goal is their first for 555 minutes. Bristol Rovers' challenge falters at fellow play-off hopefuls Wrexham while two second-half goals give Grimsby three points at Wigan and fifth place.

After a blank week, it is business as usual on the 21st but leaders Watford and Bristol City again fail to impress. A last-minute goal by Steve Palmer salvages a point for the Hornets at York while City are held at Luton. Blackpool's run is halted on the coast as Southend win 2-1 at Roots Hall but stay bottom. Oldham's poor away record costs them further ground in a 3-1 defeat at Bristol Rovers for whom Barry Hayles scores a brace, while Northampton hang on to third place with a goalless draw at Millwall. Grimsby close the gap with victory over Bournemouth. Brentford, held at Burnley, come within 13 minutes of their first away win of the season.

Bristol City's title push is back on track as midweek victory at York closes the gap on Watford to a solitary point. Defeat for Northampton at Gillingham enables Grimsby and Bristol Rovers to join Fulham, beaten at home by Bournemouth, in the top six. A number of the struggling clubs pick up good points but impressive 3-0 wins by Carlisle at Preston and Southend at home to Plymouth condemn Brentford to the foot of the table. Just three points separate the bottom seven clubs. Watford use up one of their two games in hand on Bristol City 24 hours later to move two points clear with a 1-1 draw at Millwall. It is the Hornets' first match since their chairman, Elton John, is knighted.

On the last day of the month Watford surrender a two-goal lead at home to Bristol Rovers before Tom Moody's late strike clinches another win. Bristol City stay in touch with a 1-0 success at Ashton Gate over lowly Southend. Both games attract over 12,000 spectators. Fulham go down to a second successive defeat, at Blackpool, but stay in the top six due to Gillingham's defeat at Wycombe. Bournemouth and Wrexham blow the chance to rise above the Cottagers while Northampton, through David Seal and Nigel Cleghorn, overturn Grimsby's early lead at Sixfields Stadium to move back to third position. The third highest gate of the day is at Brunton Park to see Carlisle beat Burnley in a relegation showdown.

March

The month kicks off with a busy midweek programme which sees Bristol City and Watford both slip up at home. City are held by Brentford while Watford go down to Walsall. Fellow promotion seekers Grimsby, Northampton, Bournemouth and Bristol Rovers also drop points, the latter at Fulham, who are one of seven clubs separated by just five points behind the runaway leading pair. Carlisle drag Millwall on to the fringes of the relegation battle with a 1-0 home win.

Northampton edge Bristol Rovers out of the play-off places on the 7th as goals from Chris Freestone and Jason Dozzell help the Cobblers move to within 11 points of Bristol City. Fulham match that result with victory at Chesterfield but the day's top scorers are Brentford who beat Bournemouth 3-2 through Kevin Rapley's late strike at Griffin Park. Fellow strugglers Plymouth see off Preston; Burnley, Carlisle and Luton also collect a point each from draws. A second successive home defeat for Bristol Rovers, their eighth of the season, seriously damages their promotion push and gives hope to visitors York. Leaders Watford are held by a late Phil Clarkson goal at Blackpool.

Rovers' plight worsens on the 14th as goals from Bell and Shaun Goater at Ashton Gate take neighbours City to the top of the table with a 2-0 victory. Over 17,000 witness City's success as they topple Watford, held by bottom club Southend, on goals scored. Two goals for Kevin Donovan help Grimsby to a 3-0 win over Walsall and Northampton stay close behind with a 2-0 victory over Blackpool. Wrexham continue to make ground and dent Bournemouth's aspirations with victory at Dean Court. Burnley and Luton draw at Turf Moor but the outstanding result of the day is Millwall's 2-1 win at Craven Cottage, despite having sub Tony Witter dismissed and defender Stuart Nethercott taken off with a suspected broken shoulder. Brentford's 11-month wait for an away win ends at the 22nd attempt at Carlisle as goals by Graeme Hogg and Andy Scott take the Bees out of the bottom four. Wrexham continue their run during the week with an early goal clinching the points at home to Millwall, and Southend move off the bottom with a fine 3-1 triumph at Wigan. Watford return to winning ways and pole position with a 2-1 win over Carlisle. Concerns over the running of Plymouth's club lottery lead to a charge of misconduct by the FA.

The Pilgrims make light of their off-the-field problems on the 21st as they overcome Bristol City 2-0 at Home Park with goals from Mark Saunders and Barry Conlon. A last-minute goal by Mark Allott earns Oldham a point at home to Watford and stops the Hornets from moving six points clear. Nigel Gibbs scores for only the seventh time in 14 years at Watford. Wycombe are Wrexham's latest victims as the Welsh club climb to third with a 2-0 win at the Racecourse Ground. Brentford's revival continues with a home goalless draw with Northampton but Grimsby are less happy to collect a point at Luton after leading 2-0. Fulham are back on course with victory at York. Mark Stein gives Bournemouth a 58th-minute lead at Southend but doubles for Jeroen Boere and Andy Thomson put the Shrimpers on the path to a remarkable 5-3 victory.

Grimsby put one of their two games in hand on Wrexham to good effect by reclaiming third place with a single-goal win over Plymouth midweek. Bristol City swell their coffers on transfer deadline day with the £500,000 sale of Goater to Manchester City. Southend's recovery flounders on the Friday night as Bristol Rovers breathe new life into their flagging campaign with a 2-0 victory.

A late Dean Peer goal gives Northampton an 11th away draw of the season, this time at Watford. Bristol City leave it just as late before proving there is life after Goater as £250,000 summer signing Colin Cramb scores twice in a 2-1 win at Wycombe. Burnley's poor run ends with a 2-1 home win over Grimsby, who hang on to third place thanks to Wrexham's 2-0 defeat at Plymouth. Two goals for Ade Akinbiyi move Gillingham level on points with visitors Fulham but the match, one of three played in front of more than 10,000 fans, is overshadowed by violence which culminates in the murder of a Fulham supporter. Luton's good away record –

only Watford have lost fewer times on their travels – offers hope as a 3-2 win at Walsall keeps them within two points of the four sides just above the relegation zone.

The month closes with Bristol City rising to the top courtesy of two goals in two minutes which hand Oldham only their second home defeat. Gillingham's challenge stumbles to a 1-0 defeat at Walsall but the honours are even at Wrexham where the points are shared with Grimsby.

April

Aided by Watford slipping to a 3-2 defeat at Wigan, Bristol City open a four-point lead on the 4th with a 1-0 home win over Carlisle. Grimsby move to within ten points of Watford despite only drawing with Gillingham. Wrexham, too, drop two points at home as struggling Brentford gain a creditable 2-2 draw. A second successive win for Burnley boosts their survival hopes but damages the play-off ambitions of Northampton who subsequently drop one place as Fulham beat Preston at Craven Cottage. Luton take full advantage of York going down to nine men to record a 3-0 victory. In doing so Luton convert their first penalty of the season and chalk up their first win at Kenilworth Road since January. The Hatters win and Brentford's draw drops Plymouth into the bottom four.

Burnley's revival is short lived as Blackpool come from behind to win at Turf Moor on the 7th and Wigan harm another club's play-off aspirations with a 1-0 win over Bournemouth. Luton, let down by a poor home record, witness the tenth home goal conceded by Grimsby. Wigan's bubble is well and truly burst on Good Friday as Peter Beadle hits a hat-trick during Bristol Rovers' 5-0 rout and Grimsby can only claw a point with a last-minute equaliser at Wycombe, a result which confirms Bristol City's promotion.

Watford move to within a point of promotion with Jason Lee's winner against play-off hopefuls Wrexham and the Welsh club's day is made complete by Paul Moody's two goals which give Fulham victory at Brentford and fourth place. Bristol City's hopes of celebrating promotion in style are dashed by a shock reversal at Burnley. Gillingham move into the top six with a home win over Luton. Northampton – beaten at Chesterfield – and Bristol Rovers both slip a place. Chesterfield's fourth successive win leaves them four points off a play-off position. At the foot of the table Southend, at Preston, head for a third successive defeat while Plymouth send Brentford back into the relegation places with a 3-1 win over Blackpool in a match containing two own goals.

A crowd of 19,141 see Bristol City and Watford share the spoils at Ashton Gate on Easter Monday as the Hornets join City in Division One. Paul Peschisolido sticks a hat-trick past hapless Carlisle during a 5-0 hammering and with Grimsby and Wrexham suffering home defeats against Bristol Rovers and York the Cottagers are almost certain of a play-off place. Northampton miss out on rising into the top six when Preston snatch a last-minute point-saving goal at Sixfields. Burnley are brought back to earth with a 5-1 drubbing at Wigan but Brentford raise their survival hopes with a 2-1 win at Blackpool which puts the Bees level on points with Plymouth, who draw at Millwall.

Chesterfield's winning run comes to an end on the 14th as Luton's recovery gathers pace with another 3-0 success. Walsall still need a handful of points to ensure their safety following a 1-0 defeat at Bournemouth, who may yet sneak into the play-offs.

Bristol City, on the 18th, squander another chance to take a firm grip on the destiny of the Championship as Chesterfield, through Mark Williams, secure their fifth win in six outings. High-flying Fulham also come a cropper as Burnley grab a lifeline with a 2-1 win for their fourth success in six games. Gillingham and Wrexham do neither's promotion hopes any good with a 1-1 draw at Priestfields which allows Northampton, boosted by a Chris Freestone hat-trick in a 3-1 win at lowly Plymouth, to reclaim a top six place. Bristol Rovers complete a third successive win, over Luton, to rise to fifth. Hatters defender Julian James suffers a broken leg. Bruce Grobbelaar makes his debut for Oldham in a 0-0 draw at Walsall. A Kevin Donovan penalty gives Grimsby a midweek victory at Carlisle and third place.

In front of more than 15,000 fans on the 25th, Bristol City take charge in the Championship race with a 2-1 home win over Walsall, who are assured of Second Division safety by results elsewhere. Watford are held at home by Grimsby, who secure a play-off position. Northampton climb to fifth on the back of an almost certain play-off clinching 1-0 win over Fulham at Sixfields. A last-minute Paul Smith goal carries Gillingham into the top six and drops hosts Plymouth into the bottom four, a situation compounded by Brentford's home draw with a now safe Luton. Wrexham's promotion ambitions hang by a thread after only drawing at home to Preston and Bristol Rovers drop out of the play-off places with a single goal defeat at Blackpool. Bournemouth beat Burnley 2-1 to retain a passing interest in the play-offs. Southend and Carlisle both drop into Division Three following defeats by Oldham and York respectively.

Bournemouth's hopes are finally scuppered on the 28th as Watford win 2-1 at Vicarage Road to join Bristol City on 85 points; City lead on goals scored. Burnley miss an opportunity to climb out of the relegation zone by allowing Oldham to recover from 3-1 down at Boundary Park to salvage a point – the battle to avoid the drop goes to the final day with Brentford (50 pts), Plymouth and Burnley (both 49) looking to occupy the one safe spot left.

May

The new home for the Division Two trophy is settled courtesy of two surprising results. Bristol City, needing a win to secure the title, fall 2-1 at Preston with the scoring completed by the tenth minute. Watford, facing a tricky afternoon at Fulham, pounce on City's blip and by virtue of a 2-1 victory take the title for the second time under Graham Taylor. Despite this being Fulham's third successive defeat, Ray Wilkins' side clinch the final play-off position on goals scored from Wrexham and Gillingham. With Northampton drawing at York, Grimsby can afford to lose at home to Oldham and still hold on to third place. Wrexham win 3-1 at Southend but miss out by five goals on Fulham while Gillingham suffer the frustration of a goalless draw at home to Wigan when victory would have got them into the top six. Burnley pull off an amazing escape act with two Andy Cooke goals clinching a 2-1 victory at Turf Moor which condemns visitors Plymouth to Division

Three football. Brentford conclude the quartet of relegated clubs and their misery is all the worse as their victors, Bristol Rovers, celebrate a place in the play-offs with Barry Hayles scoring his 25th goal of the season.

Two days before taking part in the play-offs, Fulham dispense with manager Ray Wilkins and hand the managerial duties to Kevin Keegan. The former Newcastle boss is fortunate not to see his first match end in defeat following a very impressive performance by visiting Grimsby who return home on the back of a 1-1 draw. Bristol Rovers, playing in front of a record 9,173 attendance at the Memorial Ground, seriously dent Northampton's hopes of a second consecutive promotion via the play-offs with a 3-1 win. Rovers take a three-goal lead by the 46th minute through Hayles' 26th goal of the season but over confidence allows the Cobblers to stay in contention through a John Gayle goal.

Through a Kevin Donovan goal, in front of 8,689 fans, Grimsby are back at Wembley for the second time in two months as they defeat Fulham 2-1 on aggregate. Fulham play more than half of the game with ten men following the dismissal of Peschisolido. Bristol Rovers are to rue their overindulgence in the first meeting as Northampton strike through Carl Heggs and Ian Clarkson to level the scores by the hour in front of a record Sixfields crowd of 7,501. Ray Warburton's 77th-minute header confirms Northampton's return to Wembley.

Millwall name Keith Stevens as the replacement for Billy Bonds as manager and Oldham turn to Andy Ritchie following the departure of Neil Warnock. Chris Waddle leaves Burnley by mutual consent.

A crowd of 63,988, the largest for a Division Two final, gather at Wembley to see Grimsby rise back to Division One at the first time of asking, at the expense of Northampton, thanks to Donovan's 21st goal of the season. Donovan missed just one of Grimsby's 68 games during the season. ■

Play-Offs 1997-98

Semi-Finals 1st Leg

| Bristol Rovers | 3 | Northampton Town | 1 | 9,173 |

Beadle (30 pen); Bennett (37); Hayles (46) — Gayle (74)

| Fulham | 1 | Grimsby Town | 1 | 13,954 |

Beardsley (45 pen) — Smith (53)

Semi-Finals 2nd Leg

| Grimsby Town | 1 | Fulham | 0 | 8,689 |

Donovan (81)

Grimsby Town win 2-1 on aggregate

| Northampton Town | 3 | Bristol Rovers | 0 | 7,501 |

Heggs (34); Clarkson (61); Warburton (77)

Northampton Town win 4-3 on aggregate

Final – *at Wembley Stadium*

| Grimsby Town | 1 | Northampton Town | 0 | 62,988 |

Donovan (19)

NATIONWIDE DIVISION 2

	Blackpool	Bournemouth	Brentford	Bristol C.	Bristol R.	Burnley	Carlisle	Chesterfield	Fulham	Gillingham	Grimsby	Luton T.
Blackpool	—	1-0	1-2	2-2	1-0	2-1	2-1	2-1	2-1	2-1	2-2	1-1
Bournemouth	2-0	—	0-0	1-0	1-1	2-1	3-2	2-0	1-1	4-0	0-1	1-1
Brentford	3-1	3-2	—	1-4	2-3	2-1	0-1	0-0	0-2	2-0	3-1	2-2
Bristol City	2-0	3-1	2-2	—	2-0	3-1	1-0	1-0	0-2	0-2	4-1	3-0
Bristol Rovers	0-3	5-3	2-1	1-2	—	1-0	1-0	3-1	0-2	1-2	0-4	2-1
Burnley	1-2	2-2	1-1	1-0	0-0	—	3-1	0-2	2-3	0-0	2-1	1-1
Carlisle United	1-1	0-1	1-2	1-0	3-1	1-0	—	1-0	2-0	1-2	0-1	0-1
Chesterfield	1-1	1-1	0-0	1-0	0-0	1-0	2-1	—	2-0	1-0	1-0	0-0
Fulham	1-0	0-1	1-1	2-0	1-1	1-0	5-0	1-1	—	3-0	1-0	0-1
Gillingham	1-1	1-1	1-2	1-0	1-0	2-0	1-0	0-0	2-0	—	0-2	0-0
Grimsby Town	1-0	2-1	4-0	1-1	1-2	4-1	1-0	3-0	1-1	0-0	—	2-1
Luton Town	3-0	1-2	2-0	0-0	2-4	2-3	3-2	0-1	1-4	0-0	2-2	—
Millwall	2-1	3-0	3-0	2-1	1-1	1-0	1-1	3-0	1-0	2-1	2-0	0-2
Northampton Town	2-0	0-2	4-0	1-2	4-4	0-1	2-1	2-0	1-0	1-0	0-0	1-0
Oldham Athletic	0-1	2-1	1-1	2-0	1-1	3-3	3-1	0-2	1-0	2-1	1-0	0-1
Plymouth Argyle	3-1	3-0	0-0	1-2	1-1	2-2	3-1	2-0	1-4	3-1	1-0	0-0
Preston NE	3-3	5-3	1-1	2-0	1-2	2-3	3-0	3-2	1-4	1-3	0-2	2-3
Southend United	2-1	5-3	3-1	1-0	1-1	1-0	2-0	1-1	3-1	0-0	2-0	1-0
Walsall	2-1	2-1	0-1	1-1	3-2	0-0	3-0	0-2	0-1	2-1	0-0	2-3
Watford	4-1	2-1	3-1	0-3	3-0	1-0	2-1	3-2	1-2	1-1	0-0	1-1
Wigan Athletic	3-0	1-0	4-0	1-1	3-0	5-1	0-2	2-1	2-0	0-2	0-0	1-1
Wrexham	3-4	2-1	2-2	0-3	1-0	0-0	2-2	2-1	0-3	1-4	0-0	2-2
Wycombe W.	2-1	1-1	0-0	1-2	1-2	2-1	1-4	0-0	2-0	0-0	1-1	2-1
York City	1-1	0-1	3-1	0-1	0-1	3-1	4-3	1-0	0-1	2-1	0-0	1-2

RESULTS 1997-98

	Millwall	Northampton	Oldham A.	Plymouth	Preston NE	Southend	Walsall	Watford	Wigan A.	Wrexham	Wycombe	York C.
Blackpool	3-0	1-1	2-2	0-0	2-1	3-0	1-0	1-1	0-2	1-2	2-4	1-0
Bournemouth	0-0	3-0	0-0	3-3	0-2	2-1	1-0	0-1	1-0	0-1	0-0	0-0
Brentford	2-1	0-0	2-1	3-1	0-0	1-1	3-0	1-2	0-2	1-1	1-1	1-2
Bristol City	4-1	1-0	1-0	—	1-0	2-0	2-0	1-2	3-0	1-1	3-1	2-1
Bristol Rovers	2-1	0-2	3-1	1-1	2-2	1-0	2-0	1-2	5-0	1-0	3-1	1-2
Burnley	1-2	2-1	0-0	2-1	1-1	1-0	2-1	2-0	0-2	1-2	2-2	7-2
Carlisle United	1-0	0-2	3-1	2-2	0-2	5-0	2-1	0-1	1-0	2-2	0-0	1-1
Chesterfield	3-1	2-1	3-1	2-1	3-2	1-0	3-1	0-1	2-3	3-1	1-0	1-2
Fulham	1-0	1-1	3-1	2-1	2-1	2-0	1-1	0-1	2-0	1-0	0-0	1-1
Gillingham	1-2	1-1	0-2	2-1	0-0	1-2	1-1	2-2	2-0	0-1	0-0	0-0
Grimsby Town	0-1	1-0	1-1	1-0	3-1	5-1	3-0	0-2	1-1	0-0	0-1	3-0
Luton Town	0-2	2-2	1-1	3-0	1-3	1-0	0-1	0-1	1-1	2-5	0-0	0-0
Millwall	—	0-0	2-1	1-1	0-2	3-1	3-2	0-4	1-0	0-1	1-0	2-3
Northampton Town	2-0	—	0-0	2-1	2-2	3-1	0-0	1-0	1-0	3-0	0-1	1-1
Oldham Athletic	1-1	2-2	—	2-0	1-0	2-0	2-1	2-2	3-1	0-1	2-0	3-1
Plymouth Argyle	3-0	1-3	0-2	—	2-0	2-3	0-0	0-1	3-2	3-0	0-1	0-0
Preston NE	1-1	1-0	1-1	0-1	—	1-0	2-1	2-0	1-0	0-1	1-1	3-2
Southend United	0-0	0-0	1-1	3-0	3-2	—	0-1	0-3	1-0	1-3	1-2	4-4
Walsall	2-0	0-2	0-0	0-1	1-1	3-1	—	0-1	1-0	3-0	0-1	2-0
Watford	0-1	1-1	2-1	1-1	3-1	1-3	1-2	—	2-1	0-1	2-1	1-1
Wigan Athletic	0-0	1-1	1-0	1-1	1-4	3-1	2-0	3-2	—	3-2	5-2	1-1
Wrexham	1-0	1-0	3-1	1-1	0-0	4-1	2-1	1-1	2-2	—	2-0	1-1
Wycombe W.	0-0	0-0	2-1	5-1	0-0	1-1	4-2	0-0	1-2	0-0	—	1-0
York City	2-3	0-0	0-0	1-0	1-1	1-1	1-0	1-1	2-2	1-0	2-0	—

DIVISION 2 RECORDS 1997-98

Top Scorers – All Competitions

Player	Club	L	F	C	Total
Barry HAYLES	Bristol Rovers	24	2	0	26
Ade AKINBIYI	Gillingham	21	1	0	22
Tony THORPE *	Fulham	17	0	3	20
Kevin DONOVAN	Grimsby Town	17	1	1	19
Ian STEVENS	Carlisle United	17	0	0	17
Mark STALLARD	Wycombe Wanderers	17	0	0	17
Carlo CORAZZIN	Plymouth Argyle	17	0	0	17

L=League, F=FA Cup, C=Coca-Cola Cup
* 14 for Luton Town

Top Scorers and Attendances by Club

Team	Psn	Top Scorer	Agg Att	Ave Att
Blackpool	12	Clarkson (14)	119,876	5,212
Bournemouth	9	Robinson (10)	108,292	4,708
Brentford	21	Taylor (13)	115,860	5,037
Bristol City	2	Goater (17)	272,463	11,846
Bristol Rovers	5	Hayles (24)	147,493	6,412
Burnley	20	Cooke (16)	240,883	10,473
Carlisle United	23	Stevens (17)	124,041	5,393
Chesterfield	10	Chesterfield (9)	109,231	4,749
Fulham	6	Moody (15)	206,298	8,969
Gillingham	8	Akinbiyi (21)	148,641	6,462
Grimsby Town	3	Donovan (17)	121,225	5,270
Luton Town	17	Thorpe (14)	135,209	5,878
Millwall	18	Shaw (11)	161,523	7,022
Northampton Town	4	Seal (12)	147,029	6,392
Oldham Athletic	13	Barlow (12)	128,513	5,587
Plymouth Argyle	22	Corazzin (7)	122,435	5,323
Preston NE	15	Ashcroft (15)	217,769	9,468
Southend United	24	Boere (15)	96,653	4,202
Walsall	19	Boli (12)	93,435	4,062
Watford	1	Kennedy (11)	256,868	11,168
Wigan Athletic	11	Lowe (16)	91,258	3,967
Wrexham	7	N.Roberts (8)	94,506	4,108

Wycombe Wanderers 14	Stallard (17)		124,514	5,413
York City 16	Rowe (11)		88,622	3,853

Division 2 Hat-tricks

Player	Gls	Match (result)	Date
O'CONNELL	3	WIGAN A. v Wycombe W (5-2)	09-Aug-97
GOATER	3 (1p)	BRISTOL C. v Wigan A. (3-0)	30-Aug-97
BOLI	3	WALSALL v Southend U. (3-1)	30-Aug-/97
ELLIS	3	Wrexham v BLACKPOOL (3-4)	02-Sep-97
CONNOLLY	3	Luton T. v WREXHAM (2-5)	20-Sep-97
KENNEDY	3	Southend U. v WATFORD (0-3)	04-Oct-97
CARPENTER	3	Brentford v BRISTOL C. (2-3)	08-Oct-97
STALLARD	3	WYCOMBE W. v Walsall (4-2)	21-Oct-97
BEADLE	3	BRISTOL R. v Bournemouth (5-3)	28-Dec-97
MOODY	3 (1p)	Luton T. v FULHAM (1-4)	24-Jan-98
BEADLE	3	BRISTOL R. v Wigan A. (5-0)	10-Apr-98
PESCHISOLIDO	3	FULHAM v Carlisle U. (5-0)	13-Apr-98
FREESTONE	3	Plymouth Ar. v NORTHAMPTON (1-3)	18-Apr-98

p = penalty

Division 2 Red Cards

Players	Opponents	Venue	Date	Official
Blackpool				
Malkin	Brentford	A	13-Dec-97	Hall
Dixon	Brentford	A	13-Dec-97	Hall
Brabin	Watford	H	07-Mar-98	Pike
Banks	York	A	28-Mar-98	Danson
Brentford				
Bent	Burnley	H	27-Sep-97	Styles
Bates	Walsall	A	24-Feb-98	Messias
Thompson	Carlisle	A	14-Mar-98	Leake
Taylor	Northampton	H	21-Mar-98	Wiley
Bristol Rovers				
Gayle	Northampton	A	01-Nov-97	Mathieson
Pritchard	Wigan	A	02-Dec-97	Lynch
Perry	Wigan	A	02-Dec-97	Lynch
Tillson	Wigan	A	02-Dec-97	Lynch
Low	Wigan	A	02-Dec-97	Lynch
Butler	Gillingham	A	31-Jan-98	Robinson
Basford	Gillingham	A	31-Jan-98	Robinson
Penrice	Brentford	H	02-May-98	Pugh

Players	Opponents	Venue	Date	Official
Burnley				
Eyres	Gillingham	H	16-Aug-97	Laws
Howey	Brentford	A	27-Sep-97	Styles
Ford	Bristol Rovers	A	17-Jan-98	Styles
Mull	Blackpool	H	07-Apr-98	Lynch
Carlisle United				
Couzens	York	A	25-Oct-97	Laws
Harrison	Wrexham	H	01-Nov-97	Robinson
Prokas	Chesterfield	H	18-Nov-97	Messias
Hopper	Fulham	A	13-Apr-98	Styles
Foster	Grimsby	H	21-Apr-98	Lynch
Chesterfield				
Hewitt	Bournemouth	H	04-Oct-97	Bates
Carr	Gillingham	A	14-Mar-98	Fletcher
Fulham				
Moody	Grimsby	H	09-May-98	Heilbron
Peschisolido	Grimsby	A	13-May-98	Wilkes
Gillingham				
Fourtune-West	Burnley	A	16-Aug-97	Laws
Statham	Brentford	A	02-Sep-97	Pierce
Smith	Northampton	A	18-Oct-97	Singh
Statham	Millwall	H	01-Nov-97	Knight
Galloway	Fulham	A	21-Nov-97	Harris
Bryant	Luton	A	02-Dec-97	Taylor
Pennock	Bournemouth	A	26-Dec-97	Bates
Luton Town				
McGowan	Northampton	A	09-Sep-97	Harris
Spring	Plymouth	H	11-Oct-97	Crick
Patterson	Gillingham	A	11-Apr-98	Stretton
Millwall				
Sturgess	Northampton	A	27-Sep-97	Baines
Law	Bristol Rovers	A	29-Nov-97	Hall
Witter	Fulham	A	14-Mar-98	Pierce
Law	Bristol Rovers	H	04-Apr-98	Danson
Northampton Town				
Bishop	Bristol Rovers	A	07-Mar-98	Rejer
Heggs	Burnley	H	04-Apr-98	Hall
Oldham Athletic				
Garnett	Luton	A	30-Aug-97	Butler
Redmond	Southend	A	25-Oct-97	Styles
Garnett	Burnley	H	28-Apr-98	Burns

Players	Opponents	Venue	Date	Official
Plymouth Argyle				
Corazzin	Bristol Rovers	A	09-Aug-97	Fletcher
Wilson	Gillingham	A	25-Oct-97	Butler
Littlejohn	Wrexham	A	22-Nov-97	Frankland
Logan	Preston	H	07-Mar-98	Orr
Logan	Wycombe	A	14-Mar-98	Wiley
Rowbotham	Blackpool	H	11-Apr-98	Knight
Preston North End				
Appleton	Millwall	A	25-Mar-98	Wilkes
Southend United				
Dublin	Wycombe	A	02-Sep-97	Leach
Harris	Millwall	H	13-Sep-97	Finch
N'Diaye	Brentford	A	26-Dec-97	Foy
Boere	Northampton	A	14-Feb-98	Leake
Walsall				
Roper	Bristol Rovers	A	09-Sep-97	Pierce
Boli	Wrexham	H	11-Oct-97	Coddington
Viveash	Brentford	H	24-Feb-98	Messias
Watford				
Lee	Gillingham	A	20-Sep-97	Styles
Wigan Athletic				
Rogers	Bournemouth	A	16-Aug-97	Butler
Jones	Bristol Rovers	H	02-Dec-97	Lynch
Wrexham				
Watkin	Fulham	A	09-Aug-97	D'Urso
Wycombe Wanderers				
McArthy	Preston	H	27-Sep-97	Bennett
Taylor	Chesterfield	A	25-Oct-97	Pike
Cornforth	Bournemouth	H	29-Nov-97	Danson
Simpson	Carlisle	A	31-Jan-98	Foy
Stallard	Bournemouth	A	04-Apr-98	Fletcher
Mohan	Chesterfield	H	25-Apr-98	Richards
York City				
McMillan	Walsall	A	20-Sep-97	Wilkes
Rennison	Luton	A	04-Apr-98	Crick
Tinkler	Luton	A	04-Apr-98	Crick
Thompson	Wrexham	A	13-Apr-98	Bates

Blackpool

Away-Day Blues

Starting the season under new manager Nigel Worthington as one of the sides tipped to challenge for promotion, Blackpool had a disappointing season with a poor away record dashing any hopes of making it into the play-offs. After winning their opening game of the season, Blackpool lost the next two and spent the rest of the season flitting about in the middle of the table. Their failure to beat any of the promoted sides bears testimony that a drop of five places on the previous campaign was justified.

After the embarrassment of the previous season's FA Cup defeat by non-league Hednesford, Blackpool were thankful to two Phil Clarkson goals, including an 89th-minute strike, for seeing the Seasiders to a 4-3 win over Blyth Spartans. Oldham ended the run in the 2nd Round.

Blackpool pulled off a sensational success in the Coca-Cola Cup. Andy Preece gave them a 1-0 1st Round 1st Leg lead over Manchester City. In the return City grabbed a late equaliser but Blackpool held their nerve to win a penalty shoot-out at Maine Road. In the 2nd Round Dave Linighan secured a 1st Leg lead over Coventry but the Premiership side won 3-2 on aggregate with three second-half goals.

Formed:	1887
Ground:	Bloomfield Road, Blackpool, Lancs, FY1 6JJ
Phone:	01253 404331 **Box Office:** 01253 405331
Info:	0898 12 16 48
Capacity:	11,047
Colours:	Tangerine shirts with white collar, white shorts with navy and tangerine, tangerine socks with white trim
Nickname:	Seasiders
Manager:	Nigel Worthington
Honours:	Division 1 Runners-up 1955-56; Division 2 Champions 1929-30; FA Cup Winners 1953; Anglo-Italian Cup Winners 1971.
Managers:	Jimmy Mullen 1989-90, Graham Carr 1990, Sam Allardyce 1994-96, Gary Megson 1996-97.
Previous Names:	South Shore combined with Blackpool St John's
Record League Win:	7-0 v Preston NE, D1, 1/5/48
Record League Defeat:	1-10 v Small Heath, D2, 2/3/1901
Most GF in Season:	98 – Division 2, 1929-30
All-time League Apps:	568 – Jimmy Armfield, 1952-71
All-time League Goals:	247 – Jimmy Hampson, 1927-38
Most Goals in a Season:	45 – Jimmy Hampson, D2, 1929-30
Most Goals in a Match:	5 – McIntosh v Preston NE, D1, 1/5/48
Record Fee Received:	£750,000 from QPR for Trevor Sinclair, 8/93

Record Fee Paid: £275,000 to Millwall for Chris Malkin, 10/96
Record Attendance: 38,098 v Wolverhampton Wanderers, D1, 17/9/55

Stats File

Division	P	W	D	L	F	A	Pts	Yr	B	W
Premier/D1:	1134	405	273	456	1733	1863	1083	27	2	22
Division 1n/2:	1694	650	409	635	2460	2436	1709	43	1	20
Division 2n/3:	644	220	174	250	860	890	792	14	3	23
Division 3n/4:	272	118	68	86	413	317	420	6	2	21

Cup Records	P	W	D	L	F	A
FA Cup:	205	79	40	86	278	291
League Cup:	130	50	32	48	197	185
A/F Members Cup:	43	15	7	21	55	60

Sequence	Games	Start		End
Winning Run:	9	21-Nov-36	to	1-Jan-37
Without Defeat:	17	6-Apr-68	to	21-Sep-68
Without Win:	19	19-Dec-70	to	24-Apr-71
Drawn Games (4):	5	26-Dec-73	to	19-Jan-74
	5	4-Dec-76	to	1-Jan-77
Without Draw:	24	23/4/1898	to	4/3/1899
Losing Run:	8	26/11/1898	to	7/1/1898
Clean Sheets (3):	5	5-Sep-49	to	1-Oct-49
	5	15-Mar-75	to	1-Apr-75
Goal Scored:	33	23-Feb-29	to	25-Dec-29
No Goals For (3):	5	11-Jan-86	to	22-Feb-86
	5	25-Nov-89	to	30-Dec-89
SOS Undefeated:	11	1900-01		
SOS No Wins:	11	1966-67		
	11	1977-78		

5-Year Record

	Div	P	W	D	L	F	A	Pts	Psn
1993-94	2	46	16	5	25	63	75	53	20
1994-95	2	46	18	10	18	64	70	64	12
1995-96	2	46	23	13	10	67	40	82	3
1996-97	2	46	18	15	13	60	47	69	7
1997-98	2	46	17	11	18	59	67	62	12

AFC Bournemouth

Local Heroes

In an age when professional football is dominated by the big clubs with their huge financial clout, the story of Bournemouth is a reassuring tale of how a club, in its hour of need, was rescued by the local community who now own the Dean Court outfit. In the summer of 1997 Bournemouth faced extinction. Eleven months later, under the astute guidance of Mel Machin, the Cherries faced Grimsby at Wembley in the Auto Windscreens Shield Final in front of 62,432. Bournemouth lost 2-1, with the Cherries' goal coming from John Bailey who had been snapped up from non-league football, but that they were there at all shows the strides made over the past year. Bournemouth's financial position was also aided by the £800,000 sale of Matt Holland to Ipswich.

Bournemouth improved their league position by six places on the previous season and, in addition to taking four points off promoted Bristol City during the season, they also put the West Country club out of the FA Cup, having already defeated Heybridge Swifts. Division One Huddersfield ended the Cherries' cup run while their Coca-Cola dream lost its fizz in the 1st Round with a disappointing extra-time defeat by Division Three Torquay United.

Formed:	1899
Ground:	Dean Court Ground, Bournemouth, Dorset, BH7 7AF
Phone:	01202 395381 **Box Office:** 01202 395381
Info:	0898 12 11 63
Capacity:	10,440
Colours:	Red shirts with white 'V', black shorts and black socks
Nickname:	The Cherries
Manager:	Mel Machin
Honours:	Division 3 Champions 1986-87; Associate Members' Cup Winners 1983-84; Runners-up 1997-98.
Managers:	Alec Stock 1979-80, David Webb 1980-82, Don Megson 1983, Harry Redknapp 1983-92, Tony Pulis 1992-94.
Previous Names:	Boscombe St Johns, 1890-99, Boscombe FC, 1899-1923, Bournemouth & Boscombe Athletic FC, 1923-71
Record League Win:	7-0 v Swindon Town, D3S, 22/9/56
Record League Defeat:	0-9 v Lincoln City, D3, 18/12/82
Most GF in Season:	88 – Division 3S, 1956-57
All-time League Apps:	423 – Sean O'Driscoll, 1984-95
All-time League Goals:	202 – Ron Eyre, 1924-33
Most Goals in a Season:	42 – 1970-71
Most Goals in a Match:	9 – Ted MacDougall v Margate, 20/11/71
Record Fee Received:	£800,000 from Everton for Joe Parkinson, 3/94

Record Fee Paid: £210,000 to Gillingham for Gavin Peacock, 8/89
Record Attendance: 28,799 v Manchester United, FA Cup 6th Round, 2/3/57

Stats File

Division	P	W	D	L	F	A	Pts	Yr	B	W
Division 1n/2:	136	43	30	63	166	206	159	3	12	22
Division 2n/3:	1334	495	368	471	1686	1658	1580	29	1	21
Division 3n/4:	368	139	118	111	441	366	419	8	2	18

Cup Records	P	W	D	L	F	A
FA Cup:	203	89	47	67	352	278
League Cup:	112	26	39	47	108	144
A/F Members Cup:	39	16	8	15	61	50

Sequence	Games	Start		End
Winning Run:	7	22-Aug-70	to	23-Sep-70
Without Defeat:	18	6-Mar-82	to	28-Aug-82
Without Win:	14	6-Mar-74	to	27-Apr-74
Drawn Games:	5	10-Nov-79	to	21-Dec-79
Without Draw:	27	7-Sep-50	to	3-Mar-51
Losing Run (3):	7	14-Sep-55	to	8-Oct-55
	7	13-Aug-94	to	13-Sep-94
Clean Sheets:	7	20-Oct-84	to	24-Nov-84
Goal Scored:	20	26-Aug-61	to	9-Dec-61
No Goals For:	6	1-Feb-75	to	8-Mar-75
SOS Undefeated:	14	1961-62		
SOS No Wins:	8	1994-95		

5-Year Record

	Div	P	W	D	L	F	A	Pts	Psn
1993-94	2	46	14	15	17	51	59	57	17
1994-95	2	46	13	11	22	49	69	50	19
1995-96	2	46	16	10	20	51	70	58	14
1996-97	2	46	15	15	16	43	45	60	16
1997-98	2	46	18	12	16	57	52	66	9

Bristol Rovers

Pirates Plundered

Having spent much of the 1997/98 season living in the shadow cast by Bristol City, Ian Holloway's Bristol Rovers side timed their charge to the play-offs to perfection. Four wins from the final five games and a convenient slip by Gillingham in their last match saw Rovers take their place in the top six. And once in the play-offs Rovers seemed to have got themselves into an unbeatable position when taking a 3-0 1st Leg lead only to concede a late consolation goal to Northampton. Sadly for Rovers it proved to be more than a consolation as Northampton powered to a 3-0 2nd Leg triumph to shatter the Pirates' promotion dreams.

Rovers had shown a dislike of sudden death competitions in the Coca-Cola Cup with a home defeat by Bristol City after an away draw, but in the FA Cup they won 2-0 at Priestfields after being held at home by Gillingham. In the 2nd Round, non-leaguers Wisbech were defeated in the Fens but another trip to East Anglia for a 3rd Round replay at Ipswich ended in a 1-0 defeat.

Rovers made one of the discoveries of the season with £250,000 signing Barry Hayles from Stevenage, who was the Division Two top scorer on 24.

Formed:	1883
Ground:	The Memorial Ground, Filton Avenue, Horfield, Bristol, BS7 0AQ
Phone:	0117 9772000 **Box Office:** 0117 9098848
Info:	0891 66 44 22
Capacity:	8,475
Colours:	Blue shirts with blue and white quarters, white shorts, blue socks
Nickname:	The Pirates
Manager:	Ian Holloway
Honours:	Division 3S Champions 1952-53; Division 3 Champions 1989-90.

Managers:	Gerry Francis 1987-91, Martin Dobson 1991, Dennis Rofe 1992, Malcolm Allison 1992-93, John Ward 1993-96.
Previous Names:	The Purdown Poachers 1883, Black Arabs 1883, Eastville Rovers 1884, Bristol Eastville Rovers 1898
Record League Win:	7-0 v Swansea City, D2, 2/10/54 7-0 v Brighton & Hove Albion, D3S, 29/11/52 7-0 v Shrewsbury Town, D3, 21/3/64
Record League Defeat:	0-12 v Luton Town, D3S, 13/4/36
Most GF in Season:	92 – Division 3S, 1952-53
All-time League Apps:	546 – Stuart Taylor, 1965-80
All-time League Goals:	242 – Geoff Bradford, 1949-64
Most Goals in a Season:	33 – Geoff Bradford, D3S, 1952-53
Most Goals in a Match:	6 – Jack Jones v Weymouth, FA Cup, 17/11/1900 (15-1)

Record Fee Received: £1m from Crystal Palace for Nigel Martyn, 11/89
Record Fee Paid: £370,000 to QPR for Andy Tilson, 11/92
Record Attendance: 9,813 v Bristol City, D2, 2/5/90 (Twerton Park),
38,472 v Preston North End, FA Cup 4th Round,
30/1/60 (at Eastville)

Stats File

Division	P	W	D	L	F	A	Pts	Yr	B	W
Division 1n/2:	810	272	209	329	1164	1317	794	19	6	24
Division 2n/3:	1196	493	320	383	1770	1549	1574	26	1	19

Cup Records	P	W	D	L	F	A
FA Cup:	221	89	47	85	342	337
League Cup:	110	36	27	47	139	167
A/F Members Cup:	45	20	11	14	52	44

Sequence	Games	Start		End
Winning Run:	12	18-Oct-52	to	17-Jan-53
Without Defeat:	32	7-Apr-73	to	27-Jan-74
Without Win:	20	5-Apr-80	to	1-Nov-80
Drawn Games:	5	18-Mar-67	to	1-Apr-67
	5	1-Nov-75	to	22-Nov-75
Without Draw:	37	15-Nov-47	to	2-Oct-48
Losing Run:	8	29-Apr-61	to	9-Sep-61
Clean Sheets (5):	6	12-Apr-88	to	2-May-88
	6	16-Sep-89	to	14-Oct-89
Goal Scored:	26	26-Mar-27	to	3-Dec-27
No Goals For:	6	14-Oct-22	to	18-Nov-22
SOS Undefeated:	27	1973-74		
SOS No Wins:	14	1980-81		

5-Year Record

	Div	P	W	D	L	F	A	Pts	Psn
1993-94	2	46	20	10	16	60	59	70	8
1994-95	2	46	22	16	8	70	40	82	4
1995-96	2	46	20	10	16	57	60	70	10
1996-97	2	46	15	11	20	47	50	56	17
1997-98	2	46	20	10	16	70	64	70	5

Burnley

Waddle Relegation Battle

With the hig- profile appointment of Chris Waddle as manager in July 1997, Burnley were looking to build upon the advances made during the previous season in a bid to reclaim the Division One place lost in 1995. Waddle spent £400,000 on bringing Mark Ford and Steve Blatherwick but the Clarets made a dreadful start and they had to wait 11 games before becoming the last side in Division Two to win a match. For a side that spent almost the entire season in the relegation places Burnley occasionally threw the form book out of the window with wins over all three of the promoted sides. Striker Andy Cooke, who ended the previous season with a hat-trick, scored twice in the final game this time around to secure a 2-1 win over Plymouth which sent the Pilgrims and Brentford down.

Burnley's FA Cup run was brief with a draw at Rotherham being followed by a humbling 3-0 home defeat by the Division Three side. Despite their early season league problems, Burnley removed Lincoln from the Coca-Cola Cup but were comprehensively beaten by Stoke in the 2nd Round.

Shortly after the end of the season Waddle announced his departure from Turf Moor.

Formed:	1882
Ground:	Turf Moor, Burnley, Lancs, BB10 4BX
Phone:	01282 700000 **Box Office:** 01282 700100
Info:	0891 12 11 53
Capacity:	22,546
Nickname:	The Clarets
Colours:	Claret shirts with light blue sleeves, white shorts and socks
Manager:	Stan Ternent
Honours:	Division 1 Champions 1920-21, 1959-60;
	Division 2 Champions 1897-98, 1972-73;
	Division 3 Champions 1981-82;
	Division 4 Champions 1991-92;
	FA Cup Winners 1914; Anglo-Scottish Cup Winners 1979.
Managers:	Brian Miller 1979-83, Frank Casper 1989-91,
	Jimmy Mullen 1991-96, Adrian Heath 1996-97,
	Chris Waddle 1997-98.
Record League Win:	9-0 v Darwen, D1, 9/1/1892
Record League Defeat:	0-10 v Aston Villa, D1, 29/8/25
	0-10 v Sheffield United, D1, 19/1/29
Most GF in Season:	102 – Division 1, 1960-61
All-time League Apps:	522 – Jerry Dawson, 1907-28
All-time League Goals:	178 – George Beel, 1923-32
Most Goals in a Season:	35 – George Beel, D1, 1927-28

Most Goals in a Match:	6 – Louis Page v Birmingham City (a), D1, 10/4/26 (7-1)	
Record Fee Received:	£500,000 from M'boro for Marlon Beresford, 3/98	
Record Fee Paid:	£200,000 to Sunderland for Lee Howey, 8/97	
Record Attendance:	54,775 v Huddersfield Town, FA Cup 3rd Round, 23/2/24	

Stats File

Division	P	W	D	L	F	A	Pts	Yr	B	W
Premier/D1:	1982	784	447	751	3163	3157	2015	51	1	21
Division 1n/2:	1264	488	306	470	1836	1830	1305	32	1	22
Division 2n/3:	414	148	121	145	580	532	547	9	1	21
Division 3n/4:	318	124	76	118	416	411	448	7	1	22

Cup Records	P	W	D	L	F	A
FA Cup:	296	128	70	98	502	400
League Cup:	123	50	25	48	192	187
A/F Members Cup:	53	27	11	15	77	65

Sequence	Games	Start		End
Winning Run:	10	16-Nov-12	to	18-Jan-13
Without Defeat:	30	6-Sep-20	to	25-Mar-21
Without Win:	24	16-Apr-79	to	17-Nov-79
Drawn Games:	6	21-Feb-31	to	28-Mar-31
Without Draw:	30	18-Jan-08	to	21-Nov-08
Losing Run (3):	8	16-Mar-1895	to	2-Sep-1895
	8	2-Jan-95	to	25-Feb-95
Clean Sheets:	7	6-Sep-80	to	4-Oct-80
Goal Scored:	27	13-Feb-26	to	30-Oct-26
No Goals For:	6	9-Aug-97	to	7-Sep-97
SOS Undefeated:	16	1972-73		
SOS No Wins:	17	1889-90		

5-Year Record

	Div	P	W	D	L	F	A	Pts	Psn	
1993-94	2	46	21	10	15	79	58	73	6	Promoted PO
1994-95	1	46	11	13	22	49	74	46	22	Relegated
1995-96	2	46	14	13	19	56	68	55	17	
1996-97	2	46	19	11	16	71	55	68	9	
1997-98	2	46	13	13	20	55	65	52	20	

Chesterfield

Tall Orders

Living up to the magnificent FA Cup run enjoyed by Chesterfield in 1997 was always going to be a tall order for manager John Duncan and his team. That success alerted clubs to the quality of certain players at Saltergate and before the new season kicked off the Blues parted company with Kevin Davies and Sean Dyche for £1.1m. A year later Davies joined Blackburn for £7.25m.

The Spireites' league position of 10th in Division Two remained unchanged but not too surprisingly the club could not match its cup achievements. Chesterfield were strong at home with only Bristol City losing less times in front of their fans but away from Saltergate Chesterfield were successful on just three occasions. Only one club drew more games than Duncan's side, and had just three of those 17 draws ended in victory, then Chesterfield would have made the play-offs.

A crowd of 5,327 watched the start of Chesterfield's FA Cup campaign (almost 80,000 saw the two semi-finals with Middlesbrough), when Northwich were beaten 1-0 but Grimsby ended dreams of further glory with a 2nd Round replay victory at Saltergate. They also survived just one round in the Coca-Cola Cup where Tony Lormor scored in three of the four games against Wigan and Barnsley.

Formed:	1866
Ground:	Recreation Ground, Chesterfield, S40 4SX
Phone:	01246 209765 **Box Office:** 01246 209765
Info:	0891 555818
Capacity:	8,880
Nickname:	The Spireites
Colours:	Royal Blue shirts with white pin stripe, white shorts with blue stripe, blue socks
Manager:	John Duncan
Honours:	Division 3N Champions 1930-31, 1935-36; Division 4 Champions 1969-70, 1984-85; Anglo-Scottish Cup Winners 1980-81.
Managers:	Frank Barlow, 1983-87 John Duncan 1983-87, Kevin Randall 1987-1988, Paul Hart 1988-91, Chris McMenemy 1991- Feb 93.
Previous Names:	Chesterfield Municipal until 1915, Chesterfield Town 1912-22, 1962-67.
Most GF in Season:	102 – Division 3N, 1930-31
Record League Win:	12-0 v Glossop, D2, 17/1/1903
Record League Defeat:	0-10 v Gillingham (a), D3, 5/9/87
All-time League Apps:	617 – Dave Blakey, 1948-76
All-time League Goals:	161 – Ernie Moss, 1968-67, 1979-81, 1984-86
Most Goals in a Season:	44 – Jimmy Cookson, D3N, 1925-26

Most Goals in a Match: 4 – 19 occasions
Record Fee Received: £200,000 from Wolverhampton W. for Alan Birch, 8/81
Record Fee Paid: £150,000 to Carlisle United for Phil Bonnyman, 3/80
Record Attendance: 30,968 v Newcastle United, D2, 7/4/39

Stats File

Division	P	W	D	L	F	A	Pts	Yr	B	W
Division 1n/2:	776	263	190	323	1070	1237	716	20	4	21
Division 2n/3:	1058	376	269	413	1332	1389	1156	23	4	24
Division 3n/4:	764	294	206	264	1026	982	935	17	1	20

Cup Records	P	W	D	L	F	A
FA Cup:	188	65	46	77	268	296
League Cup:	99	33	21	45	139	156
A/F Members Cup:	38	12	7	19	38	51

Sequence	Games	Start		End
Winning Run:	10	6-Sep-33	to	4-Nov-33
Without Defeat:	21	26-Dec-94	to	29-Apr-95
Without Win:	16	22-Oct-60	to	11-Feb-61
	16	26-Feb-83	to	14-May-83
Drawn Games:	5	19-Sep-90	to	6-Oct-90
Without Draw:	24	4-Feb-22	to	14-Oct-22
Losing Run:	9	22-Oct-60	to	27-Dec-60
Clean Sheets:	6	14-Mar-36	to	10-Apr-36
Goal Scored:	46	25-Dec-29	to	26-Dec-30
No Goals For:	7	23-Sep-77	to	22-Oct-77
SOS Undefeated:	9	1935-36		
SOS No Wins:	9	1948-49		

5-Year Record

	Div	P	W	D	L	F	A	Pts	Psn
1993-94	3	42	16	14	12	55	48	62	8
1994-95	3	42	23	12	7	62	37	81	3
1995-96	2	46	20	12	14	56	51	72	7
1996-97	2	46	18	14	14	42	39	68	10
1997-98	2	46	16	17	13	46	44	65	10

Colchester United

Onward and Upward

Since 1891 when they were relegated to the basement division of the Football League, Colchester United have sampled life outside the league with two years in the Vauxhall Conference and won the FA Trophy at Wembley. Now Steve Wignall's side, courtesy of David Gregory's successful penalty against Torquay United, have won promotion to Division Two via the play-offs in front of almost 20,000 spectators at Wembley.

With impeccable timing it was only in the last quarter of the season that Colchester, who had been languishing in the middle of the table for much of the season, climbed into the top seven and, had Lincoln slipped up on the final day, the Us would have gained an automatic promotion position. In the play-off semi-final Colchester overturned a 1st Leg deficit against Barnet to progress to the final 3-2 on aggregate. In the FA Cup, Colchester twice came from behind to draw at Brentford and put the Division Two side out in a penalty shoot-out at Layer Road following a goalless replay. But Colchester's spot kick good fortune expired in the 2nd Round when Conference side Hereford proved more accurate after two draws. Division Two Luton tipped Colchester out of the Coca-Cola Cup at the first hurdle.

Formed:	1937
Ground:	Layer Road Ground, Colchester, Essex, CO2 7JJ
Phone:	01206 508800 **Box Office:** 01206 508800
Info:	0891 66 46 46
Capacity:	7,190
Colours:	Royal blue and white striped shirts, royal blue shorts, white socks
Nickname:	The Us
Manager:	Steve Wignall
Honours:	Division 3 Play-Off Winners 1997-98; GMVC Winners 1991-92; FA Trophy Winners 1991-92.
Managers:	Jock Wallace 1989, Mick Mills 1990, Ian Atkins 1990-91, Roy McDonough 1991-94, George Burley 1994.
Record League Win:	9-1 v Bradford City, D4, 30/12/61
Record League Defeat:	0-8 v Leyton Orient, 15/10/88
Most GF in Season:	104 – Division 4, 1961-62
All-time League Apps:	713 – Mickey Cook, 1969-84
All-time League Goals:	131 – Martyn King, 1959-65
Most Goals in a Season:	37 – Bobby Hunt, D4, 1961-62
Most Goals in a Match:	4 – numerous
Record Fee Received:	£120,000 from Wimbledon for Paul McGee, 2/89
Record Fee Paid:	£50,000 to Ipswich T. for Neil Gregory, 3/98
Record Attendance:	19,073 v Reading, FA Cup 1st Round, 27/11/48

Stats File

Division	P	W	D	L	F	A	Pts	Yr	B	W
Division 2n/3:	644	211	182	251	876	1000	604	14	5	23
Division 3n/4:	1090	448	275	367	1627	1438	1437	24	2	24

Cup Records	P	W	D	L	F	A
FA Cup:	141	53	38	50	220	212
League Cup:	91	28	16	47	123	154
A/F Members Cup:	40	16	7	17	65	66

Sequence	Games	Start		End
Winning Run:	7	29-Nov-68	to	1-Feb-69
Without Defeat:	20	22-Dec-56	to	19-Apr-57
Without Win:	20	2-Mar-68	to	31-Aug-68
Drawn Games:	6	21-Mar-77	to	11-Apr-77
Without Draw:	29	6-Mar-90	to	7-Nov-92
Losing Run:	8	9-Oct-54	to	4-Dec-54
Clean Sheets:	5	13-Feb-98	to	3-Mar-98
Goal Scored:	24	15-Sep-62	to	27-Mar-63
No Goals For:	5	7-Apr-81	to	25-Apr-81
SOS Undefeated:	8	1961-62		
SOS No Wins:	7	1951-52		

5-Year Record

	Div	P	W	D	L	F	A	Pts	Psn	
1993-94	3	42	13	10	19	56	71	49	17	
1994-95	3	42	16	10	16	56	64	58	10	
1995-96	3	46	18	18	10	61	51	72	7	
1996-97	3	46	17	17	12	62	51	68	8	
1997-98	3	46	21	11	14	72	60	74	4	Promoted PO

Fulham

Cash-Crazy Cottagers

Going into the new season with a successful promotion season behind him and new club owner Mohamed Al Fayed suggesting there may be £30m available to sign players, manager Micky Adams must have felt that he was on to a good thing. But just eight games and 11 points into the season Adams was dismissed to make way for the high-profile arrival of Kevin Keegan and Ray Wilkins, the latter as team manager.

Adams had already broken the club transfer record when signing Paul Moody for £200,000 but that figure was swiftly smashed by the new regime with more than £7m being spent on nine players including £2.1m on Chris Coleman. The rapid turnover in players worked to a degree, with Fulham making the play-offs despite the Cottagers losing their last three games. That poor form cost Wilkins his job, with Keegan taking charge of the team, but the change failed to halt the slide and Grimsby duly ended Fulham's promotion hopes in the play-off.

After surviving a tricky 1st Round FA Cup tie at Margate, Fulham removed Southend before going down 3-1 at Tottenham. A Coca-Cola Cup victory over Wycombe was followed by defeat in the 2nd Round against Wolves.

Formed:	1879
Ground:	Craven Cottage, Stevenage Road, Fulham, London, SW6 6HH
Phone:	0171 736 6561 **Box Office:** 0171 736 6561
Info:	0891 44 00 44
Nickname:	The Cottagers
Capacity:	14,969
Colours:	White shirts with black trim, white shorts, white socks with black trim
Manager:	Kevin Keegan
Honours:	Division 2 Champions 1948-49; Division 3S Champions 1931-32.
Managers:	Alan Dicks 1990-1991, Don Mackay 1991-94, Ian Brantfoot 1994-96, Micky Adams 1996-97, Ray Wilkins 1997-98.
Previous Names:	Fulham St Andrews, 1879-98
Record League Win:	10-1 v Ipswich Town, D1, 26/9/63
Record League Defeat:	0-9 v Wolverhampton Wanderers, D1, 16/9/59
Most GF in Season:	111 – Division 3S, 1931-32
All-time League Apps:	594 – Johnny Haynes 1952-70
All-time League Goals:	158 – Gordon Davies, 1978-84, 1986-91
Most Goals in a Season:	43 – Frank Newton, D3S, 1931-32
Most Goals in a Match:	6 – Ronnie Rooke v Bury, 6-0, FA Cup 3rd Round, 7/1/39

Record Fee Received: £333,333 from Liverpool for Richard Money, 5/80
Record Fee Paid: £2.1m to Blackburn Rovers for Chris Coleman, 12/97
Record Attendance: 49,335 v Millwall, D2, 8/10/38

Stats File

Division	P	W	D	L	F	A	Pts	Yr	B	W
Premier/D1:	504	148	122	234	724	928	418	12	10	22
Division 1n/2:	1984	752	472	760	2917	2799	2040	48	1	22
Division 2n/3:	598	224	171	203	800	751	784	13	2	21
Division 3n/4:	134	53	43	38	189	155	202	3	2	17

Cup Records	P	W	D	L	F	A
FA Cup:	222	81	56	85	315	318
League Cup:	125	46	32	47	185	181
A/F Members Cup:	38	12	8	18	59	64

Sequence	Games	Start		End
Winning Run:	8	23-Feb-63	to	6-Apr-63
Without Defeat:	15	23-Mar-57	to	18-Sep-57
	15	17-Jan-70	to	6-Apr-70
Without Win:	15	25-Feb-50	to	23-Aug-50
Drawn Games:	6	14-Oct-95	to	18-Nov-95
Without Draw:	23	10-Sep-55	to	4-Feb-56
Losing Run:	11	2-Dec-61	to	24-Feb-62
Clean Sheets (3):	6	3-Mar-23	to	31-Mar-23
	6	28-Feb-92	to	20-Mar-92
Goal Scored:	26	28-Mar-31	to	19-Dec-31
No Goals For:	6	21-Aug-71	to	18-Sep-71
SOS Undefeated:	12	1958-59		
SOS No Wins:	10	1937-38		
	10	1953-54		

5-Year Record

	Div	P	W	D	L	F	A	Pts	Psn	
1993-94	2	46	14	10	22	50	63	52	21	Relegated
1994-95	3	42	16	14	12	60	54	62	8	
1995-96	3	46	12	17	17	57	63	53	17	
1996-97	3	46	25	12	9	72	38	87	2	Promoted
1997-98	2	46	20	10	16	60	43	70	6	

Gillingham

Drawn-Out Season
On the limited resources available at Gillingham, manager Tony Pulis, in his third season in charge at Priestfield Stadium, took the club to within a solitary point of the play-offs. Gillingham flitted between the top six and midtable throughout the campaign but the Gills looked destined to make the play-offs until drawing three of the last four games. A home draw with Wigan on the last day finally put paid to their promotion aspirations. Had Gillingham scored just two more goals during the season then they would have secured a place in the play-off lottery at the expense of money-bags Fulham.

Spearheading the Gills' promotion drive was record signing Ade Akinbiyi, whose 21 league goals made him the second highest scorer in Division Two. In March, Iffy Onuora, Gillingham's top scorer for the previous season, joined Swindon in a £120,000 deal.

Gillingham gained a good draw at Bristol Rovers in the 1st Round of the FA Cup but, as they did in the league, lost on home soil to the West Country club. The Gills also failed to make any headway in the Coca-Cola Cup with a 1-0 defeat by Birmingham at Priestfield being followed by a 3-0 reversal at St Andrews.

Formed:	1893
Ground:	Priestfield Stadium, Gillingham, ME7 4DD
Phone:	01634 851854/576828 **Box Office:** 01634 851854
Info:	0891 44 00 44
Nickname:	The Gills
Capacity:	10,600
Colours:	Blue shirts, blue shorts, white socks
Nickname:	The Gills
Manager:	Tony Pulis
Honours:	Division 4 Champions 1963-64.
Managers:	Paul Taylor 1988, Keith Burkinshaw 1988-89, Damien Richardson 1989-93, Mike Flanagan 1993-95, Neil Smillie 1995.
Previous Name:	New Brompton, 1893-1913
Record League Win:	10-0 v Chesterfield, D3, 5/9/87
Record League Defeat:	0-8 v Luton Town, D2S, 14/4/29
Most GF in Season:	90 – Division 4, 1973-74
All-time League Apps:	571 – John Simpson, 1957-72
All-time League Goals:	135 – Brian Yeo, 1963-75
Most Goals in a Season:	31 – Ernie Morgan, D3S, 1954-55
	31 – Brian Yeo, D4, 1973-74
Most Goals in a Match:	6 – Fred Cheesmuir v Merthyr Tydfil (h), D3S, 26/4/30 (6-0)

Record Fee Received: £300,000 from Tottenham H. for Peter Beadle, 6/92
Record Fee Paid: £150,000 to Plymouth Ar. for Mark Patterson, 10/97
Record Attendance: 23,002 v QPR FA Cup 3rd Round, 10/1/48

Stats File

Division	P	W	D	L	F	A	Pts	Yr	B	W
Division 2n/3:	1104	411	308	385	1462	1422	1320	24	4	24
Division 3n/4:	718	271	203	244	990	919	842	16	1	21

Cup Records	P	W	D	L	F	A
FA Cup:	192	68	48	76	289	271
League Cup:	107	32	24	51	123	170
A/F Members Cup:	37	9	9	19	47	62

Sequence	Games	Start		End
Winning Run:	7	18-Dec-54	to	29-Jan-55
Without Defeat:	20	13-Oct-73	to	10-Feb-74
Without Win:	15	1-Apr-72	to	2-Sep-72
Drawn Games:	5	29-Dec-90	to	29-Jan-91
	5	28-Aug-93	to	18-Sep-93
Without Draw:	19	24-Oct-25	to	20-Feb-26
	19	20-Sep-88	to	6-Jan-89
Losing Run:	10	20-Sep-88	to	5-Nov-88
Clean Sheets (5):	5	3-Apr-81	to	20-Apr-81
	5	26-Apr-97	to	16-Aug-97
Goal Scored:	20	31-Oct-59	to	2-Apr-60
No Goals For:	6	6-Nov-37	to	27-Dec-37
	6	11-Feb-61	to	8-Mar-61
SOS Undefeated:	13	1963-64		
SOS No Wins:	9	1961-62		

5-Year Record

	Div	P	W	D	L	F	A	Pts	Psn	
1993-94	3	42	12	15	15	44	51	51	16	
1994-95	3	42	10	11	21	46	64	41	19	
1995-96	3	46	22	17	7	49	20	83	2	Promoted
1996-97	2	46	19	10	17	60	59	67	11	
1997-98	2	46	19	13	14	52	47	70	8	

Lincoln City

Westley Transformation

The path Lincoln City took towards ending an exile of 12 years away from Division Two (Three as it was then) was bizarre in the extreme. Manager John Beck, in charge since October 1995, was dismissed on 6 March with the Imps seemingly well placed, at eighth in the table, with a game in hand on all the sides above them. What led to Beck's downfall was that Lincoln headed the table in mid December after a magnificent 18-match unbeaten run but were slipping off the pace by the spring. They had also been put out of the FA Cup in a replay by non-league Emley after a replay and penalties had been required to remove Gainsborough in the 1st Round.

In Beck's wake, Shane Westley stepped up from assistant manager and with a wel- timed run not only got the Imps into a play-off position but, with victory over Brighton on the final day, and defeat for Torquay at Leyton Orient, seized an automatic promotion place.

Lincoln's Coca-Cola Cup run was even shorter than their FA Cup saga as a 1st Round 1-1 draw at home to Burnley was followed by a 2nd Leg 2-1 defeat at Turf Moor.

Formed:	1884		
Ground:	Sincil Bank, Lincoln, LN5 8LD		
Phone:	01522 880011	**Box Office:**	01522 880011
Info:	0891 66 46 66		
Capacity:	10,918		
Colours:	Red and white striped shirts, black shorts, red stockings		
Nickname:	The Red Imps		
Manager:	Shane Westley		
Honours:	Division 3N Champions 1931-32, 1947-48, 1951-52, Division 4 Champions 1975-76, GMVC Champions 1987-88		
Managers:	Steve Thompson 1990-93, Keith Alexander 1993-94, Sam Ellis 1994-95, Steve Wicks 1995, John Beck 1995-98.		
Record League Win:	11-1 v Crewe Alexandra, D3N, 29/9/51		
Record League Defeat:	3-11 v Manchester City, D2, 23/3/1895		
	0-8 v Notts County, D2, 23/1/1897		
	0-8 v Preston North End, D2, 28/12/1901		
	1-9 v Wigan Borough, D3N, 3/3/23		
	0-8 v Stoke City, D2, 23/2/57		
Most GF in Season:	121 – Division 3N, 1951-52		
All-time League Apps:	402 – Tony Emery, 1945-59		
All-time League Goals:	144 – Andy Graver, 1950-54, 1955, 1958-61		
Most Goals in a Season:	42 – Allan Hall, D3N, 1931-32		

Most Goals in a Match:	6 – Andy Graver v Crewe Alexandra (h) D3N, 29/9/51 (11-1)	
	6 – Frank Keetly v Halifax Town (h), D3N, 16/1/32 (9-1)	
Record Fee Received:	£500,000 from Port Vale for Garry Ainsworth, 9/97	
Record Fee Paid:	£63,000 to Leicester C. for Grant Brown, 1/90	
Record Attendance:	23,196 v Derby County, LC 4th Round, 15/11/67	

Stats File

Division	P	W	D	L	F	A	Pts	Yr	B	W
Division 1n/2:	1258	376	260	622	1740	2399	1012	34	5	22
Division 2n/3:	414	132	122	160	535	587	468	9	4	24
Division 3n/4:	1226	453	338	435	1700	1649	1419	27	1	24

Cup Records	P	W	D	L	F	A
FA Cup:	184	58	41	85	272	322
League Cup:	113	38	30	45	162	177
A/F Members Cup:	36	13	5	18	45	55

Sequence	Games	Start		End
Winning Run:	10	1-Sep-30	to	18-Oct-30
Without Defeat:	18	11-Mar-80	to	13-Sep-80
Without Win:	19	22-Aug-78	to	23-Dec-78
Drawn Games:	5	26-Dec-77	to	14-Jan-78
	5	21-Feb-81	to	10-Mar-81
Without Draw:	36	23/3/1894	to	7/9/1895
Losing Run:	12	21/9/1896	to	9/1/1897
Clean Sheets (7):	5	22-Mar-80	to	7-Apr-80
	5	29-Dec-84	to	23-Feb-85
Goal Scored:	37	1-Mar-30	to	15-Jan-31
No Goals For (3):	5	15-Nov-13	to	20-Dec-13
	5	10-Jan-87	to	22-Feb-87
SOS Undefeated (3):	7	1989-90		
	7	1950-51		
SOS No Wins:	10	1919-20		

5-Year Record

	Div	P	W	D	L	F	A	Pts	Psn	
1993-94	3	42	12	11	19	52	63	47	18	
1994-95	3	42	15	11	16	54	55	56	12	
1995-96	3	46	13	14	19	57	73	53	18	
1996-97	3	46	18	12	16	70	69	66	9	
1997-98	3	46	20	15	11	60	51	75	3	Promoted

Luton Town

Houdini Lawrence

The bookies may have placed their faith in Luton Town challenging Bristol City for the Championship but Hatters supporters spent much of the season demanding the departure of manager Lennie Lawrence as the club looked destined for playing in the bottom division for the first time in 30 years. With the sale of Matthew Upson and Ceri Hughes during the close season, Lawrence lost two of his brightest prospects in deals which could eventually be worth over £2m, but precious little of it went towards team building. Come February, striker Tony Thorpe, top scorer for a second season, was sold to Fulham for £800,000 after his 19 goals had helped carry the Hatters towards safety.

Despite winning just one of their opening ten games, Lawrence conjured up some of the Houdini magic he successfully employed at Charlton and Luton recovered sufficiently to avoid the drop with seven points to spare.

The Hatters FA Cup venture was disappointingly terminated in Round One by Torquay but the Coca-Cola Cup brought some success with Colchester being ousted before West Bromwich Albion saw them off in the 2nd Round.

Luton's problems were not aided by the ongoing saga of the club's possible move to a new stadium, not necessarily in Luton.

Formed:	1885
Ground:	Kenilworth, 1 Maple Road, Luton, Beds, LU4 8AW
Phone:	01582 411622 **Box Office:** 01582 416976
Info:	0891 12 11 23
Capacity:	9,975
Nickname:	The Hatters
Colours:	White with navy/orange trim, navy blue shorts, white socks with orange/blue trim
Manager:	Lennie Lawrence
Honours:	Division 2 Champions 1981-82; Division 4 Champions 1967-68; Division 3S Champions 1936-37; FA Cup Runners-up 1958-59; Football League Cup Winners 1987-88.
Managers:	John Moore 1986-87, Ray Harford 1987-89, Jim Ryan 1990-91, David Pleat 1991-95, Terry Westley 1995.
Record League Win:	12-0 v Bristol Rovers, D3S, 13/4/36
Record League Defeat:	0-9 v Birmingham City, D2, 12/11/1898
Most GF in Season:	103 – Division 3S, 1936-37
All-time League Apps:	550 – Bob Morton, 1948-64
All-time League Goals:	265 – Gordon Turner, 1949-64
Most Goals in a Season:	55 – Joe Payne, D3S, 1936-37
Most Goals in a Match:	10 – Joe Payne v Bristol Rovers, D3S, 13/4/36 (12-0)

Record Fee Received: £1.5m from N. Forest for Kingsley Black, 8/91
Record Fee Paid: £650,000 to Odense for Lars Elstrup, 8/89
Record Attendance: 30,069 v Blackpool, FA Cup 6th Round Replay, 4/3/59

Stats File

Division	P	W	D	L	F	A	Pts	Yr	B	W
Premier/D1:	658	213	168	277	863	1011	725	16	7	22
Division 1n/2:	1332	488	343	501	1997	1945	1394	32	1	24
Division 2n/3:	276	110	76	90	397	364	331	6	2	21
Division 3n/4:	138	67	29	42	236	187	163	3	1	17

Cup Records	P	W	D	L	F	A
FA Cup:	231	90	53	88	378	374
League Cup:	114	46	31	37	174	156
A/F Members Cup:	16	8	2	6	28	28

Sequence	Games	Start		End
Winning Run:	9	22-Jan-77	to	8-Mar-77
Without Defeat:	19	20-Jan-68	to	24-Apr-68
	19	8-Apr-69	to	7-Oct-69
Without Win:	16	9-Sep-64	to	6-Nov-64
Drawn Games:	5	16-Feb-29	to	11-Mar-29
	5	28-Aug-71	to	18-Sep-71
Without Draw:	19	2-Dec-61	to	14-Apr-62
Losing Run:	8	11/11/1899	to	6-Jan-00
Clean Sheets:	7	13-Oct-23	to	24-Nov-23
	7	16-Jan-93	to	20-Feb-93
Goal Scored:	25	24-Oct-31	to	2-Apr-32
No Goals For (3):	5	10-Apr-73	to	24-Apr-73
	5	4-Apr-94	to	23-Apr-94
SOS Undefeated:	13	1969-70		
SOS No Wins:	9	1974-75		

5-Year Record

	Div	P	W	D	L	F	A	Pts	Psn	
1993-94	1	46	14	11	21	56	60	53	20	
1994-95	1	46	15	13	18	61	64	58	16	
1995-96	1	46	11	12	23	40	64	45	24	Relegated
1996-97	2	46	21	15	10	71	45	78	3	
1997-98	2	46	14	15	17	60	64	57	17	

Macclesfield Town

The Team Now Arriving...

Macclesfield Town's arrival in the Football League, 123 years after their formation, was nothing short of sensational as Sammy McIlroy's side not only won promotion to Division Two at the first attempt but also achieved the only unbeaten home record in the whole of the Premiership and Nationwide League.

Macclesfield's first ever match in the Football League was a 2-1 home win over Torquay but supporters of the Silkmen had to wait until the club's 14th away match before a victory – at Doncaster – was recorded. With that success Macclesfield's promotion campaign stepped up a gear and hopes of gaining an automatic promotion place rose with a vital win at Peterborough. A place in Division Two was secured on 25 April when Chester, who ironically ground shared at Moss Rose earlier in the decade, were beaten 3-2.

Unbeatable as Macclesfield may have been at home in the league, Moss Rose held no such fear for Walsall in the 2nd Round of the FA Cup as the visitors stormed to a sensational 7-0 win. The Silkmen won at Hartlepool in the 1st Round. The Coca-Cola Cup also provided no joy for Macclesfield as they suffered a 1st Round extra-time exit at Hull.

Formed:	1874
Ground:	The Moss Rose Ground, London Road, Macclesfield, Cheshire, SK11 7SP
Phone:	01625 264686 **Box Office:** 01625 264686
Info:	0891 88 44 82
Capacity:	6,028
Colours:	Royal blue shirts, white shorts, blue socks
Nickname:	The Silkmen
Manager:	Sammy McIlroy
Honours:	Division 3 Runners-up, 1997-98; GMVC Champions 1994-95, 1996-97; FA Trophy Winners 1969-70, 1995-96; Bob Lord Trophy Winners 1993-94.
Record League Win:	3-0 v Doncaster Rovers, D3, 23/8/97 and 24/1/98
Record League Defeat:	1-5 v Colchester United, D4, 14/3/98
Most GF in Season:	63 – Division 3, 1997-98
All-time League Apps:	46 – Ryan Price and Darren Tinson, 1997-98
All-time League Goals:	13 – Steve Wood, 1997-98
Most Goals in a Season:	13 – Steve Wood, 1997-98
Most Goals in a Match:	2 – Phil Power v Darlington, 5/9/97
	2 – Phil Power v Cambridge U., 8/11/97
	2 – Steve Wood v Doncaster R., 24/1/98
Record Fee Received:	£40,000 from Sheffield U. for Mike Lake, 1988

Record Fee Paid: £25,000 to Mansfield for Ben Sedgemore, 3/98
Record Attendance: 9,008 v Winsford U., Cheshire Snr Cup 2nd Round, 4/2/48

Stats File

Division	P	W	D	L	F	A	Pts	Yr	B	W
Division 3n/4:	46	23	13	10	63	44	82	1	2	2

Cup Records	P	W	D	L	F	A
FA Cup:	37	8	6	23	61	90
League Cup:	2	0	1	1	1	2
A/F Members Cup:	1	0	0	1	0	1

Sequence	Games	Start		End
Winning Run:	4	17-Jan-98	to	27-Jan-98
Without Defeat:	8	17-Jan-98	to	21-Feb-98
Without Win:	4	20-Sep-97	to	11-Oct-97
	4	21-Oct-97	to	4-Nov-97
Drawn Games:	3	27-Sep-97	to	11-Oct-97
Without Draw:	8	13-Dec-97	to	27-Jan-98
Clean Sheets:	3	20-Jan-98	to	27-Jan-98
	3	28-Feb-98	to	7-Mar-98
Goal Scored:	9	5-Sep-97	to	25-Oct-97

5-Year Record

	Div	P	W	D	L	F	A	Pts	Psn	
1997-98	3	46	23	13	10	63	44	82	2	Promoted

Manchester City

An All-time Low

The dramatic fall from grace of Manchester City continued during 1997/98, with the club falling into Division Two for the first time in its 111-year history. Such a scenario seemed unthinkable at the start of the season as manager Frank Clark invested close to £5m on Lee Bradbury from Portsmouth and Tony Vaughan from Ipswich. With brilliant Georgian midfielder Georgi Kinkladze staying at Maine Road and Uwe Rosler leading the attack, City seemed destined for success. But it was not to be and the club never recovered from a poor start.

As City's poor form continued in February, Clark was dismissed but only learnt of his fate through the media. Joe Royle was appointed as City's sixth manager in 18 months but could not halt the slide, and even a 5-2 win at Stoke on the final day could not stave off relegation.

Clark was not the only casualty as chairman Francis Lee resigned in the face of condemnation from fans and shareholders.

City progressed through one round of the FA Cup with victory over Bradford before going down at home to West Ham. Entering the Coca-Cola Cup in the 1st Round for the first time, City were humiliated by Blackpool who went through on the away goals rule.

Formed:	1887
Ground:	Maine Road, Moss Side, Manchester, M14 7WN
Phone:	0161 226 1191 **Box Office:** 0161 226 2224
Info:	0898 12 11 91
Capacity:	39,600
Colours:	Sky blue shirts, white shorts, sky blue stockings
Nickname:	City, The Blues
Manager:	Joe Royle
Honours:	Division 1 Champions 1936-37, 1967-68; Division 2 Champions 1898-99, 1902-03, 1909-10, 1927-28, 1946-47, 1965-66; FA Cup Winners 1903-04, 1933-34, 1955-56, 1968-69; Football League Cup Winners 1969-70, 1975-76; Cup-Winners' Cup Winners 1969-70.
Managers:	Peter Reid 1990-93, Brian Horton 1993-95, Alan Ball 1995-96, Steve Coppell 1996, Frank Clark 1996-1998.
Previous Names:	Ardwick FC 1887-95 (from amalgamation of West Gorton and Gorton A.)
Record League Win:	10-0 v Darwen, D2, 1/4/1899
Record League Defeat:	0-8 v Burton Wanderers, D2, 1894-95
	1-9 v Everton, D1, 3/9/1908
	0-8 v Wolverhampton Wndrs, D1, 23/12/33
Most GF in Season:	108 – Division 2, 1926-27

All-time League Apps:	676 – Alan Oakes, 1959-76	
All-time League Goals:	177 – Eric Brook, 1927-39	
Most Goals in a Season:	38 – Tom Johnson, D2, 1928-29	
Most Goals in a Match:	5 – Tom Johnson v Everton (a), D1, 15/9/28 (6-2) (Dennis Law scored six v Luton, FA Cup 4th Round in 1961 but match was abandoned at 6-2.)	
Record Fee Received:	£3.2m from Blackburn R. for Garry Flitcroft, 3/96	
Record Fee Paid:	£2.5m to Wimbledon for Keith Curle, 8/91 £2.5m to Wimbledon for Terry Phelan, 8/92	
Record Attendance:	84,569 v Stoke City, FA Cup 6th Round, 3/3/1934	

Stats File

Division	P	W	D	L	F	A	Pts	Yr	B	W
Premier/D1:	2936	1106	731	1099	4497	4464	3084	72	1	21
Division 1n/2:	878	431	195	252	1727	1189	1169	23	1	22

Cup Records	P	W	D	L	F	A
FA Cup:	280	133	59	88	498	358
League Cup:	149	75	32	42	263	175
A/F Members Cup:	17	8	1	8	37	29

Sequence	Games	Start		End
Winning Run:	9	8-Apr-12	to	28-Sep-12
Without Defeat:	22	26-Dec-36	to	1-May-37
	22	16-Nov-46	to	19-Apr-47
Without Win:	17	26-Dec-79	to	7-Apr-80
Drawn Games:	6	5-Apr-13	to	6-Sep-13
Without Draw:	20	12/12/1892	to	21/10/1893
Losing Run:	8	23-Aug-95	to	14-Oct-95
Clean Sheets (3):	5	28-Dec-46	to	1-Feb-47
	5	23-Feb-85	to	19-Mar-85
Goal Scored:	44	3-Oct-36	to	9-Oct-37
No Goals For:	6	30-Jan-71	to	13-Mar-71
SOS Undefeated:	11	1914-15		
SOS No Wins:	12	1980-81		

5-Year Record

	Div	P	W	D	L	F	A	Pts	Psn	
1993-94	P	42	9	18	15	38	49	45	16	
1994-95	P	42	12	13	17	53	64	49	17	
1995-96	P	38	9	11	18	33	58	38	18	Relegated
1996-97	1	46	17	10	19	59	60	61	14	
1997-98	1	46	12	12	22	56	57	48	22	Relegated

Millwall

Slide Halted – Just

Since finishing third in Division One in 1994, Millwall have been on a steady downward slide. Relegation came along two years later and, after finishing 14th in Division Three in 1997, the slump continued last season with just five points separating the Lions from the relegation zone. In a bid to buck the trend, Millwall appointed Billy Bonds as manager for the 1997/98 season but after an unsuccessful campaign Bonds departed and the managerial duties were handed to 33-year-old Lions defender Keith Stevens.

Millwall started the season with two defeats in three games but staged a good recovery and after 19 games were very nicely placed at third in the table. But they were unable to sustain that good form and gradually slid down the table, never threatening to reverse the decline, and ended the season in 18th position.

An unfortunate draw in the FA Cup took Millwall to Bristol City in the 1st Round where the Londoners lost 1-0. Progress was made in the Coca-Cola Cup where a penalty shoot-out victory was achieved over Northampton after a 2-2 aggregate draw. Millwall enjoyed no such good fortune in the 2nd Round as Wimbledon dished out convincing 5-1 and 4-1 defeats.

Formed:	1885
Ground:	The New Den, Zampa Road, London, SE16 3LN
Phone:	0171 232 1222 **Box Office:** 0171 232 9999
Info:	0891 400 300
Capacity:	20,146
Nickname:	The Lions
Colours:	Blue shirts, white shorts, blue stockings
Manager:	Keith Stevens
Honours:	Division 2 Champions 1987-88; Division 3S Champions 1927-98, 1937-38; Division 4 Champions 1961-62; Football League Trophy Winners 1982-83
Managers:	Bruce Rioch 1990-92, Mick McCarthy, 1992-96, Jimmy Nicholl 1996-97, John Docherty 1997, Billy Bonds 1997-98
Previous Names:	Millwall Rovers 1885, Millwall Athletic 1889
Record League Win:	9-1 v Torquay U., D3S, 29/8/27
Record League Defeat:	1-8 v Plymouth, D2, 16/1/32
Most GF in Season:	127 – Division 3S, 1927-28
All-time League Apps:	596 – Barry Kitchener
All-time League Goals:	111 – Teddy Sheringham, 1983-91
Most Goals in a Season:	37 – R. Parker, 1927
Most Goals in a Match:	5 – R. Parker v Norwich, D3S, 28/8/26 (6-1)
Record Fee Received:	£2m from N. Forest for Teddy Sheringham, 7/91

Record Fee Paid: £800,000 to Derby County for Paul Goddard, 12/89
Record Attendance: 48,672 v Derby County, FA Cup 5th Round, 20/2/37 (at Den)

Stats File

Division	P	W	D	L	F	A	Pts	Yr	B	W
Premier/D1:	76	19	22	35	86	117	79	2	10	20
Division 1n/2:	1286	464	348	474	1702	1766	1435	30	1	22
Division 2n/3:	552	212	154	186	736	714	684	12	2	21
Division 3n/4:	228	105	61	62	422	323	271	5	1	9

Cup Records	P	W	D	L	F	A
FA Cup:	241	84	64	93	348	362
League Cup:	120	45	33	42	172	177
A/F Members Cup:	26	11	5	10	46	40

Sequence	Games	Start		End
Winning Run:	10	10-Mar-28	to	25-Apr-28
Without Defeat:	19	22-Aug-59	to	31-Oct-59
Without Win:	20	26-Dec-89	to	5-May-90
Drawn Games (4):	5	3-Oct-59	to	24-Oct-59
	5	22-Dec-73	to	12-Jan-74
Without Draw:	26	22-Mar-30	to	29-Nov-30
Losing Run:	11	10-Apr-29	to	16-Sep-29
Clean Sheets:	11	27-Feb-26	to	10-Apr-26
Goal Scored:	22	8-Dec-23	to	19-Apr-24
	22	27-Nov-54	to	12-Apr-55
No Goals For:	6	20-Dec-47	to	17-Jan-48
	6	5-Apr-97	to	3-May-97
SOS Undefeated:	19	1959-60		
SOS No Wins:	11	1929-30		

5-Year Record

	Div	P	W	D	L	F	A	Pts	Psn	
1993-94	1	46	19	17	10	58	49	74	3	
1994-95	1	46	16	14	16	60	60	62	12	
1995-96	1	46	13	13	20	43	63	52	22	Relegated
1996-97	2	46	16	13	17	50	55	61	14	
1997-98	2	46	14	13	19	43	54	55	18	

Northampton Town

On the Fringes

For the second successive year Northampton Town had an extended league campaign as the Cobblers battled their way to Wembley for the play-off final. But unlike their visit to the Twin Towers a year earlier, Northampton were unsuccessful in 1998 as Grimsby clinched their historic Wembley double to deny the Cobblers promotion in front of a record Division Two play-off final attendance of 62,988. Manager Ian Atkins made few changes to his squad during the summer but spent a club record £90,000 on David Seal from Bristol City in September and followed it in December with the £75,000 signing of Chris Freestone from Middlesbrough.

Northampton were either in the top six or on the fringes of the play-off pack throughout the season but endured a nerve-wracking final day as a draw at York was only just enough to get into the play-offs due to results elsewhere. The Cobblers were fortunate to get away with just a 3-1 defeat at Bristol Rovers in the 1st Leg of the play-off but in the return a record Sixfields crowd of 7,501 saw goals from Carl Heggs, Ian Clarkson and Ray Warburton pull off a remarkable 4-3 aggregate victory, having been 3-0 down at one stage in the first game.

Formed:	1897
Ground:	Sixfields Stadium, Upton Way, Northampton, NN5 5QA
Phone:	01604 757773 **Box Office:** 01604 588338
Info:	0839 66 44 77
Capacity:	7,653
Nickname:	The Cobblers
Colours:	Claret with white shirts, yellow shoulder panel, white shorts, claret socks
Manager:	Ian Atkins
Honours:	Division 3 Champions 1962-63; Division 4 Champions 1986-87.
Managers:	Tony Barton 1984-85, Graham Carr 1985-90, Theo Foley 1990-92, Phil Chard 1992-93, John Barnwell 1993-95.
Record League Win:	10-0 v Walsall, D3S, 5/11/27
Record League Defeat:	0-10 v Bournemouth, D3S, 2/9/39
Most GF in Season:	109 – Division 3S, 1952-53
	109 – Division 3, 1962-63
All-time League Apps:	521 – Tommy Fowler, 1946-61
All-time League Goals:	135 – Jack English, 1948-60
Most Goals in a Season:	36 – Cliff Holton, D3, 1961-62
Most Goals in a Match:	5 – R. Hoten v Crystal Palace (h), 8-1, D3S, 27/10/28
	5 – A. Dawes v Lloyds Bank (h), 8-1 FAC 1R, 26/11/32
Record Fee Received:	£265,000 from Watford for Richard Hill, 3/87

Record Fee Paid: £90,000 to Bristol C. for David Seal, 9/97
Record Attendance: 24,523 v Fulham, D1, 23/4/66

Stats File

Division	P	W	D	L	F	A	Pts	Yr	B	W
Premier/D1:	42	10	13	19	55	92	33	1	21	21
Division 1n/2:	126	48	31	47	171	194	127	3	2	21
Division 2n/3:	414	150	110	154	605	557	473	9	1	22
Division 3n/4:	1226	452	301	473	1721	1739	1402	27	1	23

Cup Records	P	W	D	L	F	A
FA Cup:	206	73	50	83	318	307
League Cup:	109	34	26	49	135	161
A/F Members Cup:	44	18	7	19	67	59

Sequence	Games	Start		End
Winning Run:	8	27-Aug-60	to	19-Sep-60
Without Defeat:	21	27-Sep-86	to	6-Feb-87
Without Win:	18	26-Mar-69	to	20-Sep-69
Drawn Games:	6	18-Sep-83	to	15-Oct-83
Without Draw:	29	5-Feb-27	to	5-Nov-27
Losing Run:	8	26-Oct-35	to	21-Dec-35
Clean Sheets:	6	3-Sep-30	to	20-Sep-30
	6	25-Oct-75	to	29-Nov-75
Goal Scored:	27	23-Aug-86	to	6-Feb-87
No Goals For:	7	7-Apr-39	to	6-May-39
SOS Undefeated:	11	1983-84		
SOS No Wins:	13	1965-66		

5-Year Record

	Div	P	W	D	L	F	A	Pts	Psn	
1993-94	3	42	9	11	22	44	66	38	22	
1994-95	3	42	10	14	18	45	67	44	17	
1995-96	3	46	18	13	15	51	44	67	11	
1996-97	3	46	20	12	14	67	44	72	4	Promoted PO
1997-98	2	46	18	17	11	52	37	71	4	

Notts County

First to Promotion

Notts County's response to two relegations within three years was simply awesome as Sam Allardyce's side dominated Division Three to such an extent that they achieved promotion within the Football League earlier than any side had previously done. Second-placed Macclesfield were a distant 17 points away and the margin over fourth place and the play-offs was a staggering 25 points as a run of ten consecutive wins in late winter left the pack floundering.

As records tumbled one of the most amazing statistics was the 28 goals scored by top scorer Gary Jones. He found the net just three times in 27 games the previous season. During the last 22 games of the season Jones scored 23 times and he received good support from Sean Farrell who ended the campaign with 15 goals. The Magpies also conceded fewer goals than any other side in Division Three. The one setback for County came in the FA Cup where, after beating Colwyn Bay, they lost at home to Preston in a 2nd Round replay. County went past Darlington in the Coca-Cola Cup and won 1-0 at Tranmere in the 2nd Leg of their 2nd Round clash but had lost 2-0 at home to go out of the competition.

Formed:	1862
Ground:	Meadow Lane, Nottingham, NG2 3HJ
Phone:	0115 9529000 **Box Office:** 0115 9557210
Info:	0891 88 86 84
Capacity:	20,300
Nickname:	The Magpies
Colours:	Black and white striped shirts, white shorts, black socks
Manager:	Sam Allardyce
Honours:	Division 2 Champions 1896-97, 1913-14, 1922-23;
	Division 3S Champions 1930-31, 1949-50;
	Division 4 Champions 1970-71; FA Cup Winners 1893-94;
	Anglo-Italian Cup Winners 1994-95.
Managers:	Mick Walker 1993-94, Russell Slade 1994-95, Howard Kendall 1995, Colin Murphy 1995-1996, Steve Thompson 1996.
Record League Win:	10-0 v Port Vale, D2, 26/2/1895
	11-1 v Newport County, 15/1/49
Record League Defeat:	1-9 v Blackburn Rovers, D1, 16/11/1889
	1-9 v Aston Villa, D3S, 29/9/30
	1-9 v Portsmouth, D2, 9/4/27
	0-8 v West Brom Alb., D1, 25/10/19
	0-8 v Newcastle Utd, D1, 26/10/01
Most GF in Season:	107 – Division 4, 1959-60
All-time League Apps:	602 – Albert Iremonger, 1904-26
All-time League Goals:	138 – Les Bradd, 1967-78

Most Goals in a Season: 39 – Tom Keetley, 1930-31
Most Goals in a Match: 9 – Harry Curshaw v Wednesbury Strollers, FA Cup 2nd Round Replay, 10/12/1881
Record Fee Received: £2.5m from Derby County for Craig Short, 9/92
Record Fee Paid: £750,000 to Sheffield Utd for Tony Agana, 11/91
Record Attendance: 47,310 v York City, FA Cup 6th Round, 10/3/55

Stats File

Division	P	W	D	L	F	A	Pts	Yr	B	W
Premier/D1:	1068	341	253	474	1403	1712	983	30	3	22
Division 1n/2:	1516	549	378	589	2224	2325	1550	37	1	24
Division 2n/3:	644	256	169	219	926	874	815	14	2	24
Division 3n/4:	414	181	103	130	627	544	494	9	1	20

Cup Records	P	W	D	L	F	A
FA Cup:	282	122	50	110	526	419
League Cup:	112	47	20	45	169	171
A/F Members Cup:	34	13	9	12	38	42

Sequence	Games	Start		End
Winning Run:	10	3-Dec-97	to	31-Jan-98
Without Defeat:	19	26-Apr-30	to	6-Dec-30
Without Win:	20	3-Dec-96	to	31-Mar-97
Drawn Games:	5	2-Dec-78	to	26-Dec-78
Without Draw:	22	14-Feb-03	to	7-Nov-03
	22	12-Sep-59	to	9-Jan-60
Losing Run (3):	7	8-Apr-33	to	6-May-33
	7	3-Sep-83	to	16-Oct-83
Clean Sheets:	6	11-Mar-69	to	5-Apr-69
	6	21-Oct-70	to	14-Nov-70
Goal Scored:	35	26-Apr-30	to	21-Mar-31
	35	10-Oct-59	to	27-Aug-60
No Goals For (3):	5	25-Jan-64	to	22-Feb-64
	5	29-Dec-84	to	26-Jan-85
SOS Undefeated:	18	1930-31		
SOS No Wins:	11	1977-78		

5-Year Record

	Div	P	W	D	L	F	A	Pts	Psn	
1993-94	1	46	20	8	18	65	69	68	7	
1994-95	1	46	9	13	24	45	66	40	24	Relegated
1995-96	2	46	21	15	10	63	39	78	4	
1996-97	2	46	7	14	25	33	59	35	24	Relegated
1997-98	3	46	29	12	5	82	43	99	1	Promoted

Oldham Athletic

Home Champs
With a home record which saw Oldham Athletic collect as many points as champions Watford, it is not too difficult to see where their problems lay during the 1997/98 season as the Latics came to rest in 13th place. Just two away games were won when a reasonable away record would almost certainly have got them into the play-offs. No side scored more times at home than Oldham but only two sides outside the relegated clubs scored less on their travels.

Oldham, relegated the previous May, made a mediocre start to the season before a run of success at home, coupled with away draws, had them in third place by the beginning of February. A setback was suffered with a home defeat by Blackpool which sparked an indifferent run and a fall away from the top six.

With wins over Mansfield and Blackpool, Oldham survived two rounds of the FA Cup for the first time since 1994 but were defeated in the 3rd Round at Cardiff. Oldham's Coca-Cola Cup venture was less successful with a 1st Round 5-1 aggregate defeat by Grimsby. Manager Neil Warnock left at the end of the season after failing to get the support he wanted from the club.

Formed:	1894
Ground:	Boundary Park, Oldham, Lancs, OL1 2PA
Phone:	0161 624 4972 **Box Office:** 0161 624 4972
Info:	0891 12 11 42
Nickname:	The Latics
Capacity:	17,005
Colours:	Royal blue shirts, blue shorts, blue stockings
Manager:	Andy Ritchie
Honours:	Division 2 Champions 1990-91; Division 3N Champions 1952-53; Division 3 Champions 1973-74.
Managers:	Jimmy McIlroy 1966-68, Jack Rowley 1968-69, Jimmy Frizzell 1970-82, Joe Royle 1982-94, Graeme Sharp 1994-97, Neil Warnock 1997-98.
Previous Names:	Pine Villa, 1895, Oldham Athletic 1899
Record League Win:	11-0 v Southport, D4, 26/12/62
Record League Defeat:	4-13 v Tranmere Rovers, D3N, 26/12/35
Most GF in Season:	95 – Division 4, 1962-63
All-time League Apps:	570 – Ian T. Wood, 1965-80
All-time League Goals:	157 – Roger Palmer, 1980-92
Most Goals in a Season:	33 – Tom Davis, D3N, 1936-37
Most Goals in a Match:	7 – Eric Gemmill v Chester, D3N, 19/1/53
Record Fee Received:	£1.7m from Aston Villa for Earl Barrett, 2/92

Record Fee Paid: £700,000 to Aston Villa for Ian Olney, 5/92
Record Attendance: 47,671 v Sheffield Wed., FA Cup 4th Round, 25/1/30

Stats File

Division	P	W	D	L	F	A	Pts	Yr	B	W
Premier/D1:	484	159	129	196	604	713	483	12	2	22
Division 1n/2:	1526	561	396	569	2160	2195	1727	36	1	23
Division 2n/3:	460	171	112	177	655	663	469	10	1	24
Division 3n/4:	320	121	70	129	499	513	312	7	2	23

Cup Records	P	W	D	L	F	A
FA Cup:	198	76	40	82	305	330
League Cup:	103	37	19	47	151	172
A/F Members Cup:	7	0	0	7	4	18

Sequence	Games	Start		End
Winning Run:	10	12-Jan-74	to	12-Mar-74
Without Defeat:	20	1-May-90	to	10-Nov-90
Without Win:	17	4-Sep-20	to	18-Dec-20
Drawn Games:	5	26-Dec-82	to	15-Jan-83
Without Draw:	29	5-Sep-67	to	2-Mar-68
Losing Run:	8	27-Dec-32	to	18-Feb-33
	8	15-Dec-34	to	2-Feb-35
Clean Sheets:	6	26-Feb-83	to	5-Apr-83
	6	23-Aug-86	to	13-Sep-86
Goal Scored:	25	15-Jan-27	to	17-Sep-27
	25	25-Aug-62	to	2-Feb-63
No Goals For:	6	4-Feb-22	to	4-Mar-22
SOS Undefeated:	16	1990-91		
SOS No Wins:	10	1996-97		

5-Year Record

	Div	P	W	D	L	F	A	Pts	Psn	
1993-94	P	42	9	13	20	42	68	40	21	Relegated
1994-95	1	46	16	13	17	60	60	61	14	
1995-96	1	46	14	14	18	54	50	56	18	
1996-97	1	46	10	13	23	51	66	43	23	Relegated
1997-98	2	46	15	16	15	62	54	61	13	

Preston North End

Same Again

For the second time in as many seasons since winning Division Three, Preston North End finished 15th in Division Two, this despite gaining two points less than in 1996/97. Preston started the season in good nick and with just two defeats from the opening ten games sat in fifth position. But the run was not sustained by the Lillywhites and in January, with hope of FA Cup glory gone and his side drifting down the table, manager Gary Peters resigned after three years in the job.

David Moyes came in first as caretaker boss before taking the position on a permanent basis. After ending a wait of over two months for a win, Preston finished the season with a flourish. Just one of the last 13 games was lost and on the final day they beat Bristol City to deny them the Championship.

North End progressed beyond the 2nd Round of the FA Cup for the first time in four years with wins over Doncaster and Notts County, commendably after an away replay, only to be beaten by Stockport. Rotherham were comprehensively beaten in the Coca-Cola Cup but a 6-0 2nd Round defeat at Blackburn rendered a 1-0 2nd Leg home win as merely academic.

Off the field the development of Deepdale continued unabated and the new £2.6 million North End Stand should be in place for the start of the 1998-99 season, adding an additional 6,000 seats to capacity.

Formed:	1881
Ground:	Deepdale, Preston, PR1 6RU
Phone:	01772 902020
Info:	01772 902000
Capacity:	21,500
Colours:	White and navy shirts, navy shorts, navy socks
Nickname:	The Lillywhites
Manager:	David Moyes
Honours:	Division 1 Champions 1888-89, 1889-90;
	Division 2 Champions, 1903-04, 1912-13, 1950-51;
	Division 3 Champions 1970-71, 1995-96;
	FA Cup Winners 1888-89, 1937-38.
Managers;	Tommy Booth 1985-86, Brian Kidd 1986, John McGrath 1986-90,
	Lee Chapman 1990-92, John Beck 1992-94.
Record League Win:	10-0 v Stoke City (h), D1, 14/9/1889
Record League Defeat:	0-7 v Blackpool (h), D1, 1/5/48
	0-7 v Nottingham Forest (a), D2, 9/4/27
Most GF in Season:	100 – Division 2, 1927-28
	100 – Division 1, 1957-58
All-time League Apps:	447 – Alan Kelly, 1961-75
All-time League Goals:	187 – Tom Finney, 1946-60

Most Goals in a Season: 37 – Ted Harper, D2, 1932-33
Most Goals in a Match: 8 – Jimmy Ross v Hyde (h), 26-0, FAC 1R, 15/10/1887
Record Fee Received: £765,000 from Manchester City for Michael Robinson, 6/79
Record Fee Paid: £250,000 to Stoke City for Tony Ellis, 8/92
Record Attendance: 42,684 v Arsenal, D1, 23/4/38

Stats File

Division	P	W	D	L	F	A	Pts	Yr	B	W
Premier/D1:	1720	671	390	659	2701	2569	1732	46	1	22
Division 1n/2:	1270	485	340	445	1953	1843	1309	31	1	22
Division 2n/3:	782	284	200	298	1019	1066	951	17	1	23
Division 3n/4:	222	97	62	63	341	275	353	5	1	23

Cup Records	P	W	D	L	F	A
FA Cup:	301	141	59	101	592	403
League Cup:	115	42	29	44	147	181
A/F Members Cup:	50	24	9	17	77	55

Sequence	Games	Start		End
Winning Run:	14	25-Dec-50	to	27-Mar-51
Without Defeat:	21	19-Aug-95	to	1-Jan-96
Without Win:	15	14-Apr-23	to	20-Oct-23
Drawn Games:	6	24-Feb-79	to	20-Mar-79
Without Draw:	27	24/10/1891	to	22/10/1892
	27	8-Oct-58	to	4-Apr-59
Losing Run:	8	1-Oct-83	to	5-Nov-83
	8	22-Sep-84	to	27-Oct-84
Clean Sheets:	6	14-Sep-01	to	19-Oct-01
	6	9-Sep-72	to	30-Sep-72
Goal Scored:	30	15-Nov-52	to	26-Aug-53
No Goals For:	6	8/4/1897	to	1/9/1897
	6	19-Nov-60	to	26-Dec-60
SOS Undefeated:	22	1888-89		
SOS No Wins:	11	1923-24		

5-Year Record

	Div	P	W	D	L	F	A	Pts	Psn	
1993-94	3n	42	18	13	11	79	60	67	5	
1994-95	3n	42	19	10	13	58	41	67	5	
1995-96	3n	46	23	17	6	78	38	86	1	Promoted
1996-97	2n	46	18	7	21	49	55	61	15	
1997-98	2n	46	15	14	17	56	56	59	15	

Reading

New Stadium, New Division

As Reading look forward to moving into a new multi-million pound stadium, much of the sheen of what the future holds was tarnished by relegation after four seasons in Division One.

Manager Terry Bullivant bolstered his side with the club record signing of Carl Asaba for £800,000 and also spent £500,000 on Barnet players Linvoy Primus and Lee Hodges. But Reading's early form was poor with six of the first eight games lost, the last 6-0 at Tranmere. The run was ended by the Royals' first win at Portsmouth for 21 years. By the middle of January Reading had risen to 14th but, following a 2-0 win over Birmingham, their season fell away in spectacular fashion and after nine defeats in ten games, Bullivant resigned for Tommy Burns to take over. Burns couldn't halt the slide and with all their final five games lost, Reading were relegated.

Reading enjoyed better success in the cups with FA Cup progress being made against Cheltenham and Cardiff – on penalties – before losing to a late goal at Sheffield United. In the Coca-Cola Cup, Swansea, Peterborough and Wolves were beaten before Reading pulled off a shock 3-2 win at Leeds. Middlesbrough stopped the run through a last-minute winner at Elm Park.

Formed:	1871
Ground:	The Madejski Stadium, Reading, Berks.
Phone:	0118 9507878 **Box Office:** 0118 9507878
Info:	0891 12 1000
Capacity:	25,000
Colours:	Blue & white hooped shirts, white shorts and socks
Nickname:	The Royals
Manager:	Tommy Burns
Honours:	Division 3 Champions 1985-86; Division 3S Champions 1925-26; Division 4 Champions 1978-79; Division 3S Cup Winners 1937-38; Simod Cup Winners 1987-88.
Managers:	Ian Branfoot 1984-89, Ian Porterfield 1989-91, Mark McGhee 1991-94, Jimmy Quinn/Mick Gooding 1994-97, Terry Bullivant 1997-98.
Record League Win:	10-2 v Crystal Palace, D3S, 4/9/46 8-0 v Southport, D3, 22/4/70
Record League Defeat:	1-8 v Burnley, D2, 13/9/30 0-7 v Preston North End, D2, 27/8/28
Most GF in Season:	112 – Division 3S, 1951-52
All-time League Apps:	500 – Martin Hicks, 1978-91
All-time League Goals:	158 – Ronnie Blackman, 1947-54

Most Goals in a Season: 39 – Ronnie Blackman, D3S 1951-52
Most Goals in a Match: 6 – Arthur Bacon v Stoke City (h), D2, 3/4/1931
Record Fee Received: £1.575m from Newcastle U. for Shaka Hislop, 8/95
Record Fee Paid: £800,000 to Brentford for Carl Asaba, 8/97
Record Attendance: 33,042 v Brentford, FA Cup 5th Round, 19/2/27

Stats File

Division	P	W	D	L	F	A	Pts	Yr	B	W
Division 1n/2:	480	152	118	210	611	777	508	11	2	24
Division 2n/3:	1196	471	296	429	1779	1722	1422	26	1	21
Division 3n/4:	368	161	110	97	513	392	454	8	1	16

Cup Records	P	W	D	L	F	A
FA Cup:	271	106	71	94	424	420
League Cup:	119	43	29	47	174	188
A/F Members Cup:	30	10	7	13	40	53

Sequence	Games	Start		End
Winning Run:	13	17-Aug-85	to	19-Oct-85
Without Defeat:	19	21-Apr-73	to	27-Oct-73
Without Win:	14	30-Apr-27	to	29-Oct-27
Drawn Games:	5	11-Oct-97	to	1-Nov-97
Without Draw:	33	31-Aug-35	to	18-Mar-36
Losing Run:	7	28-Feb-98	to	28-Mar-98
Clean Sheets:	11	28-Mar-79	to	5-May-79
Goal Scored:	32	1-Oct-32	to	26-Apr-33
No Goals For:	6	13-Apr-25	to	30-Apr-25
SOS Undefeated:	14	1973-74		
	14	1985-86		
SOS No Wins:	12	1927-28		

5-Year Record

	Div	P	W	D	L	F	A	Pts	Psn	
1993-94	2	46	26	11	9	81	44	89	1	Promoted
1994-95	1	46	23	10	13	58	44	79	2	
1995-96	1	46	13	17	16	54	63	56	19	
1996-97	1	46	15	12	19	58	67	57	18	
1997-98	1	46	11	9	26	39	78	42	24	Relegated

Stoke City

Pottery Cracks

Stoke City's five-year stay in Division One came to a dramatic end during a shattering 5-2 home defeat by Manchester City which sent both sides down when a win for the Potteries club would have secured their future at the higher level. Demotion was not high on Stoke's list of expectations at the start of the season as the club moved into its new £15m Britannia Stadium and banked a club record £2.75m from the sale of Mike Sheron to QPR.

Manager Chic Bates saw his side make a decent start and after 11 games Stoke were seventh in the table, but an 11-match winless run culminated in a humiliating 7-0 home defeat by Birmingham. Bates, just days after chairman Peter Coates resigned, stood down as manager in January to be replaced by Chris Kamara. But the former Bradford boss failed to halt the slide and left after 16 games. Alan Durban took over for the final five games, 17 years after his previous spell as manager.

Stoke were knocked out of the FA Cup by West Brom in the 3rd Round but removed lower league sides Rochdale and Burnley from the Coca-Cola Cup before losing at home to Leeds after extra time.

Formed:	1863
Ground:	Britannia Stadium, Stoke on Trent
Phone:	01782 413511 **Box Office:** 01782 413511
Info:	0891 70 02 78
Capacity:	25,000
Colours:	Red and white striped shirts, white shorts, red and white socks
Nickname:	The Potters
Manager:	Brian Little
Honours:	Division 2 Champions 1932-33, 1962-63, 1992-93; Division 3N Champions 1926-27; Football League Cup Winners 1971-72; Autoglass Trophy Winners 1991-92.
Managers:	Lou Macari 1991-93, Joe Jordan 1993-94, Lou Macari 1994-97, Chic Bates 1997-98, Chris Kamara 1998.
Previous Names:	Stoke
Record League Win:	9-0 v Plymouth Argyle, D2, 17/12/60
Record League Defeat:	0-10 v Preston North End, D1, 4/2/37
Most GF in Season:	92 – Division 3N, 1926-27
All-time League Apps:	591 – Eric Skeels, 1959-76
All-time League Goals:	171 – John Ritchie, 1962-66 & 1969-75
Most Goals in a Season:	32 – Charles Wilson, 1927-28
Most Goals in a Match:	7 – Neville Coleman v Lincoln, D2, 23/2/57

Record Fee Received: £1.5m from Chelsea for Mark Stein, 10/93
£1.5m from Newcastle for Andrew Griffin, 1/98
Record Fee Paid: £580,000 to Birmingham C. for Paul Peschisolido, 7/94
Record Attendance: 51,380 v Arsenal, D1, 29/3/37

Stats File

Division	P	W	D	L	F	A	Pts	Yr	B	W
Premier/D1:	1992	662	474	856	2657	3134	1842	52	4	22
Division 1n/2:	1496	580	384	532	2104	1984	1695	35	1	24
Division 2n/3:	138	64	38	36	197	142	230	3	1	14

Cup Records	P	W	D	L	F	A
FA Cup:	272	91	78	103	403	392
League Cup:	130	54	33	43	177	166
A/F Members Cup:	26	14	6	6	43	29

Sequence	Games	Start		End
Winning Run:	8	30/3/1895	to	21/9/1895
Without Defeat:	25	5-Sep-92	to	20-Feb-93
Without Win:	17	15-Sep-84	to	22-Dec-84
	17	22-Apr-89	to	14-Oct-89
Drawn Games:	5	1-Sep-73	to	15-Sep-73
	5	21-Mar-87	to	11-Apr-87
Without Draw:	46	30/3/1895	to	14/11/1896
Losing Run:	11	6-Apr-85	to	17-Aug-85
Clean Sheets (3):	5	16-Apr-79	to	5-May-79
	5	17-Feb-96	to	9-Mar-96
Goal Scored:	21	24-Dec-21	to	22-Apr-22
No Goals For:	8	29-Dec-84	to	16-Mar-85
SOS Undefeated:	9	1926-27		
SOS No Wins:	11	1951-52		
	11	1989-90		

5-Year Record

	Div	P	W	D	L	F	A	Pts	Psn	
1993-94	1	46	18	13	15	57	59	67	10	
1994-95	1	46	16	15	15	50	53	63	11	
1995-96	1	46	20	13	13	60	49	73	4	
1996-97	1	46	18	10	18	51	57	64	12	
1997-98	1	46	11	13	22	44	74	46	23	Relegated

Walsall

Replacement Wanted

Walsall went into the season with £500,000 in the bank following the transfer of striker Kyle Lightbourne to Coventry but while scoring just 43 league goals all season the Saddlers failed to replace the previous season's top scorer. The lack of a cutting edge was highlighted even more by the fact that Walsall conceded the fewest number of goals of any side in the bottom 14 of Division Two. The highlight of a disappointing league campaign was a 2-1 win at champions Watford.

Walsall's FA Cup form was exceptional. A home win over Lincoln United was followed by a stunning 7-0 win at Macclesfield – Town's only home defeat of the season – and a good 2-0 success at Peterborough. One of the successes of Walsall's season was Frenchman Roger Boli. A free signing, he scored a consolation goal during a 4th Round 5-1 defeat away to Manchester United.

Walsall also excelled in the Coca-Cola Cup. A 1st Round double over Exeter was supplemented by a shock 3-2 aggregate victory over Nottingham Forest with Andy Watson scoring twice. Watson was also on target as Sheffield United were beaten 2-1 and then notched their only goal in a 4-1 4th Round reversal at West Ham.

Formed:	1888
Ground:	Bescot Stadium, Bescot Crescent, Walsall, WS1 4SA
Phone:	01922 22791 **Box Office:** 01922 22791
Info:	0891 555800
Capacity:	9,000
Colours:	Red and white halved shirts, white shorts, black socks with red tops and white trim
Nickname:	The Saddlers
Manager:	Jan Sorensen
Honours:	Division 4 Champions 1959-60.
Managers:	Ray Train 1988-89, John Barnwell 1989-90, Paul Taylor 1990, Kenny Hibbitt 1990-94, Chris Nicholl 1994-97.
Previous Names:	Walsall Swifts (1877) and Walsall Town (1879). Shifts and Town merged to played as Walsall Town Swifts until 1895.
Record League Win:	10-0 v Darwen, D2, 4/3/1899
Record League Defeat:	0-12 v Small Heath, D2, 17/12/1892
	0-12 v Darwen, D2, 26/12/1896
Most GF in Season:	102 – Division 4, 1959-60
All-time League Apps:	467 – Colin Harrison, 1964-82
All-time League Goals:	184 – Tony Richards, 1954-63
Most Goals in a Season:	40 – Gilbert Alsop, D3N, 1933-34, 1934-35

Most Goals in a Match: 5 – Johnny Devlin v Torquay United (h), D3S, 1/9/49
5 – Gilbert Alsop v Carlisle Utd (a), D3N, 2/2/35
5 – W. Evans v Mansfield Town, 5/10/35 (7-0)
Record Fee Received: £600,000 from West Ham U. for David Kelly, 8/88
Record Fee Paid: £175,000 to Birmingham City for Alan Buckley, 6/79
Record Attendance: 10,628 England 'B' v Switzerland, 20/5/91 (Bescot)
25,433 v Newcastle U., D2, 29/8/61 (Fellows Park)

Stats File

Division	P	W	D	L	F	A	Pts	Yr	B	W
Division 1n/2:	372	112	84	176	580	746	313	11	6	24
Division 2n/3:	1334	495	350	489	1808	1764	1538	29	2	24
Division 3n/4:	352	159	94	99	567	434	499	8	1	16

Cup Records	P	W	D	L	F	A
FA Cup:	217	98	48	71	341	291
League Cup:	111	42	21	48	143	165
A/F Members Cup:	44	19	4	21	70	69

Sequence	Games	Start		End
Winning Run:	7	4-Nov-33	to	25-Dec-33
Without Defeat:	21	6-Nov-79	to	22-Mar-80
Without Win:	18	15-Oct-88	to	4-Feb-89
Drawn Games:	5	29-Sep-79	to	13-Oct-79
	5	7-May-88	to	17-Sep-88
Without Draw:	44	6/1/1894	to	7/9/1896
Losing Run:	15	29-Oct-88	to	4-Feb-89
Clean Sheets:	6	30-Mar-59	to	14-Apr-59
	6	28-Dec-74	to	4-Feb-75
Goal Scored:	27	9-Feb-28	to	13-Oct-28
	27	6-Nov-79	to	19-Apr-80
No Goals For (5):	5	21-Apr-79	to	5-May-79
	5	5-Mar-91	to	20-Mar-91
SOS Undefeated:	13	1979-80		
SOS No Wins:	13	1938-39		

5-Year Record

	Div	P	W	D	L	F	A	Pts	Psn	
1993-94	3	42	17	9	16	48	53	60	10	
1994-95	3	42	24	11	7	75	40	83	2	Promoted
1995-96	2	46	19	12	15	60	45	69	11	
1996-97	2	46	19	10	17	54	53	67	12	
1997-98	2	46	14	12	20	43	52	54	19	

Wigan Athletic

On the Up
Ambitious Wigan Athletic announced their intentions for the season by spending £1.3m on six players just weeks after winning the Division Three Championship on goal difference from Fulham. Despite the influx of new blood, manager John Deehan's side was never in the promotion picture and had ground to make up after a run of five consecutive defeats a quarter of the way into the season. Consistency was Wigan's biggest problem with wins and losses running pretty much hand in hand throughout the season. High points in the Latics' league campaign came in the form of home wins over Fulham and Watford but away from Springfield Park Wigan had problems, with just five away-day successes.

Leading scorer for the Latics was David Lowe, whose 18 league goals is his best return from 16 years as a professional. The attack was strengthened on transfer deadline day by Oldham striker Stuart Barlow for a modest £45,000.

Wigan made progress in the FA Cup with victory at Carlisle and a late winner at home to York. Premiership Blackburn ended the run despite second-half goals from Lowe and £250,000 signing David Lee. Hopes of a good Coca-Cola Cup run were scuppered in the 1st Round by Chesterfield.

Formed:	1932
Ground:	Springfield Park, Wigan, Lancs, WN6 7BA
Phone:	01942 244433 **Box Office:** 01942 244433
Info:	0891 12 16 55
Capacity:	7,466
Colours:	Royal blue and black striped shirts, black shorts, blue socks with black tops
Nickname:	The Latics
Manager:	John Deehan
Honours:	Division 3 Champions 1995-96; Freight Rover Trophy 1984-85.
Managers:	Ray Mathias 1986-89, Bryan Hamilton 1989-93, Dave Philpotts 1993, Kenny Swain 1993-94, Graham Burrow 1994-95.
Record League Win:	7-2 v Scunthorpe Utd, D4, 12/3/82
	5-0 v Peterborough Utd, D4, 19/1/82
	5-0 v Swansea City, D3, 18/1/86
	6-1 v Swansea City, D3, 6/4/91
Record League Defeat:	0-5 v Bristol Rovers, D3, 26/2/83
	1-6 v Bristol Rovers, D3, 3/3/90
Most GF in Season:	83 – Division 3, 1985-86
All-time League Apps:	296 – Colin Methven, 1979-86
All-time League Goals:	62 – Peter Houghton, 1978-83
Most Goals in a Season:	21 – Warren Aspinall, D3, 1985-86
Most Goals in a Match:	4 – Paul Jewell v Aldershot, D3, 1/3/88

Record Fee Received: £350,000 from Coventry City for Peter Atherton, 8/91
Record Fee Paid: £350,000 to Hull City for Roy Carroll, 4/97
Record Attendance: 27,526 v Hereford United, 12/12/53

Stats File

Division	P	W	D	L	F	A	Pts	Yr	B	
Division 2n/3:	552	203	145	204	740	734	754	12	4	23
Division 3n/4:	360	157	91	112	520	447	502	8	1	19

Cup Records	P	W	D	L	F	A
FA Cup:	106	43	22	41	161	145
League Cup:	61	16	13	32	77	104
A/F Members Cup:	54	25	10	19	88	66

Sequence	Games	Start		End
Winning Run:	6	22-Feb-86	to	22-Mar-86
Without Defeat:	21	24-Oct-81	to	12-Mar-82
Without Win:	14	9-May-89	to	17-Oct-89
Drawn Games:	4	24-Nov-84	to	22-Dec-84
	4	9-May-89	to	19-Aug-89
Without Draw:	16	8-May-82	to	3-Nov-82
Losing Run:	7	6-Apr-93	to	4-May-93
Clean Sheets:	5	14-Oct-78	to	3-Nov-78
Goal Scored:	24	27-Apr-96	to	14-Dec-96
No Goals For:	4	12-Mar-83	to	2-Apr-83
	4	15-Apr-95	to	29-Apr-95
SOS Undefeated:	7	1987-88		
SOS No Wins:	11	1989-90		

5-Year Record

	Div	P	W	D	L	F	A	Pts	Psn	
1993-94	3	42	11	12	19	51	70	45	19	
1994-95	3	42	14	10	18	53	60	52	14	
1995-96	3	46	20	10	16	62	56	70	10	
1996-97	3	46	26	9	11	84	51	87	1	Promoted
1997-98	2	46	17	11	18	64	66	62	11	

Wrexham

Point Not Taken

By finishing seventh in Division Two, Wrexham were not only the most successful of the three Welsh clubs playing in England but were also just one point short of a possible return to the second highest Division for the first time in 16 years.

Brian Flynn, one of the longest serving single club managers in the Nationwide League, made a bare minimum of changes to his squad and it looked as though his loyalty would be rewarded with promotion. But the wheels came off the bid for a play-off place when the Robins went seven games without a win prior to a last-day success at bottom club Southend. It left Wrexham as one of four clubs on 70 points, the top two of which made it into the play-offs on goals scored.

Looking to emulate their run to the 6th Round of the FA Cup the previous season, the Robins' equal best achievement in that competition, Wrexham began well with 2-0 wins at Rochdale and Chester then took Wimbledon to a replay before losing at the Racecourse Ground. Star of the cup run was the long-serving Karl Connolly, who scored five of their six goals. Sheffield United terminated Wrexham's Coca-Cola Cup campaign in the 1st Round.

Formed:	1872
Ground:	Racecourse Ground, Mold Road, Wrexham, LL11 2AH
Phone:	01978 262129 **Box Office:** 01978 262129
Info:	0898 12 16 42
Capacity:	9,200
Colours:	Red shirts, white shorts with red stripe, white socks
Nickname:	The Robins
Manager:	Brian Flynn
Honours:	Division 3 Champions 1977-78; Welsh Cup Winners (23 times).
Managers:	John Neal 1968-77, Arfon Griffiths 1977-81, Mel Sutton 1981-82, Bobby Roberts 1982-85, Dixie McNeil 1985-89.
Record League Win:	10-1 v Hartlepool, D4, 3/3/62
Record League Defeat:	0-9 v Brentford, D3, 15/10/63
Most GF in Season:	106 – Division 3N, 1932-33
All-time League Apps:	592 – Arfon Griffiths, 1959-61 & 1962-79
All-time League Goals:	175 – Tommy Bamford, 1929-35
Most Goals in a Season:	44 – Tommy Bamford, D3N, 1933-34
Most Goals in a Match:	7 – A. Livingstone v Tranmere Rovers, Wartime Football League North, 25/10/43
Record Fee Received:	£800,000 from Birmingham C. for Bryan Hughes, 3/97
Record Fee Paid:	£210,000 to Liverpool for Joey Jones, 10/78
Record Attendance:	34,445 v Manchester United, FA Cup 4th Round, 26/1/57

Stats File

Division	P	W	D	L	F	A	Pts	Yr	B	W
Division 1n/2:	168	51	45	72	168	192	158	4	15	21
Division 2n/3:	828	311	230	287	1200	1175	950	18	1	23
Division 3n/4:	818	306	206	306	1243	1186	975	18	2	24

Cup Records	P	W	D	L	F	A
FA Cup:	201	84	45	72	353	317
League Cup:	104	33	22	49	134	187
A/F Members Cup:	43	16	11	16	65	62

Sequence	Games	Start		End
Winning Run:	7	4-Mar-78	to	27-Mar-78
Without Defeat:	16	3-Sep-66	to	19-Nov-66
Without Win:	14	8-Dec-23	to	8-Mar-24
	14	4-Mar-50	to	26-Aug-50
Drawn Games:	5	12-Jan-35	to	9-Feb-35
	5	29-Oct-66	to	19-Nov-66
Without Draw:	22	30-Mar-35	to	26-Oct-35
Losing Run:	9	2-Oct-63	to	30-Oct-63
Clean Sheets:	6	12-Apr-68	to	27-Apr-68
Goal Scored:	25	5-May-28	to	12-Jan-29
No Goals For:	6	4-Apr-51	to	21-Apr-51
	6	12-Sep-73	to	1-Oct-73
SOS Undefeated:	10	1928-29		
SOS No Wins:	6	1929-30		
	6	1951-52		

5-Year Record

	Div	P	W	D	L	F	A	Pts	Psn
1993-94	2	46	17	11	18	66	77	62	12
1994-95	2	46	16	15	15	65	64	63	13
1995-96	2	46	18	16	12	76	55	70	8
1996-97	2	46	17	18	11	54	50	69	8
1997-98	2	46	18	16	12	55	51	70	7

Wycombe Wanderers

Goal Blitz Start

Wycombe Wanderers' fifth season as members of the Nationwide League got off to a frantic start with goals – for and against – flying in from all directions. After just seven games Wycombe supporters had witnessed 28 goals as the Chairboys occupied a midtable position. It was a position from which John Gregory's side seldom moved because for much of the season the Blues were just below halfway.

Gregory was in his first full season at Adams Park but quit on 25 February to take up the vacant manager's role at Aston Villa. Neil Smillie stepped in firstly as caretaker manager and proved his worth with ten points from his first four games, including a season's best 5-1 win over relegatio- bound Plymouth.

Having equalled their best ever run in the FA Cup (3rd Round) the previous season, Wycombe suffered an embarrassing penalty shoot-out defeat by Basingstoke at the first hurdle this season, despite leading by two goals in the first meeting and twice in the replay. Their Coca-Cola Cup 1st Round clash with Fulham came during the high-scoring start to the season and, after losing 2-1 at home, Wycombe bowed out on the back of a 4-4 draw at Craven Cottage.

Formed:	1884
Ground:	Adams Park, Hillbottom Road, High Wycombe, Bucks, HP12 4HJ
Phone:	01494 472100 **Box Office:** 01494 441118
Info:	0891 446855
Capacity:	7,250
Nickname:	The Chairboys
Colours:	Light and dark blue quartered shirts, dark blue shorts, light blue socks
Honours:	GM Vauxhall Conference Champions 1992-93; FA Amateur Cup Winners 1930-31; FA Trophy Winners 1990-91, 1992-93.
Manager:	Neil Smillie
Managers:	Peter Suddaby 1987-88, Jim Kelman 1988-90, Martin O'Neill 1990-95, Alan Smith 1995-96, John Gregory 1996-98
Record League Win:	4-0 v Scarborough, D3, 2/11/93
Record League Defeat:	2-5 v Colchester United, D3, 18/9/93
Most GF in Season:	67 – Division 3, 1994-95
All-time League Apps:	171, Dave Carrol, 1993-97
All-time League Goals:	29 – Miguel de Souza, 1995-97
Most Goals in a Season:	18 – Miguel de Souza, 1995-96
Most Goals in a Match:	3 – Miguel de Souza v Bradford, 2/9/95
Record Fee Received:	£375,000 from Swindon Town for Keith Scott, 11/93
Record Fee Paid:	£140,000 to Birmingham City for Steve McGavin, 3/95
Record Attendance:	9,007 v West Ham U, FA Cup 3rd Round, 7/1/95

Stats File

Division	P	W	D	L	F	A	Pts	Yr	B	W
Division 2n/3:	184	65	58	61	225	214	253	4	6	18
Division 3n/4:	42	19	13	10	67	53	70	1	4	4

Cup Records	P	W	D	L	F	A
FA Cup:	69	18	21	30	87	102
League Cup:	16	5	4	7	21	25
A/F Members Cup:	13	6	3	4	16	21

Sequence	Games	Start		End
Winning Run:	4	26-Feb-94	to	19-Mar-94
Without Defeat:	14	29-Aug-95	to	18-Nov-95
Without Win:	10	4-May-96	to	28-Sep-96
Drawn Games:	4	16-Sep-95	to	7-Oct-95
Without Draw:	14	1-Jan-94	to	29-Mar-94
Losing Run (6):	3	12-Oct-96	to	19-Oct-96
	3	19-Nov-96	to	30-Nov-96
Clean Sheets:	4	13-Aug-94	to	30-Aug-94
Goal Scored:	11	29-Mar-94	to	20-Aug-94
No Goals For:	5	11-Mar-95	to	25-Mar-95
	5	15-Oct-96	to	2-Nov-96
SOS Undefeated:	6	1993-94		
SOS No Wins:	9	1996-97		

5-Year Record

	Div	P	W	D	L	F	A	Pts	Psn	
1993-94	3	42	19	13	10	67	53	70	4	Promoted
1994-95	2	46	21	15	10	60	46	78	6	
1995-96	2	46	15	15	16	63	59	60	12	
1996-97	2	46	15	10	21	51	56	55	18	
1997-98	2	46	14	18	14	51	53	60	14	

York City

No Cup Glory
Given the exceptional giant cup killings enjoyed by York City in recent years, this season will be seen as a disappointing one for the Bootham Crescent club. Alan Little's side increased their points tally, by seven, on the previous season but could make scant progress in the cup competitions.

With the small crowds that York attract, Little's moves in the transfer market were limited. His first signing of the season to cost a fee did not arrive until January when Barry Jones moved from Wrexham for £35,000. That figure was swamped into insignificance when 19-year-old Jonathan Greening signed for Manchester United in a deal which could ultimately earn the Minstermen £1m. Greening started in just six games before his move.

York lost their first two games of the season but recovered well to be in third place by early November, thanks in the main to a good record at Bootham Crescent. Unfortunately it was form that they failed to maintain and they ended the season in 16th place.

In the FA Cup, Southport were beaten 4-0 but a 2nd Round defeat was suffered at Wigan. After a good win over Port Vale in the Coca-Cola Cup, York were put out by Oxford United.

Formed:	1922
Ground:	Bootham Crescent, York, YO3 7AQ
Phone:	01904 624447 **Box Office:** 01904 624447
Info:	0891 12 16 48
Capacity:	9,534
Colours:	Red shirts with white flash, navy blue shorts, red socks
Nickname:	The Minstermen
Manager:	Alan Little
Honours:	Division 4 Champions 1983-84.
Managers:	Barry Lyons 198-81, Denis Smith 1982-87, Bobby Saxton 1987-88, John Bird 1988-91, John Ward 1991-93.
Record League Win:	9-1 v Southport, D3N, 2/2/57
Record League Defeat:	0-12 v Chester, D3N, 1/2/36
Most GF in Season:	96 – Division 4, 1983-84
All-time League Apps:	481 – Barry Jackson, 1958-70
All-time League Goals:	127 – Norman Wilkinson, 1954-66
Most Goals in a Season:	31 – Bill Fenton, D3N, 1951-52, 31 – Arthur Bottom, D3N, 1954-55 and 1955-56
Most Goals in a Match:	5 – Alf Patrick v Rotherham United, D3, 20/11/48
Record Fee Received:	£1m from Manchester Utd for Jonathan Greening, 3/98

Record Fee Paid: £140,000 to Burnley for Adrian Randall, 12/95
Record Attendance: 28,123 v Huddersfield Town, FA Cup 6th Round, 5/3/38

Stats File

Division	P	W	D	L	F	A	Pts	Yr	B	W
Division 1n/2:	84	24	18	42	90	126	66	2	15	21
Division 2n/3:	690	220	185	285	864	993	767	15	3	24
Division 3n/4:	1048	392	263	393	1505	1423	1187	23	1	24

Cup Records	P	W	D	L	F	A
FA Cup:	201	79	55	67	295	277
League Cup:	110	34	29	47	137	170
A/F Members Cup:	39	13	9	17	51	53

Sequence	Games	Start		End
Winning Run:	7	31-Oct-64	to	26-Dec-64
Without Defeat:	21	10-Sep-73	to	12-Jan-74
Without Win:	17	4-May-87	to	24-Oct-87
Drawn Games:	6	26-Dec-92	to	22-Jan-93
Without Draw:	22	11-Jan-69	to	2-May-69
Losing Run:	8	14-Nov-66	to	31-Dec-66
Clean Sheets:	11	1-Oct-73	to	8-Dec-73
Goal Scored:	24	1-Dec-62	to	15-May-63
	24	3-Mar-84	to	2-Oct-84
No Goals For:	7	28-Aug-72	to	26-Sep-72
SOS Undefeated:	8	1984-85		
SOS No Wins:	15	1987-88		

5-Year Record

	Div	P	W	D	L	F	A	Pts	Psn
1993-94	2	46	21	12	13	64	40	75	5
1994-95	2	46	21	9	16	67	51	72	9
1995-96	2	46	13	13	20	58	73	52	20
1996-97	2	46	13	13	20	47	68	52	20
1997-98	2	46	14	17	15	52	58	59	16

Division 2 All-Time Table

The table lists the total records of all clubs who have played in what is now Division 2. It incorporates the records of the former Division 3. Yrs=Number of years (seasons) in the division. H=Highest position achieved. L=Lowest position.

Team	P	W	D	L	F	A	Pts	Yrs	H	L
Bournemouth	1334	495	368	471	1686	1658	1580	29	1	21
Bristol R.	1196	493	320	383	1770	1549	1574	26	1	19
Walsall	1334	495	350	489	1808	1764	1538	29	2	24
Brentford	1242	459	336	447	1705	1656	1533	27	1	23
Reading	1196	471	296	429	1779	1722	1422	26	1	21
Gillingham	1104	411	308	385	1462	1422	1320	24	4	24
Plymouth Arg.	1012	378	276	358	1415	1345	1200	22	1	22
Shrewsbury T.	1150	394	326	430	1611	1639	1193	25	1	22
Chesterfield	1058	376	269	413	1332	1389	1156	23	4	24
Rotherham U.	1012	349	278	385	1256	1312	1131	22	1	23
Bury	920	347	246	327	1277	1163	1075	20	1	22
Port Vale	920	336	255	329	1240	1237	1047	20	2	23
Swindon T.	874	358	237	279	1315	1101	1016	19	1	22
Southend U.	966	330	248	388	1313	1437	1015	21	2	24
Mansfield T.	966	327	263	376	1278	1382	995	21	1	24
Bristol C.	690	301	173	216	1085	866	976	15	2	23
Hull C.	782	312	207	263	1151	1038	952	17	1	24
Preston NE	782	284	200	298	1019	1066	951	17	1	23
Wrexham	828	311	230	287	1200	1175	950	18	1	23
Bradford C.	736	269	192	275	1022	1059	902	16	1	24
Brighton & HA	782	298	209	275	1065	987	887	17	2	23
Swansea	736	242	198	296	922	1083	827	16	3	24
Grimsby T.	736	291	185	260	1031	950	822	16	1	23
Notts Co.	644	256	169	219	926	874	815	14	2	24
Peterborough U.	736	273	206	257	1074	1048	810	16	4	21
Watford	690	281	199	210	998	845	801	15	1	23
Blackpool	644	220	174	250	860	890	792	14	3	23
Fulham	598	224	171	203	800	751	784	13	2	21
York C.	690	220	185	285	864	993	767	15	3	24
Oxford U.	598	236	171	191	826	721	757	13	1	18

Team										
Wigan A.	552	203	145	204	740	734	754	12	4	23
Huddersfield T.	552	217	148	187	753	674	750	12	3	24
Tranmere R.	736	242	213	281	980	1028	743	16	4	23
Chester C.	690	203	191	296	737	960	705	15	5	24
Leyton O.	598	201	154	243	733	834	693	13	1	24
Bolton W.	506	200	134	172	667	590	692	11	1	21
Millwall	552	212	154	186	736	714	684	12	2	21
Exeter C.	598	179	165	254	759	936	611	13	8	24
Colchester U.	644	211	182	251	876	1000	604	14	5	23
Stockport Co.	460	180	116	164	642	592	602	10	2	24
Burnley	414	148	121	145	580	532	547	9	1	21
Newport Co.	506	161	130	215	684	801	537	11	4	24
Barnsley	552	183	159	210	736	838	525	12	2	24
Halifax T.	552	179	162	211	697	826	520	12	3	24
Carlisle U.	460	156	125	179	589	642	494	10	1	23
QPR	414	188	98	128	782	601	474	9	1	15
Northampton T.	414	150	110	154	605	557	473	9	1	22
Oldham A.	460	171	112	177	655	663	469	10	1	24
Lincoln C.	414	132	122	160	535	587	468	9	4	24
Doncaster R.	460	133	110	217	530	764	453	10	11	24
Torquay U.	414	145	103	166	537	592	406	9	4	23
Crewe Alex.	322	119	71	132	433	461	404	7	3	23
Cardiff C.	322	107	88	127	405	460	387	7	2	22
Portsmouth	276	108	80	88	366	331	337	6	1	24
Luton T.	276	110	76	90	397	364	331	6	2	21
Sheffield U.	230	100	49	81	366	300	317	5	2	21
Cambridge U.	276	95	65	116	363	414	314	6	1	24
Crystal Palace	276	113	86	77	419	332	312	6	2	15
Birmingham C.	184	82	55	47	258	197	301	4	1	12
Blackburn R.	230	104	59	67	299	249	267	5	1	13
Wycombe W.	184	65	58	61	225	214	253	4	6	18
Coventry C.	230	93	66	71	403	347	252	5	1	15
Scunthorpe U.	276	81	72	123	346	444	243	6	4	24
Sheffield Wed.	230	83	76	71	297	266	242	5	3	20
Stoke C.	138	64	38	36	197	142	230	3	1	14
Rochdale	276	68	84	124	310	438	220	6	9	24
Aldershot T.	230	69	56	105	289	342	216	5	8	24
Charlton A.	184	83	39	62	274	245	205	4	3	14
Hartlepool U.	184	51	51	82	180	274	194	4	11	23
Hereford U.	184	65	54	65	237	238	184	4	1	23
Wimbledon	138	50	34	54	210	232	174	3	2	24
Darlington	184	45	47	92	209	326	169	4	13	24
Southport	184	54	51	79	219	277	159	4	8	23

WBA	92	44	24	24	152	103	156	2	4	7
Derby Co.	92	42	28	22	145	95	154	2	3	7
Middlesbrough	92	51	19	22	154	94	149	2	2	2
Wolverhampton	92	37	24	31	153	147	135	2	1	23
Workington	138	48	33	57	180	215	129	3	5	24
Aston Villa	92	51	21	20	139	78	123	2	1	4
Barrow	138	46	30	62	167	210	122	3	8	23
Norwich C.	92	46	24	22	171	116	116	2	2	4
Southampton	92	43	20	29	194	155	106	2	1	14
Sunderland	46	27	12	7	92	48	93	1	1	1
Bradford PA	92	34	19	39	159	175	87	2	11	21
Accrington S.	92	26	17	49	128	210	69	2	19	24
Rotherham T.	46	14	14	18	54	62	56	1	16	16

NATIONWIDE LEAGUE DIVISION 3

Final Table 1997-98

Pn	Team	P	W	D	L	F	A	Pts		FA	LC
1	Notts County	46	29	12	5	82	43	99	P	2	2
2	Macclesfield Town	46	23	13	10	63	44	82	P	2	1
3	Lincoln City	46	20	15	11	60	51	75	P	2	1
4	Colchester United	46	21	11	14	72	60	74	P	2	1
5	Torquay United	46	21	11	14	68	59	74		2	2
6	Scarborough	46	19	15	12	67	58	72		1	1
7	Barnet	46	19	13	14	61	51	70		1	2
8	Scunthorpe United	46	19	12	15	56	52	69		3	2
9	Rotherham United	46	16	19	11	67	61	67		3	1
10	Peterborough United	46	18	13	15	63	51	67		3	2
11	Leyton Orient	46	19	12	15	62	47	66		1	2
12	Mansfield Town	46	16	17	13	64	55	65		1	1
13	Shrewsbury Town	46	16	13	17	61	62	61		1	1
14	Chester City	46	17	10	19	60	61	61		2	1
15	Exeter City	46	15	15	16	68	63	60		1	1
16	Cambridge United	46	14	18	14	63	57	60		2	1
17	Hartlepool United	46	12	23	11	61	53	59		1	1
18	Rochdale	46	17	7	22	56	55	58		1	1
19	Darlington	46	14	12	20	56	72	54		3	1
20	Swansea City	46	13	11	22	49	62	50		1	1
21	Cardiff City	46	9	23	14	48	52	50		4	1
22	Hull City	46	11	8	27	56	83	41		1	3
23	Brighton & HA	46	6	17	23	38	66	35		1	1
24	Doncaster Rovers	46	4	8	34	30	113	20	R	1	1

Play-Off Semi-Finals

Barnet v Colchester United	1-0	1-3	2-3 on aggregate
Scarborough v Torquay United	1-3	1-4	2-7 on aggregate

Final

Colchester United v Torquay United   1-0

				HOME					*AWAY*				
		P	W	D	L	F	A	W	D	L	F	A	Pts
1	Notts County	46	14	7	2	41	20	15	5	3	41	23	99
2	Macclesfield Town	46	19	4	0	40	11	4	9	10	23	33	82
3	Lincoln City	46	11	7	5	32	24	9	8	6	28	27	75
4	Colchester United	46	14	5	4	41	24	7	6	10	31	36	74
5	Torquay United	46	14	4	5	39	22	7	7	9	29	37	74
6	Scarborough	46	14	6	3	44	23	5	9	9	23	35	72
7	Barnet	46	10	8	5	35	22	9	5	9	26	29	70
8	Scunthorpe United	46	11	7	5	30	24	8	5	10	26	28	69
9	Rotherham United	46	10	9	4	41	30	6	10	7	26	31	67
10	Peterborough United	46	13	6	4	37	16	5	7	11	26	35	67
11	Leyton Orient	46	14	5	4	40	20	5	7	11	22	27	66
12	Mansfield Town	46	11	9	3	42	26	5	8	10	22	29	65
13	Shrewsbury Town	46	12	3	8	35	28	4	10	9	26	34	61
14	Chester City	46	12	7	4	34	15	5	3	15	26	46	61
15	Exeter City	46	10	8	5	39	25	5	7	11	29	38	60
16	Cambridge United	46	11	8	4	39	27	3	10	10	24	30	60
17	Hartlepool United	46	10	12	1	40	22	2	11	10	21	31	59
18	Rochdale	46	15	3	5	43	15	2	4	17	13	40	58
19	Darlington	46	13	6	4	43	28	1	6	16	13	44	54
20	Swansea City	46	8	8	7	24	16	5	3	15	25	46	50
21	Cardiff City	46	5	13	5	27	22	4	10	9	21	30	50
22	Hull City	46	10	6	7	36	32	1	2	20	20	51	41
23	Brighton & HA	46	3	10	10	21	34	3	7	13	17	32	35
24	Doncaster Rovers	46	3	3	17	14	48	1	5	17	16	65	20

Season Review

August

Nationwide League new boys Macclesfield Town enjoy a successful start to their Football League life on the 9th as goals from the debut-making Efetobore Sodje and Richard Landon give Sammy McIlroy's side a 2-1 victory over a Torquay United side tipped by the bookies for a season of struggle. Joint pre-season favourites for the title, Cardiff City, collect all three points and their first win at Leyton Orient for 22 years, through a Carl Dale goal. Beaten play-off finalists Swansea City make a winning start with victory over expected strugglers Brighton & Hove Albion. Ronnie Moore's reign as manager of relegated Rotherham United starts badly with Barnet winning 3-2 at Millmoor after two late goals. Former Bees boss Barry Fry is less successful as Peterborough United lose at home to Scunthorpe United, while the two remaining relegated clubs, Shrewsbury Town and Notts County, both win 2-1 at home. Former England striker Mark Hateley finds the going tough as Hull City manager with the Tigers beaten 2-0 at Mansfield Town.

Doncaster are the first Division Three side in Coca-Cola action on the 11th and their exit is imminent after going down 8-0 at home to Nottingham Forest, but there are some encouraging results the following night. Iyseden Christie hits a four-minute hat-trick as Mansfield beat the previous season's heroes Stockport 4-2 at Field Mill. Torquay gain a surprise victory at Bournemouth while Peterborough hold Portsmouth to a 2-2 draw. Both sides finish the match with ten men following a 21-man mêlée. Cambridge United and Lincoln City also draw at home to higher league opposition while Shrewsbury gain an excellent draw at Brentford. In three all-Division Three clashes only Scunthorpe win, at Scarborough. Brighton and Orient keep the sequence going on the 13th with a 1-1 draw.

After the second round of league games on the 18th, only two clubs, Notts County and Scunthorpe, have maximum points. County win 3-0 at Hull while United hand Orient their second 1-0 reversal. Three sides are on four points: Hartlepool who defeat Colchester with Joe Allon scoring twice, Exeter who gain a notable victory at Barnet and Macclesfield following a draw at Brighton's Priestfield Stadium lodgings. Four sides are still pointless, including Hull, who have already conceded five goals but still attracted a gate of 7,412, the biggest Division Three gate of the day by over 4,000. Doncaster Rovers' internal problems come to the fore as they crash 5-0 at home to Peterborough and manager Kerry Dixon becomes the first casualty of the season as administrators announce he is leaving by mutual consent. Rovers' poor run continues on the 25th with a 3-0 defeat at Macclesfield who now top the table. Mark Weaver steps in to replace Dixon as general manager. Victory, albeit from a Darren Rowbotham penalty, for Exeter against pointless Darlington lifts the Devon club into second place. Notts County suffer a surprise defeat when Lincoln win at Meadow Lane for the first time in 104 years. Referee Phil Richards is attacked by a spectator after sending off County player Devon White and moments later allowing a disputed Lincoln winner to stand. Hull suffer a third defeat and are still goalless after going down 2-0 at Peterborough. Rotherham record their first successes as do Orient who benefit from visitors Rochdale having two players controversially dismissed for infringements inside the penalty area, which allow Dean Smith to score twice. Torquay rise to fifth thanks to two Rodney Jack goals at Shrewsbury. Scunthorpe's winning start flounders at Vetch Field as Swansea maintain maximum points to two games.

Coca-Cola Cup glory comes the way of several Division Three sides on the 26th with pride of place going to Barnet who, at one stage, trail 3-1 on aggregate to Norwich before putting the First Division side out with three goals in 12 minutes, including two for Sean Devine. Peterborough snatch a dramatic 2-1 (4-3 aggregate) win at Division One strugglers Portsmouth and an extra-time equaliser by Rodney Jack hands Torquay a 2-1 aggregate victory over Bournemouth. Most disappointed player on the night is Shrewsbury's Lee Steele, who claims a hat-trick, but Brentford still go through 6-4 overall. Mansfield cause immense problems for Stockport but eventually bow out 8-7 on aggregate as County strike twice in the final three minutes. Hartlepool beat Tranmere on the night but still go out as do Colchester and Swansea despite drawing with Luton and Reading respectively. The following night, Cambridge take West Brom to extra time before going down 3-2 over two legs. Doncaster limit the aggregate damage against Nottingham Forest to 10-1.

On the penultimate day of the month Exeter take pole position with a 1-0 win at Doncaster but most attention is focused on Boothferry Park where Hull not only score their first goals of the season but put seven past Swansea – who score four themselves – with Duane Darby scoring a hat-trick. There are also seven goals at the Abbey Stadium where Paul Wanless scores twice in Cambridge's 4-3 win over Shrewsbury. And at Sincil Bank, Lincoln's Gareth Ainsworth scores all his side's three goals in a draw with Scarborough. A third consecutive league win for Peterborough, at Rochdale's expense, lifts them into second place ahead of Scunthorpe, 1-0 winners over Mansfield, but only by virtue of goals scored. Macclesfield protect their unbeaten start with a draw at Hartlepool but slip to fourth. Doncaster go bottom as the only club still without a point.

September

Exeter maintain their flying start on the 2nd with two Rowbotham goals clinching a derby victory at Torquay, and Scunthorpe stay just a point behind with two John Eyre goals accounting for Chester City. Macclesfield, at Rochdale, suffer their first defeat, while Cardiff, although only drawing at home with Shrewsbury, retain one of just two unbeaten records in the division. Orient add to Doncaster's miserable start with a 4-1 win at Belle Vue and Cambridge match that result courtesy of the visit of Colchester. Jan Molby's Swansea lose their second away match, going down 2-0 at Barnet. Mansfield score their first away goals with an impressive 2-0 success at Lincoln. Brighton confirm that David Bellotti's reign as chief executive is over with Dick Knight taking charge of the club. A crowd of just 1,215 celebrate the news as Albion draw at home with Peterborough.

Five matches are brought forward to Friday 6th due to the funeral on the following day of Diana, Princess of Wales. Cambridge dislodge Exeter at the top with a 2-0 win over Orient while Swansea climb to eighth with a third successive home win. Macclesfield also retain their winning streak at Moss Rose with victory over Darlington who are joined on one point by Doncaster, following a welcome draw at Mansfield. Hull are still looking for their first away point and goal after a 1-0 reverse at Chester.

On the Sunday the leadership changes hands again as Barry Fry takes delight in watching his Peterborough side smash Barnet for five at London Road. Veteran Jimmy Quinn claims a hat-trick including one goal from 40 yards. Notts County are just two points off the top and one behind Scunthorpe after beating United.

Swansea miss out on an opportunity to move into fourth place on the 9th as they lose 3-2 at Darlington after leading 2-0; Glenn Naylor scores twice for the Quakers in the final three minutes. Steve Flack's last-minute equaliser against Cardiff is enough to take Exeter back to the top. Colchester leapfrog Scunthorpe on the 13th thanks to Tony Lock's late goal. Notts County are given a warning by the FA as to their future conduct following the recent physical attack on a referee.

Peterborough have to come from behind to save a point at Rotherham on the Saturday but it is enough for them to reclaim the summit ahead of Macclesfield who sweep Swansea aside 3-0. Exeter are toppled due to Carl Griffiths' fifth goal of the season for Orient. Biggest crowd of the day is at Meadow Lane where Notts County move into third place with a 1-0 win over Mansfield. Barnet end Cambridge's good run with a 3-1 success at the Abbey Stadium while Hartlepool, four draws from their first six matches, beat Torquay 3-0 with three goals in ten minutes. Darlington take a point from Brighton despite playing for over an hour with ten men.

Chester, on the 16th, clinch their first away points of the season and end Cardiff's unbeaten home record with two early strikes at Ninian Park. Seven sides are engaged in Coca-Cola Cup ties, Hull pulling off the biggest upset with Darby's goal clinching victory over Premiership Crystal Palace. Torquay, at Ipswich, and Peterborough, at Reading, record highly creditable draws while Barnet go down by just one goal at Middlesbrough as do Scunthorpe at home to Everton. Notts County and Orient are on the brink of defeat after home losses against Tranmere and Bolton.

Peterborough, Notts County and Exeter match each other step for step at the top of the table at the weekend with victories over Shrewsbury and Rotherham respectively. All three sides have 17 points from eight matches. Swansea's slump continues with a home defeat against Colchester but Doncaster are surprisingly celebrating their third point of the season following a goalless draw with Cambridge.

All four Division Three clubs playing 2nd Round 2nd Leg Coca-Cola Cup matches on the 23rd go out. The only goal for the quartet to celebrate is teenager Craig Dudley's winner at Tranmere but Notts County still bow out 2-1 on aggregate. Barnet are defeated 2-0 at home by Middlesbrough. Peterborough do likewise against Reading and Torquay lose 3-0 at Plainmoor to Ipswich.

Notts County and Exeter continue to set the pace on the 27th with fine away wins which end the unbeaten home records of Scarborough and Colchester. The latter have David Greene sent off. Scunthorpe are third following a 2-0 win over bottom but one Hull while high flying Macclesfield and Peterborough share the spoils at Moss Rose. Brighton enjoy their first success of the season with Mark Morris scoring against Rochdale on his 500th league appearance. Hull close the month in style by doubling their aggregate Coca-Cola Cup lead over Crystal Palace and, despite eventually losing 2-1 after extra time, go through on the away goals rule. Seven different players get on the scoresheet as Leyton Orient draw 4-4 at Bolton but lose the tie 7-5 on aggregate.

October

Scunthorpe join the exodus from the Coca-Cola Cup on the opening day of the month with a 5-0 defeat at Everton and the Irons have little to smile about at the weekend when they have Michael Walsh dismissed during a 2-0 defeat at Rochdale. Home draws by Exeter and Notts County, with Scarborough and Darlington, allow Peterborough to join the top two on 21 points by completing a 3-1 win over Swansea, which includes another brace for Quinn. Darlington boss David Hodgson is ordered from the dug-out after an altercation with a linesman. Of 12 games played seven finish all square with the most unlikely draw coming at Boothferry Park where Torquay stun Hull by grabbing a point after being three down. Chester also come from behind to move into sixth spot with a 3-1 win over Hartlepool.

A run of six defeats in eight games paves the way for Jan Molby's dismissal as manager of Swansea on the 8th, and the following day the Swans appoint former Fulham boss Micky Adams as Molby's replacement. Hull sign David Rocastle on a three-month loan from Chelsea.

On the day England qualify for the World Cup, Peterborough – the division's leading scorers by nine goals – win a thrilling five-goal clash with Colchester to stay level on points at the top with Exeter who get Adams' stint as Swansea manager off to a losing start. Peterborough's tenth league match without defeat coincides with tenth goals of the season for Martin Carruthers and Quinn. Notts County have goalkeeper Darren Ward to thank for taking a point off Macclesfield, a result which allows Chester to move within three points of the top three after seeing off Brighton 2-0. Doncaster have to settle for a point after leading 2-0 against Hartlepool and are already four points adrift from the rest of the table. Bottom but one Darlington are thrashed 5-0 at Rochdale, for whom Robbie Painter and David Lancaster both score twice. Hull show signs of staging a revival with a 3-0 victory over Scarborough but their interest in the Coca-Cola Cup expires on the 15th in front of 35,856 spectators at St James's Park as two second-half goals take Newcastle through to the 4th Round. And Hull's fortunes dip again at the weekend when a 2-0 defeat at Barnet, in conjunction with Darlington's 5-1 thrashing of Doncaster, leaves the Tigers just one rung from the foot of the ladder. At the summit, there appears to be nothing to stop Peterborough and Exeter as the top two both win 3-1 at Scarborough and Brighton respectively. Boro boss Mick Wadsworth offers to stand down after the game but his resignation is refused. Swansea succumb to a sixth defeat in seven after leading against third-placed Notts County. Troubled Doncaster have a new manager as Dave Cowling takes charge.

The leading pair are finally stopped in their tracks on the 21st but a draw for Exeter at Macclesfield after leading 2-0 is sufficient for the Grecians to move a point clear of Peterborough. The Posh become the seventh visiting side to fail to win at Hartlepool and Notts County's bid to claim top spot is thwarted by Andy Hayward's last-minute equaliser for Rotherham. Torquay leave it equally late before taking a home point off Orient. Scarborough are the day's biggest winners – 4-1 over a Chester side which has lost six of its seven away games. Swansea, at home to Mansfield, lose again. Of the 11 games played that night, seven clubs record their lowest home attendance of the season to date. Two European matches are live on television at the same time. And barely a thousand people are at Priestfield the following night to witness Lincoln rising to fourth place with a 1-0 win over Brighton.

Micky Adams complains of a lack of funds at Swansea and quits after just 13 days in charge. His assistant Alan Cork is appointed manager.

Swansea end their nightmare run of sixth consecutive away defeats on the Friday with a 3-0 win at Doncaster. The following day sees Peterborough return to winning ways with a 2-0 home success over Torquay but Exeter suffer their first home defeat of the campaign as David D'Auria clinches a 3-2 win for Scunthorpe. Carruthers and Quinn again do the damage for the Posh. Notts County seize the chance to take second place with a single goal triumph over Cambridge and Lincoln consolidate in fourth place with Lee Thorpe scoring twice in a 3-1 win over Darlington. Mansfield's recovery is halted by fast-improving Barnet who win 2-1 at Field Mill after falling behind. Chester are still undefeated at the Deva Stadium following a 1-1 draw with Macclesfield, their fifth draw from seven away games. Quite amazingly, 5,686 turn up to see struggling Hull and Brighton draw a blank.

Dave Cowling serves the fifth shortest managerial term in Football League history as he steps down at Doncaster after ten days, citing interference. Danny Bergara steps in as caretaker.

November

On the 1st just under 6,000 spectators see the top two, Exeter and Peterborough, finish goalless at St James's Park. Notts County are quick to pounce and with their fifth away win of the season, at Barnet, move to the summit. Lincoln and Scarborough stay in contention with wins over Orient and Doncaster. The most exciting encounter of the afternoon is at Feethams where two sides inside the bottom four, Darlington and Hull, find the net seven times, with the Quakers' Darren Roberts scoring the decider. Rochdale still have just one point from eight away games following a 4-0 drubbing at Chester. Hartlepool, at home to Brighton, draw for the ninth time in 15 games. Macclesfield slip to tenth with defeat at Rotherham. In the Welsh derby on the Sunday, Cardiff have Scott Young sent off inside 14 minutes on their way to a 1-0 home defeat against Swansea.

A series of remarkable results on the 4th see only Chester of the sides in the top 11 win and their success at Notts County, secured by Gary Bennett's 87th-minute goal, lifts them to fifth. Peterborough, although held at home by Shrewsbury, reclaim top spot while Exeter are surprisingly defeated by lowly Hull. Lincoln can only draw at Rochdale as can Scunthorpe at home to Cambridge but Scarborough go down at Orient. Swansea's revival ends with a home defeat by Hartlepool. The following night Barnet move to within five points of the top with a 3-0 victory at Brighton.

Again the leading clubs struggle to pick up points on the 8th which allows Macclesfield, 3-1 winners over Cambridge, to climb to seventh. Peterborough can manage no better than a point from the visit of Darlington and the big showdown at Meadow Lane between Notts County and Exeter also ends all square after Rowbotham puts the visitors ahead before Gary Strodder ensures equality. Even more unexpected than Peterborough's slip is Barnet's draw with Doncaster at Underhill. Lincoln hang on to fourth place with a draw at Swansea and Shrewsbury follow up their good draw at Peterborough with an emphatic 4-1 victory at Hull. Brighton celebrate their first goal for seven and a half hours but still lose to Rotherham.

In amongst some disappointing FA Cup 1st Round results on the 15th, Torquay pull off an outstanding 1-0 win at Luton through Paul Gibbs' second-half penalty. Cambridge, Colchester, Exeter, Mansfield, Rotherham and Shrewsbury all draw with higher league opposition while Cardiff, Darlington, Lincoln – who have Mark Hone dismissed after just eight minutes – and Orient, are all held by non-league clubs. Definitely through are Chester, Macclesfield – 4-2 winners at Hartlepool – Scunthorpe, who beat Scarborough 2-1, and on the Sunday Notts County. But there are two embarrassing casualties. Brighton lose at Hereford in one of the most intriguing ties and Hull are put out 2-0 at home by Hednesford. Doncaster put up a brave fight before going down 3-2 at Preston.

A full programme of matches on the 18th finishes with just one point separating the top four sides. Peterborough lead after taking a point from the Deva Stadium but Notts County miss out when losing 2-0 at Colchester. Exeter surge back into contention with victory over Mansfield taking Peter Fox's side into second place. Lincoln strengthen their position with a laboured 2-1 win over Doncaster. Scunthorpe's good week continues with three points taken from a trip to Rotherham but the player with most to celebrate is Shrewsbury striker Devon White who scores a hat-trick during a 4-3 win over Macclesfield. Hull lose again, this time presenting Cardiff with their second home win of the season.

The leadership changes hands again on the penultimate weekend of the month thanks to Peterborough drawing at home for the third successive match, this time with Mansfield, and Lincoln winning at Colchester. Exeter's problems in winning at St James's Park again cost them dear as Shrewsbury continue their good run with a 2-2 draw. Notts County are down to fourth following a 1-1 draw at Orient but Scunthorpe, helped by two Alex Calvo-Garcia goals, win 4-2 at Torquay. Hartlepool's 2-0 win over Barnet, on the back of a brace from Jon Cullen, lifts them above the Bees into sixth position. Rochdale, one point from nine away games, record their first away success not too surprisingly at Doncaster. Swansea's problems pile up, with the latest setback being the postponement of their match with Chester due to a failure to complete certain safety works.

Cambridge and Rotherham are the toast of Division Three on the 25th following outstanding FA Cup replay victories. Cambridge, 14 games without a win, come from two down to beat Plymouth 3-2 with a Paul Wilson penalty in extra time at the Abbey Stadium. Rotherham's success is decisive as Burnley are turfed out 3-0 in Lancashire. Colchester also beat Division Two opposition but it is a case of keeping their nerve as the Us win a penalty shoot-out. Cardiff are taken to extra time before seeing off Slough Town 3-2 at Ninian Park and Lincoln, three up inside 18 minutes at Gainsborough, scrape through 3-2. Exeter fall to a late goal at Northampton, Mansfield are put out by Oldham and Shrewsbury are well beaten 4-0 at Grimsby. Orient suffer the humiliation of losing at home to non-leaguers Hendon. The following night 2,000 cram into Solihull's tiny ground and see the non-league side evenly share six goals with Darlington before succumbing in a penalty shoot-out. Chester and Swansea finally face each other in the league with Chester winning 2-0 at the Deva Stadium.

Chester stretch their unbeaten home run to 11 games on the 29th with a 1-1 draw with Exeter and the three sides surrounding the Grecians also draw. Leaders Lincoln are held by Macclesfield while Peterborough take a point from Notts County in front of a gate of 8,006 at Meadow Lane. Boosted by their cup success, Cambridge end their lean league run with a 2-0 win over Hartlepool and there are also wins for lowly sides Swansea, at Shrewsbury, Brighton at Scunthorpe and Hull at home to Doncaster. Rovers are now nine points adrift and, providing they survive their financial difficulties, already seem certain to drop out of the league come May.

December

Danny Bergara is the latest manager to say farewell to Doncaster, and Mark Weaver is back in the hottest seat in football. Weaver weaves some magic as Rovers, at the 21st attempt, win a league match for the first time this season on the 2nd with Chester defeated 2-1 at Belle Vue. Sadly, only 864 people can be bothered to watch the match. At the top of the table, Lincoln bolster their position with a 2-1 win at Exeter after the Devon club take an early lead. Quinn's winner five minutes from time against Cambridge moves Peterborough four points clear of Exeter in second place. Victory for Barnet would take them into third place but the Bees lose 2-0 to Orient.

Four Division Three sides are through to the 3rd Round of the FA Cup following 2nd Round ties on the 6th. Rotherham, after a goalless first half, progress with a 6-0 thrashing of Kings Lynn while Cardiff, Darlington and Peterborough also dispose of sides from the pyramid. Lincoln require eight minutes of injury time to gain only a draw at home to non-league opposition, a fate which also befalls Cambridge, Colchester and Scunthorpe. Torquay do well to hold Watford and Notts County achieve a creditable draw at Preston. The only casualty is Macclesfield as their unbeaten home record disappears under an avalanche as Walsall win 7-0.

In a bid to cut costs, Brighton release five of their most experienced players. Cambridge's fifth home win of the season on the Friday denies Exeter a return to the top of the table.

The following day, Notts County are three up inside 20 minutes against Doncaster and eventually win 5-2 to replace Lincoln as league leaders. A last-minute equaliser denies Lincoln maximum points against Hartlepool and, with third-placed Peterborough only drawing at Cardiff, County assume pole position. Barnet beat Macclesfield 3-1 to climb above Exeter on goals scored.

Cambridge take an early lead in their FA Cup 2nd Round replay at Stevenage on the 15th but when goalscorer Martin Butler and Paul Wanless are dismissed United crash to a 2-1 defeat. Three more Division Three sides bow out 24 hours later. Notts County are one minute away from beating Preston but concede a late equaliser and go out during extra time. Colchester take Hereford to extra time at Edgar Street but are defeated in a penalty shoot-out. Torquay do well to force extra time at Watford but eventually join the exodus with a 2-1 reversal. In one of the biggest upsets of the round, Lincoln, leading 2-0 with just 15 minutes remaining, also depart after failing to win a penalty shoot-out following a 3-3 draw with tiny Emley. Scunthorpe, however, continue to fly the flag with a 2-1 victory at Ilkeston. Chester and Barnet have their play-off hopes dashed on the 19th with defeats at Colchester and Scarborough.

Sean Farrell notches both Notts County goals on the 20th as the Magpies stay a point clear of Peterborough with victory at Torquay. The Posh are equally impressive as Carruthers and David Farrell grab two goals each in a 5-1 destruction of one-time leaders Lincoln. City are still three points clear of fourth-placed Exeter who hand Rochdale their 10th away defeat with three first-half goals. Hull also suffer their 10th reversal on their travels with a 2-1 defeat at Orient. Hopes of a Welsh side making a second-half to the season challenge for the play-offs look bleak as Cardiff lose at Macclesfield and Swansea have only Brighton and Doncaster below them following a 1-1 draw with Cambridge. Swansea have Richard Appleby sent off for the third time in five weeks.

Notts County extend their lead to four points on Boxing Day with two Gary Jones goals accounting for one of his former clubs, Scarborough. County's position is strengthened by a 2-0 defeat for Peterborough at Barnet which takes the Bees into the top six. Lincoln, although third, fall further off the pace with a 1-0 home defeat against Rotherham, who climb to fifth. Exeter stay in contention by becoming the 14th side to draw with Cardiff this season. Darlington chalk up their second home win of the week with a 4-2 success over Macclesfield and there are a further eight goals at Brighton where Paul Emblen scores a hat-trick as the Seagulls come back from three down to draw with Colchester.

Another brace for Sean Farrell, against Hartlepool, takes Notts County seven points clear on the 27th as Peterborough lose at home to Brighton with defender Ashley Vickers dismissed on his debut. Lincoln stay third with a point at Mansfield but in a remarkable match at Millmoor, Rotherham move to fourth with a 5-4 victory over Hull. Rotherham striker Lee Glover bags four as the Yorkshire club's biggest gate of the season see their side take a 5-1 lead before Hull hit back with three goals in six minutes. Barnet keep pace with Rotherham after a 2-0 win at Swansea while Chester maintain their unbeaten home record at the expense of Scunthorpe. Over 8,000 attend a 1-1 draw between Exeter and Torquay at St James's Park while half that number see Orient striker Carl Griffiths put three past Doncaster during an 8-0 slaughter at Brisbane Road.

January

Just two league games are played on the first Saturday of the new year and, with a 2-1 win at Colchester, Hartlepool nudge Exeter out of the top six. With poor weather putting paid to several matches, just three Division Three clubs play in the 3rd Round of the FA Cup. The pick of the results comes from Ninian Park where Cardiff beat Division Two Oldham 1-0 with a solo effort from Jason Fowler. Rotherham's good run counts for little as visitors Sunderland help themselves to five goals and Scunthorpe become the first visiting side this season to lose to Crystal Palace at Selhurst Park.

In-form sides Barnet and Rotherham draw a blank at Underhill on the 10th and fellow play-off hopefuls Hartlepool and Exeter also finish level at Victoria Park. But leaders Notts County march on with a 2-1 success at Rochdale and Peterborough open a three-point gap on third place with a 3-1 win at Scunthorpe. County's club record sixth successive victory is the perfect way for the Magpies to celebrate being the first club to play 4,000 Football League matches. Scarborough are into the top three for the first time with two goals from Steve Brodie helping to clinch a 3-2 win at Cambridge. Lincoln lose more ground as they go down 3-1 at home to Chester, who move to within three points of second-placed Peterborough. With a 2-0 defeat at Torquay, Macclesfield are stuck in 12th place but just six points off the play-off positions. Doncaster double their total of successes for the season with a 1-0 win over Shrewsbury.

Delayed and replayed FA Cup ties take place on the 14th and 15th. On the Tuesday Peterborough, in front of 12,809, lose 2-0 at home to Walsall, while on Wednesday night Darlington's good home run cannot save them from a 4-0 defeat by Wolves.

Notts County continue their winning streak the following weekend with a 3-1 win over Cardiff but with the Nationwide League's top scorer Jimmy Quinn bagging two against Rochdale, Peterborough stay seven points behind. Scarborough's charge is slowed by a draw at home with Lincoln, Boro' have keeper Andy Rhodes sent off for handball in the build-up to City's last-minute equaliser. That result allows Rotherham to claim third place following victory over Rochdale. Barnet, on the back of inflicting on Chester their first home defeat of the season, move to fourth.

Exeter hammer Doncaster 5-1 and three days later the Grecians draw at home for the seventh time when Barnet are the visitors. With Peterborough not playing, Notts County move ten points clear as Hull's away record still shows just four points from 15 games. Scarborough and Macclesfield, the first two sides to complete ten at home wins, are successful again with both Torquay and Scunthorpe being the latest sides to return home pointless.

Cardiff find an unusual way to prepare for an FA Cup tie by dismissing manager Russell Osman. Former boss Kenny Hibbitt takes temporary control of team matters. Despite the upheaval, Cardiff, Division Three's last representatives, manage a draw at home to Reading. Notts County are now a formidable 13 points clear after a 5-3 win at Lincoln which includes two more goals for Farrell. Lincoln come back from three to level before losing again. Peterborough go down at Hull which allows Barnet to join them on 49 points following a 3-2 win over Colchester; Bees keeper Lee Harrison concedes his first goal in over nine hours. Scarborough slip up when dropping two points at Brighton while Rotherham's draw at Hartlepool is less of a surprise. Chester get back to winning ways courtesy of Rod McDonald's last-minute goal at Cambridge and Macclesfield, at the 14th attempt, celebrate their first away win in the Nationwide League – their victims are Doncaster.

Swansea romp to their best win of the season with a 4-0 trouncing of Darlington on the 27th but both Chester and Rotherham drop two points with home draws; indeed, Rotherham are thankful for two injury-time goals saving the day against Cambridge.

Gary Jones is the toast of Notts County on the last day of the month as his two goals, at Mansfield, give County a tenth successive league win and a club record of six away wins on the trot. Quinn scores again for Peterborough as they stay second in the table ahead of Barnet on goals scored. The Bees beat Cambridge. Posh's victims, Rotherham, lose little ground as Scarborough, Chester, Macclesfield and Exeter all draw but Lincoln stay close behind with a 1-0 win over Hull.

February

Cardiff's FA Cup venture ends at the hands of Reading keeper Nicky Hammond who saves three spot kicks after the sides are tied at 1-1 at the end of extra time. Peterborough squander their game in hand on Notts County with a 1-0 defeat at Brisbane Road on the 6th which enables Orient to move into seventh place. County's winning run comes to an end the following day and only a last-minute Jones goal staves off defeat against

Shrewsbury. Barnet move into second place with a 1-1 draw at Scunthorpe and Macclesfield's upturn in fortunes continues with a 3-1 home win over fellow promotion chasers Scarborough. Torquay are also back in the frame after winning 4-1 at Brighton and Lincoln stay close with a 1-0 success at Cardiff. Rotherham, in fifth place, are just three points behind Barnet following a 1-0 victory over Exeter, who drop to tenth. Lincoln pick up another point on the Friday with a draw at Cambridge.

Normality is restored on the 14th with Notts County winning 2-0 at Darlington, making it their 12th away success, five more than any other side. Barnet come from two down to draw at home with Cardiff but lose second place to Peterborough who beat Swansea for the fourth time this season. Macclesfield also win, against Orient, to move into third place and Torquay turn up the heat with a 5-1 thrashing of Hull. Exeter's bid falters with a 4-1 drubbing at Scarborough and injury-hit Rotherham stumble at home to Shrewsbury. Bizarrely, 6,339 turn up to see the league's bottom two clubs, Brighton and Doncaster, draw 0-0 at Gillingham.

Scarborough's promotion hopes are slightly dented on the 21st as they become Notts County's 12th victims in 13 games. Macclesfield climb to the highest position of their brief league career, 2nd, as a John Askey goal secures an important win at Peterborough. Torquay leave it late before winning at Doncaster to move into third place. Lincoln are within a point of Barnet after cutting down the Bees 2-0 at Sincil Bank. Rotherham suffer a second successive defeat as Chester notch up their tenth win of the season at the Deva Stadium. Steve Harper scores a hat-trick as Mansfield turn over Darlington 4-0 at Field Mill.

A full midweek programme serves to help Notts County move a massive 16 points clear. Sam Allardyce's side, still struggling to attract crowds of above 5,000 despite their tremendous run, beat Swansea with two more Gary Jones goals and then see Macclesfield go down to their eighth away defeat, this time at Mansfield. Torquay underline their credentials with a 3-1 success at Chester which lifts them into second place. Barnet continue their excellent form with a 2-0 win at Hull which takes on even greater importance as Peterborough and Scarborough both drop two points when drawing 0-0 at London Road. Lincoln also lose ground when held at home by Scunthorpe while Darlington, after four draws and 12 defeats, at last win away from home, naturally enough at poor Doncaster. Brighton part company with manager Steve Gritt after just four league wins.

After a poor first half to the season, Colchester continue to climb and, with a 1-0 victory over fading Peterborough on the 27th, are just one place outside of the top six. On the last day of the month, Macclesfield delight their best crowd of the season, 5,122, with a 2-0 victory over leaders Notts County. Goals from Askey and Steve Wood end County's long unbeaten run and help the Silkmen protect the best home record in English professional football. Torquay are given a fright by Lincoln before hanging on to second place with a club record seventh successive win. Barnet are surprisingly held at home by Shrewsbury and Chester go down to Brighton in Brian Horton's first match in charge. But Scarborough and Rotherham – with two goals in the dying moments against Orient – bolster their play-off claims with home wins.

March

Notts County show no signs of slowing up in a full midweek programme which starts the month as they hand out a 5-2 thrashing for Exeter in Devon; Farrell and Jones notch two apiece. With Macclesfield drawing at Cambridge, Torquay move three points clear in second place following a 1-0 win over Cardiff. Barnet move to within a point of third-placed Macclesfield with two second-half goals clinching victory at Belle Vue in front of

Doncaster's lowest ever attendance, 739. A last-minute goal denies Scarborough full points against Mansfield while Peterborough lose at Darlington. Chester, Lincoln and Rotherham all miss out on a possible top six place when only drawing at home. Lincoln's draw with Swansea proves to be John Beck's last in charge as the Imps' manager is dismissed.

The first Saturday of the month is a bad day for several of the leading sides although Notts County have few problems in dishing out a third home defeat of the season for Barnet and moving 16 points clear; Jones scores for the 15th time in 13 games. Torquay become only Cambridge's second away victims as the Us end the Gulls' record eight match winning run with a 3-0 success and Macclesfield and Rotherham cancel out each other at Moss Rose. Peterborough's poor run continues with a home draw against Exeter while Lincoln's first match under caretaker manager Shane Westley ends in a 1-0 defeat by Orient, which takes the Londoners to within a point of the top six. Swansea and Cardiff play on the Sunday and end all square at Vetch Field.

Scarborough boost their play-off aspirations with a midweek success at Doncaster. Following the collapse of a proposed take-over, Doncaster dispense with coaches Dave Cowling and Paul Ward. The players are told only to turn up on matchdays.

Just to prove that things can get worse for the league's bottom club, Doncaster have goalkeeper Wayne O'Sullivan dismissed during a 7-1 defeat at Ninian Park on the 14th; six different players share the Cardiff goals. Chester become Notts County's latest victims as Allardyce's side close in on promotion. Torquay bounce back in style with Jack's last-minute goal at Feethams denting Darlington's impressive home record. Barnet and Scarborough reclaim third place and fourth place respectively with home wins. Both cash-ins as Macclesfield are despatched 5-1 by Colchester and the Essex side move into the top six. Only six points separate Colchester from 13th placed Hartlepool.

Notts County's promotion celebrations are put on hold on the 21st as Colchester collect a point and become the first team to stop County from scoring at Meadow Lane this season. Torquay are held goalless at home by Barnet and that result enables Macclesfield to reclaim third place on the strength of a 2-1 victory over Shrewsbury. Scarborough draw at Swansea and Rotherham do likewise at Scunthorpe but Lincoln and Peterborough keep their play-off hopes going with wins over Doncaster and Chester. The latter are facing a winding-up order.

After a slight delay, the Notts County promotion party gets into full swing as Mark Robson's 50th-minute goal sees off Orient and ensures County of the earliest Championship in Football League history. An expectant 8,383 join in the celebrations at Meadow Lane. As the Magpies open a 19-point lead, the race for second place intensifies. Fifth placed Scarborough maintain a six-point lead over Rotherham with a goalless draw at Millmoor but it is a pointless day for second-placed Torquay who lose at Scunthorpe. Lincoln's chance to move into third place is thwarted by Colchester, whose 1-0 win at Sincil Bank takes them to within three points of the Imps. Barnet can only draw at home with Hartlepool but that setback is offset by Macclesfield doing no better at Hull.

April

Steve Castle puts the first goal past Notts County keeper Darren Ward for five games as Peterborough, on the 3rd, move to a point outside the top six and hand the champions a rare defeat. Colchester stay a point and two places ahead of Peterborough with a 2-1 win which ends Rotherham's run of five successive draws. Scarborough move above Macclesfield and Barnet with a 3-1 win over Cardiff but that duo reclaim the initiative 24 hours later with respective wins over Lincoln and Darlington. Macclesfield and Lincoln both go down to ten men – Lincoln lose keeper Barry Richardson – before Steve Wood's late decider. The Bees are toasting Sean Devine after their leading scorer adds a hat-trick to his season's collection. Torquay's indifferent run continues in a home draw with Rochdale while Orient salvage a point from the visit of Mansfield after being two down but are as good as out of the play-offs. Doncaster retain the mathematical possibility of not finishing bottom with Adie Mike's last-minute winner against their nearest rivals Hull. Brighton rise to their highest position for two years when defeating Scunthorpe for their first double of the season.

Better news for Orient on the 11th as two late goals at Underhill clinch a 2-1 win and give Barnet their first home defeat since November. The Os position is further boosted by defeat for Peterborough at Cambridge and Rotherham only drawing at home to Swansea. For the visit of Brighton, Notts County 'lose' around 3,000 of the revellers who watched their previous home game. The Seagulls have the audacity to plunder a point. Torquay, with a 2-2 draw at Mansfield, move a point clear of third-placed Macclesfield following their defeat at Scunthorpe. Scarborough's surge is stifled by a 4-0 drubbing at Rochdale while Colchester's third consecutive win cements their fifth position. Doncaster's 75 years of life in the Football League – their third stint in the league – is over as they lose 2-1 at Chester.

Notts County pick up their 15th away win of the season on Easter Monday, at Doncaster, but there is a new face behind them as Macclesfield take second place with victory over Barnet. Torquay suffer a second successive setback at Plainmoor as visitors Rotherham gain a 2-1 victory which leaves them three points adrift of sixth-placed Peterborough. Posh beat Cardiff at London Road but Lincoln drop out of the top six courtesy of a draw at Victoria Park where Hartlepool have lost just once all season. Orient's promotion push is derailed by Shrewsbury striker Lee Steele, who scores all three of the Town's goals in a 3-2 victory at Brisbane Road. Orient were two up shortly after the interval at which point Shrewsbury had already had Austen Berkeley dismissed. Colchester trail to Hull at Layer Road, having earlier led 2-0, before rising to third place with a dramatic 4-3 win. Scarborough drop to fourth after a goalless afternoon with Scunthorpe.

Orient have already been fined £20,000, of which £12,500 is suspended, for fielding suspended players in several games earlier in the season. Now they have the added burden of three points deducted for the same offence. Chairman Barry Hearn blames one of the Orient staff for an administration error and vows to appeal. To complete Orient's week they go down 3-2 at Hull on the 18th. Torquay have their hopes of grabbing the second automatic promotion place knocked back by a 3-0 defeat at Notts County, but with Colchester losing at Chester and Barnet and Scarborough drawing at Underhill the Gulls hang on to the third and final guaranteed promotion position. With two games to play, Macclesfield now seem almost certain of going up at the first attempt as a 2-1 win at Cardiff puts them five points clear in second place. Lincoln, with the advantage of a game in hand on all their play-off rivals, hammer Peterborough 3-0 to leapfrog them into sixth position. Rotherham stay in the hunt with a 3-0 win over Doncaster. Mansfield veteran Tony Ford, 38, becomes only the third player to make 800 Football League appearances but he cannot celebrate with a win as Hartlepool take a point from Field Mill.

Lincoln move a giant step closer to promotion in the week with two goals from Steve Holmes seeing off Exeter and taking the Imps into third place. The Football Association uphold the Football League's right to dock Leyton Orient three points for a breach of rules.

Macclesfield make sure of the runners-up position with a 3-2 victory over Chester which gives Sammy McIlroy's side their 19th home win of the season, six more than champions Notts County. County will miss out on reaching a century of points following a 2-2 draw at Cambridge. Torquay go into their final game of the season knowing that a draw could ensure automatic promotion following a 3-1 win over Peterborough at Plainmoor. Lincoln, Colchester and Scarborough can only draw but all three are into the play-offs. Barnet's future lies in the balance as a 1-0 home defeat by Mansfield could yet open the door for Rotherham who make it hard for themselves by falling behind by two goals at home to Rochdale before rescuing a point.

The Lincoln trio of Barry Richardson, Jason Barrett and Lee Thorpe are called to the FA to answer misconduct charges following the Imps' defeat at Macclesfield earlier in the month.

May

Barnet's play-off dream looks to be shattered as Rochdale record their 15th home win of the season to leave the Bees stranded on 70 points. Fortunately for Barnet though, Rotherham's final game of the season is at Notts County and the champions are in party mood as they hammer the Yorkshire side 5-2, thus taking Barnet into the play-offs. Torquay's poor run-in costs them dear as a 2-1 defeat at Orient allows Lincoln to grab the final automatic promotion place with a 2-1 win over Brighton in front of a crowd of 9,890. Scarborough round off their league programme with a 1-1 draw and sixth place at Chester. Rochdale, despite finishing 18th, win the second highest number of home games in the division. Doncaster's final game in the Football League is witnessed by 3,572 fans who see Colchester take fourth place with a 1-0 win.

In the 1st Leg of the play-off semi-finals on the 9th, both home sides secure leads. Barnet beat Colchester 1-0 at Underhill, to go with the four points they took from United during the season, but top scorer Sean Devine is out of the return match after being dismissed. Scarborough, one win in six games, see their hopes almost completely destroyed at the McCain Stadium by Torquay, who secure a commanding 3-1 lead. Four days later Torquay's St Vincent international Rodney Jack takes his season's total to 16 with two goals in the opening seven minutes as the Gulls go on to complete an aggregate 7-2 win; Scarborough finish the game with just nine men. Barnet's 1st Leg lead lasts just 12 minutes at Layer Road before David Gregory puts Colchester level from the penalty spot. Former Barnet Youth player Warren Goodhind equalises but David Greene restores Colchester's lead to take the tie into extra time where Gregory's second goal gives the Essex club an aggregate 3-2 victory.

Gregory ensures his place in Colchester folklore by converting another penalty to give the Us victory over Torquay at Wembley in the final. The attendance of 19,486 is the lowest for a play-off final. ■

Play-Offs 1997-98

Semi-Finals 1st Leg
Barnet 1 Colchester United 0 3,612
Heald (48)

Scarborough 1 Torquay United 3 5,246
Rockett (40) Jack (22); Gittens (50);
 McFarlane (72)

Semi-Finals 2nd Leg
Colchester United 3 Barnet 1 5,863
Gregory (12 pen, 95); Goodhind (41)
Greene (65)
aet. Colchester United win 3-2 on aggregate

Torquay United 4 Scarborough 1 5,386
Jack (6, 7); McCall (38); Rockett (22)
Gibbs (55)
Torquay United win 7-2 on aggregate

Final – *at Wembley Stadium*
Colchester United 1 Torquay United 0 19,486
Gregory (22 pen)

DIVISION 3 RECORDS 1997-98

Top Scorers – All Competitions

Player	Club	L	F	C	Total
Gary JONES	Notts County	25	0	0	25
Steve WHITEHALL	Mansfield Town	24	1	0	25
Darren ROWBOTHAM	Exeter City	21	1	0	22
Jimmy QUINN	Peterborough U.	20	3	1	24
Carl GRIFFITHS	Leyton Orient	18	1	3	22
Lee GLOVER	Rotherham	18	1	0	19
Robbie PAINTER	Rochdale	17	0	1	18

L=League, F=FA Cup, C=Coca-Cola Cup

Top Scorers & Attendances by Club

Team	Psn	Top Scorer	Agg Att	Ave Att
Barnet	7	Devine (16)	52,847	2,297
Brighton & HA	23	Mayon, Minton (6)	53,540	2,327
Cambridge United	16	Kyd (12)	66,672	2,898
Cardiff City	21	Saville (11)	82,205	3,574
Chester City	14	Bennett (12)	51,876	2,255
Colchester United	4	Abrahams, N. Gregory, Sale, Skelton (7)	72,367	3,146
Darlington	19	Roberts (12)	54,418	2,366
Doncaster Rovers	24	Moncrieffe (8)	39,455	1,715
Exeter City	15	Rowbotham (21)	91,770	3,990
Hartlepool United	17	Cullen (12)	51,540	2,240
Hull City	22	Darby (13)	107,725	4,683
Leyton Orient	11	Griffiths (18)	100,491	4,369
Lincoln City	3	Thorpe (15)	91,258	3,967
Macclesfield Town	2	Wood (14)	66,823	2,905
Mansfield Town	12	Whitehall (24)	62,566	2,720
Notts County	1	G. Jones (25)	131,674	5,724
Peterborough United	10	Quinn (20)	142,240	6,184
Rochdale	18	Painter (17)	43,122	1,874
Rotherham	9	Glover (18)	83,972	3,650
Scarborough	6	Williams (14)	57,238	2,488
Scunthorpe	8	Eyre, Forrester (11)	69,142	3,006
Shrewsbury	13	Steele (13)	55,266	2,402
Swansea	20	Bird (14)	75,812	3,296
Torquay United	5	Jack (12)	61,620	2,679

Division 3 Hat-tricks

Player	Goals	Match (result)	Date
HARLE	3	Rotherham U. v BARNET (2-3)	09-Aug-97
DARBY	3	HULL C. v Swansea C. (7-4)	30-Aug-97
AINSWORTH	3	LINCOLN C. v Scarborough (3-3)	30-Aug-97
QUINN	3 (1p)	PETERBOROUGH U. v Barnet (5-1)	07-Sep-97
WHITE	3	SHREWSBURY T. v Macclesfield T. (4-3)	18-Nov-97
EMBLEN	3	BRIGHTON & HA v Colchester U. (4-4)	26-Dec-97
GRIFFTHS	3	L. ORIENT v Doncaster R. (8-0)	28-Dec-97
GLOVER	4	ROTHERHAM U. v Hull C. (5-4)	28-Dec-97
HARPER	3	MANSFIELD T. v Darlington (4-0)	21-Feb-98
STEELE	3	L. Orient v SHREWSBURY T. (2-3)	13-Apr-98

p = penalty

Division 3 Red Cards

Players	Opponents	Venue	Date	Official
Barnet				
Manuel	Shrewsbury	A	11-Oct-97	Messias
Charley	Leyton Orient	A	02-Dec-97	D'Urso
Wilson	Leyton Orient	H	11-Apr-98	Wilkes
Doolan	Mansfield T.	H	25-Apr-98	Knight
Devine	Colchester U.	H	10-May-98	Wolstenholme
Howarth	Colchester U.	A	13-May-98	Heilbron
Brighton & Hove Albion				
Baird	Chester C.	A	11-Oct-97	Pike
Linger	Leyton Orient	A	17-Jan-98	Robinson
Cambridge United				
Joseph, Marc	Torquay U.	H	01-Nov-97	Bennet
Cardiff City				
Young	Swansea C.	H	02-Nov-97	Harris
Middleton	Torquay U.	H	08-Nov-97	Hall
Middleton	Darlington	H	02-May-98	Bennet
Chester City				
Shelton	Torquay U.	A	18-Oct-97	Styles
Sinclair	Torquay U.	A	18-Oct-97	Styles
Murphy	Exeter C.	A	04-Apr-98	Knight
Colchester United				
Greene	Exeter C.	H	27-Sep-97	Butler
Cawley	Lincoln C.	H	22-Nov-97	Pearson
Branston	Barnet	A	10-May-98	Wolstenholme
Darlington				
Brydon	Colchester U.	H	09-Aug-97	Knight
Preece	Brighton & HA	A	13-Sep-97	Crick
Brydon	Peterborough	A	08-Nov-97	Messias
Hope	Peterborough	A	08-Nov-97	Messias
Shaw	Mansfield T.	A	21-Feb-98	Bailey
Oliver	Cardiff C.	A	02-May-98	Bennet
Doncaster Rovers				
Esdaille, Dar	Shrewsbury	A	9-Aug-97	Crick
McDonald	Leyton Orient	H	02-Sep-97	Pike
Cunningham	Darlington	A	18-Oct-97	Richards
Davis	Cardiff C.	A	14-Mar-98	Halsey

Players	Opponents	Venue	Date	Official
Exeter				
Minett	Darlington	H	23-Aug-97	Hall
Cyrus	Torquay U.	A	02-Sep-97	Wilkes
Baddeley	Chester C.	A	22-Nov-97	Laws
Blake	Swansea C.	A	28-Feb-98	Lomas
Flack	Cambridge U.	H	13-Apr-98	Crick
Hartlepool United				
Beech	Scarborough	A	07-Sep-97	Dean
Clark	Leyton Orient	A	24-Feb-98	Styles
Ingram	Leyton Orient	A	24-Feb-98	Styles
Hull City				
Doncel	Peterborough	A	23-Aug-97	Bates
Rioch	Swansea C.	A	30-Aug-97	Laws
Doncel	Brighton HA	A	25-Sep-98	Bennet
Leyton Orient				
Hicks	Barnet	H	02-Dec-97	D'Urso
McKenzie	Shrewsbury	A	13-Dec-97	Wolstenholme
Lincoln City				
Flemming	Leyton Orient	A	07-Mar-98	Bates
Richardson	Macclesfield T.	A	04-Apr-98	Lomas
Macclesfield Town				
Power	Colchester U.	A	14-Mar-98	Bennet
Sedgemore	Lincoln C.	H	04-Apr-98	Lomas
Mansfield Town				
Christie	Hull City	H	09-Aug-97	Jones
Sedgemore	Macclesfield T.	A	18-Oct-97	Laws
Hackett	Macclesfield T.	A	18-Oct-97	Laws
Doolan	Hartlepool U.	A	20-Dec-97	Richards
Christie	Notts County	H	31-Jan-98	Pearson
Bowling	Swansea C.	H	02-May-98	Frankland
Notts County				
White	Lincoln C.	H	23-Aug-97	Richards
Farrel	Darlington	H	08-Nov-97	Messias
Vickers	Brighton HA	H	28-Dec-97	Hall
Rochdale				
Hill	Leyton Orient	A	23-Aug-97	Styles
Leonard	Leyton Orient	A	23-Aug-97	Styles

Players	Opponents	Venue	Date	Official
Rotherham United				
Richardson	Shrewsbury T.	A	04-Oct-97	Leake
Warner	Shrewsbury T.	A	04-Oct-97	Leake
Glover	Shrewsbury T.	A	04-Oct-97	Leake
Roscoe	Chester C.	A	21-Feb-98	Robinson
Mimms	Chester C.	A	21-Feb-98	Robinson
Monington	Macclesfield T.	A	07-Mar-98	Leake
Scarborough				
Rhodes	Lincoln C.	H	17-Jan-98	Kirkby
Snodin	Chester C.	A	02-May-98	Fletcher
Williams	Torquay U.	A	13-May-98	Harris
Robinson	Torquay U.	A	13-May-98	Harris
Scunthorpe United				
Walsh	Rochdale	A	04-Oct-97	Hall
Wilcox	Chester C.	A	28-Dec-97	Stretton
Sertori	Macclesfield T.	H	11-Apr-98	Hall
Wilcox	Scarborough	A	13-Apr-98	Pike
Shrewsbury Town				
Currie	Lincoln C.	A	16-Aug-97	Dean
Naylor	Cambridge U.	A	30-Aug-97	Fletcher
Steele	Rotherham U.	H	04-Oct-97	Leake
Berkley	Leyton Orient	A	13-Apr-98	Pierce
Swansea City				
Ampadu	Macclesfield T.	A	13-Sep-97	Hall
Appleby	Scarborough	A	18-Nov-97	Jones
Ampadu	Rochdale	A	13-Dec-97	Messias
Appleby	Cambridge U.	H	20-Dec-97	Hall
Bird	Notts County	A	24-Feb-98	Dean
Bird	Cambridge C.	A	18-Apr-98	Dean
Hartfield	Mansfield T.	A	02-May-98	Frankland
Torquay United				
Mitchell	Exeter C.	H	02-Sep-97	Wilkes
Jack	Hartlepool U.	A	13-Sep-97	Messias
Veysey	Leyton Orient	A	02-May-98	Leake

NATIONWIDE DIVISION 3

	Barnet	Brighton	Cambridge	Cardiff	Chester	Colchester	Darlington	Doncaster	Exeter	Hartlepool	Hull	L. Orient
Barnet	—	2-0	2-0	2-2	2-1	3-2	2-0	1-1	1-2	1-1	2-0	1-2
Brighton & HA	0-3	—	0-2	0-1	3-2	4-4	0-0	0-0	1-3	0-0	2-2	0-1
Cambridge United	1-3	1-1	—	2-2	1-2	4-1	1-0	2-1	2-1	2-0	0-1	1-0
Cardiff City	1-1	0-0	0-0	—	0-0	1-1	1-0	7-1	1-1	3-1	2-1	1-1
Chester City	0-1	2-0	1-1	2-1	—	3-1	2-1	2-1	1-1	3-1	1-0	1-1
Colchester United	1-1	3-1	3-2	2-1	2-0	—	2-1	2-1	1-2	1-2	4-3	1-0
Darlington	2-3	0-0	1-1	0-0	1-0	4-2	—	5-1	3-2	1-1	4-3	1-1
Doncaster Rovers	1-3	1-0	0-0	1-1	2-1	0-1	0-2	—	0-1	2-2	1-0	1-4
Exeter City	0-0	2-1	1-0	1-1	5-0	0-1	1-0	5-1	—	1-1	3-0	2-2
Hartlepool United	2-0	0-0	3-3	0-1	0-1	3-1	2-2	1-0	1-1	—	2-2	2-2
Hull City	0-2	0-0	0-1	0-1	1-2	0-2	1-1	3-0	3-2	2-1	—	3-2
Leyton Orient	2-0	3-1	0-2	0-1	1-0	0-0	2-0	8-0	1-0	2-1	2-1	—
Lincoln City	2-0	2-1	0-1	1-0	1-3	0-0	3-1	2-0	1-1	2-2	0-0	1-0
Macclesfield Town	1-2	1-1	3-1	1-2	3-2	0-0	4-0	1-0	2-2	2-2	2-1	0-0
Mansfield Town	2-0	0-0	3-2	3-1	4-1	1-1	3-1	3-0	3-2	1-1	1-0	1-1
Notts County	1-2	2-2	1-0	2-1	1-2	1-1	4-0	1-1	2-3	2-1	1-0	0-0
Peterborough United	5-1	1-2	3-1	3-1	1-1	0-3	1-2	5-2	1-0	0-0	0-1	2-0
Rochdale	2-1	2-0	0-0	0-0	1-1	2-1	5-0	0-1	2-2	1-1	0-0	2-1
Rotherham United	2-3	0-0	2-2	1-1	4-2	3-2	3-0	4-1	3-0	2-1	5-4	2-2
Scarborough	1-0	2-1	2-1	3-1	4-1	1-0	4-0	3-0	4-1	0-0	2-0	2-2
Scunthorpe United	1-1	0-2	3-3	3-3	1-1	0-2	1-0	4-0	1-1	2-1	2-0	1-0
Shrewsbury Town	2-0	2-1	1-1	3-2	1-1	1-1	3-0	2-1	3-2	1-1	2-0	1-2
Swansea City	0-2	1-0	0-0	1-1	1-1	0-2	4-0	0-0	4-1	0-2	1-1	2-0
Torquay United	0-0	0-3	0-3	1-0	3-1	1-1	2-1	2-1	1-2	2-1	5-1	1-1

RESULTS 1997-98

	Lincoln C.	Macclesfield	Mansfield	Notts Co.	Peterborough	Rochdale	Rotherham	Scarborough	Scunthorpe	Shrewsbury	Swansea	Torquay
Barnet	0-0	3-1	0-1	1-2	2-0	3-1	0-0	1-1	0-1	1-1	2-0	3-3
Brighton & HA	0-1	1-1	1-1	0-1	2-2	1-1	1-2	1-1	2-2	0-3	0-1	1-4
Cambridge United	1-1	0-0	2-0	2-2	1-0	1-1	2-1	2-3	2-2	4-3	4-1	1-1
Cardiff City	2-0	1-2	4-1	1-1	0-0	2-1	2-2	1-1	0-0	2-2	0-1	1-3
Chester City	2-0	1-2	1-1	2-1	0-0	4-0	4-0	1-0	0-1	2-0	2-0	1-0
Colchester United	0-1	5-1	2-0	2-0	1-0	0-0	0-1	1-0	3-3	1-1	1-2	1-0
Darlington	2-2	4-2	0-0	0-2	3-1	1-0	1-1	1-2	1-0	3-1	3-2	0-1
Doncaster Rovers	2-4	0-3	1-0	1-1	0-5	0-3	0-3	1-0	2-3	1-0	0-3	1-0
Exeter City	1-1	1-3	1-0	2-5	0-0	1-0	1-1	1-2	1-2	2-2	1-0	0-1
Hartlepool United	1-1	0-0	2-2	1-1	2-1	2-0	0-0	1-1	2-3	2-1	4-2	3-0
Hull City	0-2	0-0	0-0	0-3	3-1	0-2	0-0	3-0	0-1	0-1	7-4	3-3
Leyton Orient	1-0	1-1	2-2	1-1	2-0	1-1	1-1	3-3	2-1	2-3	2-2	2-1
Lincoln City	—	1-1	0-2	3-5	3-0	1-0	0-1	3-1	1-1	1-0	1-1	1-1
Macclesfield Town	1-0	—	1-0	2-0	1-1	1-0	0-1	3-1	0-1	2-1	3-0	2-2
Mansfield Town	2-2	1-0	—	0-2	2-0	3-0	3-3	3-2	2-1	0-0	1-0	3-0
Notts County	1-2	1-1	1-0	—	2-2	2-1	5-2	1-0	1-0	0-0	2-1	2-0
Peterborough United	5-1	0-1	1-1	1-0	—	3-1	1-0	4-0	2-1	1-1	3-1	1-0
Rochdale	0-0	2-0	2-2	1-0	1-2	—	0-0	1-1	0-1	0-1	3-0	0-1
Rotherham United	3-1	1-0	2-2	1-1	2-2	2-2	—	0-0	0-1	3-1	3-0	0-1
Scarborough	2-2	2-1	2-2	1-2	1-3	1-0	1-2	—	0-0	0-1	3-2	4-1
Scunthorpe United	2-2	1-0	1-0	1-2	1-3	2-2	1-1	1-3	—	1-1	1-0	0-1
Shrewsbury Town	0-2	4-3	3-2	1-2	4-1	1-0	2-1	1-1	0-2	—	0-1	1-2
Swansea City	0-0	1-1	0-1	1-2	0-1	3-0	1-1	0-1	2-0	0-1	—	2-0
Torquay United	3-2	2-0	2-1	0-2	3-1	0-0	1-2	1-1	2-4	3-0	2-0	—

Barnet

Winning In-Stilled

The dramatic eight-year Football League life of Barnet took an upward swing during 1997/98 when new manager John Still brought in six players on free transfers and, just a year after finishing 15th in Division Three, took the Bees to the play-offs. Still also made £500,000 with the sale of Livoy Primus and Lee Hodges to Reading.

At one stage Barnet looked likely to take an automatic promotion place but eventually claimed a top seven place thanks to results elsewhere on the final day. Through Greg Heald, Barnet took a 1st Leg play-off lead to Colchester but went down 3-2 on aggregate at Layer Road. Even so, just to have reached the play-off semi-final was clearly a bonus. For the second consecutive year Sean Devine was top scorer and the club record fee of £70,000 invested in Leyton Orient striker Scott McGleish in October was justified by his 13 league goals.

A Ken Charley goal almost provoked an FA Cup upset against county rivals Watford but it was in the Coca-Cola Cup that the Bees enjoyed success with an excellent two-legged victory over Division One side Norwich. In the 2nd Round the Bees went out to Middlesbrough.

Formed:	1888
Ground:	Underhill Stadium, Barnet Lane, Herts, EN5 2BE
Phone:	0181 441 6932
Box Office:	0181 441 6932
Info:	0898 12 15 44
Capacity:	4,072
Colour:	Amber and black shirts, black shorts, black socks.
Nickname:	The Bees
Manager:	John Still
Honours:	GMVC Winners 1990-91
	FA Amateur Cup Winners 1945-46.
Managers:	Edwin Stein, Gary Philips 1993-94, Ray Clemence 94-96, Alan Mullery 1996-97, Terry Bullivant 1997.
Previous Names:	Barnet, 1888-1901, Alston Works, 1901-1906, Barnet Alston FC, 1906-1919.
Record League Win:	6-0 v Lincoln City, D4, 4/9/1991
Record League Defeat:	0-6 v Port Vale, D2, 21/8/1993
Most GF in Season:	81 – Division 4, 1991-92
All-time League Apps:	174 – Paul Wilson, 1991-97
All-time League Goals:	37 – Gary Bull, 1991-96
Most Goals in a Season:	20 – Gary Bull, 1991-92
Most Goals in a Match:	4 – Douglas Freedman v Rochdale, 13/9/95
	4 – Lee Hodges v Rochdale, 8/4/96

Record Fee Received: £800,000 from C. Palace for Dougie Freedman, 9/95
Record Fee Paid: £80,000 to Stockport C. for Ken Charley, 8/97
Record Attendance: 11,026 v Wycombe Wanderers,
FA Amateur Cup 4th Round, 1951-52

Stats File

Division	P	W	D	L	F	A	Pts	Yr	B	W
Division 2n/3:	46	5	13	28	41	86	28	1	24	24
Division 3n/4:	264	110	72	82	375	319	402	6	3	15

Cup Records	P	W	D	L	F	A
FA Cup:	74	19	18	37	101	151
League Cup:	22	6	6	10	30	36
A/F Members Cup:	15	4	1	10	25	31

Sequence	Games	Start		End
Winning Run:	5	29-Jan-93	to	2-Mar-93
Without Defeat:	12	5-Dec-92	to	2-Mar-93
Without Win:	14	24-Apr-93	to	10-Oct-93
	14	11-Dec-93	to	8-Mar-94
Drawn Games:	4	22-Jan-94	to	12-Feb-94
Without Draw:	12	28-Sep-91	to	26-Dec-91
Losing Run:	11	8-May-93	to	2-Oct-93
Clean Sheets:	5	26-Dec-97	to	20-Jan-98
Goal Scored:	12	18-Mar-95	to	19-Aug-95
No Goals For (5):	3	14-Feb-95	to	25-Feb-95
	3	8-Mar-97	to	22-Mar-97
SOS Undefeated:	3	15-Aug-92	to	19-Aug-92
SOS No Wins:	11	1993-94		

5-Year Record

	Div	P	W	D	L	F	A	Pts	Psn	
1993-94	2	46	5	13	28	41	86	28	24	Relegated
1994-95	3	42	15	11	16	56	63	56	11	
1995-96	3	46	18	16	12	65	45	70	9	
1996-97	3	46	14	16	16	46	51	58	15	
1997-98	3	46	19	13	14	61	51	70	7	

Brentford

Problem Bees

In January 1997 Brentford set a new club record of 25 home games without defeat. Sixteen months later the west London club had got through three managers and suffered relegation to the bottom division of the Football League for the first time in two decades. Brentford's problems began with the eve-of-season departure of manager Dave Webb. His replacement, Eddie May, lasted only until November when he and assistant manager Clive Walker were dismissed. Brought in to save the Bees from relegation was Micky Adams who was doing a good job at Fulham before his surprising dismissal at Craven Cottage. Adams made several signings and oversaw the sale of Marcus Bent to Crystal Palace for a possible £300,000. Although Adams did drag Brentford off the foot of the table a 2-1 defeat at Bristol Rovers on the final day of the season, coupled with Burnley's win over Plymouth, sent the Bees down.

Brentford's FA Cup sortie floundered in a penalty shoot-out at the first hurdle against Colchester but in the Coca-Cola Cup the Bees, after being held at home by Shrewsbury, pulled off a remarkable 5-3 win in the 2nd Leg. But in the 2nd Round Brentford were beaten home and away by Southampton.

Formed:	1889
Ground:	Griffin Park, Braemar Road, Brentford, Middx, TW8 0NT
Phone:	0181 847 2511
Box Office:	0181 847 2511
Info:	0891 12 11 08
Capacity:	12,763
Colours:	Red and white striped shirts, black shorts, red socks with white trim
Nickname:	The Bees
Manager:	Ron Noades
Honours:	Division 2 Champions 1934-35; Division 3 Champions 1991-92; Division 3S Champions 1932-33; Division 4 Champions 1962-63.
Managers:	Steve Perryman 1987-90, Phil Holder 1990-93, David Webb 1993-1998, Eddie May 1998, Micky Adams June 1998
Record League Win:	9-0 v Wrexham, D3, 15/10/63
Record League Defeat:	0-7 v Swansea, D3S, 8/11/24
Most GF in Season:	98 – Division 4, 1962-63
All-time League Apps:	514 – Ken Coote, 1949-64
All-time League Goals:	153 – Jim Towers, 1954-61
Most Goals in a Season:	38 – Jack Holliday, D3S 1932-33
Most Goals in a Match:	5 – Jack Holliday v Luton Town, D3S, 28/1/33 5 – Billy Scott v Barnsley, D2, 15/12/34 5 – Peter McKennan v Bury, D2, 18/2/49

Record Fee Received: £800,000 from Reading for Carl Asaba 8/97
Record Fee Paid: £720,000 to Chelsea for Joe Allon, 11/92
Record Attendance: 38,678 v Leicester City, FA Cup 6th Round, 20/2/49

Stats File

Division	P	W	D	L	F	A	Pts	Yr	B	W
Premier/D1:	210	76	46	88	330	359	198	5	5	21
Division 1n/2:	424	156	109	159	588	625	434	10	1	22
Division 2n/3:	1242	459	336	447	1705	1656	1533	27	1	23
Division 3n/4:	552	226	138	188	801	679	590	12	1	19

Cup Records	P	W	D	L	F	A
FA Cup:	203	82	44	77	320	280
League Cup:	107	32	22	53	143	186
A/F Members Cup:	51	27	7	17	87	62

Sequence	Games	Start		End
Winning Run:	9	30-Apr-32	to	24-Sep-32
Without Defeat:	16	30-Apr-32	to	12-Nov-32
	16	14-Jan-67	to	15-Apr-67
Without Win:	16	19-Feb-94	to	7-May-94
Drawn Games:	5	16-Mar-57	to	6-Apr-57
Without Draw:	26	15-Oct-76	to	26-Mar-77
Losing Run:	9	13-Apr-25	to	12-Sep-25
	9	20-Oct-28	to	25-Dec-28
Clean Sheets:	7	1-Oct-57	to	9-Nov-57
Goal Scored:	26	4-Mar-63	to	14-Sep-63
No Goals For:	6	19-Apr-97	to	16-Aug-97
SOS Undefeated:	14	1932-33		
SOS No Wins:	10	1925-26		

5-Year Record

	Div	P	W	D	L	F	A	Pts	Psn	
1993-94	2	46	13	19	14	57	55	58	16	
1994-95	2	46	25	10	11	81	39	85	2	
1995-96	2	46	15	13	18	43	49	58	15	
1996-97	2	46	20	14	12	56	43	74	4	
1997-98	2	46	11	17	18	50	71	50	21	Relegated

Brighton & HA

Going Home

With a highly publicised last day of the season draw at Hereford in May 1997, Brighton avoided relegation to the Vauxhall Conference but is it merely a stay of execution for the south coast club which has been on the brink of financial ruin for some considerable time? Manager Steve Gritt retained the previous season's squad and his prospects for the season were not aided by the club having to ground-share with Gillingham some 70 miles away.

The faithful who made the regular trips to Priestfield Stadium received scant reward with the Seagulls winning just three times at 'home'. Plans to relocate within Brighton for the new season will be well received by supporters although not local residents.

Hopes of a money-spinning FA Cup run floundered in the 1st Round as Hereford gained some measure of revenge for their demotion with a 2-1 win. Jeff Minton scored an equaliser at home to Leyton Orient in the 1st Round of the Coca-Cola Cup but defeat at Brisbane Road in the return match was one of three reversals the Os inflicted on the Seagulls during the season.

Brighton and Gritt parted company in February, which paved the way for the return of Brian Horton. The prospect of a temporary move back to Brighton's Withdean Stadium is very much on the cards while a new stadium is constructed.

Formed:	1900
Ground:	Withdean Stadium, Brighton.
Phone:	01273 778855
Box Office:	01273 778855
Info:	0891 44 00 66
Capacity:	tbc
Colours:	Blue and white striped shirts, blue shorts, blue socks
Nickname:	The Seagulls
Manager:	Brian Horton
Honours:	Division 3S Champions 1957-58; Division 4 Champions 1964-65; Charity Shield Winners 1910.
Managers:	Alan Mullery 1986-87, Barry Lloyd 1987-93, Liam Brady 1993-95, Jimmy Case 1995-96, Steve Gritt 1996-98.
Previous Names:	Brighton United, 1898-1900, Brighton & Hove Rangers 1900-1901
Record League Win:	9-1 v Newport, D3S, 18/4.51; 9-1 v Southend, D3, 27/11/65
Record League Defeat:	0-9 v Middlesbrough, D2, 23/8/58
Most GF in Season:	112 – Division 3, 1955-56
All-time League Apps:	509 – E 'Tug' Wilson, 1922-36
All-time League Goals:	113 – Tommy Cook, 1922-29

Most Goals in a Season: 32 – Peter Ward, 1976-77
Most Goals in a Match: 6 – Arthur Attwood v Shoreham, 12-0, FA Cup, 1/10/32
Record Fee Received: £900,000 from Liverpool for Mark Lawrenson, 8/81
Record Fee Paid: £500,000 to Manchester United for Andy Ritchie, 10/80
Record Attendance: 36,747 v Fulham, D2, 27/12/58

Stats File

Division	P	W	D	L	F	A	Pts	Yr	B	W
Premier/D1:	168	47	48	73	182	244	164	4	13	22
Division 1n/2:	646	229	155	262	881	983	737	15	2	23
Division 2n/3:	782	298	209	275	1065	987	887	17	2	23
Division 3n/4:	184	64	50	70	264	245	195	4	1	23I

Cup Records	P	W	D	L	F	A
FA Cup:	235	93	61	81	377	311
League Cup:	108	37	26	45	127	162
A/F Members Cup:	30	12	4	14	49	61

Sequence	Games	Start		End
Winning Run:	9	2-Oct-26	to	20-Nov-26
Without Defeat:	16	8-Oct-30	to	28-Jan-31
Without Win:	15	20-Sep-47	to	17-Jan-48
	15	21-Oct-72	to	27-Jan-73
Drawn Games:	6	16-Feb-80	to	15-Mar-80
Without Draw:	25	14-Feb-25	to	14-Oct-25
Losing Run:	12	11-Nov-72	to	27-Jan-73
Clean Sheets (5):	5	29-Jan-77	to	26-Feb-77
	5	25-Feb-95	to	15-Mar-95
Goal Scored:	31	4-Feb-56	to	6-Oct-56
No Goals For (3):	6	8-Nov-24	to	20-Dec-24
	6	23-Sep-70	to	16-Oct-70
SOS Undefeated:	8	1977-78		
	8	1953-54		
SOS No Wins:	8	1966-67		
	8	1997-98		

5-Year Record

	Div	P	W	D	L	F	A	Pts	Psn	
1993-94	2	46	15	14	17	60	67	59	14	
1994-95	2	46	14	17	15	54	53	59	16	
1995-96	2	46	10	10	26	46	69	40	23	Relegated
1996-97	3	46	13	10	23	53	70	47	23	
1997-98	3	46	6	17	23	38	66	35	23	

Cambridge United

Wonder Worker

Cambridge United ended the 1996/97 season with just two wins from 15 games but still missed the play-off places by just four points. Manager Roy McFarland looked to have worked wonders during the close season as, with seven games of the new season gone, United were just a point off the top of the table. But it proved to be a short-lived fling near the summit as the Us then endured a 13-match run without a win and dropped quickly down the table. Cambridge retained a reasonable home record with just four games lost at the Abbey Stadium all season. But with just three away successes and ten games drawn, they failed to pick up sufficient points on their travels to stay in contention.

With their finances stretched, McFarland only signed players on free transfers but did swell the club's coffers by almost £600,000 following the departure of Jody Craddock and Micah Hyde.

Having already defeated Plymouth in the FA Cup, Cambridge had two players dismissed during a 2nd Round replay defeat at Vauxhall Conference side Stevenage. The Us battled well in the Coca-Cola Cup and only went out in extra time to Division One West Brom following two 1-1 draws.

Formed:	1919
Ground:	Abbey Stadium, Newmarket Road, Cambridge, CB5 8LL
Phone:	01223 566500
Box Office:	01223 566500
Info:	0891 555885
Capacity:	9,667
Colours:	Amber shirts with black stripe, black shorts, black socks with amber trim
Nickname:	Us
Manager	Roy McFarland
Honours:	Division 3 Champions 1990-91; Division 4 Champions 1976-77
Managers:	Chris Turner 1985-90, John Beck 1990-92, Ian Atkins 1992-93, Gary Johnson 1993-95, Tommy Taylor 1995-96.
Previous Names:	Abbey United until 1951.
Record League Win:	6-0 v Darlington, D4, 18/9/71
	6-0 v Hartlepool United, D4, 11/2/89
Record League Defeat:	0-6 v Aldershot, D3, 13/4/74
	0-6 v Darlington, D4, 28/9/74
	0-6 v Chelsea, D2, 15/1/83
Most GF in Season:	87 – Division 4, 1976-77
All-time League Apps:	416 – Steve Spriggs, 1975-87
All-time League Goals:	74 – Alan Biley, 1975-80
Most Goals in a Season:	24 – David Crown, 1977-78

Most Goals in a Match:	4 – Brian Greenhalgh v Darlington, D4, 18/9/71
Record Fee Received:	£1m from Manchester United for Dion Dublin, 8/92
Record Fee Paid:	£230,000 to Luton Town for Steve Claridge, 11/92
Record Attendance:	14,000 v Chelsea (friendly), 1/5/70

Stats File

Division	P	W	D	L	F	A	Pts	Yr	B	W
Division 1n/2:	344	103	104	137	389	476	370	8	5	23
Division 2n/3:	276	95	65	116	363	414	314	6	1	24
Division 3n/4:	644	245	184	215	886	838	807	14	1	22

Cup Records	P	W	D	L	F	A
FA Cup:	79	30	16	33	95	103
League Cup:	73	22	15	36	83	121
A/F Members Cup:	32	9	7	16	49	66

Sequence	Games	Start		End
Winning Run:	7	19-Feb-77	to	1-Apr-77
Without Defeat:	14	9-Sep-72	to	10-Nov-72
Without Win:	31	8-Oct-83	to	23-Apr-84
Drawn Games:	6	6-Sep-86	to	30-Sep-86
Without Draw:	25	4-Apr-81	to	5-Dec-81
Losing Run (4):	7	29-Dec-84	to	26-Feb-85
	7	8-Apr-85	to	30-Apr-85
Clean Sheets:	5	23-Jan-82	to	9-Feb-82
	5	22-Feb-87	to	10-Mar-87
Goal Scored:	19	19-Aug-72	to	25-Nov-72
No Goals For:	5	29-Sep-73	to	20-Oct-73
SOS Undefeated:	9	1986-87		
SOS No Wins:	5	1989-90		

5-Year Record

	Div	P	W	D	L	F	A	Pts	Psn	
1993-94	2n	46	19	9	18	79	73	66	10	
1994-95	2n	46	11	15	20	52	69	48	20	Relegated
1995-96	3n	46	14	12	20	61	71	54	16	
1996-97	3n	46	18	11	17	53	59	65	10	
1997-98	3n	46	14	18	14	63	57	60	16	

Cardiff City

Draw of the Draws

Cardiff City, along with Hartlepool, were very much the Nationwide League draw specialists with exactly half of their 46 Division Three matches finishing all square. The high number of draws meant that Cardiff lost fewer away games than any other of the bottom 11 sides in the League, but only two clubs won less home Nationwide League matches.

The bookies had great faith in the Bluebirds, making them favourites for promotion after they made the play-offs the previous season. After six games Russell Osman's side were undefeated but 40 games later had recorded just nine wins as only three clubs separated them from the Vauxhall Conference.

Cardiff brought in four players during the summer at a cost of £85,000 and made £500,000 from Simon Haworth's transfer to Coventry. During the season £60,000 was invested in Wigan striker Andy Sackville.

Cardiff's poor league form cost Osman his job in January, with Kenny Hibbitt returning to the hotseat. Osman's exit came two days before a 4th Round FA Cup draw with Reading; the Division One side went through on a cruel penalty shoot-out victory. Cardiff had already beaten Slough, Hendon and Oldham. The Ninian Park club were knocked out of the Coca-Cola Cup in the 1st Round by Southend.

Formed:	1899
Ground:	Ninian Park, Sloper Road, Cardiff, CF1 8SX
Phone:	01222 398636
Box Office:	01222 398636
Info:	0891 121171
Capacity:	14,980
Colours:	Royal blue shirts with white collar, white shorts, blue stockings
Nickname:	The Bluebirds
Manager:	Kenny Hibbitt
Honours:	Division 3S Champions 1946-47; Division 3 Champions 1992-93; FA Cup Winners 1926-27; Charity Shield Winners 1927; Welsh FA Cup Winners 22 times.
Managers:	Kenny Hibbitt 1995, Phil Neal 1996, Russell Osman 1996, Kenny Hibbitt 1996, Russell Osman 1996-98.
Previous Names:	Riverside FC, 1899-1908
Record League Win:	9-2 v Thames, D3S, 6/2/32
	7-0 v Burnley, D1, 1/9/28
	7-0 v Barnsley, D2, 7/12/57
	7-1 v Doncaster Rovers, D3, 1997-98
Record League Defeat:	2-11 v Sheffield United, D1, 1/1/26
	0-9 v Preston North End, D2, 7/5/66
Most GF in Season:	93 – Division 3S, 1946/47

All-time League Apps:	471 – Phil Dwyer, 1972-85	
All-time League Goals:	128 – Len Davies, 1920-23	
Most Goals in a Season:	30 – Stan Richards, 1946-47	
Most Goals in a Match:	6 – Derek Tapscott v Knighton Town, Welsh FA Cup, 20/01/61	
Record Fee Received:	£300,000 from Sheffield Utd for Nathan Blake, 2/94	
Record Fee Paid:	£200,000 to San Jose Earthquake for Godfrey Ingram, 9/82	
Record Attendance:	57,893 v Arsenal, D1, 22/5/53	
	61,566, Wales v England, 14/10/61	

Stats File

Division	P	W	D	L	F	A	Pts	Yr	B	W
Premier/D1:	630	224	154	252	865	993	602	15	2	22
Division 1n/2:	1344	480	340	524	1838	1994	1336	32	2	22
Division 2n/3:	322	107	88	127	405	460	387	7	2	22
Division 3n/4:	360	136	111	113	445	415	519	8	1	22

Cup Records	P	W	D	L	F	A
FA Cup:	194	76	46	72	252	246
League Cup:	100	37	17	46	138	178
A/F Members Cup:	32	8	6	18	39	58

Sequence	Games	Start		End
Winning Run:	9	26-Oct-46	to	28-Dec-46
Without Defeat:	21	21-Sep-46	to	1-Mar-47
Without Win:	15	21-Nov-36	to	6-Mar-37
Drawn Games:	6	29-Nov-80	to	17-Jan-81
Without Draw:	17	25-Aug-62	to	17-Nov-62
Losing Run:	7	4-Nov-33	to	25-Dec-33
Clean Sheets:	7	7-Apr-76	to	21-Aug-76
Goal Scored:	23	24-Oct-92	to	20-Mar-93
No Goals For:	8	20-Dec-52	to	14-Feb-53
SOS Undefeated:	11	1923-24		
SOS No Wins:	11	1964-65		

5-Year Record

	Div	P	W	D	L	F	A	Pts	Psn	
1993-94	2n	46	13	15	18	66	79	54	19	
1994-95	2n	46	9	11	26	46	74	38	22	Relegated
1995-96	3n	46	11	12	23	41	64	45	22	
1996-97	3n	46	20	9	17	56	54	69	7	
1997-98	3n	46	9	23	14	48	52	50	21	

Carlisle United

Day Light Gone

The gulf between the Premiership and Division One causes many a debate, while the fortunes of Carlisle United suggest that an equally unassailable void exists between the bottom two divisions. United went into the 1997/98 campaign as Division Three champions only to return there a year later after a bizarre turn of events. Mervyn Day was charged with keeping the Cumbrians in Division Two but colourful chairman Michael Knighton dispensed with his services in September and then successfully took the club to relegation himself. Knighton, who chose to stay in his Isle of Man home when Carlisle's relegation was confirmed, faced predictable calls for his head from the fans.

Prior to the start of the season Day made two six-figure signings but it was local-born goalkeeper Tony Caig who, despite conceding 75 league goals, picked up the club's Player of the Year Award.

The FA Cup offered no respite from Carlisle's league failings with a 1-0 1st Round defeat suffered at the hands of Wigan at Brunton Park. Carlisle competently disposed of Chester in the Coca-Cola Cup for the second successive year. In the 2nd Round the Blues led 2-1 at Tottenham before the Premiership side eventually pulled through 5-2 on aggregate.

Formed:	1904
Ground:	Brunton Park, Warwick Road, Carlisle, Cumbria, CA1 1LL
Phone:	01228 26237
Box Office:	01228 26237
Info:	0891 230011
Capacity:	16,651
Colours:	Blue shirts with white pinstripe and collar, white shorts, blue socks
Nickname:	Cumbrians
Manager:	Michael Knighton
Honours:	Division 3 Champions 1964-65.
Managers:	Cliff Middlemas 1987-91, Aidan McCaffery 1991-92, David McCreery 1992-93, Mick Wadsworth 1993-96, Mervyn Day 1996-97.
Previous Names:	Shaddongate United
Record League Win:	8-0 v Hartlepool, D3N, 1/9/29
	8-0 v Scunthorpe United, D2N, 25/12/52
Record League Defeat:	1-11 v Hull City, D2N, 14/1/39
Most GF in Season:	113 – Division 4, 1963-64
All-time League Apps:	466 – Alan Ross, 1963-79
All-time League Goals:	126 – Jimmy McConnell, 1928-32
Most Goals in a Season:	42 – Jimmy McConnell, D3N, 1928-29
Most Goals in a Match:	5 – H. Mills v Halifax Town, D2N, 11/9/37
	5 – Jim Whitehouse, v Scunthorpe U., D3N, 25/12/52

Record Fee Received: £1m (> £2m) from C. Palace for Matt Jansen, 2/98
Record Fee Paid: £121,000 to Notts County for David Reeves, 12/93
Record Attendance: 27,500 v Birmingham City, FAC R3, 5/1/57 and
v Middlesbrough, FA Cup 5th Round, 7/2/70

Stats File

Division	P	W	D	L	F	A	Pts	Yr	B	W
Premier/D1:	42	12	5	25	43	59	29	1	22	22
Division 1n/2:	630	229	158	243	837	857	670	15	3	20
Division 2n/3:	460	156	125	179	589	642	494	10	1	23
Division 3n/4:	626	242	150	234	852	867	782	14	1	23

Cup Records	P	W	D	L	F	A
FA Cup:	177	73	33	71	287	278
League Cup:	108	39	25	44	147	171
A/F Members Cup:	51	28	8	15	79	56

Sequence	Games	Start		End
Winning Run:	6	27-Feb-37	to	27-Mar-37
Without Defeat:	19	1-Oct-94	to	11-Feb-95
Without Win:	14	19-Jan-35	to	19-Apr-35
Drawn Games:	6	11-Feb-78	to	11-Mar-78
Without Draw:	26	15-Mar-30	to	22-Nov-30
Losing Run:	8	19-Jan-35	to	9-Mar-35
	8	8-Nov-86	to	3-Jan-87
Clean Sheets:	7	9-Oct-68	to	16-Nov-68
Goal Scored:	26	23-Aug-47	to	17-Jan-48
No Goals For:	5	24-Aug-68	to	14-Sep-68
SOS Undefeated:	10	1989-90		
SOS No Wins:	12	1968-69		

5-Year Record

	Div	P	W	D	L	F	A	Pts	Psn	
1993-94	3n	42	18	10	14	57	42	64	7	
1994-95	3n	42	27	10	5	67	31	91	1	Promoted
1995-96	2n	46	12	13	21	57	72	49	21	Relegated
1996-97	3n	46	24	12	10	67	44	84	3	Promoted
1997-98	2n	46	12	8	26	57	73	44	23	Relegated

Chester City

Home High, Away Low

Although Chester City finished well down the Division Three table in 14th place, they were only nine points short of a play-off position, mainly on the strength of a useful home record – they won more home games than promoted Lincoln. The Blues also completed the league double with a win at Notts County and a home success against Colchester. Conversely, City also suffered the indignity of being the only side to lose away to both Brighton and Doncaster.

Chester faced an embarrassing FA Cup exit at home to Winsford United before goals from Nick Richardson and Chris Priest turned the tie round. At home to Wrexham in the 2nd Round, Chester bowed out 2-0 in front of the Sky television cameras. For the second year running, Chester parted company with the Coca-Cola Cup at the 1st Round stage courtesy of Division Two Carlisle.

Manager Kevin Ratcliffe boosted the club's coffers on transfer deadline day with the sale of teenager Matt McKay to Everton. McKay was a first-year professional at the Deva Stadium and his transfer could eventually earn Chester £750,000.

Formed:	1884
Ground:	Deva Stadium, Bumpers Lane, Chester, Cheshire, CH1 4LT
Phone:	01244 371376
Box Office:	01244 371376
Info:	0891 121633
Capacity:	6,000
Colours:	Blue and white striped shirts, black shorts, blue and white socks
Nickname:	Blues or City
Manager	Kevin Ratcliffe
Honours:	Division 3N Cup Winners 1935-36, 1936-37; Welsh Cup Winners (3); Debenhams Cup Winners 1976-77.
Managers:	John McGrath 1984, Harry McNally 1985-92, Graham Barrow 1992-94, Mike Pejic 1994-95, Derek Mann 1995.
Previous Name:	Chester until 1983.
Record League Win:	12-0 v York City, D3N, 1/2/36
Record League Defeat:	0-9 v Barrow, D3N, 10/2/34
	2-11 v Oldham Athletic, D3N, 19/1/52
Most GF in Season:	119 – Division 4 1964-65
All-time League Apps:	408 – Ray Gill, 1951-62
All-time League Goals:	125 – Stuart Rimmer, 1985-88, 1991-97
Most Goals in a Season:	36 – Dick Yates, D3N, 1946-47
Most Goals in a Match:	5 – T. Jennings v Walsall, 5-1, D3N, 30/1/32
	5 – Barry Jepson v York City, 9-2, D4, 8/2/58
Record Fee Recieved:	£500,000 (>£750,000) from Everton for Matt McKay, 3/98

Record Fee Paid: £120,000 to Barnsley for Stuart Rimmer, 8/91
Record Attendance: 20,500 v Chelsea, FA Cup R3 Replay, 16/1/1952 (Sealand Rd)

Stats File

Division	P	W	D	L	F	A	Pts	Yr	B	W
Division 2n/3:	690	203	191	296	737	960	705	15	5	24
Division 3n/4:	1144	410	290	444	1599	1649	1244	25	2	24

Cup Records	P	W	D	L	F	A
FA Cup:	156	64	27	65	235	227
League Cup:	101	26	21	54	122	197
A/F Members Cup:	41	13	8	20	41	63

Sequence	Games	Start		End
Winning Run:	8	21-Apr-34	to	5-Sep-34
	8	1-Feb-36	to	14-Mar-36
Without Defeat:	18	27-Oct-34	to	16-Feb-35
Without Win:	25	19-Sep-61	to	3-Mar-62
Drawn Games:	6	11-Oct-86	to	1-Nov-86
Without Draw:	24	16-Oct-76	to	22-Mar-77
Losing Run:	9	7-Apr-93	to	21-Aug-93
	9	30-Apr-94	to	13-Sep-94
Clean Sheets (3):	5	21-Sep-74	to	5-Oct-74
	5	4-Feb-97	to	22-Feb-97
Goal Scored:	24	31-Aug-32	to	21-Jan-33
No Goals For (6):	5	3-Apr-82	to	21-Apr-82
	5	3-Nov-90	to	15-Dec-90
SOS Undefeated:	9	1936-37		
SOS No Wins:	9	1994-95		
	9	1956-57		

5-Year Record

	Div	P	W	D	L	F	A	Pts	Psn	
1993-94	3	42	21	11	10	69	46	74	2	Promoted
1994-95	2	46	6	11	29	37	84	29	23	Relegated
1995-96	3	46	18	16	12	72	53	70	8	
1996-97	3	46	18	16	12	55	43	70	6	
1997-98	3	46	17	10	19	60	61	61	14	

Darlington

Quaking Season
Since making the play-offs in 1995/96, Darlington have spent two seasons down in the lower reaches of Division Three. Whilst there is nothing particularly startling about that fact, it must be frustrating for manager David Hodgson that a fine home record was badly let down by away performances which produced the second worst return in the whole of the Nationwide League. With just a mediocre away record the Quakers could have attained a comfortable mid-table or even play-off position. But for the dire circumstances Doncaster find themselves in, Darlington would not have won a single game on their travels.

It was a different story in the FA Cup where, technically, they chalked up two away successes. In the 1st Round Darlington were held at home by non-leaguers Solihull Borough despite taking a first-minute lead through Glenn Naylor. The replay was a six-goal thriller ending all square with Darlington's Canadian international Jason Devos striking home the deciding penalty shoot-out winner. And it was a Darren Roberts penalty which gave the Quakers victory at Hednesford before Wolves ended the party with a 4-0 romp at Feethams. Darlington went out of the Coca-Cola Cup in the 1st Round when facing Division Three champions-elect Notts County.

Formed:	1883
Ground:	Feethams, Darlington, Co. Durham, DL1 5JB
Phone:	01325 465097
Box Office:	01325 465097
Info:	0898 12 11 49
Capacity:	7,046
Colours:	White shirts with diagonal black stripes, black shorts, white socks
Nickname:	The Quakers
Manager:	David Hodgson
Honours:	Division 3N Champions 1924-25;
	Division 3N Cup Winners 1933-34;
	Division 4 Champions 1990-91;
	GMVC Champions 1989-90.
Managers:	Billy McEwan 1992-93, Alan Murray 1993-95, Paul Futcher 1995, David Hodgson/Jim Platt 1995, Jim Platt 1995-96.
Record League Win:	9-2 v Lincoln City, D2N, 7/1/28
Record League Defeat:	0-10 v Doncaster Rovers, D4, 25/1/64
Most GF in Season:	108 – Division 3N, 1929-30
All-time League Apps:	442 – Ron Greener, 1955-68
All-time League Goals:	87 – Alan Walsh, 1978-84
Most Goals in Season:	39 – David Brown, D3N, 1924-25

Most Goals in a Match:	5 – Tom Ruddy v South Shields, D2, 23/4/27	
	5 – Maurice Wellock v Rotherham U., D3N, 15/2/30	
Record Fee Received:	£250,000 from Newcastle for James Coppinger, 3/98	
Record Fee Paid:	£250,000 from Newcastle for Paul Robinson, 3/98	
	£95,000 to Motherwell for Nick Cusack, 1/92	
Record Attendance:	21,023 v Bolton Wanderers, LC 3rd Round, 14/11/60	

Stats File

Division	P	W	D	L	F	A	Pts	Yr	B	W
Division 1n/2:	84	26	16	42	151	175	68	2	15	21
Division 2n/3:	184	45	47	92	209	326	169	4	13	24
Division 3n/4:	1596	531	430	635	2047	2288	1690	35	1	24

Cup Records	P	W	D	L	F	A
FA Cup:	188	69	41	78	262	295
League Cup:	99	32	20	47	113	172
A/F Members Cup:	35	10	5	20	62	75

Sequence	Games	Start		End
Winning Run:	5	7-Jan-28	to	11-Feb-28
Without Defeat:	17	27-Apr-68	to	19-Oct-68
Without Win:	19	27-Apr-88	to	8-Nov-88
Drawn Games:	5	24-Feb-87	to	14-Mar-87
	5	31-Dec-88	to	28-Jan-89
Without Draw:	25	1-Jan-32	to	7-Sep-32
Losing Run:	8	31-Aug-85	to	19-Oct-85
Clean Sheets:	7	16-Sep-68	to	19-Oct-68
	7	2-Feb-91	to	5-Mar-91
Goal Scored:	22	3-Dec-32	to	15-Apr-33
No Goals For:	7	5-Sep-75	to	11-Oct-75
	7	25-Feb-95	to	25-Mar-95
SOS Undefeated:	14	1968-69		
SOS No Wins:	15	1988-89		

5-Year Record

	Div	P	W	D	L	F	A	Pts	Psn
1993-94	3	42	10	11	21	42	64	41	21
1994-95	3	42	11	8	23	43	57	41	20
1995-96	3	46	20	18	8	60	42	78	5
1996-97	3	46	14	10	22	64	78	52	18
1997-98	3	46	14	12	20	56	72	54	19

Exeter City

All-Point High

With relegation to the Vauxhall Conference in 1997 having been averted by a single point, Exeter City were strongly fancied to drop out of the Nationwide League a year later. But to the immense credit of manager Peter Fox, the Grecians made a fine start to the 1997/98 season – they were just two points off the top after 20 games – and were in contention for a play-off position until the final stages of the season. Exeter finished the season in 15th place. Their total of 60 points is the Grecians' highest since being relegated to Division Three in 1994 but it did leave them ten points adrift of a place in the top seven.

Top scorer Darren Rowbotham, whose first league goal of the season was his 100th in the Football League, put Exeter ahead in their 1st Round FA Cup tie with Northampton but the Cobblers forced a draw and won the replay. Exeter went out of the Coca-Cola Cup in the 1st Round for the fourth consecutive year with Walsall winning 2-0 at the Bescot Stadium and 1-0 at St James's Park. Exeter have scored in just one of their last six matches in this competition.

Formed:	1904
Ground:	St James's Park, Well Street, Exeter, Devon, EX4 6PX
Phone:	01392 254073
Box Office:	01392 254073
Info:	0891 44 68 68
Capacity:	10,570
Colours:	Red and white striped shirts, black shorts, red socks
Nickname:	The Grecians
Manager:	Peter Fox
Honours:	Division 4 Champions 1989-90; Division 3 South Cup Winners 1933-34.
Managers:	Gerry Francis 1983-84, Jim Iley 1984-85, Colin Appleton 1985-87, John Delve (Caretaker) 1988, Terry Cooper 1988-91.
Record League Win:	8-1 v Coventry, D3S, 4/12/26 8-1 v Aldershot, D3S, 4/5/35 7-0 v Crystal Palace, D3S, 9/1/54
Record League Defeat:	0-9 v Notts County, D3S, 16/10/48 0-9 v Northampton Town, D3S, 12/4/58
Most GF in Season:	88 – Division 3S, 1932-33
All-time League Apps:	495 – Arnold Mitchell, 1952-66
All-time League Goals:	129 – Tony Kellow, 1976-78, 1980-83 & 1985-87
Most Goals in a Season:	33 – Fred Whitlow, D3S, 1932-33
Most Goals in a Match:	6 – James Bell v Weymouth, FAV 1PR, 3/10/08 6 – Fred Whitlow v Crystal Palace, D3S Cup, 24/1/34

Record Fee Received: £500,000 from Rangers for Chris Vinnicombe, 11/98 and from Manchester City for Martin Phillips, 11/95
Record Fee Paid: £65,000 to Blackpool for Tony Kellow, 3/80
Record Attendance: 20,984 v Sunderland, FA Cup 6th Round Replay, 4/3/31

Stats File

Division	P	W	D	L	F	A	Pts	Yr	B	W
Division 2n/3:	598	179	165	254	759	936	611	13	8	24
Division 3n/4:	1235	433	339	463	1617	1693	1347	27	1	22

Cup Records	P	W	D	L	F	A
FA Cup:	176	60	41	75	272	280
League Cup:	104	29	26	49	119	176
A/F Members Cup:	45	13	12	20	45	56

Sequence	Games	Start		End
Winning Run:	7	23-Apr-77	to	20-Aug-77
Without Defeat:	13	23-Aug-86	to	25-Oct-86
Without Win:	18	14-Jan-84	to	21-Apr-84
	18	21-Feb-95	to	19-Aug-95
Drawn Games:	6	13-Sep-86	to	4-Oct-86
Without Draw:	19	12-Sep-73	to	22-Dec-73
Losing Run (5):	7	22-Feb-36	to	28-Mar-36
	7	14-Jan-84	to	25-Feb-84
Clean Sheets (3):	5	20-Sep-86	to	11-Oct-86
	5	19-Aug-95	to	9-Sep-95
Goal Scored:	22	15-Sep-58	to	28-Feb-59
No Goals For:	6	24-Nov-23	to	29-Dec-23
	6	17-Jan-86	to	21-Feb-86
SOS Undefeated:	13	1986-87		
SOS No Wins (4):	7	1992-93		
	7	1966-67		

5-Year Record

	Div	P	W	D	L	F	A	Pts	Psn	
1993-94	2	46	11	12	23	52	83	45	22	Relegated
1994-95	3	42	8	10	24	36	70	34	22	
1995-96	3	46	13	18	15	46	53	57	14	
1996-97	3	46	12	12	22	48	73	48	22	
1997-98	3	46	15	15	16	68	63	60	15	

Halifax Town

Shay Return

Halifax Town supporters could be forgiven if, five years ago, they wondered whether they would have a club to support come the millennium as the Shaymen dropped out of the Football League. But now, with 61-year-old Scot George Mulhall at the helm, Halifax can look forward to the new century with genuine optimism, having reclaimed their Nationwide League status and invested around £750,000 on improving the once dilapidated facilities at the Shay.

Halifax made a flying start to the season with a dozen unbeaten games before being hammered 4-0 at Cheltenham Town. At the turn of the year Cheltenham were just four points behind Halifax with two games in hand but a month later Mulhall's side were ten points clear of the pack and well on the way to adding their name to those of Colchester, Darlington and Lincoln as clubs which have won their way back into the league following relegation to the Conference. Promotion was secured on 18th April with a 2-0 win at Kidderminster, with goals from top Conference scorer Geoff Horsfield and Jamie Paterson. Horsfield scored 30 times in the Conference as Halifax became only the fourth club in the league's history to go through an entire campaign unbeaten at home.

Formed:	1911
Ground:	The Shay Stadium, Shaw Hill, Halifax,
Phone:	01422 345543
Box Office:	01422 345543
Info:	0891 22 73 23
Capacity:	8,049
Colours:	Blue shirts, blue shorts, white socks
Nickname:	The Shaymen
Manager:	George Mulhall
Honours:	Division 3N Runners-up 1934-35; Division 4 Runners-up 1968-69; GMVC Champions 1997-98.
Managers:	(Football League) Bill Ayre 1986-90, Jim McCalliog (1990-91), John McGrath 1991-92, Peter Wragg 1992-. (Conference) John Bird.
Record League Win:	6-0 v Bradford PA, D3N, 3/12/55
Record League Defeat:	0-13 v Stockport County, D3N, 6/1/34
Most GF in Season:	83 – Division 3N, 1957-58
All-time League Apps:	367 – John Pickering, 1965-74
All-time League Goals:	129 – Ernest Dixon, 1922-30
Most Goals in a Season:	34 – Albert Valentine, D3N, 1934-35
Most Goals in a Match:	-

Record Fee Received: £250,000 from Watford for Wayne Allison, 7/89
Record Fee Paid: £50,000 to Hereford U. for Ian Juryeff, 9/90
Record Attendance: 36,885 v Tottenham H., FA Cup 5th Round, 15/2/53

Stats File

Division	P	W	D	L	F	A	Pts	Yr	B	W
Division 2n/3:	552	179	162	211	697	826	520	12	3	24
Division 3n/4:	1050	298	284	468	1234	1606	1030	23	2	23

Cup Records	P	W	D	L	F	A
FA Cup:	160	51	42	67	220	253
League Cup:	72	14	16	42	86	140
A/F Members Cup:	29	10	7	12	37	48

Sequence	Games	Start		End
Winning Run:	7	22-Feb-64	to	21-Mar-64
Without Defeat:	17	14-Jan-69	to	21-Apr-69
Without Win:	22	26-Aug-78	to	10-Feb-79
Drawn Games:	7	22-Jan-82	to	20-Feb-82
Without Draw:	23	30-Sep-33	to	24-Feb-34
Losing Run:	8	7-Dec-46	to	13-Jan-47
Clean Sheets:	5	3-May-69	to	9-Aug-69
	5	11-Jan-71	to	6-Feb-71
Goal Scored:	19	2-May-88	to	26-Nov-88
No Goals For:	8	25-Aug-90	to	6-Oct-90
SOS Undefeated:	5	1959-60		
	5	1961-62		
SOS No Wins:	9	1954-55		

5-Year Record

	Div	P	W	D	L	F	A	Pts	Psn	
1993-94	VC	42	13	16	13	55	49	55	13	
1994-95	VC	42	17	12	13	68	54	63	8	
1995-96	VC	42	13	13	16	49	68	52	15	
1996-97	VC	42	12	12	18	55	74	48	19	
1997-98	VC	42	25	12	5	74	43	87	1	Promoted

Hartlepool United

Home Base
Finishing in 17th place in Division Three of the Nationwide League is unlikely to result in a rush on season tickets at Victoria Park for the 1998/99 season, but it was Hartlepool United's most successful campaign since being relegated four years earlier.

The most remarkable feature of Hartlepool's season was that the club which made more applications for re-election to the league than any other lost just one of their 23 home Division Three matches. Just one other side matched that achievement and only Macclesfield could better it in the whole of the Premiership and the Nationwide Leagues. Hartlepool were also the only side to record ten or more draws both home and away, with exactly half of their league games ending all square.

Despite their near invincibility at home in the league, Hartlepool suffered a 1st Round FA Cup exit for the fifth consecutive year as Macclesfield won 4-2 in Cleveland. 'Pool recorded a notable 2-1 home win over Tranmere in the Coca-Cola Cup but departed the competition 4-3 on aggregate.

Manager Mick Tait traded mostly with free transfer players during the season but made a handsome profit when selling Jon Cullen to Sheffield United in January for £250,000.

Formed:	1908
Ground:	Victoria Park, Hartlepool, Cleveland, TS24 8BZ
Phone:	01429 272584
Box Office:	01429 222077
Info:	0891 12 11 47
Capacity:	7,229
Colours:	Sky blue shirts with dark blue trim, dark blue shorts, blue socks
Nickname:	The Pool
Manager:	Mick Tait
Honours:	Division 3N Runners-up 1956-57.
Managers:	Alan Murray 1991-93, Viv Busby 1993, John MacPhail 1993-94, David McCreery 1994-95, Keith Houchen 1995-96.
Previous Names:	Hartlepools United until 1968; Hartlepool, 1968-77
Record League Win:	10-1 v Barrow, D4, 4/4/59
Record League Defeat:	1-10 v Wrexham, D4, 3/3/62
Most GF in Season:	90 – Division 3N, 1956-57
All-time League Apps:	447 – Watty Moore 1948-60
All-time League Goals:	98 – Ken Johnson, 1949-64
Most Goals in a Season:	28 – Billy Robinson, D3N, 1928-28
	28 – Joe Allon, D4, 1990-91
Most Goals in a Match:	7 – Billy Smith v St Peters Albion, FAC, 17/11/23

Record Fee Received: £275,000 from Plymouth Argyle for Paul Dalton, 5/92
Record Fee Paid: £75,000 to Plymouth Argyle for Ryan Cross, 5/92
Record Attendance: 17,426 v Manchester United, FA Cup 3rd Round, 18/1/57

Stats File

Division	P	W	D	L	F	A	Pts	Yr	B	W
Division 2n/3:	184	51	51	82	180	274	194	4	11	23
Division 3n/4:	1650	507	400	743	1993	2647	1612	36	3	24

Cup Records	P	W	D	L	F	A
FA Cup:	158	56	33	69	233	272
League Cup:	90	20	20	50	99	183
A/F Members Cup:	35	11	3	21	39	76

Sequence	Games	Start		End
Winning Run:	7	4-Sep-56	to	24-Sep-56
	7	1-Apr-68	to	26-Apr-68
Without Defeat:	17	24-Feb-68	to	10-Aug-68
	18	9-Jan-93	to	3-Apr-93
Without Win:	18	1-Dec-62	to	20-Apr-63
	18	9-Jan-93	to	3-Apr-93
Drawn Games (5):	4	23-Aug-86	to	13-Sep-86
	4	28-Oct-95	to	18-Nov-95
Without Draw (4):	22	2-May-55	to	3-Dec-55
	22	17-Jan-70	to	15-Aug-70
Losing Run (3):	8	28-Mar-70	to	15-Aug-70
	8	27-Jan-93	to	27-Feb-93
Clean Sheets (3):	5	29-Apr-67	to	1-Sep-67
	5	27-Jan-73	to	23-Feb-73
Goal Scored:	17	28-Feb-64	to	29-Aug-64
No Goals For:	11	9-Jan-93	to	2-Mar-93
SOS Undefeated:	6	1992-93		
SOS No Wins:	10	1976-77		

5-Year Record

	Div	P	W	D	L	F	A	Pts	Psn	
1993-94	2	46	9	9	28	41	87	36	23	Relegated
1994-95	3	42	11	10	21	43	69	43	18	
1995-96	3	46	12	13	21	47	67	49	20	
1996-97	3	46	14	9	23	53	66	51	20	
1997-98	3	46	12	23	11	61	53	59	17	

Hull City

Tiger Service

A poor run-in to the 1996/97 season led to the end of Terry Dolan's seven-year tenure as manager of Hull City and opened the door for former England striker Mark Hateley to take his first steps in management. Hull's first season in the bottom division for 13 years saw the Tigers finish in 17th position but hopes of an instant improvement in results were not fulfilled. Hull were pointless and bottom of the Nationwide League after three games before an astonishing first win was recorded with a 7-4 rout of Swansea at Boothferry Park with the previous season's top scorer, Duane Darby, notching a hat-trick. Just one away game was won all season, at Cambridge, while Hull also suffered the indignity of defeat at Conference-bound Doncaster. Come the end of the season only Brighton and Doncaster were still below the Tigers.

Hull suffered a nightmare in the FA Cup with a 2-0 1st Round defeat at Boothferry Park by Hednesford. The Tigers saved their best form for the Coca-Cola Cup. Macclesfield were defeated before Premiership Crystal Palace were beaten on the away goals rule thanks to Ian Wright's goal at Selhurst Park. The run ended in the 3rd Round at Newcastle.

Formed:	1904
Ground:	Boothferry Park, Boothferry Road, Hull, North Humberside, HU4 6EU
Phone:	01482 351119
Box Office:	01482 351119
Info:	0891 66 45 50
Capacity:	12,996
Colours:	Amber and black striped shirts, black shorts, black and amber socks
Nickname:	The Tigers
Manager:	Mark Hateley
Honours:	Division 3 Champions 1965-66; Division 3N Champions 1932-33, 1948-49.
Managers:	Brian Horton 1984-88, Eddie Gray 1988-90, Colin Appleton 1990, Stan Ternant 1990-91, Terry Dolan 1991-97.
Record League Win:	10-0 v Halifax Town, D3N, 26/12/30 11-1 v Carlisle Utd, D3N, 14/1/39
Record League Defeat:	0-8 v Wolverhampton W., D2, 4/11/11
Most GF in Season:	109 – Division 3, 1965-66
All-time League Apps:	520 – Andy Davidson 1952-67
All-time League Goals:	195 – Chris Chilton, 1960-71
Most Goals in a Match:	5 – Ken McDonald v Bristol City, D2, 17/11/28 5 – Slim Raleigh v Halifax Town, D3N, 26/12/30
Most Goals in a Season:	39 – Bill McNaughton, D3N, 1932-33

Record Fee Received: £750,000 from Middlesbrough for Andy Payton, 11/91
Record Fee Paid: £200,000 to Leeds United for Peter Swan, 3/89
Record Attendance: 55,019 v Manchester United, FA Cup 6th Round, 26/2/49

Stats File

Division	P	W	D	L	F	A	Pts	Yr	B	W
Division 1n/2:	2074	723	547	804	2818	3017	2072	50	3	24
Division 2n/3:	782	312	207	263	1151	1038	952	17	1	24
Division 3n/4:	184	68	53	63	245	228	257	4	2	22

Cup Records	P	W	D	L	F	A
FA Cup:	235	88	66	81	343	322
League Cup:	93	26	20	47	108	159
A/F Members Cup:	35	16	4	15	49	46

Sequence	Games	Start		End
Winning Run:	10	1-May-48	to	28-Sep-48
	10	23-Feb-66	to	20-Apr-66
Without Defeat:	15	12-Dec-64	to	13-Mar-65
	15	23-Apr-83	to	18-Oct-83
Without Win:	27	27-Mar-89	to	4-Nov-89
Drawn Games:	5	3-Feb-21	to	12-Mar-21
	5	30-Mar-29	to	15-Apr-29
Without Draw:	29	27-Sep-19	to	27-Mar-20
Losing Run:	8	7-Apr-34	to	8-Sep-34
Clean Sheets:	6	26-Sep-08	to	31-Oct-08
Goal Scored:	26	10-Apr-90	to	23-Nov-90
No Goals For:	6	13-Nov-20	to	18-Dec-20
SOS Undefeated:	11	1983-84		
	11	1948-49		
SOS No Wins:	16	1989-90		

5-Year Record

	Div	P	W	D	L	F	A	Pts	Psn	
1993-94	2	46	18	14	14	62	54	68	9	
1994-95	2	46	21	11	14	70	57	74	8	
1995-96	2	46	5	16	25	36	78	31	24	Relegated
1996-97	3	46	13	18	15	44	50	57	17	
1997-98	3	46	11	8	27	56	83	41	22	

Leyton Orient

Lost on Points

Barry Hearn's desire to revive the fortunes of Leyton Orient is taking time to come to fruition although improved form during the second-half of the 1997/98 season offers hope of better days ahead. Orient, with Tommy Taylor at the helm for his first full campaign, experienced a disappointing first half to the season but rallied well in the latter stages and, with just five games to go, had closed the gap on the play-off places to just two points. This made the three points they had deducted for 'an administration muddle' that saw them unwittingly field suspended players all the more unpalatable. Unfortunately the Os could not quite bridge that gap but their total of 66 points was their best since being relegated in 1995.

Looking to the FA Cup for glory proved unsuccessful with Orient drawing away in the 1st Round to Ryman League side Hendon and then embarrassingly losing the replay at Brisbane Road. The Coca-Cola Cup brought slightly more cheer with the Os making a rare excursion past the 1st Round. Victory in the 2nd leg at home clinched a 4-2 aggregate win over Brighton, but in the 2nd Round Orient found a 3-1 deficit from the home leg against Bolton too much of a handicap despite battling for a bold 4-4 draw in Lancashire. In October McGleish was sold to Barnet for £70,000.

Formed:	1881
Ground:	Brisbane Road, Leyton, London, E10 5NE
Phone:	0181 539 2223
Box Office:	0181 539 2223
Info:	0898 12 11 50
Capacity:	13,842
Colours:	Red with white shirts, white shorts, red stockings
Nickname:	The Os
Manager:	Tommy Taylor
Honours:	Division 3 Champions 1969-70; Division 3S Champions 1955-56.
Managers:	Ken Knighton 1981, Frank Clark 1982-91, Peter Eustace 1991, Chris Turner/John Sitton 1994-95, Pat Holland 1995-96.
Previous Names:	1981-86 Glyn Cricket and Football Club; 1886-88 Eagle FC; 1988-98 Orient FC; 1898-1946 Clapton Orient; 1946-47 Leyton Orient; 1967-86 Orient.
Record League Win:	8-0 v Crystal Palace, D3, 12/11/55 8-0 v Rochdale, D4, 20/10/87, 8-0 v Colchester United, D4, 15/10/88 8-0 v Doncaster Rovers, D3, 1997-98
Most Goals in a Match:	9-2 v Aldershot, D3S, 10/2/34

Record League Defeat:	1-7 v Torquay United, D3S, 16/4/49
	1-7 v Stoke City, D2, 7/9/56,
	0-6 on seven different occasions
Most GF in Season:	106 – Division 3S, 1955-56
All-time League Goals:	121 – Tom Johnston, 1956-58, 1959-61
All-time League Apps:	432 – Peter Allen
Most Goals in a Season:	35 – Tom Johnston, D2, 1957-58
Most Goals in a Match:	5 – R. Heckman v Lovells Athletic, FAC 1R, 19/8/55
Record Fee Received:	£600,000 from Notts County for John Chiedozie, 8/81
Record Fee Paid:	£175,000 to Wigan Athletic for Paul Beesley, 10/89
Record Attendance:	34,345 v West Ham U., FA Cup 4th Round, 25/1/64

Stats File

Division	P	W	D	L	F	A	Pts	Yr	B	W
Premier/D1:	42	6	9	27	37	81	21	1	22	22
Division 1n/2:	1682	540	447	695	1970	2380	1537	41	2	22
Division 2n/3:	598	201	154	243	733	834	693	13	1	24
Division 3n/4:	322	126	80	116	470	406	455	7	5	21

Cup Records	P	W	D	L	F	A
FA Cup:	211	79	52	80	286	309
League Cup:	98	27	28	43	126	154
A/F Members Cup:	46	18	10	18	64	65

Sequence	Games	Start		End
Winning Run:	10	21-Jan-56	to	30-Mar-56
Without Defeat:	14	30-Oct-54	to	19-Feb-55
Without Win:	23	6-Oct-62	to	13-Apr-63
Drawn Games:	6	16-Sep-72	to	7-Oct-72
	6	30-Nov-74	to	28-Dec-74
Without Draw:	29	16-Dec-11	to	5-Oct-12
Losing Run:	9	1-Apr-95	to	6-May-95
Clean Sheets:	6	6-Feb-71	to	10-Mar-71
Goal Scored:	22	12-Mar-27	to	8-Oct-27
No Goals For:	8	19-Nov-94	to	7-Jan-95
SOS Undefeated:	8	1968-69		
SOS No Wins:	9	1979-80		

5-Year Record

	Div	P	W	D	L	F	A	Pts	Psn	
1993-94	2	46	14	14	18	57	71	56	18	
1994-95	2	46	6	8	32	30	75	26	24	Relegated
1995-96	3	46	12	11	23	44	63	47	21	
1996-97	3	46	15	12	19	50	58	57	16	
1997-98	3	46	19	12	15	62	47	66	11	

Mansfield Town

Impressive Stag

Mansfield Town manager Steve Parkin can afford to be optimistic about the Stags' chances for the forthcoming season after seeing his side end the 1997/98 campaign with an impressive 11-match unbeaten run. Unfortunately for Mansfield, though, only four of those 11 games were won, which left them just a point better off than a year earlier and five points short of the play-offs.

One of the big bonuses for Mansfield was the form of striker Steve Whitehall who more than justified his £20,000 move from Rochdale with 24 goals. The cheque book came out again in October with Lee Peacock joining from Carlisle for £150,000, almost double Mansfield's previous record purchase.

Mansfield's search for FA Cup glory was swiftly blunted by a home defeat at the hands of Oldham, after the Stags had done well to draw away to the Division Two side. In the Coca-Cola Cup Iyseden Christie scored a hat-trick in a 1st Round 1st Leg tie to secure a 4-2 victory over Stockport. Seven minutes from time in the return, 38-year-old Tony Ford, the Stags' assistant manager, put his side 7-6 ahead on aggregate only for Stockport to score twice in the time remaining to grab a sensational victory.

Formed:	1910
Ground:	Field Mill Ground, Quarry Lane, Mansfield, Nottingham, NG18 5DA
Phone:	01623 23567
Box Office:	01623 23567
Info:	0891 12 13 11
Capacity:	10,315
Colours:	Amber shirts with dark blue trim, amber shorts with dark blue trim, amber socks
Nickname:	The Stags
Manager:	Steve Parkin
Honours:	Division 3 Champions 1976-77; Division 4 Champions 1974-75; Freight Rover Trophy Winners 1986-87.
Managers:	Mick Jones 1979-81, Stuart Boam 1981-83, Ian Greaves 1983-89, George Foster 1989-93, Andy King 1993-96.
Previous Names:	Mansfield Wesleyans 1891-1910
Record League Win:	9-2 v Rotherham United, D3N, 27/12/32 8-1 v QPR, D3, 15/3/61 7-0 v Scunthorpe United, D4, 21/4/75
Record League Defeat:	1-8 v Walsall, D3N, 19/1/1933
Most GF in Season:	108 – Division 4, 1962-63
All-time League Apps:	440 – Rod Arnold, 1973-84
All-time League Goals:	104 – Harold Johnston, 1931-36

Most Goals in a Season: 55 – Ted Harston, D3N, 1936-37
Most Goals in a Match: 7 – Ted Harston v Hartlepool United, D3N, 23/1/37
Record Fee Received: £638,500 from Swindon Town for Colin Calderwood (Original fee was £27,500 but Orient received a further lump sum when he then moved on to Tottenham.)
Record Fee Paid: £150,000 to Carlisle U. for Lee Peacock, 10/97
Record Attendance: 24,467 v Nottingham Forest, FAC 3R, 10/1/63

Stats File

Division	P	W	D	L	F	A	Pts	Yr	B	W
Division 1n/2:	42	10	11	21	49	69	31	1	21	21
Division 2n/3:	966	327	263	376	1278	1382	995	21	1	24
Division 3n/4:	814	317	221	276	1226	1061	1030	18	1	20

Cup Records	P	W	D	L	F	A
FA Cup:	170	72	31	67	285	268
League Cup:	98	30	21	47	140	184
A/F Members Cup:	49	20	10	19	57	65

Sequence	Games	Start		End
Winning Run:	7	28-Apr-62	to	8-Sep-62
Without Defeat:	20	14-Feb-76	to	21-Aug-76
Without Win (3):	12	3-Mar-74	to	15-Apr-74
	12	10-Nov-79	to	16-Feb-80
Drawn Games:	5	18-Oct-86	to	22-Nov-86
Without Draw:	17	8-Mar-52	to	6-Sep-52
Losing Run:	7	18-Jan-47	to	15-Mar-47
Clean Sheets:	6	13-Oct-84	to	7-Nov-84
	6	22-Mar-97	to	11-Apr-97
Goal Scored:	27	1-Oct-62	to	22-Apr-63
No Goals For:	5	4-Mar-78	to	21-Mar-78
SOS Undefeated:	10	1962-63		
	10	1949-50		
SOS No Wins:	7	1996-97		

5-Year Record

	Div	P	W	D	L	F	A	Pts	Psn
1993-94	3	42	15	10	17	53	62	55	12
1994-95	3	42	18	11	13	84	59	65	6
1995-96	3	46	11	20	15	54	64	53	19
1996-97	3	46	16	16	14	47	45	64	11
1997-98	3	46	16	17	13	64	55	65	12

Peterborough United

Posh Fry-up

Under the unique management of Barry Fry, life is never likely to be dull at London Road and for a long while it looked as though one of the busiest dealers in the transfer market was going to guide the Posh to promotion at the first attempt, following the previous season's relegation.

Posh had a tremendous first half to the season, losing just twice in 23 Division Three matches. But the wheels started to come off two days after Christmas with a 3-0 defeat at one of Fry's former clubs, Barnet. By mid February Peterborough were still placed at second in the table with just 14 games to go but a 4-1 defeat at Shrewsbury on 14th March edged them out of the promotion and play-off places and they eventually missed the boat by four points.

A convincing start was made to their FA Cup campaign with a 4-1 success at Swansea and a more laboured 3-2 win over Dagenham before Walsall won 2-0 at London Road in the 3rd Round. After being held at home by Portsmouth in the Coca-Cola Cup, the Posh went through to the 2nd Round with victory at Fratton Park but, having held Reading at Elm Park, lost the 2nd Leg.

Formed:	1934
Ground:	London Road Ground, Peterborough, PE2 8AL
Phone:	01733 63947
Box Office:	01733 63947
Info:	0898 12 16 54
Capacity:	15,500
Colours:	Royal blue shirts, white shorts, blue socks
Nickname:	The Posh
Manager:	Barry Fry
Honours:	Division 3 Champions 1976-77; Division 4 Champions 1974-75; Freight Rover Trophy Winners 1987.
Managers:	Mark Lawrenson 1989-90, Chris Turner 1991-92, Lil Fuccillo 1992-93, John Still 1994-95, Mick Halsall 1995-96.
Record League Win:	8-1 v Oldham Ath, D4, 26/11/69 7-0 v Barrow, D4, 9/10/71
Record League Defeat:	0-7 v Tranmere Rov., D4, 29/10/85
Most GF in Season:	134 – Division 4, 1960-61
All-time League Apps:	562 – Tommy Robson, 1968-81
All-time League Goals:	137 – Jim Hall, 1967-75
Most Goals In a Season:	52 – Terry Bly, 1960-61
Most Goals in a Match:	6 – J. Laxton v Rushden, FA Cup, 6/10/1945

Record Fee Received: £350,000 from Watford for Ken Charlery, 10/92
£350,000 from Walsall for Martin O'Connor, 7/96
Record Fee Paid: £450,000 to Birmingham for Martin O'Connor, 11/96
Record Attendance: 30,096 v Swansea, FA Cup 5th Round, 20/2/65

Stats File

Division	P	W	D	L	F	A	Pts	Yr	B	W
Division 1n/2:	92	24	27	41	103	139	99	2	10	24
Division 2n/3:	736	273	206	257	1074	1048	810	16	4	21
Division 3n/4:	920	367	266	287	1352	1134	1195	20	1	19

Cup Records	P	W	D	L	F	A
FA Cup:	174	84	37	53	314	251
League Cup:	128	44	32	52	164	197
A/F Members Cup:	42	21	6	15	64	59

Sequence	Games	Start		End
Winning Run:	9	1-Feb-92	to	14-Mar-92
Without Defeat:	17	17-Dec-60	to	8-Apr-61
Without Win:	17	23-Sep-78	to	30-Dec-78
Drawn Games:	8	18-Dec-71	to	12-Feb-72
Without Draw:	15	8-Mar-71	to	14-Aug-71
Losing Run (3):	5	13-Apr-94	to	8-May-94
	5	8-Oct-96	to	26-Oct-96
Clean Sheets:	7	6-Oct-73	to	10-Nov-73
Goal Scored:	33	20-Sep-60	to	18-Apr-61
No Goals For:	5	18-Jan-64	to	15-Feb-64
SOS Undefeated:	8	1973-74		
SOS No Wins:	7	1988-89		

5-Year Record

	Div	P	W	D	L	F	A	Pts	Psn	
1993-94	1	46	8	13	25	48	76	37	24	Relegated
1994-95	2	46	14	18	14	54	69	60	15	
1995-96	2	46	13	13	20	59	66	52	19	
1996-97	2	46	11	14	21	55	73	47	21	Relegated
1997-98	3	46	18	13	15	63	51	67	10	

Plymouth Argyle

Pilgrims Progress

Ending the 1996/97 season with one win from ten games was bad enough and perhaps a sign of things to come as Plymouth Argyle kicked off the following campaign with eight winless matches, before two goals from the long serving Martin Barlow saw off Walsall. But that was the Pilgrims' only success from 14 league games before a three-match-winning run put seven clubs between them and the bottom of the table.

Although Plymouth signed off the year with a draw at Watford, they still ended in the relegation zone and, despite occasionally climbing a couple of places, the possibility of returning to Division Three after a two-year absence was very real. Plymouth slipped back into the bottom four with just one game to go and after defeat at Burnley – who subsequently avoided the drop – the Pilgrims went down.

Plymouth's good FA Cup record of recent years was ended by Cambridge winning a 1st Round replay at the Abbey Stadium in extra time. In the Coca-Cola Cup the Pilgrims wiped out a two-goal 1st Round 1st Leg deficit against Oxford United to take a 3-2 lead at Home Park, only to eventually fall 5-3 on the night.

In the close season former Plymouth player Kevin Hodges returned to Home Park as manager after taking neighbours Torquay United to the Play-offs in his first season in management.

Formed:	1886
Ground:	Home Park, Plymouth, Devon, PL2 3DQ
Phone:	01752 562561
Box Office:	01752 562561
Info:	0839 442270
Capacity:	19,630
Colours:	Green/white striped shirts, black shorts, black socks with green trim
Nickname:	The Pilgrims
Manager:	Kevin Hodges
Honours:	Division 3S Champions 1929-30, 1951-52; Division 3 Champions 1958-59.
Managers:	Ken Brown 1988-90, David Kemp 1990-92, Peter Shilton 1992-95, Steve McCall 1995, Neil Warnock 1995-97, Mick Jones 1997-1998
Previous Names:	Argyle Athletic Club 1886-1903
Record League Win:	8-1 v Millwall, D2, 16/1/32
	7-0 v Doncaster Rovers, D2, 5/9/36
Record League Defeat:	0-9 v Stoke City, D2, 17/12/60
Most GF in Season:	107 – Division 3S, 1925-26
	107 – Division 3S, 1951-52
All-time League Apps:	530 – Kevin Hodges, 1978-93
All-time League Goals:	176 – Sam Black, 1924-27

Most Goals in a Season: 32 – Jack Cock, 1926-27
Most Goals in a Match: 5 – Wilf Carter v Charlton Athletic, D2, 27/12/60
Record Fee Received: £750,000 from Southampton for Mickey Evans, 3/97
Record Fee Paid: £250,000 to Hartlepool for Paul Dalton, 6/92
Record Attendance: 43,596 v Aston Villa, Division 2, 10/10/36

Stats File

Division	P	W	D	L	F	A	Pts	Yr	B	W
Division 1n/2:	1446	474	373	599	2066	2337	1406	34	4	22
Division 2n/3:	1012	378	276	358	1415	1345	1200	22	1	22
Division 3n/4:	46	22	12	12	68	49	78	1	4	4

Cup Records	P	W	D	L	F	A
FA Cup:	190	73	31	86	250	274
League Cup:	110	33	27	50	130	159
A/F Members Cup:	28	8	4	16	32	47

Sequence	Games	Start		End
Winning Run:	9	22-Mar-30	to	21-Apr-30
Without Defeat:	22	20-Apr-29	to	21-Dec-29
Without Win:	13	27-Apr-63	to	2-Oct-63
Drawn Games (3):	5	29-Mar-97	to	12-Apr-97
	5	3-May-97	to	30-Aug-97
Without Draw:	31	23-Nov-46	to	30-Aug-47
Losing Run:	9	26-Apr-47	to	30-Aug-47
	9	12-Oct-63	to	7-Dec-63
Clean Sheets:	6	8-Sep-24	to	4-Oct-24
Goal Scored:	39	15-Apr-39	to	7-Apr-40
No Goals For (3):	5	20-Sep-47	to	18-Oct-47
	5	11-Mar-50	to	8-Apr-50
SOS Undefeated:	18	1929-30		
SOS No Wins:	11	1963-64		
	11	1981-82		

5-Year Record

	Div	P	W	D	L	F	A	Pts	Psn	
1993-94	2	46	25	10	11	88	56	85	3	
1994-95	2	46	12	10	24	45	83	46	21	Relegated
1995-96	3	46	22	12	12	68	49	78	4	Promoted
1996-97	2	46	12	18	16	47	58	54	19	
1997-98	2	46	12	13	21	55	70	49	22	Relegated

Rochdale

Home Win Winners

Given that Rochdale achieved more home wins than any other side in the Nationwide League not to finish the season in a play-off position, it is a big disappointment to the Dale that their final position in the 1997/98 table was four places lower than 12 months earlier. The reason was entirely down to a dreadful away record, with just ten points being collected from 23 matches.

Manager Graham Barrow traded mainly with free transfers during the summer but in February he sold 17-year-old goalkeeper Stephen Bywater to West Ham for an initial £300,000. In an intricate deal of 20 stages, that fee could eventually rise to £2.3m.

With five wins from their opening six home games, Rochdale enjoyed a top half of the table position, but their away form quickly dragged them further down to a more familiar position. A pitiful return of just one point from nine away games was improved upon towards the end of November with a 3-0 victory at Conference-bound Doncaster. But come the end of the season only one more away success had been recorded.

Rochdale bowed out of both the FA and Coca-Cola Cups at the first hurdles with defeats by Wrexham and Stoke respectively.

Formed:	1907
Ground:	Spotland, Willbutts Lane, Rochdale, OL11 5DS
Phone:	01706 44648
Box Office:	01706 44648
Info:	0891 12 15 03
Capacity:	6,448
Colours:	Royal blue shirts, royal blue shorts, royal blue stockings
Nickname:	The Dale
Manager:	Graham Barrow
Honours:	–
Managers:	Eddie Gray 1986-88 , Danny Bergara 1988-89, Terry Dolan 1989-91, Dave Sutton 1991-94, Mick Docherty 1995-96.
Record League Win:	8-1 v Chesterfield, D3N, 18/12/26
	7-0 v Walsall, D 3N, 24/12/21
	7-0 v York City, D3N, 14/1/39
	7-0 v Hartlepool, D3N, 2/11/57
Record League Defeat:	1-9 v Tranmere Rovers, D3N, 25/12/31
	0-8 v Wrexham, D3, 28/9/29
	0-8 v Leyton Orient, D4, 20/10/87
Most GF in Season:	105 – Division 3N, 1926-27
All-time League Apps:	316 – Graham Smith, 1966-74
All-time League Goals:	119 – Reg Jenkins 119 1964-73

Most Goals in a Season:	44 – Albert Whitehurst, 1926-27
Most Goals in a Match:	6 – Tommy Tippett v Hartlepool, D3N, 21/4/30
Record Fee Received:	£500,000 from Blackburn R. for Stephen Bywater, 11/97
Record Fee Paid:	£80,000 to Scunthorpe Utd for Andy Flounders, 7/91
Record Attendance:	24,231 v Notts County, FA Cup 2nd Round, 10/12/49

Stats File

Division	P	W	D	L	F	A	Pts	Yr	B	W
Division 2n/3:	276	68	84	124	310	438	220	6	9	24
Division 3n/4:	1546	485	429	632	1901	2238	1635	34	3	24

Cup Records	P	W	D	L	F	A
FA Cup:	150	43	35	72	214	263
League Cup:	97	25	20	52	120	185
A/F Members Cup:	40	12	9	19	44	71

Sequence	Games	Start		End
Winning Run:	8	29-Sep-69	to	3-Nov-69
Without Defeat:	20	15-Sep-23	to	19-Jan-24
Without Win:	28	14-Nov-31	to	29-Aug-32
Drawn Games:	6	17-Aug-68	to	14-Sep-68
Without Draw:	33	26-Dec-25	to	9-Oct-26
Losing Run:	17	14-Nov-31	to	12-Mar-32
Clean Sheets:	5	21-Sep-68	to	12-Oct-68
	5	14-Feb-76	to	6-Mar-76
Goal Scored:	29	8-Jan-27	to	15-Oct-27
No Goals For:	9	14-Mar-80	to	26-Apr-80
SOS Undefeated:	9	1925-26		
SOS No Wins:	22	1973-74		

5-Year Record

	Div	P	W	D	L	F	A	Pts	Psn
1993-94	3	42	16	12	14	63	51	60	9
1994-95	3	42	12	14	16	44	67	50	15
1995-96	3	46	14	13	19	57	61	55	15
1996-97	3	46	14	16	16	58	58	58	14
1997-98	3	46	17	7	22	56	55	58	18

Rotherham United

Moore Free Deals

In the aftermath of relegation Rotherham United turned to a one-time hero of the terraces, Ronnie Moore, to help the Merry Millers regain their Division Two place. Moore made several signings, mostly on free transfers, and splashed out £20,000 on 6' 5" striker Gijsbert Bos, formerly of Lincoln. But it was the well-travelled Lee Glover who topped United's list of goalscorers with a career best 17 – only one short of his total during his previous 11 seasons as a professional.

Rotherham lost their first two games of the season but went on to be one of the most consistent sides in the division with only four clubs losing less games. United hovered around the edge of the play-off positions all season and victory in their final game would have clinched a top seven place. Unfortunately for Moore, that match was at runaway champions Notts County and a 5-2 defeat curtailed the celebrations.

Rotherham's FA Cup campaign began encouragingly with a 3-0 win at Burnley after a home draw. Six different players scored in the 6-0 win over Kings Lynn only for Sunderland to win 5-1 at Millmoor in the 3rd Round. Their Coca-Cola Cup run fizzled out in Round 1 against Preston.

Formed:	1884
Ground:	Millmoor Ground, Rotherham, South Yorks, YO12 4HF
Phone:	01709 512434
Box Office:	01709 512434
Info:	0891 66 44 42
Capacity:	11,514
Colours:	Red shirts with white sleeves and collar, white shorts with red trim, red socks
Nickname:	The Merry Millers
Manager:	Ronnie Moore
Honours:	Division 3N Champions 1950-51; Division 3 Champions 1980-81; Division 4 Champions 1988-89.
Managers:	Dave Cusack 1987-88, Billy McEwan 1988-91, Phil Henson 1991-94, Archie Gemmill/John McGovern 1994-96, Danny Bergara 1996-97.
Previous Names:	Thornhill United 1884; Rotherham County 1905; amalgamated with Rotherham Town to form Rotherham United in 1925.
Record League Victory:	8-0 v Oldham Athletic, D3N, 26/5/47
Record League Defeat:	1-11 v Bradford City, D3N, 25/8/28
Most GF in Season:	114 – Division 3N, 1946-47
All-time League Apps:	459 – Danny Williams, 1946-60
All-time League Goals:	130 – Gladstone Guest, 1946-56

Most Goals in a Season: 38 – Wally Ardron, D3N, 1946-47
Most Goals in a Match: 4 – numerous occasions
Record Fee Received: £180,000 from Everton for Bobby Mimms, 5/85
Record Fee Paid: £100,000 to Cardiff City for Ronnie Moore, 8/80
Record Attendance: 25,000 v Sheffield United, D2, 13/12/52

Stats File

Division	P	W	D	L	F	A	Pts	Yr	B	W
Division 1n/2:	966	344	219	403	1435	1614	937	23	3	21
Division 2n/3:	1012	349	278	385	1256	1312	1131	22	1	23
Division 3n/4:	226	97	74	55	340	232	328	5	1	15

Cup Records	P	W	D	L	F	A
FA Cup:	187	72	48	67	302	291
League Cup:	136	56	30	50	192	195
A/F Members Cup:	42	17	12	13	60	52

Sequence	Games	Start		End
Winning Run:	9	2-Feb-82	to	6-Mar-82
Without Defeat:	18	4-Nov-50	to	3-Mar-51
	18	13-Oct-69	to	7-Feb-70
Without Win:	14	30-Mar-34	to	15-Sep-34
	14	8-Oct-77	to	2-Jan-78
Drawn Games:	6	13-Oct-69	to	22-Nov-69
Without Draw:	28	18-Jan-58	to	4-Oct-58
Losing Run:	8	7-Apr-56	to	18-Aug-56
Clean Sheets:	7	13-Feb-82	to	13-Mar-82
Goal Scored:	30	3-Apr-54	to	27-Dec-54
No Goals For:	5	4-Apr-86	to	19-Apr-86
SOS Undefeated:	11	1948-49		
SOS No Wins:	8	1933-34		
	8	1996-97		

5-Year Record

	Div	P	W	D	L	F	A	Pts	Psn	
1993-94	2	46	15	13	18	63	60	58	15	
1994-95	2	46	14	14	18	57	61	56	17	
1995-96	2	46	14	14	18	54	62	56	16	
1996-97	2	46	7	14	25	39	70	35	23	Relegated
1997-98	3	46	16	19	11	67	61	67	9	

Scarborough

On the Verge

Scarborough's 11th season as members of the Football League came close to being their most successful yet as manager Mike Wadsworth led the club to the play-offs and the prospect of their first promotion. Wadsworth's first season in charge saw Boro finish midtable. To improve on that he brought in around half a dozen players and released just a couple.

Scarborough timed their charge into the play-off positions to perfection and victory in their final match would have clinched automatic promotion. The Seamer Road club came within four minutes of achieving their goal only for Chester to grab a late equaliser at the Deva Stadium. In the play-off semi-final Scarborough made little impression, with defeats of 3-1 and 4-1 by Torquay.

It is a touch ironic that four of Scarborough's five best seasons in the FA Cup came during their non-league days and there was little chance of the balance being altered in 1997/98 as they suffered a 1st Round defeat at Scunthorpe. The Coca-Cola Cup also brought no joy as Scunthorpe won both legs of their 1st Round meeting but at least Scarborough did take four points from the two league games between the two clubs.

Formed:	1897
Ground:	The McCain Stadium, Seamer Road, Scarborough, YO12 4HF
Phone:	01723 375094
Box Office:	01723 375094
Capacity:	6,899
Colours:	All white with red trim and shorts
Nickname:	The Boro
Manager:	Mick Wadsworth
Honours:	FA Trophy Winners 1972-73, 1975-76, 1976-77; GMVC Champions 1986-87.
Managers:	Ray McHale 1989-93, Phil Chambers 1993, Steve Wicks 1993-94, Billy Ayre 1994, Ray McHale 1994-96, Mitch Cook 1996.
Record League Win:	4-0 v Bolton Wanderers, D4, 29/8/87 4-0 v Newport County, D4, 12/4/88
Record League Defeat:	1-5 v Barnet, D4, 8/2/92
Most GF in Season:	67 – Division 4, 1988-89
All-time League Apps:	164 – Steve Richards, 1987-91
All-time League Goals:	34 – Darren Foreman, 1991-93
Most Goals in a Season:	27 – Darren Foreman, D3, 1992-93
Most Goals in a Match:	3 – Darren Foreman v Northampton, D3, 10/10/92 3 – Darren Foreman v York City, D3 19/12/22

Record Fee Received: £350,000 from Notts County for Craig Short, 7/89 (£100,000 then £250,000 when he moved on to Everton)
Record Fee Paid: £100,000 to Leicester City for Martin Russell, 2/89
Record Attendance: 11,162 v Luton Town, FA Cup 3rd Round, 1937-38

Stats File

Division	P	W	D	L	F	A	Pts	Yr	B	W
Division 3n/4:	490	168	135	187	647	694	639	11	5	23

Cup Records	P	W	D	L	F	A
FA Cup:	79	21	14	44	93	159
League Cup:	40	12	11	17	61	77
A/F Members Cup:	25	5	5	15	30	40

Sequence	Games	Start		End
Winning Run (8):	3	23-Jan-93	to	6-Feb-93
	3	1-Jan-94	to	8-Jan-94
Without Defeat (4):	9	26-Dec-90	to	16-Feb-91
	9	28-Sep-96	to	2-Nov-96
Without Win:	16	17-Sep-94	to	14-Jan-95
Drawn Games (4):	4	27-Jan-90	to	17-Feb-90
	4	13-Apr-98	to	2-May-98
Without Draw:	20	27-Sep-89	to	20-Jan-90
Losing Run:	7	19-Mar-96	to	13-Apr-96
Clean Sheets (3):	3	14-Oct-95	to	28-Oct-95
	3	14-Mar-98	to	28-Mar-98
Goal Scored:	15	1-Apr-89	to	16-Sep-89
No Goals For:	4	12-Mar-88	to	2-Apr-88
	4	9-Mar-96	to	23-Mar-96
SOS Undefeated:	4	1988-89		
	4	1996-97		
SOS No Wins:	5	1997-98		
	5	1991-92		

5-Year Record

	Div	P	W	D	L	F	A	Pts	Psn
1993-94	3	42	15	8	19	55	61	53	14
1994-95	3	42	8	10	24	49	70	34	21
1995-96	3	46	8	16	22	39	69	40	23
1996-97	3	46	16	15	15	65	68	63	12
1997-98	3	46	19	15	12	67	58	72	6

Scunthorpe United

Out of the Basement

Scunthorpe United, after two seasons sat in midtable obscurity, came within one win of a shot at the play-offs. Such was the tightness of Division Three that Brian Laws' side, despite only scoring two goals more than they conceded, were only six points short of an automatic promotion place.

Having finished the previous season with a disappointing run, Laws traded seven players for six during the summer in an attempt to get the club out of the basement division for the first time in 14 years. Scunthorpe made a fine start to the season with 19 points from nine games putting them into third place but it was form they could not sustain and most of the season was spent on the edge of the play-off places.

A good run towards the end of the season took the Irons to within a point of seventh-placed Barnet but ultimately a late-season defeat at Brighton proved costly.

Scunthorpe put Scarborough out of the FA Cup and took two games to see off Ilkeston before being one of the few sides to lose to Crystal Palace at Selhurst Park. A cup double was completed over Scarborough in the Coca-Cola Cup but Everton halted any further progress.

Formed:	1904
Ground:	Glanford Park, Doncaster Road, Scunthorpe, DN15 8TD
Phone:	01724 848077
Box Office:	01724 848077
Info:	0898 12 16 52
Capacity:	9,185
Colours:	Sky blue shirts with claret hoops on sleeves, white shorts, white socks
Nickname:	The Irons
Manager:	Brian Laws
Honours:	Division 3N Champions 1957-58.
Managers:	Mick Buxton 1987-91, Bill Green 1991-93, Richard Money 1993-94, David Moore 1994-96, Mick Buxton 1996-97.
Previous Names:	Merged with Lindsey United in 1910 to become Scunthorpe and Lindsey United. Dropped Lindsey in 1958.
Record League Win:	8-1 v Luton Town, D3, 24/4/1965
Record League Defeat:	0-8 v Carlisle United, D3N, 25/12/1952
Most GF in Season:	88 – D3N, 1957-58
All-time League Apps:	595 – Jack Brownsword, 1950-65
All-time League Goals:	110 – Steve Cammack, 1979-81 & 1981-86
Most Goals in a Season:	31 – Barrie Thomas, D2, 1961-62
Most Goals in a Match:	5 – Barrie Thomas v Luton Town, D3, 24/4/65
Record Fee Received:	£400,000 from Aston Villa for Neil Cox, 2/91

Record Fee Paid: £80,000 to York City for Ian Helliwell, 8/91
Record Attendance: 8,775 v Rotherham, D4, 1/5/89
23,935 v Portsmouth, FA Cup 4th Round, 30/1/1954
(at Old Show Ground)

Stats File

Division	P	W	D	L	F	A	Pts	Yr	B	W
Division 1n/2:	252	86	63	103	376	431	235	6	4	22
Division 2n/3:	276	81	72	123	346	444	243	6	4	24
Division 3n/4:	1271	459	359	453	1697	1682	1561	28	4	24

Cup Records	P	W	D	L	F	A
FA Cup:	169	60	50	59	243	257
League Cup:	95	23	24	48	93	151
A/F Members Cup:	45	14	10	21	59	71

Sequence	Games	Start		End
Winning Run:	6	18-Oct-69	to	25-Nov-69
Without Defeat:	15	30-Nov-57	to	29-Mar-58
	15	13-Nov-71	to	26-Feb-72
Without Win:	14	20-Apr-74	to	28-Sep-74
	14	22-Mar-75	to	6-Sep-75
Drawn Games:	6	2-Jan-84	to	25-Feb-84
Without Draw:	21	25-Sep-65	to	26-Feb-66
Losing Run:	8	29-Nov-97	to	20-Jan-98
Clean Sheets:	6	27-Jan-90	to	3-Mar-90
Goal Scored:	23	18-Aug-51	to	26-Dec-51
No Goals For:	7	19-Apr-75	to	6-Sep-75
SOS Undefeated:	9	1982-83		
SOS No Wins:	12	1963-64		

5-Year Record

	Div	P	W	D	L	F	A	Pts	Psn
1993-94	3	42	15	14	13	64	56	59	11
1994-95	3	42	18	8	16	68	63	62	7
1995-96	3	46	15	15	16	67	61	60	12
1996-97	3	46	18	9	19	59	62	63	13
1997-98	3	46	19	12	15	56	52	69	8

Shrewsbury Town

Taming of the Shrew

Shrewsbury Town went into the 1997/98 season looking to rebuild after three seasons of struggle in Division Two which culminated in relegation. New manager Jake King greatly changed the squad he inherited, but this was never likely to be anything more than a season of consolidation. Certainly the Blues had little trouble in living up to that billing as they did enough to stay well clear of the foot of the table but were never in the running for honours. Even so, Shrewsbury did reasonably well against the top sides by drawing at Notts County and defeating Macclesfield 4-3 at Gay Meadow.

The FA Cup brought no relief to Shrewsbury's plight after a home draw with Grimsby was followed by a 4-0 hammering in the replay on Humberside. In the Coca-Cola Cup £30,000 signing Lee Steele scored a hat-trick in the 2nd Leg at home to Brentford but visitors Brentford spoilt his day with a 5-3 victory at Gay Meadow, giving the Bees a 6-4 aggregate victory.

Although most of King's work involved low-cost signings and free transfers, he also set a new club record with the sale of defender David Walton to Division One side Crewe for £750,000.

Formed:	1886
Ground:	Gay Meadow, Shrewsbury, SY2 6AB
Phone:	01743 360111
Box Office:	01743 360111
Capacity:	8,000
Colours:	Blue shirts, blue shorts, blue socks
Nickname:	The Town or Blues
Manager:	Jake King
Honours:	Division 3 Champions 1978-79; Welsh Cup Winners (6 times).
Managers:	Chic Bates 1984-87, Ken Brown 1987, Ian McNeil 1987-90, Asa Hartford 1990-91, John Bond 1991-93, Fred Davies 1994-97.
Record League Win:	7-0 v Swindon Town, D3S, 6/5/55
Record League Defeat:	1-8 v Norwich City, D3S, 13/9/52
	1-8 v Coventry City, D3, 22/10/63
	0-7 v Bristol Rovers, D3, 21/3/64
Most GF in Season:	101 – Division 4, 1958-59
All-time League Apps:	406 – Colin Griffin, 1975-89
All-time League Goals:	152 – Arthur Rowley, 1958-65
Most Goals in a Season:	38 – Arthur Rowley, D3, 1958-59
Most Goals in a Match:	5 – Alf Wood v Blackburn Rovers, D3, 2/10/71
Record Fee Received:	£750,000 to Crewe A. for David Walton, 10/97

Record Fee Paid: £100,000 to Aldershot for John Dungworth, 11/79
£100,000 to Southampton for Mark Blake, 8/90
Record Attendance: 18,917 v Walsall, D3, 26/4/61

Stats File

Division	P	W	D	L	F	A	Pts	Yr	B	W
Division 1n/2:	426	138	119	169	481	549	504	10	8	22
Division 2n/3:	1150	394	326	430	1611	1639	1193	25	1	22
Division 3n/4:	222	105	57	60	362	259	322	5	1	13

Cup Records	P	W	D	L	F	A
FA Cup:	151	60	39	52	257	235
League Cup:	107	29	33	45	137	177
A/F Members Cup:	34	11	7	16	47	55

Sequence	Games	Start		End
Winning Run:	7	28-Oct-95	to	16-Dec-95
Without Defeat:	16	30-Oct-93	to	26-Feb-94
Without Win:	17	25-Jan-92	to	11-Apr-92
Drawn Games:	6	9-Apr-60	to	25-Apr-60
	6	30-Oct-63	to	14-Dec-63
Without Draw:	22	10-Nov-79	to	1-Apr-80
Losing Run (3):	7	25-Dec-51	to	24-Jan-52
	7	17-Oct-87	to	14-Nov-87
Clean Sheets:	6	12-Mar-94	to	9-Apr-94
Goal Scored:	28	7-Sep-60	to	8-Mar-61
No Goals For:	6	1-Jan-91	to	19-Feb-91
SOS Undefeated:	6	1957-58		
	6	1978-79		
SOS Undefeated:	6	1961-62		
SOS No Wins:	10	1988-89		

5-Year Record

	Div	P	W	D	L	F	A	Pts	Psn	
1993-94	3	42	22	13	7	63	39	79	1	Promoted
1994-95	2	46	13	14	19	54	62	53	18	
1995-96	2	46	13	14	19	58	70	53	18	
1996-97	2	46	11	13	22	49	74	46	22	Relegated
1997-98	3	46	16	13	17	61	62	61	13	

Southend United

Down, Down, Deeper and…

Just 12 months after finishing bottom of Division One, Southend United achieved the unenviable record of doing likewise in the Nationwide League Division Two. Following their demotion from Division One, manager Ronnie Whelan made way for Alvin Martin, who made relatively few changes to the squad he took on.

The Shrimpers' season seldom got out of first gear as they rolled along at roughly a point per game until a run of ten games without a win after the turn of the year sent them plummeting to the foot of the table. The winless run expired when Southend beat Blackpool at Roots Hall 2-1, having only scored two goals in the previous six games. Bottom place could have been avoided by victory in the last game of the season but, despite top scorer Jeroen Boere scoring his 14th goal of the season, United still lost 3-1 at home to Wrexham.

Southend did well not to be added to Woking's list of giant killings in the FA Cup with two late goals at Kingfield clinching a place in the 2nd Round where Martin's side lost 1-0 at Fulham. Cardiff were successfully removed from the Coca-Cola Cup but Southend were emphatically beaten by Premiership team Derby in the 2nd Round.

Formed:	1906
Ground:	Roots Hall, Victoria Avenue, Southend-on-Sea, SS2 6NQ
Phone:	01702 304050
Box Office:	01702 304090
Info:	0839 66 44 44
Capacity:	12,306
Colours:	Blue shirts with gold collar and cuffs, yellow shorts, blue socks
Nickname:	The Shrimpers
Manager:	Alvin Martin
Honours:	Division 4 Champions 1980-81.
Managers:	Colin Murphy 1992-93, Barry Fry 1993, Peter Taylor 1993-95, Steve Thompson 1995, Ronnie Whelan 1995-97.
Record League Win:	9-2 v Newport Co., D3S, 5/9/36
	8-1 v Cardiff City, D3S, 20/2/37
	7-0 v QPR, D3S, 7/4/1928
	7-0 v Workington, D4, 29/3/68
Record League Defeat:	0-8 v Northampton Town, D3S, 22/3/24
	1-9 v Brighton, D3, 27/11/65
Most GF in Season:	92 – Division 3S, 1950-51
All-time League Apps:	452 – AW 'Sandy' Anderson, 1950-63
All-time League Goals:	120 – Roy Hollis, 1953-60
Most Goals in a Season:	34 – Jim Shankley, 1928-29

Most Goals in a Match:	5 – Jim Shankly v Merthyr Tydfil, D3S, 1/3/30
	5 – H. Johnson v Golders Green, FAC 1R, 24/11/34
	5 – Billy Best v Brentwood, 10-1, FAC 2R, 7/12/68
Record Fee Received:	£2.2m from N. Forest for Stan Collymore, 7/93
Record Fee Paid:	£350,000 to Plymouth Argyle for Gary Poole, 7/93
Record Attendance:	31,033 v Liverpool, FA Cup 3rd Round, 10/1/79

Stats File

Division	P	W	D	L	F	A	Pts	Yr	B	W
Division 1n/2:	276	88	69	119	328	414	333	6	12	24
Division 2n/3:	966	330	248	388	1313	1437	1015	21	2	24
Division 3n/4:	598	262	144	192	871	742	746	13	1	20

Cup Records	P	W	D	L	F	A
FA Cup:	182	79	28	75	318	266
League Cup:	96	31	22	43	114	157
A/F Members Cup:	28	13	1	14	60	50

Sequence	Games	Start		End
Winning Run:	7	4-Oct-24	to	6-Dec-24
Without Defeat:	16	20-Feb-32	to	29-Aug-32
Without Win:	17	31-Dec-83	to	14-Apr-84
Drawn Games:	6	30-Jan-82	to	19-Feb-82
Without Draw:	26	7-Apr-62	to	17-Nov-62
Losing Run (3):	6	5-Feb-55	to	12-Mar-55
	6	29-Aug-87	to	19-Sep-87
Clean Sheets:	6	8-Apr-69	to	28-Apr-69
Goal Scored:	24	23-Mar-29	to	9-Nov-29
No Goals For:	6	28-Oct-33	to	16-Dec-33
	6	6-Apr-79	to	24-Apr-79
SOS Undefeated:	15	1931-32		
SOS No Wins:	9	1982-83		
	9	1956-57		

5-Year Record

	Div	P	W	D	L	F	A	Pts	Psn	
1993-94	1	46	17	8	21	63	67	59	15	
1994-95	1	46	18	8	20	54	73	62	13	
1995-96	1	46	15	14	17	52	61	59	14	
1996-97	1	46	8	15	23	42	86	39	24	Relegated
1997-98	2	46	11	10	25	47	79	43	24	Relegated

Swansea City

Cardiff Eclipsed

Football supporters in the principality had little to cheer during 1997/98 although Swansea City fans had the marginal joy of seeing their side finish one place above rivals Cardiff; but 20th in Division Three offers little cause for a street party.

A season of struggle on the pitch for the Swans was matched by difficulties off it as manager Jan Molby was sacked in October only for his replacement, Micky Adams, to walk out 13 days later. Molby, who took the Swans to the play-offs the previous season, was dismissed after a run of six defeats in eight games, which included a remarkable 7-4 reversal at Hull. Former Wimbledon hero Alan Cork became Swansea's third manager of the season only to leave in mid-Summer.

Swansea's FA Cup escapade was short lived with Peterborough winning 4-1 at Vetch Field in the 1st Round, and their Coca-Cola Cup dreams went the same way with a 1st Round defeat by Reading.

Swansea spent precious little in the transfer market but collected almost £700,000 when David Thomas, Steve Torpey and Christian Edwards all moved on. One transfer which did pay off was the capture of Tony Bird from Barry Town for £30,000, as he finished the season as top scorer with 14 league goals.

Formed:	1900
Ground:	Vetch Field, Swansea, SA1 3SU
Phone:	01792 474114
Box Office:	01792 474114
Info:	0891 12 16 39
Capacity:	11,477
Colours:	All white shirts, white shorts, white socks
Nickname:	The Swans
Manager:	John Hollins
Honours:	Division 3S Champions 1924-25, 1948-49; Welsh Cup Winners (10 times); Autoglass Trophy Winners 1993-94
Managers:	Terry Yorath 1990-91, Frank Burrows 1991-95, Kevin Cullis 1996, Jan Molby 1996-97, Micky Adams 1997, Alan Cork 1997-Jun-98
Previous Names:	Swansea Town until February 1970
Record League Win:	8-0 v Hartlepool United, D4, 1977-78
Record League Defeat:	1-8 v Fulham, D2, 22/1/38
	1-8 v Newcastle United, D2, 2/9/39
	0-7 v Tottenham Hotspur, D2, 3/12/32
	0-7 v Bristol Rovers, D2, 2/10/54
	0-7 v Workington, D3, 4/10/60
	4-7 v Hull City, D3, 1997-98

Most GF in Season:	92 – Division 4, 1976-77
All-time League Apps:	585 – Wilfy Milne, 1920-37
All-time League Goals:	166 – Ivor Allchurch, 1949-58 and 1965-68
Most Goals in a Season:	35 – Cyril Pearce, 1931-32
Most Goals in a Match:	5 – Jack Fowler v Charlton Athletic, D3S, 27/9/24
Record Fee Received:	£400,000 from Bristol C. for Steve Torpey, 8/97
Record Fee Paid:	£340,000 to Liverpool for Colin Irwin, 8/81
Record Attendance:	32,796 v Arsenal, FA Cup 4th Round, 17/2/68

Stats File

Division	P	W	D	L	F	A	Pts	Yr	B	W
Premier/D1:	84	31	17	36	109	120	110	2	6	21
Division 1n/2:	1428	497	321	610	2156	2489	1322	34	3	22
Division 2n/3:	736	242	198	296	922	1083	827	16	3	24
Division 3n/4:	552	222	129	201	752	704	644	12	3	22

Cup Records	P	W	D	L	F	A
FA Cup:	185	75	37	73	282	285
League Cup:	98	28	21	49	133	169
A/F Members Cup:	46	17	15	14	50	44

Sequence	Games	Start		End
Winning Run:	8	4-Feb-61	to	18-Mar-61
Without Defeat:	19	4-Feb-61	to	26-Aug-61
	19	19-Oct-70	to	9-Mar-71
Without Win:	15	25-Mar-89	to	2-Sep-89
Drawn Games (4):	5	28-Mar-92	to	11-Apr-92
	5	5-Jan-93	to	5-Feb-93
Without Draw:	26	26-Nov-32	to	29-Apr-33
Losing Run:	9	26-Jan-91	to	19-Mar-91
Clean Sheets:	6	16-Feb-82	to	20-Mar-82
Goal Scored:	27	28-Aug-47	to	7-Feb-48
No Goals For:	6	6-Feb-96	to	24-Feb-96
SOS Undefeated (4):	7	1968-69		
	7	1978-79		
SOS No Wins:	11	1938-39		

5-Year Record

	Div	P	W	D	L	F	A	Pts	Psn	
1993-94	2	46	16	12	18	56	58	60	13	
1994-95	2	46	19	14	13	57	45	71	10	
1995-96	2	46	11	14	21	43	79	47	22	Relegated
1996-97	3	46	21	8	17	62	58	71	5	
1997-98	3	46	13	11	22	49	62	50	20	

Torquay United

Final Day Decides

The transformation of Torquay United in 1997/98 after two seasons of struggle in Division Three is of great credit to manager Kevin Hodges as he took the Devon club to the play-offs. But for a dramatic late-season collapse and defeat at Leyton Orient on the final day, the Gulls would have gained one of the three automatic promotion places.

Hodges made only minimal changes to his squad but the side which recorded just one win from their last 18 games the previous season got off to an indifferent start before climbing the table steadily. By February they were into the top seven and promotion looked a certainty as they held second place for a month, only for a run of draws and three defeats from the last four games to nudge them back into the play-off places. Torquay made no mistake in the semi-final with Scarborough, recording an emphatic 7-2 aggregate victory, but lost 1-0 to Colchester in the final.

Torquay pulled off a shock win at Luton in the FA Cup before taking Watford to extra time in the 2nd Round. The Gulls also distinguished themselves in the Coca-Cola Cup with victory over Bournemouth before bowing out to Ipswich.

In the close season manager Kevin Hodges shocked everyone at Plainmoor by resigning and moving back to the club where he spent much of his playing carreer – Plymouth.

Formed:	1898
Ground:	Plainmoor Ground, Torquay, Devon TQ1 3PG
Phone:	01803 328666
Box Office:	01803 328666
Info:	0891 12 16 41
Colours:	Yellow and white stripes with navy trimmed shirts, navy with yellow with white trim shorts, yellow socks with navy trim
Capacity:	6,000
Nickname:	The Gulls
Manager:	
Honours:	Sherpa Van Trophy Finalists 1988-89
Managers:	John Impey 1991-92, Ivan Golac 1992, Paul Compton 1992-93, Don O'Riordan 1993-95, Eddie May 1995-96, Kevin Hodges 1996-1998.
Previous Names:	Torquay Town until 1910
Record League Win:	9-0 v Swindon Town, D3S, 8/3/52
Record League Defeat:	2-10 v Fulham, D3S, 7/9/31
	2-10 v Luton Town, D3S, 2/9/33
	1-9 v Millwall, D3S, 29/8/27
Most GF in Season:	89 – Division 3S, 1956-57
All-time League Apps:	443 – Dennis Lewis, 1947-59

All-time League Goals: 204 – Sammy Collins, 1948-58
Most Goals in a Season: 40 – Sammy Collins, D3S, 1955-56
Most Goals in a Match: 5 – Robin Stubbs v Newport County, D4, 19/10/63
Record Fee Received: £185,000 from Manchester U. for Lee Sharpe, 6/88
Record Fee Paid: £60,000 to Dundee for Wes Saunders, 7/90
Record Attendance: 21,908 v Huddersfield, FA Cup 4th Round, 29/1/55

Stats File

Division	P	W	D	L	F	A	Pts	Yr	B	W
Division 2n/3:	414	145	103	166	537	592	406	9	4	23
Division 3n/4:	1368	486	368	514	1743	1860	1557	30	3	24

Cup Records	P	W	D	L	F	A
FA Cup:	165	61	38	66	261	249
League Cup:	102	25	27	50	115	171
A/F Members Cup:	43	15	7	21	48	67

Sequence	Games	Start		End
Winning Run:	8	24-Jan-98	to	3-Mar-98
Without Defeat:	15	14-Sep-60	to	10-Dec-60
	15	5-May-90	to	3-Nov-90
Without Win:	17	5-Mar-38	to	10-Sep-38
Drawn Games:	8	25-Oct-69	to	13-Dec-69
Without Draw:	20	16-Sep-50	to	20-Jan-51
	20	17-Oct-92	to	6-Mar-93
Losing Run (3):	8	29-Sep-71	to	6-Nov-71
	8	30-Sep-95	to	18-Nov-95
Clean Sheets:	5	30-Apr-66	to	20-Aug-66
	5	13-Jan-90	to	17-Feb-90
Goal Scored:	19	3-Oct-53	to	6-Feb-54
No Goals For:	7	8-Jan-72	to	4-Mar-72
SOS Undefeated:	14	1990-91		
SOS No Wins:	6	1929-30		
	6	1983-84		

5-Year Record

	Div	P	W	D	L	F	A	Pts	Psn
1993-94	3	42	17	16	9	64	56	67	6
1994-95	3	42	14	13	15	54	57	55	13
1995-96	3	46	5	14	27	30	84	29	24
1996-97	3	46	13	11	22	46	62	50	21
1997-98	3	46	21	11	14	68	59	74	5

Division 3 All-Time Table

The table lists the total records of all clubs who have played in what is now Division 3. It incorporates the records of the former Division 4. Yrs=Number of years (seasons) in the division. H=Highest position achieved. L=Lowest position.

Team	P	W	D	L	F	A	Pts	Yrs	H	L
Darlington	1596	531	430	635	2047	2288	1690	35	1	24
Rochdale	1546	485	429	632	1901	2238	1635	34	3	24
Hartlepool U.	1650	507	400	743	1993	2647	1612	36	3	24
Crewe Alex.	1458	505	377	576	1907	2086	1565	32	3	24
Scunthorpe U.	1271	459	359	453	1697	1682	1561	28	4	24
Torquay U.	1368	486	368	514	1743	1860	1557	30	3	24
Doncaster R.	1362	472	344	546	1780	1974	1441	30	1	24
Colchester U.	1090	448	275	367	1627	1438	1437	24	2	24
Lincoln C.	1226	453	338	435	1700	1649	1419	27	1	24
Northampton T.	1226	452	301	473	1721	1739	1402	27	1	23
Aldershot	1286	468	334	484	1829	1851	1393	28	4	23
Stockport Co.	1332	438	352	542	1600	1896	1380	29	1	24
Exeter C.	1235	433	339	463	1617	1693	1347	27	1	22
Chester C.	1144	410	290	444	1599	1649	1244	25	2	24
Peterborough U.	920	367	266	287	1352	1134	1195	20	1	19
York C.	1048	392	263	393	1505	1423	1187	23	1	24
Halifax T.	1050	298	284	468	1234	1606	1030	23	2	23
Mansfield T.	814	317	221	276	1226	1061	1030	18	1	20
Wrexham	818	306	206	306	1243	1186	975	18	2	24
Tranmere R.	780	318	185	277	1179	1057	953	17	2	21
Chesterfield	764	294	206	264	1026	982	935	17	1	20
Bradford C.	780	307	205	268	1174	1089	845	17	2	23
Gillingham	718	271	203	244	990	919	842	16	1	21
Cambridge U.	644	245	184	215	886	838	807	14	1	22
Newport Co.	874	300	198	376	1167	1365	803	19	3	24
Hereford U.	686	225	186	275	804	884	801	15	2	24
Carlisle U.	626	242	150	234	852	867	782	14	1	23
Bury	540	230	151	159	830	635	767	12	3	15
Southend U.	598	262	144	192	871	742	746	13	1	20
Port Vale	598	220	185	193	802	715	704	13	1	20
Southport	734	229	200	305	931	1147	658	16	1	24
Workington	734	227	200	307	873	1071	654	16	3	24

Swansea	552	222	129	201	752	704	644	12	3	22
Scarborough	490	168	135	187	647	694	639	11	5	23
Brentford	552	226	138	188	801	679	590	12	1	19
Cardiff C.	360	136	111	113	445	415	519	8	1	22
Wigan A.	360	157	91	112	520	447	502	8	1	19
Walsall	352	159	94	99	567	434	499	8	1	16
Notts Co.	414	181	103	130	627	544	494	9	1	20
Barnsley	460	177	127	156	628	555	481	10	2	16
Leyton O.	322	126	80	116	470	406	455	7	5	21
Reading	368	161	110	97	513	392	454	8	1	16
Burnley	318	124	76	118	416	411	448	7	1	22
Grimsby T.	368	155	92	121	520	460	441	8	1	23
Barrow	504	151	127	226	685	897	429	11	3	24
Blackpool	272	118	68	86	413	317	420	6	2	21
Bournemouth	368	139	118	111	441	366	419	8	2	18
Bradford PA	460	146	110	204	647	817	402	10	4	24
Preston NE	222	97	62	63	341	275	353	5	1	23
Rotherham U.	226	97	74	55	340	232	328	5	1	15
Shrewsbury T.	222	105	57	60	362	259	322	5	1	13
Oldham A.	320	121	70	129	499	513	312	7	2	23
Swindon T.	184	87	39	58	263	211	300	4	1	17
Millwall	228	105	61	62	422	323	271	5	1	9
Watford	230	110	51	69	387	296	271	5	1	15
Huddersfield	230	100	64	66	337	246	264	5	1	11
Wimbledon	184	91	47	46	304	204	258	4	1	13
Hull C.	184	68	53	63	245	228	257	4	2	22
Fulham	134	53	43	38	189	155	202	3	2	17
Brighton & HA	184	64	50	70	264	245	195	4	1	23
Wolverhampton	92	51	16	25	151	93	169	2	1	4
Crystal Palace	138	68	30	40	284	204	166	3	2	8
Maidstone U.	134	43	37	54	188	188	166	3	5	19
Luton T.	138	67	29	42	236	187	163	3	1	17
Oxford U.	138	50	43	45	216	178	143	3	4	18
Bristol C.	92	37	27	28	129	114	138	2	4	14
Portsmouth	92	44	24	24	153	97	112	2	4	7
Sheffield U.	46	27	15	4	94	41	96	1	1	1
Macclesfield T.	46	23	13	10	63	44	82	1	2	2
Bolton W.	46	22	12	12	66	42	78	1	3	3
Plymouth Arg.	46	22	12	12	68	49	78	1	4	4
Gateshead	92	28	17	47	114	171	73	2	20	22
Wycombe W.	42	19	13	10	67	53	70	1	4	4
Barnet	42	21	6	15	81	61	69	1	7	7
Coventry C.	46	24	12	10	84	47	60	1	2	2
Accrington S.	46	16	8	22	74	88	40	1	18	18

Also available now:

FA Carling PREMIERSHIP 1998-99

Pocket Annual

The 6th edition of the Premiership *bible* is now available.

384 pages – £4.99

FA CHALLENGE CUP
1997-98 Sponsored by Littlewoods

First Round

AFC Bournemouth	v	Heybridge Swifts	3-0	3,385
Barnet	v	Watford	1-2	4,040
Billericay Town	v	Wisbech	2-3	1,947
Blackpool	v	Blyth Spartans	4-3	4,814
Brentford	v	Colchester United	2-2	2,899
Bristol City	v	Millwall	1-0	8,413
Bristol Rovers	v	Gillingham	2-2	4,825
Carlisle United	v	Wigan Athletic	0-1	5,182
Carshalton	v	Stevenage Borough	0-0	1,405
Cheltenham Town	v	Tiverton Town	2-1	2,781
Chester City	v	Winsford	2-1	3,885
Chesterfield	v	Northwich Victoria	1-0	5,327
Darlington	v	Solihull Borough	1-1	2,318
Exeter City	v	Northampton Town	1-1	4,605
Farnborough Town	v	Dagenham & Redbridge	0-1	1,236
Hartlepool United	v	Macclesfield Town	2-4	3,165
Hayes	v	Boreham Wood	0-1	1,343
Hendon	v	Leyton Orient	2-2	2,421
Hereford United	v	Brighton & HA	2-1	5,787
Hull City	v	Hednesford Town	0-2	6,091
Ilkeston Town	v	Boston United	2-1	2,504
Kings Lynn	v	Bromsgrove Rovers	1-0	2,847
Lincoln City	v	Gainsborough Trinity	1-1	6,014
Luton Town	v	Torquay United	0-1	3,446
Margate	v	Fulham	1-2	6,000
Morecambe	v	Emley	1-1	1,496
Notts County	v	Colwyn Bay	2-0	3,074
Oldham Athletic	v	Mansfield Town	1-1	5,253
Plymouth Argyle	v	Cambridge United	0-0	4,793
Preston North End	v	Doncaster Rovers	3-2	7,953
Rochdale	v	Wrexham	0-2	3,956
Rotherham United	v	Burnley	3-3	5,709
Scunthorpe United	v	Scarborough	2-1	3,039
Shrewsbury Town	v	Grimsby Town	1-1	3,193
Slough Town	v	Cardiff City	1-1	2,262
Southport	v	York City	0-4	3,952
Swansea City	v	Peterborough United	1-4	2,821
Walsall	v	Lincoln United	2-0	3,279

| Woking | v | Southend United | 0-2 | 5,000 |
| Wycombe Wanderers | v | Basingstoke | 2-2 | 3,932 |

First Round Replays

Basingstoke	v	Wycombe Wanderers	2-2	5,085
aet. Basingstoke win 5-4 on penalties				
Burnley	v	Rotherham United	0-3	3,118
Cambridge United	v	Plymouth Argyle	† 3-2	3,139
Cardiff City	v	Slough Town	† 3-2	2,343
Colchester United	v	Brentford	0-0	3,613
aet. Colchester win 4-2 on penalties				
Emley	v	Morecambe	3-3	2,709
aet. Emley win 3-1 on penalties				
Gainsborough Trinity	v	Lincoln City	2-3	5,726
Played at Lincoln City				
Gillingham	v	Bristol Rovers	0-2	4,459
Grimsby Town	v	Shrewsbury Town	4-0	3,242
Leyton Orient	v	Hendon	0-1	3,355
Mansfield Town	v	Oldham Athletic	0-1	4,097
Northampton Town	v	Exeter City	2-1	5,259
Solihull Borough	v	Darlington	3-3	2,000
aet. Darlington win 4-2 on penalties				
Stevenage Borough	v	Carshalton Athletic	5-0	2,377

Second Round

AFC Bournemouth	v	Bristol City	3-1	
Cambridge United	v	Stevenage Borough	1-1	4,847
Cardiff City	v	Hendon	3-1	2,578
Cheltenham Town	v	Boreham Wood	1-1	3,525
Chester City	v	Wrexham	0-2	5,224
Colchester United	v	Hereford United	1-1	3,558
Fulham	v	Southend United	1-0	8,537
Grimsby Town	v	Chesterfield	2-2	
Hednesford Town	v	Darlington	0-1	1,900
Lincoln City	v	Emley	2-2	3,729
Macclesfield Town	v	Walsall	0-7	3,566
Northampton Town	v	Basingstoke	1-1	5,881
Oldham Athletic	v	Blackpool	2-1	6,590
Peterborough United	v	Dagenham & Redbridge	3-2	5,572
Preston North End	v	Notts County	2-2	7,583
Rotherham United	v	King's Lynn	6-0	5,883
Scunthorpe United	v	Ilkeston Town	1-1	4,187
Torquay United	v	Watford	1-1	3,416
Wigan Athletic	v	York City	2-1	4,021
Wisbech	v	Bristol Rovers	0-2	

Second Round Replays

Basingstoke	v	Northampton Town	0-0	3,052
	aet. Northampton Town win 4-3 on penalties			
Boreham Wood	v	Cheltenham Town	0-2	1,615
Chesterfield	v	Grimsby Town	0-2	4,553
Emley	v	Lincoln City	3-3	4,891
	aet. Emley win 4-3 on penalties			
Hereford United	v	Colchester United	1-1	3,725
	aet. Hereford United win 5-4 on penalties			
Ilkeston Town	v	Scunthorpe United	1-2	14,114
Notts County	v	Preston North End	† 1-2	3,052
Stevenage Borough	v	Cambridge United	2-1	4,886
Watford	v	Torquay United	† 2-1	5,848

Third Round

AFC Bournemouth	v	Huddersfield Town	0-1	7,385
Arsenal	v	Port Vale	0-0	37,471
Barnsley	v	Bolton Wanderers	1-0	15,042
Blackburn Rovers	v	Wigan Athletic	4-2	22,402
Bristol Rovers	v	Ipswich Town	1-1	8,610
Crystal Palace	v	Scunthorpe United	2-0	11,624
Cardiff City	v	Oldham Athletic	1-0	6,635
Charlton Athletic	v	Nottingham Forest	4-1	13,827
Chelsea	v	Manchester United	3-5	34,792
Cheltenham	v	Reading	1-1	6,000
Crewe Alexandra	v	Birmingham City	1-2	4,607
Darlington	v	Wolverhampton W.	0-4	5,018
Derby County	v	Southampton	2-0	27,992
Everton	v	Newcastle United	0-1	20,885
Grimsby Town	v	Norwich City	3-0	8,161
Hereford United	v	Tranmere Rovers	0-3	7,473
Leeds United	v	Oxford United	4-0	20,568
Leicester City	v	Northampton Town	4-0	20,608
Liverpool	v	Coventry City	1-3	33,888
Manchester City	v	Bradford City	2-0	23,686
Peterborough United	v	Walsall	0-2	12,809
Portsmouth	v	Aston Villa	2-2	16,013
Preston North End	v	Stockport County	1-2	12,180
QPR	v	Middlesbrough	2-2	13,379
Rotherham United	v	Sunderland	1-5	11,500
Sheffield United	v	Bury	1-1	14,009
Swindon Town	v	Stevenage Borough	1-2	9,422
Tottenham Hotspur	v	Fulham	3-1	27,909
Watford	v	Sheffield Wednesday	1-1	18,306
WBA	v	Stoke City	3-1	17,598
West Ham United	v	Emley	2-1	18,629
Wimbledon	v	Wrexham	0-0	6,349

Third Round Replays

Aston Villa	v	Portsmouth	1-0	23,365
Bury	v	Sheffield United	1-2	4,920
Ipswich Town	v	Bristol Rovers	1-0	11,362
Middlesbrough	v	QPR	2-0	21,817
Port Vale	v	Arsenal	1-1	14,964
	aet. Arsenal win 4-3 on penalties			
Reading	v	Cheltenham	2-1	9,686
Sheffield Wednesday	v	Watford	0-0	18,707
	aet. Sheffield Wednesday win 5-3 on penalties			
Wrexham	v	Wimbledon	2-3	9,539

Fourth Round

Aston Villa	v	WBA	4-0	39,372
Birmingham City	v	Stockport County	2-1	15,882
Crystal Palace	v	Leicester City	3-0	15,489
Cardiff City	v	Reading	1-1	10,174
Charlton Athletic	v	Wolverhampton W.	1-1	15,540
Coventry City	v	Derby County	2-0	22,864
Huddersfield Town	v	Wimbledon	0-1	14,533
Ipswich Town	v	Sheffield United	1-1	14,654
Leeds United	v	Grimsby Town	2-0	29,598
Manchester City	v	West Ham United	1-2	26,495
Manchester United	v	Walsall	5-1	54,669
Middlesbrough	v	Arsenal	1-2	28,264
Sheffield Wednesday	v	Blackburn Rovers	0-3	15,940
Stevenage Borough	v	Newcastle United	1-1	8,040
Tottenham Hotspur	v	Barnsley	1-1	28,722
Tranmere Rovers	v	Sunderland	1-0	14,055

Fourth Round Replays

Barnsley	v	Tottenham Hotspur	3-1	18,220
Newcastle United	v	Stevenage Borough	2-1	36,705
Reading	v	Cardiff City	1-1	11,808
	aet. Reading win 4-3 on penalties			
Sheffield United	v	Ipswich Town	1-0	14,144
Wolverhampton W.	v	Charlton Athletic	3-0	20,429

Fifth Round

Arsenal	v	Crystal Palace	0-0	37,164
Aston Villa	v	Coventry City	0-1	26,979
Leeds United	v	Birmingham City	3-2	35,463
Manchester United	v	Barnsley	1-1	54,700
Newcastle United	v	Tranmere Rovers	1-0	36,675
Sheffield United	v	Reading	1-0	17,845
West Ham United	v	Blackburn Rovers	2-2	25,729
Wimbledon	v	Wolverhampton W.	1-1	15,322

Fifth Round Replays

Barnsley	v	Man. United	3-2	18,655
Blackburn Rovers	v	West Ham United	1-1	21,972
	aet. West Ham United win 5-4 on pens			
Crystal Palace	v	Arsenal	1-2	15,674
Wolverhampton W.	v	Wimbledon	2-1	25,112

Sixth Round

Arsenal	v	West Ham United	1-1	38,077
Coventry City	v	Sheffield United	1-1	23,084
Leeds United	v	Wolverhampton W.	0-1	39,902
Newcastle United	v	Barnsley	3-1	36,695

Sixth Round Replays

Sheffield United	v	Coventry City	1-1	29,034
	aet. Sheffield United win 3-1 on pens			
West Ham United	v	Arsenal	1-1	25,859
	aet. Arsenal win 4-3 on pens			

Semi-Finals

Sheffield United	v	Newcastle United	0-1	53,452
		at Old Trafford, Manchester		
Wolverhampton W.	v	Arsenal	0-1	39,372
		at Villa Park, Birmingham		

Final – 16 May 1998 at Wembley Stadium

Arsenal	v	Newcastle United	2-0	79,183

Overmars (23); Anelka (69)

Arsenal: Seaman, Dixon, Keown, Adams, Winterburn, Parlour, Vieira, Petit, Overmars, Wreh (Platt 63), Anelka. *Subs not used:* Bould, Wright, Manninger, Grimandi.

Newcastle United: Given, Pistone, Dabizas, Howey, Pearce (Andersson 72), Barton (Watson 77), Lee, Batty, Speed, Ketsbaia (Barnes 85), Shearer. *Subs not used:* Hislop, Albert.

Referee: Mr Paul Durkin (Portland)

† after extra time

FA CHALLENGE CUP FINALS 1872-1998

Year	Winners	Runners-up	Score
1872	The Wanderers	Royal Engineers	1-0
1873	The Wanderers	Oxford University	2-0
1874	Oxford University	Royal Engineers	2-0
1875	Royal Engineers	Old Etonians	1-1
	Royal Engineers	Old Etonians	2-0
1876	The Wanderers	Old Etonians	1-1 †
	The Wanderers	Old Etonians	3-0
1877	The Wanderers	Oxford University	2-1 †
1878	The Wanderers*	Royal Engineers	3-1
1879	Old Etonians	Clapham Rovers	1-0
1880	Clapham Rovers	Oxford University	1-0
1881	Old Carthusians	Old Etonians	3-0
1882	Old Etonians	Blackburn Rovers	1-0
1883	Blackburn Olympic	Old Etonians	2-1 †
1884	Blackburn Rovers	Queen's Park, Glasgow	2-1
1885	Blackburn Rovers	Queen's Park, Glasgow	2-0
1886	Blackburn Rovers**	West Bromwich Albion	0-0
	Blackburn Rovers**	West Bromwich Albion	2-0
1887	Aston Villa	West Bromwich Albion	2-0
1888	West Bromwich Albion	Preston North End	2-1
1889	Preston North End	Wolverhampton Wanderers	3-0
1890	Blackburn Rovers	Sheffield Wednesday	6-1
1891	Blackburn Rovers	Notts County	3-1
1892	West Bromwich Albion	Aston Villa	3-0
1893	Wolverhampton Wanderers	Everton	1-0
1894	Notts County	Bolton Wanderers	4-1
1895	Aston Villa	West Bromwich Albion	1-0
1896	Sheffield Wednesday	Wolverhampton Wanderers	2-1
1897	Aston Villa	Everton	3-2
1898	Nottingham Forest	Derby County	3-1
1899	Sheffield United	Derby County	4-1
1900	Bury	Southampton	4-0
1901	Tottenham Hotspur	Sheffield United	2-2
	Tottenham Hotspur	Sheffield United	3-1
1902	Sheffield United	Southampton	1-1
	Sheffield United	Southampton	2-1
1903	Bury	Derby County	6-0

Year	Winners	Runners-up	Score
1904	Manchester City	Bolton Wanderers	1-0
1905	Aston Villa	Newcastle United	2-0
1906	Everton	Newcastle United	1-0
1907	Sheffield Wednesday	Everton	2-1
1908	Wolverhampton Wanderers	Newcastle United	3-1
1909	Manchester United	Bristol City	1-0
1910	Newcastle United	Barnsley	1-1
	Newcastle United	Barnsley	2-0
1911	Bradford City	Newcastle United	0-0
	Bradford City	Newcastle United	1-0
1912	Barnsley	West Bromwich Albion	0-0 †
	Barnsley	West Bromwich Albion	1-0
1913	Aston Villa	Sunderland	1-0
1914	Burnley	Liverpool	1-0
1915	Sheffield United	Chelsea	3-0
1920	Aston Villa	Huddersfield Town	1-0 †
1921	Tottenham Hotspur	Wolverhampton Wanderers	1-0
1922	Huddersfield Town	Preston North End	1-0
1923	Bolton Wanderers	West Ham United	2-0
1924	Newcastle United	Aston Villa	2-0
1925	Sheffield United	Cardiff City	1-0
1926	Bolton Wanderers	Manchester City	1-0
1927	Cardiff City	Arsenal	1-0
1928	Blackburn Rovers	Huddersfield Town	3-1
1929	Bolton Wanderers	Portsmouth	2-0
1930	Arsenal	Huddersfield Town	2-0
1931	West Bromwich Albion	Birmingham	2-1
1932	Newcastle United	Arsenal	2-1
1933	Everton	Manchester City	3-0
1934	Manchester City	Portsmouth	2-1
1935	Sheffield Wednesday	West Bromwich Albion	4-2
1936	Arsenal	Sheffield United	1-0
1937	Sunderland	Preston North End	3-1
1938	Preston North End	Huddersfield Town	1-0 †
1939	Portsmouth	Wolverhampton Wanderers	4-1
1946	Derby County	Charlton Athletic	4-1 †
1947	Charlton Athletic	Burnley	1-0 †
1948	Manchester United	Blackpool	4-2
1949	Wolverhampton Wanderers	Leicester City	3-1
1950	Arsenal	Liverpool	2-0
1951	Newcastle United	Blackpool	2-0
1952	Newcastle United	Arsenal	1-0
1953	Blackpool	Bolton Wanderers	4-3

Year	Winners	Runners-up	Score
1954	West Bromwich Albion	Preston North End	3-2
1955	Newcastle United	Manchester City	3-1
1956	Manchester City	Birmingham City	3-1
1957	Aston Villa	Manchester United	2-1
1958	Bolton Wanderers	Manchester United	2-0
1959	Nottingham Forest	Luton Town	2-1
1960	Wolverhampton Wanderers	Blackburn Rovers	3-0
1961	Tottenham Hotspur	Leicester City	2-0
1962	Tottenham Hotspur	Burnley	3-1
1963	Manchester United	Leicester City	3-1
1964	West Ham United	Preston North End	3-2
1965	Liverpool	Leeds United	2-1 †
1966	Everton	Sheffield Wednesday	3-2
1967	Tottenham Hotspur	Chelsea	2-1
1968	West Bromwich Albion	Everton	1-0 †
1969	Manchester City	Leicester City	1-0
1970	Chelsea	Leeds United	2-2 †
	Chelsea	Leeds United	2-1 †
1971	Arsenal	Liverpool	2-1 †
1972	Leeds United	Arsenal	1-0
1973	Sunderland	Leeds United	1-0
1974	Liverpool	Newcastle United	3-0
1975	West Ham United	Fulham	2-0
1976	Southampton	Manchester United	1-0
1977	Manchester United	Liverpool	2-1
1978	Ipswich Town	Arsenal	1-0
1979	Arsenal	Manchester United	3-2
1980	West Ham United	Arsenal	1-0
1981	Tottenham Hotspur	Manchester City	1-1 †
	Tottenham Hotspur	Manchester City	3-2
1982	Tottenham Hotspur	Queens Park Rangers	1-1 †
	Tottenham Hotspur	Queens Park Rangers	1-0
1983	Manchester United	Brighton & Hove Albion	2-2
	Manchester United	Brighton & Hove Albion	4-0
1984	Everton	Watford	2-0
1985	Manchester United	Everton	1-0 †
1986	Liverpool	Everton	3-1
1987	Coventry City	Tottenham Hotspur	3-2 †
1988	Wimbledon	Liverpool	1-0
1989	Liverpool	Everton	3-2 †
1990	Manchester United	Crystal Palace	3-3 †
	Manchester United	Crystal Palace	1-0
1991	Tottenham Hotspur	Nottingham Forest	2-1 †

Year	Winners	Runners-up	Score
1992	Liverpool	Sunderland	2-0
1993	Arsenal	Sheffield Wednesday	1-1 †
	Arsenal	Sheffield Wednesday	2-1 †
1994	Manchester United	Chelsea	4-0
1995	Everton	Manchester United	1-0
1996	Manchester United	Liverpool	1-0
1997	Chelsea	Middlesbrough	2-0
1998	Arsenal	Newcastle	2-0

Final Venues

1872	Kennington Oval
1873	Lillie Bridge
1874-92	Kennington Oval
1893	Fallowfield, Manchester
1894	Everton
1895-1914	Crystal Palace
1915	Old Trafford
1920-22	Stamford Bridge
1923-1998	Wembley

Replay Venues

1886	Derby
1901	Bolton
1910	Everton
1911	Old Trafford
1912	Bramall Lane
1970	Old Trafford
1981	Wembley
1982	Wembley
1983	Wembley
1990	Wembley
1993	Wembley

* *Trophy won outright by The Wanderers, but restored to the FA.*
** *Special trophy awarded for a third consecutive win.*
† *after extra time.*

FA CHALLENGE CUP WINS BY CLUB

Manchester United (9)	1909, 1948, 1963, 1977, 1983, 1985, 1990, 1994, 1996
Tottenham Hotspur (8)	1901, 1921, 1961, 1962, 1967, 1981, 1982, 1991
Aston Villa (7)	1887, 1895, 1897, 1905, 1913, 1920, 1957
Arsenal (7)	1930, 1936, 1950, 1971, 1979, 1993, 1998
Blackburn Rovers (6)	1884, 1885, 1886, 1890, 1891, 1928
Newcastle United (6)	1910, 1924, 1932, 1951, 1952, 1955
Everton (5)	1894, 1906, 1933, 1966, 1995
Liverpool (5)	1965, 1974, 1986, 1989, 1992
The Wanderers (5)	1872, 1873, 1876, 1877, 1878
West Bromwich Albion (5)	1888, 1892, 1931, 1954, 1968
Bolton Wanderers (4)	1923, 1926, 1929, 1958
Manchester City (4)	1904, 1934, 1956, 1969
Sheffield United (4)	1899, 1902, 1915, 1925
Wolverhampton Wdrs (4)	1893, 1908, 1949, 1960
Sheffield Wednesday (3)	1896, 1907, 1935
West Ham United (3)	1964, 1975, 1980
Bury (2)	1900, 1903
Chelsea (2)	1970, 1997
Nottingham Forest (2)	1898, 1959
Old Etonians (2)	1879, 1882
Preston North End (2)	1889, 1938
Sunderland (2)	1937, 1973

Club	Year	Club	Year
Barnsley	1912	Notts County	1894
Blackburn Olympic	1883	Old Carthusians	1881
Blackpool	1953	Oxford University	1874
Bradford City	1911	Portsmouth	1939
Burnley	1914	Royal Engineers	1875
Cardiff City	1927	Southampton	1976
Charlton Athletic	1947	Wimbledon	1988
Clapham Rovers	1880		
Coventry City	1987		
Derby County	1946		
Huddersfield Town	1922		
Ipswich Town	1978		
Leeds United	1972		

COCA-COLA FOOTBALL LEAGUE CUP 97-98

First Round

AFC Bournemouth	v	Torquay United	0-1	3,215
Torquay United	v	AFC Bournemouth	1-1	2,278
aet. Torquay win 2-1 on aggregate				
Blackpool	v	Manchester City	1-0	8,084
Manchester City	v	Blackpool	1-0	12,563
aet. 1-1 on aggregate. Blackpool win 4-2 on penalties				
Brentford	v	Shrewsbury Town	1-1	2,040
Shrewsbury Town	v	Brentford	3-5	2,136
Brentford win 6-4 on aggregate				
Brighton & HA	v	Leyton Orient	1-1	1,073
Leyton Orient	v	Brighton & HA	3-1	3,690
Leyon Orient win 4-2 on aggregate				
Bristol City	v	Bristol R.	0-0	9,341
Bristol R.	v	Bristol City	1-2	5,872
aet. Bristol City win 2-1 on aggregate				
Cambridge United	v	WBA	1-1	3,520
WBA	v	Cambridge United	2-1	10,264
aet. WBA win 3-2 on aggregate				
Cardiff City	v	Southend United	1-1	2,804
Southend United	v	Cardiff City	3-1	3,002
Southend United win 4-2 on aggregate				
Charlton Athletic	v	Ipswich Town	0-1	6,598
Ipswich Town	v	Charlton Athletic	3-1	10,989
Ipswich Town win 4-1 on aggregate				
Chester City	v	Carlisle United	1-2	2,367
Carlisle United	v	Chester City	3-0	2,586
Carlisle United win 5-1 on aggregate				
Colchester United	v	Luton Town	0-1	2,840
Luton Town	v	Colchester United	1-1	2,816
Luton Town win 2-1 on aggregate				
Crewe Alexandra	v	Bury	2-3	2,618
Bury	v	Crewe Alexandra	3-3	3,296
aet. Bury win 6-5 on aggregate				
Darlington	v	Notts County	1-1	2,700
Notts County	v	Darlington	2-1	1,925
aet. Notts County win 3-2 on aggregate				

Doncaster Rovers	v	Nottingham Forest	0-8	4,547
Nottingham Forest	v	Doncaster Rovers	2-1	9,908

Nottingham Forest win 10-1 on aggregate

Gillingham	v	Birmingham City	0-1	5,246
Birmingham City	v	Gillingham	3-0	7,921

Birmingham City win 4-0 on aggregate

Huddersfield Town	v	Bradford City	2-1	8,720
Bradford City	v	Huddersfield Town	1-1	8,065

Huddersfield Town win 3-2 on aggregate

Lincoln City	v	Burnley	1-1	3,010
Burnley	v	Lincoln City	2-1	4,644

Burnley win 3-2 on aggregate

Macclesfield Town	v	Hull City	0-0	2,249
Hull City	v	Macclesfield Town	2-1	3,300

aet. Hull City win 2-1 on aggregate

Mansfield Town	v	Stockport County	4-2	2,170
Stockport County	v	Mansfield Town	6-3	2,840

Stockport County win 8-7 on aggregate

Northampton	v	Millwall	2-1	3,773
Millwall	v	Northampton Town	2-1	4,364

aet. 3-3 on aggregate. Millwall win 2-0 on penalties

Norwich City	v	Barnet	2-1	5,429
Barnet	v	Norwich City	3-1	2,846

Barnet win 4-3 on aggregate

Oldham Athletic	v	Grimsby Town	1-0	5,656
Grimsby Town	v	Oldham Athletic	5-0	5,078

Grimsby Town win 5-1 on aggregate

Oxford United	v	Plymouth Argyle	2-0	5,083
Plymouth Argyle	v	Oxford United	3-5	3,037

Oxford United win 7-3 on aggregate

Peterborough United	v	Portsmouth	2-2	3,613
Portsmouth	v	Peterborough United	1-2	6,395

Peterborough United win 4-3 on aggregate

Port Vale	v	York City	1-2	2,749
York City	v	Port Vale	1-1	3,195

York City win 3-2 on aggregate

QPR	v	Wolverhampton W.	0-2	8,355
Wolverhampton W.	v	QPR	1-2	18,398

Wolverhampton W. win 3-2 on aggregate

Reading	v	Swansea City	2-0	4,829
Swansea City	v	Reading	1-1	3,333

Reading win 3-1 on aggregate

| Rochdale | v | Stoke City | 1-3 | 2,509 |
| Stoke City | v | Rochdale | 1-1 | 12,768 |

Stoke City win 4-2 on aggregate

| Rotherham United | v | Preston NE | 1-3 | 2,901 |
| Preston NE | v | Rotherham United | 2-0 | 9,441 |

Preston NE win 5-1 on aggregate

| Scarborough | v | Scunthorpe United | 0-2 | 1,907 |
| Scunthorpe United | v | Scarborough | 2-1 | 2,149 |

Scunthorpe United win 4-1 on aggregate

| Swindon Town | v | Watford | 0-2 | 6,271 |
| Watford | v | Swindon Town | 1-1 | 7,712 |

Watford win 3-1 on aggregate

| Tranmere Rovers | v | Hartlepool United | 3-1 | 3,878 |
| Hartlepool United | v | Tranmere Rovers | 2-1 | 1,626 |

Tranmere Rovers win 4-3 on aggregate

| Walsall | v | Exeter City | 2-0 | 2,321 |
| Exeter City | v | Walsall | 0-1 | |

Walsall win 3-0 on aggregate

| Wigan Athletic | v | Chesterfield | 1-2 | 3,413 |
| Chesterfield | v | Wigan Athletic | 1-0 | 4,076 |

Chesterfield win 3-1 on aggregate

| Wrexham | v | Sheffield United | 1-1 | 3,644 |
| Sheffield United | v | Wrexham | 3-1 | 7,181 |

Sheffield United win 4-2 on aggregate

| Wycombe W. | v | Fulham | 1-2 | 4,360 |
| Fulham | v | Wycombe W. | 4-4 | 5,055 |

Fulham win 6-5 on aggregate

Second Round

| Birmingham City | v | Stockport Co. | 4-1 | 4,900 |
| Stockport Co. | v | Birmingham City | 2-1 | 2,074 |

Birmingham City win 5-3 on aggregate

| Blackburn Rovers | v | Preston NE | 6-0 | 22,564 |
| Preston NE | v | Blackburn Rovers | 1-0 | 11,472 |

Blackburn Rovers win 6-1 on aggregate

| Blackpool | v | Coventry City | 1-0 | 5,884 |
| Coventry City | v | Blackpool | 3-1 | 9,565 |

Coventry City win 3-2 on aggregate

| Burnley | v | Stoke City | 0-4 | 4,175 |
| Stoke City | v | Burnley | 2-0 | 6,041 |

Stoke City win 6-0 on aggregate

| Chesterfield | v | Barnsley | 1-2 | 6,318 |
| Barnsley | v | Chesterfield | 4-1 | 8,417 |

Barnsley win 6-2 on aggregate

Fulham	v	Wolverhampton W.	0-1	5,933
Wolverhampton W.	v	Fulham	1-0	17,862

Wolverhampton W. win 2-0 on aggregate

Grimsby Town	v	Sheffield Wednesday	2-0	6,429
Sheffield Wednesday	v	Grimsby Town	3-2	11,120

Grimsby Town win 4-3 on aggregate

Huddersfield Town	v	West Ham United	1-0	8,525
West Ham United	v	Huddersfield Town	3-0	16,137

West Ham United win 3-1 on aggregate

Hull City	v	Crystal Palace	1-0	9,323
Crystal Palace	v	Hull City	2-1	6,407

aet. 2-2 on aggregate. Hull City win on away goals

Ipswich Town	v	Torquay United	1-1	8,031
Torquay United	v	Ipswich Town	0-3	3,598

Ipswich Town win 4-1 on aggregate

Leeds United	v	Bristol City	3-1	8,806
Bristol City	v	Leeds United	2-1	10,857

Leeds United win 4-3 on aggregate

Leyton Orient	v	Bolton Wanderers	1-3	4,128
Bolton Wanderers	v	Leyton Orient	4-4	6,444

Bolton Wanderers win 7-5 on aggregate

Luton Town	v	WBA	1-1	3,437
WBA	v	Luton Town	4-2	7,227

WBA win 5-3 on aggregate

Middlesbrough	v	Barnet	1-0	9,611
Barnet	v	Middlesbrough	0-2	3,968

Middlesbrough win 3-0 on aggregate

Nottingham Forest	v	Walsall	0-1	7,841
Walsall	v	Nottingham Forest	2-2	6,037

aet. Walsall win 3-2 on aggregate

Notts County	v	Tranmere Rovers	0-2	1,779
Tranmere Rovers	v	Notts County	0-1	3,287

Tranmere Rovers win 2-1 on aggregate

Oxford United	v	York City	4-1	2,923
York City	v	Oxford United	1-2	1,555

Oxford United win 6-2 on aggregate

Reading	v	Peterborough United	0-0	
Peterborough United	v	Reading	0-2	6,067

Reading win 2-0 on aggregate

Scunthorpe United	v	Everton	0-1	7,145
Everton	v	Scunthorpe United	5-0	11,562

Everton win 6-0 on aggregate

Southampton	v	Brentford	3-1	8,004
Brentford	v	Southampton	0-1	3,957

Southampton win 4-1 on aggregate

| Southend United | v | Derby County | 0-1 | 4,011 |
| Derby County | v | Southend United | 5-0 | 18,490 |

Derby County win 6-0 on aggregate

| Sunderland | v | Bury | 2-1 | 18,775 |
| Bury | v | Sunderland | 1-2 | 3,928 |

Sunderland win 4-2 on aggregate

| Tottenham Hotspur | v | Carlisle United | 3-2 | 19,255 |
| Carlisle United | v | Tottenham Hotspur | 0-2 | 13,571 |

Tottenham Hotspur win 5-2 on aggregate

| Watford | v | Sheffield United | 1-1 | 7,154 |
| Sheffield United | v | Watford | 4-0 | 7,511 |

Sheffield United win 5-1 on aggregate

| Wimbledon | v | Millwall | 5-1 | 6,949 |
| Millwall | v | Wimbledon | 1-4 | 3,591 |

Wimbledon win 9-2 on aggregate

Byes: Arsenal, Aston Villa, Leicester City, Liverpool, Manchester United, Newcastle United.

Third Round

| Chelsea | v | Blackburn Rovers | 1-1 | 18,671 |

aet. Chelsea win 4-1 on penalties

Coventry City	v	Everton	4-1	10,087
Middlesbrough	v	Sunderland	2-0	26,451
Newcastle United	v	Hull City	2-0	35,856
Stoke City	v	Leeds United	1-3 †	16,203
Tottenham Hotspur	v	Derby County	1-2	20,390
WBA	v	Liverpool	0-2	21,986
West Ham United	v	Aston Villa	3-0	20,360
Arsenal	v	Birmingham City	4-1	27,097
Barnsley	v	Southampton	1-2	9,019
Bolton Wanderers	v	Wimbledon	2-0 †	9,875
Grimsby Town	v	Leicester City	3-1	7,738
Ipswich Town	v	Man. United	2-0	22,173
Oxford United	v	Tranmere Rovers	1-1	3,878

aet Oxford United win 6-5 on penalties

| Reading | v | Wolverhampton W. | 4-2 | 11,080 |
| Walsall | v | Sheffield United | 2-1 | 8,239 |

Fourth Round

Arsenal	v	Coventry City	1-0 †	30,199
Chelsea	v	Southampton	2-1 †	20,968
Derby County	v	Newcastle United	0-1	27,364

Leeds United	v	Reading	2-3	15,069
Liverpool	v	Grimsby Town	3-0	28,515
Middlesbrough	v	Bolton Wanderers	2-1	22,801
Oxford United	v	Ipswich Town	1-2 †	5,723
West Ham United	v	Walsall	4-1	17,463

Fifth Round

Reading	v	Middlesbrough	0-1	13,072
West Ham United	v	Arsenal	1-2	24,770
Ipswich Town	v	Chelsea	2-2	22,088

aet. Chelsea win 4-1 on penalties

| Newcastle United | v | Liverpool | † 0-2 | 33,207 |

Semi-Finals First Leg

| Arsenal | v | Chelsea | 2-1 | 38,114 |
| Liverpool | v | Middlesbrough | 2-1 | 33,438 |

Semi-Finals Second Leg

| Chelsea | v | Arsenal | 3-1 | 34,330 |

Chelsea win 4-3 on aggregate

| Middlesbrough | v | Liverpool | 2-0 | 29,824 |

Middlesbrough win 3-2 on aggregate

Final – 29th March 1998 at Wembley Stadium

| Chelsea | v | Middlesbrough | 2-0 | 77,698 |

Sinclair (95);
di Matteo (107)
aet

Chelsea: de Goey, Sinclair, Leboeuf, Duberry, Le Saux, Petrescu (Clarke, 74), Wise, Newton, di Matteo, Zola, M.Hughes (Flo, 81). Sub not used: Hitchcock.
Booked: M.Hughes (34 foul), Le Saux (40 dissent), Wise (75 foul), Leboeuf (87 foul).
Middlesbrough: Schwarzer, Festa, Kinder, Vickers, Pearson, Mustoe, Maddison (Beck, 101), Ricard (Gascoigne, 63), Branca, Merson, Townsend. Sub not used: Fleming.
Booked: Townsend (52 foul), Gascoigne (69 foul).

Ref: Mr P. Jones (Loughborough)

† = after extra time

FOOTBALL LEAGUE CUP FINALS 1961-1998

Year	Winners	Runners-up	1st	2nd	Agg
1961	Aston Villa	Rotherham United	0-2	†3-0	3-2
1962	Norwich City	Rochdale	3-0	1-0	4-0
1963	Birmingham City	Aston Villa	3-1	0-0	3-1
1964	Leicester City	Stoke City	1-1	3-2	4-3
1965	Chelsea	Leicester City	3-2	0-0	3-2
1966	West Bromwich Albion	West Ham United	1-2	4-1	5-3
1967	Queens Park Rangers	West Bromwich Albion	3-2		
1968	Leeds United	Arsenal	1-0		
1969	Swindon Town	Arsenal	†3-1		
1970	Manchester City	West Bromwich Albion	2-1		
1971	Tottenham Hotspur	Aston Villa	†2-0		
1972	Stoke City	Chelsea	2-1		
1973	Tottenham Hotspur	Norwich City	1-0		
1974	Wolverhampton W.	Manchester City	2-1		
1975	Aston Villa	Norwich City	1-0		
1976	Manchester City	Newcastle United	2-1		
1977	Aston Villa	Everton	†3-2		
	after 0-0 draw and 1-1 draw aet				
1978	Nottingham Forest	Liverpool	1-0		
	after 0-0 draw aet				
1979	Nottingham Forest	Southampton	3-2		
1980	Wolverhampton W.	Nottingham Forest	1-0		
1981	Liverpool	West Ham United	2-1		
	after 1-1 draw aet				

Milk Cup

Year	Winners	Runners-up	Score
1982	Liverpool	Tottenham Hotspur	†3-1
1983	Liverpool	Manchester United	†2-1
1984	Liverpool	Everton	1-0
	after 0-0 draw aet		
1985	Norwich City	Sunderland	1-0
1986	Oxford United	Queens Park Rangers	3-0

Littlewoods Cup

Year	Winners	Runners-up	Score
1987	Arsenal	Liverpool	2-1
1988	Luton Town	Arsenal	3-2

| 1989 | Nottingham Forest | Luton Town | 3-1 |
| 1990 | Nottingham Forest | Oldham Athletic | 1-0 |

Rumbelows League Cup
| 1991 | Sheffield Wednesday | Manchester United | 1-0 |
| 1992 | Manchester United | Nottingham Forest | 1-0 |

Coca-Cola Cup
1993	Arsenal	Sheffield Wednesday	2-1
1994	Aston Villa	Manchester United	3-1
1995	Liverpool	Bolton Wanderers	2-1
1996	Aston Villa	Leeds United	3-0
1997	Leicester City	Middlesbrough	† 1-0
	after 1-1 aet draw at Wembley		
1998	Chelsea	Middlesbrough	† 2-0

† *after extra time*

FOOTBALL LEAGUE CUP WINS BY CLUB

Aston Villa (5) … … … … 1961, 1975, 1977, 1994, 1996
Liverpool (5) … … … … 1981, 1982, 1983, 1984, 1995
Nottingham Forest (4) … … 1978, 1979, 1989, 1990
Arsenal (2) … … … … … 1987, 1993
Manchester City (2) … … … 1970, 1976
Tottenham Hotspur (2) … … 1971, 1973
Norwich City (2) … … … … 1962, 1985
Wolverhampton Wders (2)   1974, 1980
Leicester City (2) … … … … 1964, 1997
Chelsea (2) … … … … … 1965, 1998
Birmingham City   … … … 1963
WBA   … … … … … … 1966
QPR … … … … … … … 1967
Leeds United … … … … 1968
Swindon Town   … … … 1969
Stoke City … … … … … 1972
Oxford United … … … … 1986
Luton Town   … … … … 1988
Sheffield Wednesday   … … 1991
Manchester United   … … … 1992

FA CHARITY SHIELD WINNERS 1908-97

1908	Manchester United v Queens Park Rangers 4-0	
	after 1-1 draw	
1909	Newcastle United v Northampton Town 2-0	
1910	Brighton & Hove Albion v Aston Villa 1-0	
1911	Manchester United v Swindon Town 8-4	
1912	Blackburn Rovers v Queens Park Rangers 2-1	
1913	Professionals v Amateurs 7-2	
1919	West Bromwich Albion v Tottenham Hotspur 2-0	
1920	Tottenham Hotspur v Burnley 2-0	
1921	Huddersfield Town v Liverpool 1-0	
1922	*Not Played*	
1923	Professionals v Amateurs 2-0	
1924	Professionals v Amateurs 3-1	
1925	Amateurs v Professionals 6-1	
1926	Amateurs v Professionals 6-3	
1927	Cardiff City v Corinthians 2-1	
1928	Everton v Blackburn Rovers 2-1	
1929	Professionals v Amateurs 3-0	
1930	Arsenal v Sheffield Wednesday 2-1	
1931	Arsenal v West Bromwich Albion 1-0	
1932	Everton v Newcastle United 5-3	
1933	Arsenal v Everton 3-0	
1934	Arsenal v Manchester City 4-0	
1935	Sheffield Wednesday v Arsenal 1-0	
1936	Sunderland v Arsenal 2-1	
1937	Manchester City v Sunderland 2-0	
1938	Arsenal v Preston North End 2-1	
1948	Arsenal v Manchester United 4-3	
1949	Portsmouth v Wolverhampton Wanderers 1-1	*
1950	World Cup Team v Canadian Touring Team 4-2	
1951	Tottenham Hotspur v Newcastle United 2-1	
1952	Manchester United v Newcastle United 4-2	
1953	Arsenal v Blackpool 3-1	*
1954	Wolverhampton Wanderers v West Bromwich Albion 4-4	*
1955	Chelsea v Newcastle United 3-0	
1956	Manchester United v Manchester City 1-0	
1957	Manchester United v Aston Villa 4-0	

1958	Bolton Wanderers v Wolverhampton Wanderers	4-1
1959	Wolverhampton Wanderers v Nottingham Forest	3-1
1960	Burnley v Wolverhampton Wanderers	2-2 *
1961	Tottenham Hotspur v FA XI	3-2
1962	Tottenham Hotspur v Ipswich Town	5-1
1963	Everton v Manchester United	4-0
1964	Liverpool v West Ham United	2-2 *
1965	Manchester United v Liverpool	2-2 *
1966	Liverpool v Everton	1-0
1967	Manchester United v Tottenham Hotspur	3-3 *
1968	Manchester City v West Bromwich Albion	6-1
1969	Leeds United v Manchester City	2-1
1970	Everton v Chelsea	2-1
1971	Leicester City v Liverpool	1-0
1972	Manchester City v Aston Villa	1-0
1973	Burnley v Manchester City	1-0
1974	Liverpool v Leeds United	1-1
	Liverpool won on penalties	
1975	Derby County v West Ham United	2-0
1976	Liverpool v Southampton	1-0
1977	Liverpool v Manchester United	0-0 *
1978	Nottingham Forest v Ipswich Town	5-0
1979	Liverpool v Arsenal	3-1
1980	Liverpool v West Ham United	1-0
1981	Aston Villa v Tottenham Hotspur	2-2 *
1982	Liverpool v Tottenham Hotspur	1-0
1983	Manchester United v Liverpool	2-0
1984	Everton v Liverpool	1-0
1985	Everton v Manchester United	2-0
1986	Everton v Liverpool	1-1 *
1987	Everton v Coventry City	1-0
1988	Liverpool v Wimbledon	2-1
1989	Liverpool v Arsenal	1-0
1990	Liverpool v Manchester United	1-1 *
1991	Arsenal v Tottenham Hotspur	0-0 *
1992	Leeds United v Liverpool	4-3
1993	Manchester United v Arsenal	1-1
	Manchester United won on penalties	
1994	Manchester United v Blackburn Rovers	2-0
1995	Everton v Blackburn Rovers	1-0
1996	Manchester United v Newcastle United	4-0
1997	Manchester United v Chelsea	1-1

* Each club retained shield for six months

AUTO WINDSCREENS SHIELD 1997-98

The competition, which is currently sponsored by Auto Windscreens, is officially called The Associate Members Cup and was conceived for clubs in the lower two divisions of the Football League. It takes its name from the fact that, prior to the restructuring of the league (on formation of the FA Premier League), clubs in these two divisions had just four votes between them. Clubs in the former Divisions 1 and 2 had one vote and were termed Full Members. (A Full Members Cup was run from 1985-86 to 1991-92.)

The competition was initially organised into 16 leagues of three clubs, who played each other to decide which clubs went through to the knock-out stages. In 1995-96, one group finished with the three clubs having identical records; Bradford City were eliminated by the drawing of lots. The knock-out phase was played in regions (north and south) to save travelling costs, leaving a club from each region to play in the final at Wembley Stadium.

From the 1996-97 season, the competition became a straight knock-out tournament, with some clubs given byes to the second round. Teams are grouped into north and south regions with the winners of each meeting in the final which has been held at Wembley since 1985.

Previous Finals

1984 Bournemouth v Hull City	2-1	
1985 Wigan Athletic v Brentford	3-1	
1986 Bristol City v Bolton Wanderers	3-0	
1987 Mansfield Town v Bristol City	1-1	Mansfield on penalties
1988 Wolverhampton W. v Burnley	2-0	
1989 Bolton Wanderers v Torquay United	4-1	
1990 Tranmere Rovers v Bristol Rovers	2-1	
1991 Birmingham City v Tranmere Rovers	3-2	
1992 Stoke City v Stockport County	1-0	
1993 Port Vale v Stockport County	2-1	
1994 Swansea v Huddersfield Town	1-1	Swansea on penalties
1995 Birmingham City v Carlisle United	1-0	Birmingham win sdo
1996 Rotherham United v Shrewsbury Town	2-1	
1997 Carlisle United v Colchester United	0-0	Carlisle on penalties
1998 Grimsby Town v AFC Bournemouth	2-1	Grimsby win sdo

sdo = Sudden death overtime
All finals were played at Wembley Stadium except 1984 which was at Hull City FC.

Competition Review

1st Round

Holders Carlisle United became the first side during the 1997/98 season to benefit from the golden goal rule with Gareth McAllindon's goal confirming that Oldham's problems in winning away from home were not confined to league games. Ironically it was another side with a dreadful away record, Darlington, who also lost to a golden goal as Preston went through to the 2nd Round. Grimsby, already building a reputation as a cup-fighting unit in the FA and Coca-Cola Cups, won at Chesterfield while lowly Hull disposed of Scarborough. The most attractive game of the round was at Craven Cottage where Fulham beat Watford, and was the only match in the 1st Round to attract a gate in excess of 3,000. Five matches failed to break the thousand mark, with just 580 witnessing Doncaster's exit at home to Rochdale.

2nd Round

Chris Waddle's Burnley, then bottom of Division Two, beat runaway Division Three champions Notts County 2-0 in one of the upsets of the round but there was no stopping Grimsby who avoided a shock defeat with a home win over Hull. Macclesfield may have been invincible at Moss Rise in the league but in addition to a home FA Cup defeat they also bowed out of the AWS on their own soil, with Preston doing the damage. Fulham, again playing in front of the largest attendance of the round, marched on against Wycombe. Northampton thrashed promotion rivals Torquay 5-1 at Sixfields but the biggest winners were Walsall and Carlisle. The latter trounced Rochdale 6-1, Dale doing little to suggest that they may have been unfortunate to lose 12 of their 14 away games. Walsall added to Brighton's woes with a 5-0 hammering at Bescot Stadium. Division One Bournemouth comfortably beat Leyton Orient 2-0 at Dean Court while Wigan striker Graeme Jones, having scored twice in the previous round against Lincoln, repeated the dose against Rotherham. Both Bristol clubs successfully negotiated a path to the quarter-finals; City won at home to Millwall while Rovers removed Exeter at St James's Park. But Wales' representatives, Swansea and Wrexham, both departed in the 2nd round against Peterborough and Mansfield respectively.

Quarter-Finals

Jones' goal spree came to an end at Bloomfield Road as Blackpool went through to the semi-final in front of just 1,687 spectators and the Tangerines were joined in the last four (Northern Section) by close rivals Preston who beat Mansfield. Two late goals gave Grimsby an impressive 2-0 win at Scarborough, and completing the final four in the north were Burnley, who soundly ensured that Carlisle would not retain the trophy with a 4-1 success at Turf Moor. Down south it was the end of the road for the Bristol pair, with Rovers falling to Roger Boli's golden goal for Walsall and City losing to a late goal by Bournemouth's Jamie Vincent. The biggest surprise was at Fulham where Tony Thorpe's goal – shortly before joining the Cottagers – gave Luton a last-minute 2-1 win. Division Three triumphed over Division Two with Peterborough beating Northampton 2-1 at London Road thanks to goals from Steve Castle and Andy Edwards.

Semi-Finals

In front of the first attendance of over 10,000 in this season's competition, Burnley took their minds off a relegation battle to book a place in the Northern final with a home victory over Preston, while another Lancashire club also said farewell with Grimsby beating Blackpool 1-0 at Blundell Park. Bournemouth took full advantage of being drawn at home for the third successive round with a home win over Luton but Peterborough failed to do likewise and were beaten 2-1 at home by Walsall, who scored twice in the final ten minutes.

Regional Finals

In front of a disappointing attendance of 6,064, Grimsby could only draw at home to Burnley. But in the return, goals by Lee Nogan and top scorer Kevin Donovan booked the Mariners' first appearance at Wembley. The Southern Final was a fluctuating affair but looked to be clear cut when Frenchman Franck Rolling and Russell Beardsmore, the latter back after 13 weeks on the injury list, clinched a 2-0 win for Bournemouth at Walsall. Within 53 minutes of the 2nd Leg at Dean Court Walsall had pulled level through Wayne Thomas and Boli, who maintained his record of scoring in every round. An own goal put the Cherries back in control before a thrilling finale saw Didier Tholot restore Walsall's two-goal lead with ten minutes remaining, only for Rolling to secure Bournemouth's first ever trip to Wembley.

Final

For Grimsby this was the first of two trips to the home of football in consecutive months while for Bournemouth it was a remarkable achievement, coming barely a year after the south coast club had been within a handful of minutes of being wound up. Both clubs did themselves and the Nationwide League proud and with 62,432 at the stadium it was watched by the third highest attendance in the competition's 15-year history. Bournemouth took a first-half lead through the diminutive John Bailey but an unfortunate own goal by Cherries keeper Jimmy Glass, following a Kingsley Black header, took the game into extra time in which Wayne Burnett, a £100,000 purchase from Huddersfield just two months earlier, scored the decisive golden goal winner.

Northern Section
First Round
Carlisle U. v Oldham A.	1-0	s
Chesterfield v Grimsby T.	0-1	s
Doncaster R. v Rochdale	0-1	
Shrewsbury T. v Hartlepool U.	1-2	
Hull City v Scarborough	2-1	
Preston NE v Darlington	3-2	s
Scunthorpe U. v Chester C.	2-1	
Wigan A. v Lincoln C.	2-0	

Second Round
Blackpool v York C.	1-1	†

Blackpool win on penalties

Burnley v Notts Co.	2-0
Carlisle U. v Rochdale	6-1
Grimsby T. v York C.	1-0
Hartlepool U. v Scunthorpe U.	1-2
Macclesfield T. v Preston NE	0-1
Mansfield T. v Wrexham	1-0
Wigan A. v Rotherham U.	3-0

Third Round
Blackpool v Wigan A.	1-0
Burnley v Carlisle U.	4-1
Preston NE v Mansfield T.	1-0
Scunthorpe U. v Grimsby T.	0-2

Semi-Finals
Burnley v Preston NE	1-0
Grimsby T. v Blackpool	1-0

Final
Grimsby T. v Burnley	1-1
Burnley v Grimsby T.	0-2

Grimsby T. win 3-1 on aggregate.

Southern Section
First Round
Barnet v Walsall	1-2	
Bristol R. v Cambridge U.	1-0	
Cardiff C. v Millwall	0-2	
Fulham v Watford	1-0	
Gillingham v Peterborough U.	0-1	
Leyton Orient v Colchester U.	1-0	
Northampton T. v Plymouth Ar.	1-1	†

Northampton win 5-3 on penalties

Southend U. v Wycombe W.	0-1

Second Round
Bournemouth v Leyton Orient	2-0
Bristol C. v Millwall	1-0
Exeter C. v Bristol R.	1-2
Fulham v Wycombe W.	3-1
Luton T. v Brentford	2-1
Northampton T. v Torquay U.	5-1
Swansea C v Peterborough U.	1-2
Walsall v Brighton & HA	5-0

Third Round
Bournemouth v Bristol C.	1-0	
Bristol R. v Walsall	0-1	s
Fulham v Luton T.	1-2	
Peterborough v Northampton T.	2-1	

Semi-Finals
Bournemouth v Luton T.	1-0
Peterborough v Walsall	1-2

Final
Walsall v Bournemouth	0-2
Bournemouth v Walsall	2-3

Bournemouth win 4-3 on aggregate.

Final – 19th April 1998 at Wembley Stadium
AFC Bournemouth	v	Grimsby Town	1-2	62,432
Bailey (31)		OG (Glass, 75); Burnett (112)		

after sudden death overtime

FWA FOOTBALLER OF THE YEAR WINNERS

Season	Winner	Club
1947-48	Stanley Matthews	Blackpool & England
1948-49	Johnny Carey	Manchester United & Rep of Ireland
1949-50	Joe Mercer	Arsenal & England
1950-51	Harry Johnston	Blackpool & England
1951-52	Billy Wright	Wolverhampton Wanderers & England
1952-53	Nat Lofthouse	Bolton Wanderers & England
1953-54	Tom Finney	Preston North End & England
1954-55	Don Revie	Manchester City & England
1955-56	Bert Trautmann	Manchester City
1956-57	Tom Finney	Preston North End & England
1957-58	Danny Blanchflower	Tottenham Hotspur & Northern Ireland
1958-59	Syd Owen	Luton Town & England
1959-60	Bill Slater	Wolverhampton Wanderers & England
1960-61	Danny Blanchflower	Tottenham Hotspur & Northern Ireland
1961-62	Jimmy Adamson	Burnley
1962-63	Stanley Matthews	Stoke City & England
1963-64	Bobby Moore	West Ham United & England
1964-65	Bobby Collins	Leeds United & Scotland
1965-66	Bobby Charlton	Manchester United & England
1966-67	Jack Charlton	Leeds United & England
1967-68	George Best	Manchester United & Northern Ireland
1968-69	Dave Mackay	Derby County & Scotland
	Tony Book	Manchester City
1969-70	Billy Bremner	Leeds United & Scotland
1970-71	Frank McLintock	Arsenal & Scotland
1971-72	Gordon Banks	Stoke City & England
1972-73	Pat Jennings	Tottenham Hotspur & Northern Ireland
1973-74	Ian Callaghan	Liverpool & England
1974-75	Alan Mullery	Fulham & England
1975-76	Kevin Keegan	Liverpool & England
1976-77	Emlyn Hughes	Liverpool & England
1977-78	Kenny Burns	Nottingham Forest & Scotland
1978-79	Kenny Dalglish	Liverpool & Scotland
1979-80	Terry McDermott	Liverpool & England
1980-81	Frans Thijssen	Ipswich Town & Holland
1981-82	Steve Perryman	Tottenham Hotspur & England
1982-83	Kenny Dalglish	Liverpool & Scotland
1983-84	Ian Rush	Liverpool & Wales
1984-85	Neville Southall	Everton & Wales

1985-86	Gary Lineker	Everton & England
1986-87	Clive Allen	Tottenham Hotspur & England
1987-88	John Barnes	Liverpool & England
1988-89	Steve Nicol	Liverpool & England
1989-90	John Barnes	Liverpool & England
1990-91	Gordon Strachan	Leeds United & Scotland
1991-92	Gary Lineker	Tottenham Hotspur & England
1992-93	Chris Waddle	Sheffield Wednesday & England
1993-94	Alan Shearer	Blackburn Rovers & England
1994-95	Jurgen Klinsmann	Tottenham Hotspur & Germany
1995-96	Eric Cantona	Manchester United & France
1996-97	Gianfranco Zola	Chelsea & Italy
1997-98	Dennis Bergkamp	Arsenal & Holland

PFA AWARDS 1997-98

Player of the Year
1. Dennis Bergkamp — Arsenal
2. Andy Cole — Manchester United
3. Michael Owen — Liverpool

Young Player of the Year
1. Michael Owen — Liverpool
2. Kevin Davies — Southampton
3. Rio Ferdinand — West Ham United

Merit Award
Steve Ogrizovic — Coventry City

Division 1 Team
Miller (WBA), Dyer (Ipswich Town), Tricco (Ipswich Town), Pearson (Middlesbrough), Cooper (N. Forest), Clark (Sunderland), Kinkladze (Man. City), Keane (Wolves), Robinson (Charlton A.), Van Hooijdonk (N. Forest), Merson (Middlesbrough).

Division 2 Team
Chamberlain (Watford), Parkinson (Preston), Kennedy (Watford), Taylor (Bristol City), Coleman (Fulham), Donovan (Grimsby), Hodge (Walsall), Bracewell (Fulham), Groves (Grimsby), Boli (Walsall), Goater (Bristol City, now Man. City).

Division 3 Team
Ward (Notts Co.), Hendon (Notts Co.), Pearce (Notts Co.), Strodder (Notts Co.), Walling (Lincoln), Parnell (Peterborough), Houghton (Peterborough), Culolen (Hartlepool, now Sheff. Utd), Ling (Orient), Quinn (Peterborough), Jack (Torquay).

ENGLAND

Wembley, September 10th 1997 – World Cup Qualifying Group Two
ENGLAND   MOLDOVA   4-0   74,102
Scholes (28), Wright (46, 90),
Gascoigne (81)
England: Seaman, G. Neville, Southgate, Campbell, Beckham (Ripley 67)
(Butt 75), Batty, Gascoigne, P. Neville, Scholes, L. Ferdinand (Collymore
82), Wright. Subs not used: Pallister, Walker, Le Saux, Lee.
Moldova: Roumanenco, Stroenco, Fistican, Tistimitstanu, Spinu, Shishkin
(Popovici 60), Curtean, Culibaba (Suharev 52), Rebetadj, Miterev, Rogaciov
(Cibotari 74).

Rome, October 11th 1997 – World Cup Qualifying Group Two
ITALY   ENGLAND   0-0   81,200
Italy: Peruzzi, Nesta, Costacurta, Cannavaro, Maldini (Benarrivo 31), Di
Livio (sent off), Dino Baggio, Albertini, Zola (Del Piero 64),
Inzaghi (Chiesa 46), Vieri.
England: Seaman, Beckham, Campbell, Adams, Southgate, Le Saux, Ince,
Gascoigne (Butt 88), Batty, Sheringham, Wright. Subs not used: G. Neville,
Walker, P. Neville, Scholes, McManaman, Fowler.

Wembley, November 15th 1997 – International
ENGLAND   CAMEROON   2-0   46,176
Scholes (45), Fowler (45)
England: Martyn, Campbell, P. Neville, Ince, Southgate, (R. Ferdinand 38),
Hinchcliffe, Beckham, Gascoigne (R. Lee 73), Fowler, Scholes (Sutton 79),
McManaman. Subs not used: Seaman, Batty, Butt, Cole.
Cameroon: Ongandzi, Song, Wome, Mimboe, Kalla, Job, Mboma
(Njitap 75), Etchi, Etame (Olembe 73), Foe, Ipoua (Billong 46). Subs not
used: Mangan, Mettomo, Njeukam, Zoalang.

Wembley, February 2nd 1998 – International
ENGLAND   CHILE   0-2   65,228
Salas (45, 79))
England: Martyn, G. Neville, Campbell, Batty (Ince 62), Adams, P. Neville
(Le Saux 46), Lee, Butt, Dublin, Sheringham (Shearer 62), Owen. Subs not
used: Southgate, Hislop, McManaman, Gascoigne.
Chile: Tapia, Villarroel, Reyes, Fuentes, Margas, Rojas, Parraguez, Acuna,
Sierra (Valenzuela 88), Barrera (Carreno 77), Salas. Subs not used: Ramirez,
Cornejo, Vega, Galdames, Rozental.

Berne, March 25th 1998 – International
SWITZERLAND ENGLAND 1-1 17,000
Vega (37) Merson (70)

England: Flowers, Keown, Hinchcliffe, Ince, Southgate, R. Ferdinand, McManaman, Merson (Batty 81), Shearer, Owen (Sheringham 69), Lee. Subs not used: Campbell, Redknapp, Dublin, Matteo, Martyn.
Switzerland: Corminboeuf, Vogel, Fornier, Henchoz, Vega, Yakin, Sesa (Kunz 88), Wicky (Lonfat 81), Grassi, Sforza, Chapuisat. Subs not used: Jeanneret, Wolf, Muller, Zuberbuhler.

Wembley, April 22nd 1998 – International
ENGLAND PORTUGAL 3-0 63,463
Shearer (5, 65),
Sheringham (46)

England: Seaman, G. Neville, (P. Neville 82), Le Saux, Adams, Campbell, Ince, Batty, Scholes, Beckham, (Merson 46), Sheringham (Owen 76), Shearer. Subs not used: Martyn, Southgate, Parlour, Dublin.
Portugal: Baia, Xavier, Dimas, (Pedro Barbosa 53), Beto, Fernando Couto, Paulo Sousa (Oceano 75 mins), Figo, Joao Pinto (Capucho 68 – sent off), Calado, Paulinho Santos, Cadete. Subs not used: Silvino, Joao Manuel Pinto, Sergio Conceicao, Gomes.

Wembley, May 24th 1998 – International
ENGLAND SAUDI ARABIA 0-0 63,733
England: Seaman, G. Neville, Hinchcliffe (P. Neville 74), Batty, Adams, Southgate, Beckham (Gascoigne 60), Anderton, Shearer (L. Ferdinand 74), Sheringham (Wright 60), Scholes. Subs not used: Campbell, Flowers, Merson.
Saudi Arabia: Al-Daye, Al-Jahni, Al-Khlaiwi, Zebramawi, Amin (Al-Dosary 78), Al-Shahrani, Al-Jaber, S Al-Owairan (Al-Temiyat 75), Solaimani, Al-Muwalid, K Al-Owairan, Subs not used: Madani, Al-Thyniyan, Saleh, Al-Sadiq, Al-Dossary.

Wembley, May 27th 1998 – International
MOROCCO ENGLAND 0-1 80,000
 Owen (59)

Morocco: Benzekri, Saber, Rossi, Negrouz, Hadrioui, Chiba (Amzine 63), Taher, Chippo (Sellami 79), Bassir, Ouakili (Reda 73), Robbi (El Khattabi 63). Subs not used: Triki, Abrami, Azzouzi, Laroussi, Abdeiaoui, Chadi, Chadili.
England: Flowers, Keown, Le Saux, Ince, Campbell, Southgate, Anderton, Gascoigne, Dublin (L. Ferdinand 79), Wright (Owen 26), McManaman. Subs not used: R. Ferdinand, Walker, Neville, Butt, Lee.

Wembley, May 29th 1998 – International
BELGIUM   ENGLAND   0-0 25,000
Belgium: Van de Walle, Deflandre, Van Meir, Verstraeten, Borkelmans, De Boeck, Verheyen (Claessens 62), L. M'Penza, Goossens (M. M'Penza 45), Scifo, Boffin. Subs not used: De Wilde, Staerens, Crasson, Leonard.
England: Martyn, G. Neville (R. Ferdinand 45). P. Neville (Owen 45), Butt, Campbell (Dublin 76), Keown, Lee, Gascoigne (Beckham 50), L. Ferdinand, Merson, Le Saux. Subs not used: Walker, Batty, Sheringham, Shearer, McManaman, Scholes, Anderton.

Marseille, June 15th 1998 – World Cup Finals, Group G
ENGLAND   TUNISIA   2-0 54,587
Shearer (42), Scholes (90)
England: Seaman, Campbell, Adams, Southgate, Le Saux, Anderton, Ince, Batty, Scholes, Sheringham (Owen 85), Shearer. Subs not used: Flowers, Martyn, Keown, R. Ferdinand, G. Neville, Beckham, Lee, McManaman, Merson, L. Ferdinand.
Tunisia: El Ouaer, H Trabelsi (Thabet 79 mins), S Trabelsi, Badra, Boukadida, Clayton, Ghadhbane, Chihi, Souayah (Beya 45 mins), Ben Slimane (Ben Younes 65 mins), Sellimi. Subs not used: Boumnijel, Salhi, Chouchane, Jabaliah, Bouazizi, Ben Ahmen, Jelassi, Melki.

Toulouse, June 22nd 1998 – World Cup Finals, Group G
ENGLAND   ROMANIA   1-2 37,500
Owen (83)   Moldovan (47); Petrescu (90)
England: Seaman, G. Neville, Campbell, Adams, Le Saux, Anderton, Ince (Beckham 33), Batty, Scholes, Sheringham (Owen 73), Shearer. Subs not used: Flowers, Martyn, Keown, R. Ferdinand, Lee, McManaman, Merson, L. Ferdinand.
Romania: Stelea, Petrescu, Ciobotariu, Gheorghe Popescu, Filipescu, Munteanu, Hagi (Stanga 73, Marinescu 84), Galca, Gabriel Popescu, Moldovan (Lacatus 86), Ilie.

Lens, June 26th 1998 – World Cup Finals, Group G
ENGLAND   COLOMBIA   2-0 41,275
Anderton (20); Beckham (30)
England: Seaman, G. Neville, Campbell, Adams, Le Saux, Anderton (Lee 79), Ince (Batty 82), Beckham, Scholes (McManaman 73), Owen, Shearer. Subs not used: Flowers, Martyn, Keown, R. Ferdinand, Merson, L. Ferdinand.
Colombia: Mondragon, Cabrera, Bermudez, Palacios, Moreno, Ricon, Serna (Aristazabal 46), Lozano, Valderrama, Preciado (Valencia 46), De Avila (Ricard 56).

St Etienne, June 30th 1998 – World Cup Finals, Second Round
ARGENTINA   ENGLAND   2-2   30,600
Batistuta (6 pen); Zanetti (45)   Shearer (10 pen); Owen (16)
aet Argentina win 4-3 on penalties.

Argentina: Roa, Vivas, Ayala, Charmot, Zanetti, Almeyda, Simone (Berti 91), Ortega, Veron, Batistuta (Balbo 68), Lopez (Gallardo 68).
England: Seaman, G. Neville, Campbell, Adams, Le Saux (Southgate 70), Anderton (Batty 96), Ince, Beckham (sent off), Scholes (Merson 78), Owen, Shearer. Subs not used: Flowers, Martyn, Keown, R. Ferdinand, Sheringham, L. Ferdinand.

Post-War England Manager Records

Manager	Tenure	P	W	D	L	F	A
Glenn Hoddle	7/96-	24	15	4	5	36	10
Terry Venables	01/94-06/96	23	11	11	1	35	13
Graham Taylor	08/90-11/93	38	18	12	8	62	32
Bobby Robson	08/82-07/90	95	47	30	18	158	60
Ron Greenwood	08/77-07/82	56	33	13	10	93	40
Don Revie	10/74-07/77	29	14	8	7	49	25
Joe Mercer	04/74-10/74	7	3	3	1	9	7
Sir Alf Ramsey	01/63-03/74	110	67	26	17	224	98
Sir Walter Winterbottom	08/46-12/62	139	78	33	28	383	196

Goalscorer Summary 1997-98

	Player	Goals	
Alan	SHEARER	4	Portugal (2), Tunisia, Argentina (pen)
Michael	OWEN	3	Morocco, Romania, Argentina
Paul	SCHOLES	3	Moldova, Cameroon, Tunisia
Ian	WRIGHT	2	Moldova (2),
Paul	GASCOIGNE	1	Moldova
Robbie	FOWLER	1	Cameroon
Paul	MERSON	1	Switzerland
Teddy	SHERINGHAM	1	Portugal
Darren	ANDERTON	1	Colombia
David	BECKHAM	1	Colombia

Appearance Summary 1997-98

	Player	Club	Tot	St	Sub	SNU	PS
Tony	ADAMS	Arsenal	8	8	0	0	0
Darren	ANDERTON	Tottenham Hotspur	6	6	0	1	2
David	BATTY	Newcastle United	10	7	3	2	1
David	BECKHAM	Manchester United	9	7	2	1	3
Nicky	BUTT	Manchester United	4	2	2	2	0
Sol	CAMPBELL	Tottenham Hotspur	11	11	0	2	1
Andy	COLE	Manchester United	0	0	0	1	0
Stan	COLLYMORE	Liverpool	1	0	1	0	0
Dion	DUBLIN	Coventry City	3	2	1	2	1
Les	FERDINAND	Tottenham Hotspur	4	1	2	4	1
Rio	FERDINAND	West Ham United	3	1	2	5	0
Tim	FLOWERS	Blackburn Rovers	2	2	0	5	0
Robbie	FOWLER	Liverpool	1	1	0	1	0
Paul	GASCOIGNE	Rangers/Middlesbro'	6	5	1	1	3
Andy	HINCHCLIFFE	Everton	3	3	0	0	1
Shaka	HISLOP	Newcastle United	0	0	0	1	0
Paul	INCE	Liverpool	10	9	1	0	2
Martin	KEOWN	Arsenal	3	3	0	0	4
Graeme	LE SAUX	Chelsea	9	8	1	0	1
Robert	LEE	Newcastle United	5	3	2	6	1
Nigel	MARTYN	Leeds United	3	0	0	6	0
Steve	McMANAMAN	Liverpool	4	3	1	6	0
Paul	MERSON	Middlesbrough	4	2	2	4	1
Gary	NEVILLE	Manchester United	8	8	0	3	2
Phil	NEVILLE	Manchester United	6	4	2	1	2
Michael	OWEN	Liverpool	9	4	5	0	1
Gary	PALLISTER	Manchester United	0	0	0	1	0
Ray	PARLOUR	Arsenal	0	0	0	1	0
Jamie	REDKNAPP	Liverpool	0	0	0	1	0
Stuart	RIPLEY	Blackburn Rovers	1	0	1	0	1
Paul	SCHOLES	Manchester United	8	8	0	2	3
David	SEAMAN	Arsenal	8	8	0	1	0
Alan	SHEARER	Newcastle United	8	7	1	1	1
Teddy	SHERINGHAM	Manchester United	7	6	1	3	5
Gareth	SOUTHGATE	Aston Villa	8	7	1	2	1
Chris	SUTTON	Blackburn Rovers	1	0	1	0	0
Ian	WALKER	Tottenham	0	0	0	3	0
Ian	WRIGHT	Arsenal	4	3	1	0	1

1997-98 APPEARANCE CHART

	Moldova	Italy	Cameroon	Chile	Switzerland	Portugal	Saudi Arabia	Morocco	Belgium	Tunisia	Romania	Colombia	Argentina
ADAMS	–	•	–	•	•	–	•	•	–	–	•	•	•
ANDERTON	–	–	–	–	–	–	•	•	*	–	–	•(79)	•(96)
BATTY	•	•	*	•(62)	*(81)	–	•	•	*	–	•	*(82)	•(96)
BECKHAM	•(67)	•	•	–	–	•(46)	•(60)	–	*(50)	*	*(33)	•	•
BUTT	*(75)	*(88)	*	•	–	–	–	*	•	–	–	–	–
CAMPBELL	•	•	•	•	–	*	•	*	•	•(76)	•	•	•
COLE	–	–	•	*	–	–	–	–	–	–	–	–	–
COLLYMORE	*(82)	–	–	–	–	–	–	–	–	–	–	–	–
DUBLIN	–	–	–	–	*	*	–	–	•(79)	*(76)	–	–	–
FERDINAND, L.	•(82)	–	–	–	–	–	*(74)	*(79)	–	*	*	*	*
FERDINAND, R.	–	–	*(38)	–	•	–	–	*	•(46)	*	*	*	*
FLOWERS	–	–	–	–	–	*	*	–	–	*	*	*	*
FOWLER	–	*	•	–	–	–	–	–	–	–	–	–	–
GASCOIGNE	•	•(88)	•(73)	*	–	–	*(60)	–	•	•(50)	–	–	–
HINCHCLIFFE	–	–	•	–	•	–	•(74)	–	–	–	–	–	–
HISLOP	–	–	–	*	–	–	–	–	–	–	–	–	–
INCE	–	•	•	*(62)	•	•	–	•	•	–	•(33)	•(82)	•
KEOWN	–	–	–	–	–	–	–	–	–	*	*	*	*
LE SAUX	*	•	–	*(46)	–	•	•	•	•	–	–	•	•(70)
LE TISSIER	–	–	–	–	–	–	–	–	–	–	–	–	–
LEE	*	–	*(73)	•	•	–	–	*	•	–	*	*(79)	•
MARTYN	–	–	•	–	*	*	–	•	*	*	*	*	*
MATTEO	–	–	–	–	*	–	–	–	–	–	–	–	–
McMANAMAN	–	*	•	*	•	–	–	•	*	•	*	*(73)	*
MERSON	–	–	–	–	–	•(81)	*(46)	*	–	•	•	*	*(78)
NEVILLE, G.	•	*	–	–	•(82)	–	*	–	•(46)	•	•	•	•
NEVILLE, P.	–	–	•	•(46)	–	*(82)	*(74)	–	•(46)	–	–	–	–
OWEN	–	–	–	•	•(69)	*(76)	–	*(26)	*(46)	*(85)	*(73)	•	–
PALLISTER	*	–	–	–	–	–	–	–	–	–	–	–	–
PARLOUR	–	–	–	–	–	*	–	–	–	–	–	–	–

• Started match. * Substitute - No appearance. A number next to an * indicates an appearance as substitute, the number giving the minute the player entered the match.

	Moldova	Italy	Cameroon	Chile	Switzerland	Portugal	Saudi Arabia	Morocco	Belgium	Tunisia	Romania	Colombia	Argentina
REDKNAPP	–	–	–	–	*	–	–	–	–	–	–	–	–
RIPLEY	*(67)	(75)	–	–	–	–	–	–	–	–	–	–	–
SCHOLES	•	*	•(79)	–	–	•	•	–	*	•	•	•(73)	•(78)
SEAMAN	•	•	*	–	–	•	•	–	–	•	•	•	•
SHEARER	–	•	–	*(62)	•	•	•(74)	–	*	•	•	•	•
SHERINGHAM	–	•	–	•(62)	*(69)	•(76)	•(60)	–	*	•(85)	•(73)	*	*
SOUTHGATE	•	•	•(38)	*	•	*	•	•	–	–	•	–	*(70)
SUTTON	–	–	*(79)	–	–	–	–	–	–	–	–	–	–
WALKER	*	*	–	–	–	–	–	*	*	–	–	–	–
WRIGHT	•	•	–	–	–	–	*(60)	•(26)	–	–	–	–	–

England Red Cards

Player	Opponents	Venue	Year	Score
Alan Mullery	Yugoslavia	Florence	1968	0-1
Alan Ball	Poland	Chorzow	1973	0-2
Trevor Cherry	Argentina	Buenos Aires	1977	1-1
Ray Wilkins	Morocco	Monterrey	1986	0-0
David Beckham	Argentina	Saint-Etienne	1998	2-2 aet

England have never won a game in which they have had a player sent off.

FRANCE '98

First Phase Results

GROUP A
Brazil v Scotland 2-1
Morocco v Norway 2-2
Scotland v Norway 1-1
Brazil v Morocco 3-0
Scotland v Morocco 0-3
Brazil v Norway 1-2

	P	W	D	L	F	A	Pt
Brazil *	3	2	0	1	6	3	6
Norway *	3	1	2	0	5	4	5
Morocco	3	1	1	1	5	5	4
Scotland	3	0	1	2	2	6	1

GROUP B
Italy v Chile 2-2
Cameroon v Austria 1-1
Chile v Austria 1-1
Italy v Cameroon 3-0
Chile v Cameroon 1-1
Italy v Austria 2-1

	P	W	D	L	F	A	Pt
Italy *	3	2	1	0	7	3	7
Chile *	3	0	3	0	4	4	3
Austria	3	0	2	1	3	4	2
Cameroon	3	0	2	1	2	5	2

GROUP C
Saudi Arabia v Denmark 0-1
France v South Africa 3-0
South Africa v Denmark 1-1
France v Saudi Arabia 4-0
France v Denmark 2-1
South Africa v Saudi Arabia ... 2-2

	P	W	D	L	F	A	Pt
France *	3	3	0	0	9	1	9
Denmark *	3	1	1	1	3	3	4
S.Africa	3	0	2	1	3	6	2
S.Arabia	3	0	1	2	1	7	1

GROUP D
Paraguay v Bulgaria 0-0
Spain v Nigeria 2-3
Nigeria v Bulgaria 1-0
Spain v Paraguay 0-0
Spain v Bulgaria 6-1
Nigeria v Paraguay 1-3

	P	W	D	L	F	A	Pt
Nigeria *	3	2	0	1	5	5	6
Paraguay *	3	1	2	0	3	1	5
Spain	3	1	1	1	8	4	4
Bulgaria	3	0	1	2	1	7	1

GROUP E
S. Korea v Mexico 1-3
Holland v Belgium 0-0
Belgium v Mexico 2-2
Holland v S. Korea 5-0
Belgium v S. Korea 1-1
Holland v Mexico 2-2

	P	W	D	L	F	A	Pt
Holland *	3	1	2	0	7	2	5
Mexico *	3	1	2	0	7	5	5
Belgium	3	0	3	0	3	3	3
S. Korea	3	0	1	2	2	9	1

GROUP F

Yugoslavia v Iran							1-0
Germany v USA							2-0
Germany v Yugoslavia							2-2
USA v Iran							1-2
Germany v Iran							2-0
USA v Yugoslavia							0-1

	P	W	D	L	F	A	Pt
Germany *	3	2	1	0	6	2	7
Yugoslavia *	3	2	1	0	4	2	7
Iran	3	1	0	2	2	4	3
USA	3	0	0	3	1	5	0

GROUP G

England v Tunisia	2-0
Romania v Colombia	1-0
Colombia v Tunisia	1-0
Romania v England	2-1
Colombia v England	0-2
Romania v Tunisia	1-1

	P	W	D	L	F	A	Pt
Romania *	3	2	1	0	4	2	7
England *	3	2	0	1	5	2	6
Colombia	3	1	0	2	1	3	3
Tunisia	3	0	1	2	1	4	1

GROUP H

Argentina v Japan	1-0
Jamaica v Croatia	1-3
Japan v Croatia	0-1
Argentina v Jamaica	5-0
Argentina v Croatia	1-0
Japan v Jamaica	1-2

	P	W	D	L	F	A	Pt
Argentina *	3	3	0	0	7	0	9
Croatia *	3	2	0	1	4	2	6
Jamaica	3	1	0	2	3	9	3
Japan	3	0	0	3	1	4	0

* *qualify for Second Round*

SECOND ROUND

Saturday, June 27th

Italy v Norway	1-0
Brazil v Chile	4-1

Sunday, June 28th

France v Paraguay †*	1-0
Nigeria v Denmark	1-4

Monday, June 29th

Germany v Mexico	2-1
Holland v Yugoslavia	2-1

Tuesday, June 30th

Romania v Croatia	0-1
Argentina v England †	2-2

Argentina 4-3 on pens

† *aet.* * *golden goal*

Euro 2000 Group 5 Fixtures

05/09/98	Sweden	v	England
10/10/98	England	v	Bulgaria
14/10/98	Luxembourg	v	England
27/03/99	England	v	Poland
05/06/99	England	v	Sweden
09/06/99	Bulgaria	v	England
04/09/99	England	v	Luxembourg
08/09/99	Poland	v	England

Sixteen countries will make the Finals: the co-hosts, Belgium and Holland; the nine group winners; the best runner-up; and four teams from a play-off system, which will take place in November 1999.

England v Sweden – The Record

Date	Result	Venue	Competiton
20/10/08	12-1	London	OGr1
21/05/23	4-2	Stockholm	Friendly
17/05/37	4-0	Stockholm	Friendly
19/11/47	4-2	London	Friendly
13/05/49	1-3	Stockholm	Friendly
16/05/56	0-0	Stockholm	Friendly
28/10/59	2-3	London	Friendly
16/05/65	2-1	Gothenburg	Friendly
22/05/68	3-1	London	Friendly
10/06/79	0-0	Stockholm	Friendly
10/09/86	0-1	Stockholm	Friendly
19/10/88	0-0	London	World Cup Qualifier
06/09/89	0-0	Stockholm	World Cup Qualifier
17/06/92	1-2	Stockholm	Euro Championship Finals
08/06/95	3-3	Leeds	Umbro Cup

England v Poland – The Record

05/01/66	1-1	Liverpool	Friendly
05/07/66	1-0	Chorzow	Friendly
06/06/73	0-2	Chorzow	World Cup Qualifier
17/10/73	1-1	London	World Cup Qualifier
11/06/86	3-0	Monterrey	World Cup Group
03/06/89	3-0	London	World Cup Qualifier
11/10/89	0-0	Chorzow	World Cup Qualifier
17/10/90	2-0	London	European Cup Qualifier
13/11/91	1-1	Poznan	European Cup Qualifier
29/05/93	1-1	Katowice	World Cup Qualifier

08/09/93	3-0	Wembley	World Cup Qualifier
09/10/96	2-0	Wembley	World Cup Qualifier
31/05/96	2-0	Katowice	World Cup Qualifier

England v Bulgaria – The Record

07/06/62	0-0	Rancagua	World Cup Group Four
11/12/68	1-1	London	Friendly
01/06/74	1-0	Sofia	Friendly
06/06/79	3-0	Sofia	European Cup Qualifier
22/11/79	2-0	London	European Cup Qualifier
02/03/96	1-0	Wembley	Friendly

England v Luxembourg – The Record

21/05/27	5-2	Luxembourg	Friendly
19/10/60	9-0	Luxembourg	World Cup Qualifier
28/09/61	4-1	London	World Cup Qualifier
30/03/77	5-0	London	World Cup Qualifier
12/10/77	2-0	Luxembourg	World Cup Qualifier
15/12/82	9-0	London	European Cup Qualifier
16/11/83	4-0	Luxembourg	European Cup Qualifier

NATIONWIDE LEAGUE CLUB TRANSFERS 1997-98

August 1997

Player	From	To	Fee
Neil Emblen	Wolverhampton W.	C. Palace	£2m
Itzhik Zohar	Royal Antwerp	C. Palace	£1.2m
Deon Burton	Portsmouth	Derby Co.	£1m
Carl Asaba	Brentford	Reading	£800,000
Darren Barnard	Bristol C.	Barnsley	£750,000
Steve Torpey	Swansea C.	Bristol C.	£400,000
Traianos Dellas	Aris Salonika	Sheffield U.	£300,000
Tony Scully	C. Palace	Manchester C.	£300,000
John Aloisi	Cremonese	Portsmouth	£300,000
Sean Flynn	Derby Co.	WBA	£260,000
Lee Howey	Sunderland	Burnley	£200,000
Mixu Paatelainen	Bolton W.	Wolverhampton W.	£200,000
Peter Grant	Celtic	Norwich C.	£200,000
Robert Zabica	Spearwood (A)	Bradford C.	£150,000
Paul Hartley	Millwall	Raith R.	£150,000
Kevin Cooper	Derby Co.	Stockport Co.	£150,000
Ken Charlery	Stockport Co.	Barnet	£80,000
Tony Bird	Barry T.	Swansea C.	Joint fee – £60,000
Dave O'Gorman	Barry T.	Swansea C.	Joint fee – £60,000
Vasilis Kalogeracos	Perth Glory	Stoke City	£60,000
Peter Swan	Burnley	Bury	£50,000
Danny Wilson	Ashton U.	Plymouth Ar.	£40,000
Mikhail Kavelashvili	Manchester C.	Grasshopper	1-year loan+£40,000
Gijsbert Bos	Lincoln C.	Rotherham U.	£20,000
Steve Whitehall	Rochdale	Mansfield T.	£20,000
Charlie Oatway	Torquay U.	Barnet	£10,000
Martin MacInosh	Hamilton Ac.	Stockport Co.	Undisclosed
Martin Butler	Walsall	Cambridge U.	Undisclosed
Ian Gray	Rochdale	Stockport Co.	Tribunal
Jason Van Blerk	Millwall	Manchester C.	Free
Ronny Rosenthal	Tottenham H.	Watford	Free
Andrew Brownrigg	Norwich C.	Rotherham U.	Free
David Kerkslake	Charlton Ath.	Ipswich T.	Free
Stephen Tweed	Ionikos	Stoke C.	Free
Roger Boll	Le Havre	Walsall	Free
Dariusz Kubicki	Sunderland	Wolverhampton W.	Free
Roger Joseph	WBA	L. Orient	Free
Chris Beech	Manchester C.	Cardiff C.	Free

September 1997

Player	From	To	Fee
Fabrizio Ravanelli	Middlesbrough	Marseille	£5.3m
Jon McCarthy	Port Vale	Birmingham C.	£1.85m
Andy Impey	QPR	West Ham U.	£1.3m
Garry Ainsworth	Lincoln C.	Port Vale	£500,000
Phil Gray	Fortuna Sittard	Luton T.	£400,000
Craig Foster	Marconi-Field	Portsmouth	£300,000
Alan Fettis	N. Forest	Blackburn R.	£300,000
Jason Roberts	Hayes	Wolverhampton W.	£250,000
Paul Shaw	Arsenal	Millwall	£250,000
Paul Wilkinson	Barnsley	Millwall	£150,000
David Seal	Bristol C.	Northampton T.	£90,000
Ricky Reina	Dover	Brentford	£50,000 > £100,000
Nigel Spink	WBA	Millwall	£50,000
Leon Townley	Tottenham H.	Brentford	£50,000
Alan White	Middlesbrough	Luton T.	£40,000
Devon White	Notts County	Shrewsbury T.	£35,000
Justin Jackson	Woking	Notts County	£30,000
Ian Ormondroyd	Oldham A.	Scunthorpe U.	£25,000
Jason Harris	C. Palace	L. Orient	£25,000
Bruce Grobbelaar	Oxford U.	Sheffield W.	Nominal
Neil Campbell	York C.	Scarborough	Unknown
Kim Grant	Luton T.	Millwall	Unknown
Stephen Grant	Shamrock R	Stockport Co.	Unknown
Matthew Hocking	Sheffield U.	Hull C.	Unknown
Steve Watkin	Wrexham	Swansea	Unknown
Mark Bowen	Shimizu S-Pulse	Charlton A.	Free
Damien Brennan	Belvedere	Huddersfield T.	Free
Andrew Brown	Hull C.	Clydebank	Free
James Bunch	Doncaster R.	Evesham	Free
Garry Childs	Grimsby T.	Wisbech T.	Free
Jason Dair	Millwall	Raith R.	Free
Cec Edey	Macclesfield T.	Stalybridge Ce.	Free
Collin Foster	Watford	Cambridge U.	Free
Kevin Gage	Preston NE	Hull C.	Free
Matthew George	Aston Villa	Sheffield U.	Free
Dirk Heber	Bursaspor	Tranmere R.	Free
Darren Hughes	Exeter C.	Morecambe	Free
David Hunt	Cardiff C.	Newport AFC	Free
Paul Linger	Charlton A.	L. Orient	Free
Carlos Merino	Urdaneta Italy	N. Forest	Free
George Parris	Southend U.	St Leonards	Free
Steve Perkins	Plymouth Ar.	Stevenage B.	Free
Mark Snijders	AZ Alkmaar	Port Vale	Free
Paul White	Birmingham C.	Nuneaton B.	Free
Paul Agnew	WBA	Swansea	Non-contract
Mark Gavin	Scunthorpe U.	Hartlepool U.	Non-contract
Paul Harries	NSW Soccer	Portsmouth	Non-contract
David Hogan	Accrington S.	Rochdale	Non-contract

Paul Newell	Sittingbourne	Colchester U.	Non-contract
Guy Nzamba	Trieste	Southend U.	Non-contract
John O'Loughlin	B'carana Hearts	Middlesbrough	Non-contract
Andrew Thorpe	Chorley	Doncaster R.	Non-contract
Kon Anastasirioris	Univ NSW	Scarborough	Non-contract
Andy Dibble	Rangers	Luton T.	Monthly
Jesus Sanjuan	Real Zaragoza	Wolverhampton W.	Monthly

October 1997

Player	From	To	Fee
Paul Peschisolido	WBA	Fulham	£1.1m
Mike Evans	Southampton	WBA	£750,000
David Walton	Shrewsbury T.	Crewe Alex.	£750,000
Chris Marsden	Stockport Co.	Birmingham C.	£500,000
Ian Selley	Arsenal	Fulham	£500,000
Mertas Sheleilah	Alania V	Manchester C.	£500,000
Marcelo Cipriano	Dep Alaves	Sheffield U.	£400,000
Micky Mellon	Blackpool	Tranmere R.	£300,000
Gary Walsh	Middlesbrough	Bradford C.	£300,000
Paul Cook	Tranmere R.	Stockport Co.	£250,000
Neil Maddison	Southampton	Middlesbrough	£250,000
Robert Ines	Sydney U.	Portsmouth	£175,000
Mark Patterson	Plymouth Ar.	Gillingham	£150,000
Lee Peacock	Carlisle U.	Mansfield	£150,000
Jorg Smeets	Hercules	Wigan A.	£100,000
Nicky Mohan	Bradford C.	Wycombe W.	£85,000
David Evres	Burnley	Preston NE	£80,000
Paul Bracewell	Sunderland	Fulham	£75,000
Dean Walling	Carlisle U.	Lincoln C.	£75,000
Scott McGleish	L. Orient	Barnet	£70,000
Lee Richardson	Oldham A.	Huddersfield T.	£65,000
Andy Saville	Wigan A.	Cardiff C.	£60,000
Nick Cusack	Fulham	Swansea	£50,000
Christer Warren	Southampton	Bournemouth	£50,000
Graham Lancashire	Wigan A.	Rochdale	£40,000
Aidan Newhouse	Fulham	Swansea	£30,000
Jason White	Northampton T.	Rotherham	£25,000
Paul Harries	NSW Soccer	Portsmouth	£25,000
James Smith	Wolverhampton W.	C. Palace	Swap
Kevin Muscat	C. Palace	Wolverhampton W.	Swap
Doughie Freedman	C. Palace	Wolverhampton W.	Swap
Gareth Bough	N. Forest	Corby T.	Free
Carl Bradshaw	Norwich C.	Wigan A.	Free
Darren Bradshaw	Blackpool	Rushden & D.	Free
John Butler	Rochdale	Stalybridge Ce.	Free
Billy Clark	Bristol R.	Exeter C.	Free
Ian Clark	Doncaster R.	Hartlepool U.	Free
Regis Coulbault	Toulon	Southend U.	Free
Mario Doner	Motherwell	Darlington	Free
Wayne Dowell	Rochdale	Northwich V.	Free

Steve Fraser	Lincoln C.	Grantham	Free
Erik Fuglestad	V. Stavanger	Norwich C.	Free
Nathan Freeman	Manchester C.	Farnborough T.	Free
Ryan Green	Danes Court	Wolverhampton W.	Free
Barry Horne	Birmingham C.	Huddersfield T.	Free
John Jeffers	Stockport Co.	Hednesford	Free
Ben Lewis	Colchester U.	Southend U.	Free
Neil Moore	Norwich C.	Burnley	Free
Richard Moore	Birmingham C.	Gateshead	Free
Sada N'Diaye	Troyes	Southend U.	Free
Jason Peake	Brighton & HA	Bury	Free
Daniel Potter	Chelsea	Colchester U.	Free
Franz Resch	Motherwell	Darlington	Free
Marc Robertson	Marconi	Burnley	Free
Michael Rodosthenous	WBA	Cambridge U.	Free
Robert Sawyers	Wolverhampton W.	Barnet	Free
Lauren Croci	Bordeaux	Carlisle U.	Non-contract
Jason Dozzell	Tottenham H.	Ipswich T.	Non-contract
Wayne Dver	Birmingham C.	Oxford U.	Non-contract
Sasa Llic	Australia	Charlton A.	Non-contract
Alexandros Kiratzoglou	Heidelberg U	Oldham A.	Non-contract
Michael Love	Wycombe W.	Northampton T.	Non-contract
Chris Mackenzie	Hereford U.	L. Orient	Non-contract
David Regis	Barnsley	L. Orient	Non-contract
Jonathan Scargil	Sheffield W.	Chesterfield	Non-contract
David Smith	Bramhall	Doncaster R.	Non-contract
Rod Thornley	Warrington	Doncaster R.	Non-contract
Nick Buxton	Bury	Scarborough	Monthly
Darren Lonerghan	Oldham A.	Bury	Monthly
Jan Pedersen	Brann	Hartlepool U.	Monthly
Richard Perry	Bristol C.	Bristol R.	Monthly
David Whyte	Charlton A.	Ipswich T.	Monthly
Thomas Wright	Bradford C.	Oldham A.	Monthly

November 1997

Player	From	To	Fee
Craig Russell	Sunderland	Manchester C.	£1m
Nicky Summerbee	Manchester C.	Sunderland	£1m
Wayne Allison	Swindon T.	Huddersfield T.	£800,000
David Johnson	Bury	Ipswich T.	£800,000
Maik Taylor	Southampton	Fulham	£700,000
John McGinlay	Bolton W.	Bradford C.	£625,000
Paul Trollope	Derby Co.	Fulham	£600,000
George Ndah	C. Palace	Swindon T.	£500,000
Graham Stuart	Everton	Sheffield U.	£500,000
Bobby Ford	Oxford U.	Sheffield U.	£400,000
Alan Neilson	Southampton	Fulham	£250,000
Chris Swailes	Ipswich T.	Bury	£200,000
Chris Byrne	Sunderland	Stockport Co.	£200,000
Tony Lormor	Chesterfield	Preston NE	£130,000

Owen Archdeacon	Carlisle U.	G. Morton	£100,000
Steve McAnespie	Bolton W.	Fulham	£100,000
Ian Johnson	Dundee U.	Huddersfield T.	£90,000
Andy Scott	Sheffield U.	Brentford	£75,000
Paul Simpson	Derby Co.	Wolverhampton W.	£75,000
Warren Aspinall	Carlisle U.	Brentford	£50,000
Neil Edwards	Stockport Co.	Rochdale	£25,000
Andy Milner	Chester C.	Morecambe	£8,000
Vance Warner	N. Forest	Rotherham	Undisclosed
Gavin Gordon	Hull C.	Lincoln C.	Unknown
Matthew Bound	Stockport Co.	Swansea	Unknown
Steve Gaughen	Chesterfield	Darlington	Unknown
David Reeves	Preston NE	Chesterfield	Swap
Carl Tiler	Sheffield U.	Everton	Swap
Mitch Ward	Sheffield U.	Everton	Swap
Sam Ayorinde	L. Orient	Dover A.	Free
Dave Beasant	Southampton	N. Forest	Free
Brian Borrows	Coventry C.	Swindon T.	Free
Scott Bennetts	Exeter C.	Farnborough T.	Free
Natham Freeman	Manchester C.	Farnborough T.	Free
Tommy Gallagher	Notts County	Stafford R.	Free
Kyle Hayton	Preston NE	Morecambe	Free
Colin Hill	Trelleborgs	Northampton T.	Free
Anthony Jones	L. Orient	Chelmsford C.	Free
Andy Lomas	Cambridge U.	Stevenage B.	Free
Darren Lonergan	Oldham A.	Stalybridge Ce.	Free
Steve Norman	Gillingham	St Leonards	Free
David Phillips	N. Forest	Huddersfield T.	Free
Mark Smith	Cardiff C.	Rushden & D.	Free
Ole Bjorn Sundgot	Bradford C.	Molde	Free
Steve Sutton	Notts County	Grantham	Free
Clive Walker	Brentford	Cheltenham T.	Free
Peter Whiston	Shrewsbury T.	Stafford R.	Free
Andrea Silenzi	N. Forest	Released	Free
Sam Tydeman	Gillingham	St Leonards	Free
Steve Winter	Torquay U.	Dorchester T.	Free
Andy Ansah	L. Orient	Brighton & HA	Non-contract
Glenn Cockerill	Fulham	Brentford	Non-contract
Leo Cotterill	Bournemouth	Rushden & D.	Non-contract
Craig Davis	Gateshead	Doncaster R.	Non-contract
Charlie Hartfield	Sheffield U.	Swansea	Non-contract
Martin Hollund	SK Brann Bergen	Hartlepool U.	Non-contract
Paul Holsgrove	Reading	Crewe Alex.	Non-contract
Sasa Ilic	Charlton A.	Welling U.	Non-contract
Matthew Kerr	Ballymena U.	Blackpool	Non-contract
Chris Leadbitter	Plymouth Ar.	Torquay U.	Non-contract
Danny O'Hagan	Weston-s-Mare	Plymouth Ar.	Non-contract
Jonathan Scargill	Chesterfield	Oldham A.	Non-contract
Andrew Tretton	Derby Co.	Chesterfield	Non-contract
Leon Woodley	Knowle	Birmingham C.	Non-contract
Graham Anthony	Plymouth Ar.	Carlisle U.	Monthly

Steve Lenagh	Sheffield W.	Chesterfield	Monthly
Brian McGinty	Rangers	Hull C.	Monthly
Colin Omogbehin	Baldock T.	Luton T.	Monthly
Danielle Tiatto	FC Baden	Stoke C.	Monthly

December 1997

Player	From	To	Fee
Chris Coleman	Blackburn R.	Fulham	£2.1m
George Kulcsar	Bradford C.	QPR	£250,000
Jason Bowen	Birmingham C.	Reading	£200,000
Ian Hughes	Bury	Blackpool	£200,000
Gareth Davies	C. Palace	Reading	£175,000
Scott Murray	Aston Villa	Bristol C.	£150,000
Mark Patterson	Sheffield U.	Bury	£125,000
Chris Freestone	Middlesbrough	Northampton T.	£75,000
Tony Ellis	Blackpool	Bury	£70,000
Carl Veart	C. Palace	Millwall	£50,000
Paul Watson	Fulham	Brentford	£50,000
Charlie Bishop	Wigan A.	Northampton T.	£20,000
Paul Smith	N. Forest	Lincoln C.	£20,000
Mark Foran	Peterborough U.	Crewe Alex.	£45,000
Martin McDonald	Doncaster R.	Macclesfield T.	Undisclosed
Derek Whyte	Middlesbrough	Aberdeen	Undisclosed
Kevin Henderson	Morpeth Town	Burnley	Unknown
Shaun Maher	Bohemians	Fulham	Unknown
Ashley Vickers	Heybridge S.	Peterborough U.	£5,000
Ian Baird	Brighton & HA	Salisbury C.	Free
Shaun Chapple	Swansea	Merthr Ty.	Free
Isidro Diaz	Wolverhampton W.	Wigan A.	Free
Mark Gardiner	Macclesfield T.	Northwich V.	Free
Guiliano Grazioli	Peterborough U.	Stevenage B.	Free
Gary Ingham	Doncaster R.	Stalybridge Ce.	Free
Jason Jones	Liverpool	Swansea	Free
Paul Linger	L. Orient	Brighton & HA	Free
Ryan Morgan	Bristol R.	Clevedon T.	Free
Mark Morris	Brighton & HA	Hastings	Free
Andy Porteous	N. Forest	Manchester C.	Free
John Ramsey	Doncaster R.	Stalybridge Ce.	Free
Ian Reed	Shrewsbury T.	Halesowen	Free
David Rennie	Northampton T.	Peterborough U.	Free
Dean Saunders	N. Forest	Sheffield U.	Free
K Sigurdsson	KA Akureyri	Stoke C.	Free
Nicky Southall	Grimsby T.	Gillingham	Free
Andrew Tretton	Chesterfield	Shrewsbury T.	Free
Nial Inman	Peterborough U.	Stevenage B.	Free
Geoff Aunger	Seattle S.	Stockport Co.	Non-contract
Darren Beckford	Walsall	Bury	Non-contract
Michael Bennett	Cardiff C.	L. Orient	Non-contract
Mark Cooper	Hartlepool U.	L. Orient	Non-contract
Nelson Da Costa	Stockport Co.	Macclesfield T.	Non-contract

James Dungay	Plymouth Ar.	Exeter C.	Non-contract
Andy Hammond	Scunthorpe U.	Stalybridge Ce.	Non-contract
Neil Illman	Plymouth Ar.	Exeter C.	Non-contract
Stig Larsen	Fana IL	Hartlepool U.	Non-contract
Per-Ola Ljung	Helsingborgs	Watford	Non-contract
David Regis	L. Orient	Lincoln C.	Non-contract
Colin Simpson	Watford	L. Orient	Non-contract
Gary Tallon	Kilmarnock	Notts Co.	Non-contract
Dean Williams	Doncaster R.	Gateshead	Non-contract
Kris Winters	N. Forest	Manchester C.	Non-contract
Gustavo Di Lella	Blyth Sp.	Darlington	Mon
Jason Dozzell	Ipswich T.	Northampton T.	Mon
Marco Gabbiadini	Panionios	Stoke C.	Mon
Brian Gayle	Bristol R.	Shrewsbury T.	Mon
Bruce Grobbelaar	Unattached	Oldham A.	Mon
Andy Kiwomya	Bradford C.	Notts Co.	Mon
A. Stephenson	Kilkenny	Darlington	Mon

January 1998

Player	From	To	Fee
Emerson	Middlesbrough	Tenerife	£4.2m
Andy Hinchcliffe	Everton	Sheffield W.	£3m
Trevor Sinclair	QPR	West Ham U.	£2.3m
Includes swap of Dowie and Rowland valued at £500,000			
Andrew Griffin	Stoke C.	Newcastle U.	£1.5m
Plus £500,000 after unspecified number of appearances and £250,000 if capped			
Brian Deane	Sheffield U.	Benfica	£1m
Matt Carbone	Derby Co.	WBA	£800,000
Jan Aage Fjortoft	Sheffield U.	Barnsley	£800,000
Shaun Derry	Notts Co.	Sheffield U.	£500,000
Daniele Dichio	Sampdoria	Sunderland	£750,000
Wayne Collins	Sheffield W.	Fulham	£400,000
Plus £150,000 after a number of appearances			
Rufus Brevett	QPR	Fulham	£375,000
Carl Leaburn	Charlton A.	Wimbledon	£300,000
Kakhaber Tshkadaze	Al. Vladikavkaz	Manchester C.	£300,000
Simon Charlton	Southampton	Birmingham C.	£250,000
Jon Cullen	Hartlepool U.	Sheffield U.	£250,000
Frode Grodas	Chelsea	Tottenham H.	£250,000
John O'Kane	Manchester U.	Everton	£250,000
Rising to £450,000			
Luke Weaver	L. Orient	Sunderland	£250,000
Alon Hazan	I.Hashdor (Israel)	Watford	£200,000
Dave Smith	WBA	Grimsby T.	£200,000
Jurgen Sommer	QPR	Columbus Cr.	£175,000
Marcus Bent	Brentford	C. Palace	£150,000
Plus £150,000 after a number of appearances			
Anti Heinola	Hercules	QPR	£100,000
Stephen Frail	Hearts	Tranmere R.	£90,000
John Doolan	Mansfield	Barnet	£60,000

Player	From	To	Fee
Andrew Cook	Portsmouth	Millwall	£50,000
Ville Lehtinen	HJK Helsinki	Sheffield U.	£50,000
Barry Jones	Wrexham	York C.	£35,000
Stephen Howe	N. Forest	Swindon T.	£30,000
Ronnie Jepson	Bury	Oldham A.	£30,000
Steven Kerrigan	Ayr U.	Shrewsbury T.	£25,000
Matt Joseph	Cambridge U.	L. Orient	£10,000
Robert Ryan	Huddersfield T.	Millwall	£10,000
Andy Gray	Bury	Millwall	Nominal
Neil Mustoe	Manchester U.	Wigan A.	Unknown
Derek Whyte	Middlesbrough	Aberdeen	Unknown
Paul Barnes	Burnley	Huddersfield T.	Swap
Andy Payton	Huddersfield T.	Burnley	Swap
Iain Dowie	West Ham U.	QPR	Swap
Keith Rowland	West Ham U.	QPR	Swap
Chris Adamson	WBA	Moor Green	Free
Tomas Brolin	Leeds U.	C. Palace	Free
Leon Cort	Dulwich H.	Millwall	Free
Mark Devlin	Stoke C.	Exeter C.	Free
Jan Eriksson	Sunderland	TB Mutiny	Free
Dave Hanson	L. Orient	Halifax T.	Free
Graeme Hogg	Notts Co.	Brentford	Free
Alan Kernaghan	Manchester C.	St Johnstone	Free
Kevin Mather	Tottenham H.	Southend U.	Free
Neil Inman	Peterborough U.	Stevenage B.	Free
Ricky Lampkin	Tranmere R.	Northwich V.	Free
David Terrier	West Ham U.	Newcastle U.	Free
Paul Wilson	Plymouth Ar.	Doncaster R.	Free
Denny Mundee	Brighton & HA	Dorchester T.	Free
Mark Williams	Tranmere R.	Northwich V.	Free
Itzak Zohar	C. Palace	M. Haifa	Free
Paul Holsgrove	Crewe Alex.	Stoke C.	Monthly
Davide Xausa	Vancouver	Port Vale	Monthly
Daniel Anderson	WI Lakers (Can)	Plymouth Ar.	Non-contract
Gavin Lewis	East Fife	Plymouth Ar.	Non-contract
Antony Skedd	Gateshead	Hartlepool U.	Non-contract
Phil Startbuck	Sheffield U.	Oldham A.	Non-contract
Oscar Valle	Villareal	Walsall	Non-contract
David Whyte	Ipswich T.	Bristol R.	Non-contract

February 1998

Player	From	To	Fee
Hamilton Ricard	Dep. Cali	Middlesbrough	£2m
Alun Armstrong	Stockport Co.	Middlesbrough	£1.5m
Don Hutchison	Sheffield U.	Everton	£1m
Matt Jansen	Carlisle U.	C. Palace	£1m
	Rising to £2m after number of appearances		
Dele Adebola	Crewe Alex.	Birmingham C.	£1m
Marco Branca	Internazionale	Middlesbrough	£1m
Tony Thorpe	Luton T.	Fulham	£800,000

Darren Purse	Oxford U.	Birmingham C.	£600,000
Rory Delap	Carlisle U.	Derby Co.	£500,000 > £1m
Kyle Lightbourne	Coventry C.	Stoke C.	£500,000
James Quinn	Blackpool	WBA	£500,000
Stephen Bywater	Rochdale	West Ham U.	£300,000 > £2.3m
Kevin Francis	Birmingham C.	Oxford U.	£100,000
Nigel Jemson	Oxford U.	Bury	£100,000
Wayne Burnett	Huddersfield T.	Grimsby T.	£100,000
Gerry McMahon	Stoke C.	St Johnstone	£85,000
Danny Cullip	Fulham	Brentford	£75,000
John Hills	Everton	Blackpool	£75,000
Andy Legg	Birmingham C.	Reading	£75,000
Matthew Robinson	Southampton	Portsmouth	£50,000
Nick Wright	Derby Co.	Carlisle U.	£35,000
Jermaine Wright	Wolverhampton W.	Crewe Alex.	£25,000
Bryan Gunn	Norwich C.	Hibernian	Nominal
Jon O'Connor	Everton	Sheffield U.	Swap
Earl Barrett	Everton	Sheffield W.	Free
Jon Connelly	Ipswich T.	Albion R.	Free
Gustavo de Lilla	Darlington	Blyth Sp.	Free
Simon Coleman	Bolton W.	Southend U.	Free
Anthony Elliot	Cardiff C.	Scarborough	Free
Daniel George	N. Forest	Doncaster R.	Free
Glyn Hodges	Hull C.	N. Forest	Free
Sean Mannion	Stella Maris	Stockport Co.	Free
Jehad Muntasser	Arsenal	Bristol C.	Free
Greg Shannon	Maghera Colts	Sunderland	Free
Habib Sissoko	Louhans	Preston NE	Free
Alex Smith	Swindon T.	Huddersfield T.	Free
Dave Thompson	Cambridge U.	Yeovil T.	Free
Colin West	L. Orient	Rushden & D.	Free
Davide Xausa	Stoke C.	St. Johnstone	Free
Pasquale Bruno	Hearts	Wigan A.	Non-contract
Andrew Catley	Southampton	Exeter C.	Non-contract
Paul Edwards	Ashton U.	Doncaster R.	Non-contract
Steven Hawes	Sheffield U.	Doncaster R.	Non-contract
Mark Quayle	Everton	Southport	Non-contract
Paul Raynor	Guang Deong	L. Orient	Non-contract
David Regis	Lincoln C.	Scunthorpe U.	Non-contract
Niall Thompson	Zulte VV	Brentford	Non-contract
Neil Wallace	Victoria	Plymouth Ar.	Non-contract
Peter Zois	Purfleet	Cardiff C.	Non-contract
Franz Carr	Bolton W.	WBA	Monthly
Richard Liburb	Bradford C.	Carlisle U.	Monthly
Paul Newell	Colchester U.	Northampton T.	Monthly
Jon Pagal	Austria	Carlisle U.	Monthly
Adem Poric	Sheffield W.	Rotherham	Monthly
Russell Watkinson	Southampton	Bristol C.	Monthly
Davide Xausa	Port Vale	Stoke C.	Monthly

March 1998

Player	From	To	Fee
Paul Gascoigne	Rangers	Middlesbrough	£3.45m
Jamie Pollock	Bolton W.	Manchester C.	£1m
Jonathan Greening	York C.	Manchester U.	£1m
Neil Emblen	C. Palace	Wolverhampton W.	£900,000
Eddie Youds	Bradford C.	Charlton A.	£550,000
Matt McKay	Chester C.	Everton	£500,000 > £750,000
Shaun Goater	Bristol C.	Manchester C.	£500,000
Marlon Beresford	Burnley	Middlesbrough	£500,000
Vinnie Jones	Wimbledon	QPR	£500,000
Jim McIntyre	Kilmarnock	Reading	£420,000
Steve Claridge	Leicester C.	Wolverhampton W.	£350,000
Danny Mills	Norwich C.	Charlton A.	£350,000
Jamie Clapham	Tottenham H.	Ipswich T.	£300,000
James Coppinger	Darlington	Newcastle U.	£250,000 >
Paul Robinson	Darlington	Newcastle U.	£250,000 >
	Could rise to combined fee of £1.8m		
Paul Devlin	Birmingham C.	Sheffield U.	£200,000
Christian Edwards	Swansea	N. Forest	£175,000
Tony Scully	Manchester C.	QPR	£155,000
Chris Wilder	Bradford C.	Sheffield U.	£150,000
Andrew Hughes	Oldham A.	Notts Co.	£150,000
Ifem Onuora	Gillingham	Swindon T.	£120,000
Paul Brayson	Newcastle U.	Reading	£100,000
Stuart Gray	Celtic	Reading	£100,000
Robbie Slater	Southampton	Wolverhampton W.	£75,000
Steve Davies	Barnsley	Oxford U.	£75,000
Lee Makel	Huddersfield T.	Hearts	£75,000
Mike Pollitt	Notts Co.	Sunderland	£75,000
Mathew Brazier	QPR	Fulham	£65,000
Ian Baraclough	Notts Co.	QPR	£50,000
Neil Gregory	Ipswich T.	Colchester U.	£50,000
Jason Van Blerk	Manchester C.	WBA	£50,000
Mike Conroy	Fulham	Blackpool	£50,000
Jimmy Crawford	Newcastle U.	Reading	£50,000
Robert Fleck	Norwich C.	Reading	£50,000
Stuart Barlow	Oldham A.	Wigan A.	£45,000
Scott Howey	Motherwell	Reading	£30,000
Julian Alsop	Bristol R.	Swansea	£15,000
Neil Harris	Chelmsford C.	Millwall	£30,000
Ben Sedgemore	Mansfield	Macclesfield T.	£25,000
Francis Green	Ilkeston T.	Peterborough U.	£11,000
Craig Midgley	Bradford C.	Hartlepool U.	£10,000
Richard Goddard	Brentford	Woking	£7,500
Ian Hamilton	WBA	Sheffield U.	Undisclosed
Johann Gudmundsson	Keflavik	Watford	Undisclosed
Gary Martindale	Notts Co.	Rotherham	Nominal
Jorg Sobiech	NEC Nijmegen	Stoke C.	Nominal
Scott Partridge	Cardiff C.	Torquay U.	Nominal
Lee Jones	Swansea	Bristol R.	Swap with Alsop

Adrian Littlejohn	Plymouth Ar.	Oldham A.	Swap
Phil Starbuck	Oldham A.	Plymouth Ar.	Swap
Keiron Durkan	Stockport Co.	Macclesfield T.	Undisclosed
Bryan Small	Bolton W.	Bury	Undisclosed
Graeme Atkinson	Preston NE	Brighton & HA	Free
Vince Bartram	Arsenal	Gillingham	Free
Ian Bishop	West Ham U.	Manchester C.	Free
O'Neill Donaldson	Sheffield W.	Stoke C.	Free
Alex Dyer	Huddersfield T.	Notts Co.	Free
Gary Germaine	WBA	Moor Green	Free
Shane Fogarty	Walsall	Peterborough U.	Free
Sean Hessey	Leeds U.	Huddersfield T.	Free
Damien Hilton	Norwich C.	Brighton & HA	Free
Lee Holsgrove	Millwall	Wycombe W.	Free
Richard Jobson	Leeds U.	Manchester C.	Free
David Kerslake	Ipswich T.	Swindon T.	Free
Martin Neilsen	FC Copenhagen	Huddersfield T.	Free
Joe Omigie	Brentford	Welling U.	Free
Ben Smith	Reading	Yeovil T.	Free
Neville Southall	Everton	Stoke C.	Free
Paul Stephenson	York C.	Hartlepool U.	Free
Richard Tracey	Sheffield U.	Rotherham	Free
Stephen Tutill	York C.	Darlington	Free
Sam Winston	L. Orient	Yeovil T.	Free
Steven Blaney	West Ham U.	Brentford	Free
Lee Colkin	Northampton T.	Hednesford	Free
Jason Drysdale	Swindon T.	Northampton T.	Free
John Foster	Manchester C.	Carlisle U.	Free
Stuart Nethercott	Tottenham H.	Millwall	Free
Justin O'Reilly	Port Vale	Southport	Free
Martin Pemberton	Doncaster R.	Scunthorpe U.	Free
Adem Poric	Rotherham	Notts Co.	Free
Russell Watkinson	Southampton	Millwall	Free
Jean Eydelie	FC Sion	Walsall	Monthly
Didier Tholot	FC Sion	Walsall	Monthly
Simon Wormull	Brentford	Brighton & HA	Monthly
Dean Craven	WBA	Shrewsbury T.	Monthly
Jeffrey Woolsey	QPR	Brighton & HA	Monthly
Paul Carden	Blackpool	Rochdale	Monthly
Michael Anderson	Notts Co.	Telford U.	Non-contract
Dennis Bailey	Gillingham	Lincoln C.	Non-contract
Steve Cherry	Rotherham	Notts Co.	Non-contract
Jonathan Cross	Wrexham	Tranmere R.	Non-contract
Darren Currie	Shrewsbury T.	Plymouth Ar.	Non-contract
Claudio De Vito	Northampton T.	Barnet	Non-contract
Jim Dobbin	Doncaster R.	Grimsby T.	Non-contract
James Gibson	L. Orient	Welling U.	Non-contract
Jeremy Goss	Hearts	Colchester U.	Non-contract
Alex Finlayson	Swindon T.	Cambridge U.	Non-contract
James Holmshaw	Worksop T.	Rotherham	Non-contract

Leon Jackson	Port Vale	Leek T.	Non-contract
Gary Jermaine	WBA	Leek T.	Non-contract
Scott Lindsey	L. Orient	Welling U.	Non-contract
Craig Maskell	Hong Kong	L. Orient	Non-contract
Robin Moody	L. Orient	Woking	Non-contract
Kelechi Okorie	Sardsberg	Rochdale	Non-contract
Colin Rose	Macclesfield T.	Gateshead	Non-contract
Adam Stonier	Scunthorpe U.	Leek T.	Non-contract
David Swanick	Wrexham	Morecambe	Non-contract
Gustavo Di Lella	Darlington	Hartlepool U.	Non-contract
James Dobbin	Doncaster R.	Scarborough	Non-contract
Colin Flood	Stantondale	Crewe Alex.	Non-contract
Marco Gabbiadini	Stoke C.	York C.	Non-contract
Owen Jame	Sheffield U.	Exeter C.	Non-contract
Jim Larkin	Cambridge U.	Walsall	Non-contract
Anthony Lynch	Taunton T.	Torquay U.	Non-contract
Paul Mahorn	Tottenham H.	Port Vale	Non-contract
Jean Misse-Misse	Dundee U.	Chesterfield	Non-contract
Zach Nedimovic	Soham T.	Walsall	Non-contract
Arns Pjetursson	Fram	Reading	Non-contract
Michael Phelan	Blackpool	Stockport Co.	Non-contract
Neil Wallace	Plymouth Ar.	Exeter C.	Non-contract
David Whyte	Bristol R.	Southend U.	Non-contract

PLAYER LOANS 1997-98

August 1997
Dave Beasant - Southampton to N. Forest; Mark Stein - Chelsea to Ipswich T.; Craig Smith - Derby Co. to Rochdale; John Hills - Everton to Swansea C.; Jason Harris - C. Palace to Lincoln C.; Drewe Broughton - Norwich C. to Wigan Ath.; David Gilbert - WBA to Grimsby T.; Lee Richardson - Oldham Ath. to Stockport Co.; Paul Crichton - WBA to Aston Villa; David Regis - Barnsley to Scunthorpe U.; Kelvin Davis - Luton T. to Hartlepool U.; Kim Grant - Luton T. to Millwall; Neil Moss - Southampton to Gillingham; David Seal - Bristol C. to Northampton T.

September 1997
Martin Allen - Portsmouth to Southend U.; Chris Bettney - Sheffield U. to Hull C.; Paul Bodin - Reading to Wycombe W.; Brian Borrows - Coventry C. to Swindon T.; Jason Bowell - Birmingham C. to Southampton; Chris Casper - Manchester U. to Swindon T.; Billy Clark - Bristol R. to Cheltenham T.; Nigel Clough - Manchester C. to Sheffield W.; Simon Coleman - Bolton W. to Wolverhampton W.; Mark N. Cooper - Hartlepool U. to Macclesfield T.; Gerry Creany - Manchester C. to Burnley; Steve Davis - Barnsley to York C.; Simon Davey - Preston NE to Darlington; David Hanson - L. Orient to Dover A.; Steven Hawes - Sheffield U. to Doncaster R.; Paul Hosgrove - Reading to Grimsby T.; Scott Honeyball - L. Orient to Gravesend; Andy Kiwomya - Bradford C. to Burnley; Lee Martin - Bristol R. to Huddersfield T.; Stephen Morgan - Wigan to Bury; Ian Moore - N. Forest to West Ham U.; Ricky Otto - Birmingham C. to Notts Co.; Vince Overson - Burnley to Shrewsbury T.; Isiah Rankin - Arsenal to Colchester U.; Zeke Rowe - Peterborough U. to Kettering T.; Lee Sanford - Sheffield U. to Reading; Justin Skinner - Bristol R. to Walsall; Bryan Small - Bolton W. to Luton T.; David Town - Bournemouth to Dorchester T.; Arjan Van Heusden - Port Vale to Oxford U.; Gary Walsh - Middlesbrough to Bradford C.; Colin West - L. Orient to Northampton T.; Jason White - Northampton T. to Rotherham; Stuart Whittacker - Macclesfield T. to Stalybridge Ce.

October 1997
Sammy Ayorinde - L. Orient to Dover A.; Jamie Barnwell-Edinboro - Cambridge U. to Rushden & D.; Vince Bartram - Arsenal to Huddersfield T.; Mark Beard - Sheffield U. to Southend U.; Michael Black - Arsenal to Millwall; Brian Borrows - Coventry C. to Swindon T.; Wayne Brown - Ipswich T. to Colchester U.; Billy Clark - Cheltenham to Bristol R.; Nicky Colgan - Chelsea to Brentford; Glen Crowe - Wolverhampton W. to Cardiff C.; Mark Devlin - Stoke C. to Exeter C.; Tamer Fernandes - Brentford to Peterborough U.; Alex Finlayson - Swindon T. to Salisbury; Steve Finney - Crewe Alex. to Chesterfield; Richard Flash - Watford to Lincoln C.; Mark Gayle - Crewe Alex. to Chesterfield; Paul Gibson - Manchester U. to Mansfield; Valur Gislason - Arsenal to Brighton & HA; Richard Goddard - Brentford to Woking; Gareth Hall - Sunderland to Scarborough; Christ Hurst -

Huddersfield T. to Halifax T.; Scott Jones - Barnsley to Notts Co.; Raymond Kelly - Manchester C. to Wrexham; Phil King - Swindon T. to Blackpool; Leon McKenzie - C. Palace to Fulham; Lee McRobert - Millwall to Dover A.; Andy Milner - Chester C. to Hereford U.; John O'Kane - Manchester U. to Bradford C.; Graham Potter - WBA to Northampton T.; David Rocastle - Chelsea to Hull C.; Paul Simpson - Derby Co. to Wolverhampton W.; Paul Smith - N. Forest to Lincoln C.; Nicky Ward - Shrewsbury T. to Telford U.

November 1997

Chris Adamson - WBA to Moor Green; Chris Allen - N. Forest to Luton T.; Daniel Boxall - C. Palace to Oldham A.; Scott Bundy - Portsmouth to Dorchester T.; James Collins - Crewe Alex. to Northwich V.; Paul Dalglish - Newcastle U. to Bury; Paul Emblen - Charlton A. to Brighton & HA; Nigel Gleghorn - Burnley to Brentford; Neil Gregory - Ipswich T. to Peterborough U.; Paul Heckingbottom - Sunderland to Scarborough; Ian Helliwell - Burnley to Doncaster R.; Lee Hodges - West Ham U. to Plymouth Ar.; Jamie Hoyland - Burnley to Carlisle U.; Andrew Legg - Birmingham C. to Ipswich T.; Jaime Moreno - DC United to Middlesbrough; Scott Paterson - Bristol C. to Cardiff C.; Robert Pell - Rotherham to Doncaster R.; Lee Hodges - West Ham U. to Plymouth Ar.; Jamie Hoyland - Burnley to Carlisle U.; Andrew Legg - Birmingham C. to Ipswich T.; Jaime Moreno - DC United to Middlesbrough; Scott Paterson - Bristol C. to Cardiff C.; Robert Pell - Rotherham to Doncaster R.; Greg Strong - Bolton W. to Blackpool; Wayne Thomas - Walsall to Kidderminster H.; David Thompson - Liverpool to Swindon T.; Darren Utley - Doncaster R. to Stalybridge Ce.; Tony Warner - Liverpool to Swindon T.; Neil Woods - Grimsby T. to Wigan A.; Nicky Wright - Derby Co. to Carlisle U.

December 1997

Marc Anthony - Celtic to Tranmere R.; Graeme Atkinson - Preston NE to Rochdale; Richard Barker - Linfield to Brighton & HA; Paul Beesley - Manchester C. to Port Vale; Chris Bettney - Sheffield U. to Hull C.; Graham Branch - Tranmere R. to Wigan A.; Simon Brown - Tottenham H. to Lincoln C.; Simon Charlton - Southampton to Birmingham C.; Paul Conway - Northampton T. to Scarborough; Lawrence Davies Bradford C. to Darlington; Mark Dempsey - Shrewsbury T. to Dover A.; Martin Foster - Leeds U. to Bury; Andy Gray - Leeds U. to Bury; Steve Harper - Newcastle U. to Huddersfield T.; Barry Jones - Wrexham to York C.; David Kerslake - Ipswich T. to Wycombe W.; David Lee - Chelsea to Sheffield U.; Craig Midgley - Bradford C. to Darlington; Matt Murphy - Oxford U. to Scunthorpe U.; Mike Pollitt - Notts Co. to Gillingham; Adam Reed - Blackburn R. to Rochdale; Jason Roberts - Wolverhampton W. to Torquay U.; Jake Sedgemore - WBA to Hednesford; Neville Southall - Everton to Southend U.; Bryan Small - Bolton W. to Bradford C.; Paul Teather - Manchester U. to AFC Bournemouth; Paul Tait - Birmingham C. to Northampton T.; Scott Taylor - Bolton W. to Rotherham; Stuart Thom - N. Forest to Mansfield T.; Neil Thompson - Barnsley to Oldham A.; Paul Tisdale - Bristol C. to Exeter C.; Simon Trevitt - Hull C. to Swansea C.; Ryan van Dullerman - Northampton T. to Kettering C.; Andy Walker - Sheffield U. to Hibernian; Ronnie Wallwork - Manchester U. to Carlisle U.

January 1998

Julian Alsop - Bristol R. to Swansea C.; Steven Barnes - Birmingham C. to Brighton & HA; Earl Barrett - Everton to Sheffield U.; Grant Brebner - Manchester U. to Cambridge U.; Tony Briscoe - Shrewsbury T. to Weymouth; Andy Brownrigg - Rotherham to Stalybridge Ce.; Wayne Burnett - Huddersfield T. to Grimsby T.; James Clapham Tottenham H. to Ipswich T.; Steve Claridge - Leicester C. to Portsmouth; Gerry Creaney - Manchester C. to Chesterfield; O'Neill Donaldson - Sheffield W. to Oxford U.; Craig Dudley - Notts Co. to Shrewsbury T.; Andrew Duncan - Manchester C. to Cambridge U.; Andy Freeman - Reading to Yeovil T.; Neale Fenn Tottenham H. to L. Orient; Ben Gallagher - Manchester C. to Stafford R.; Danny George - N. Forest to Doncaster R.; Gary Germaine - WBA to Shrewsbury T.; Neil Gregory - Ipswich T. to Colchester U.; Matthew Hale - Bristol C. to Weymouth; Paul Harries - Portsmouth to Basingstoke T.; John Hills - Everton to Blackpool; Steven Hitchen - Macclesfield T. to Flixton; Andrew Hughes - Oldham A. to Notts Co.; Richard Jobson - Leeds U. to Southend U.; Damien Johnson - Blackburn R. to N. Forest; Gary Jones - Swansea to Rochdale; Lee Jones - Swansea to Bristol R.; Mark Kennedy - Liverpool to QPR; Richard Leadbeater - Wolverhampton W. to Hereford U.; Kyle Lightbourne - Coventry C. to Fulham; Tosh McKinlay - Celtic to Stoke C.; Stuart Nethercott Tottenham H. to Millwall; Darren Pitcher - C. Palace to L. Orient; Martin Phillips - Bristol C. to Scunthorpe U.; Steve Phillips - Bristol C. to Clevedon T.; Tony Philliskirk - Cardiff C. to Halifax T.; Michael Pollitt - Notts Co. to Brentford; Paul Rees - Portsmouth to Basingstoke T.; Tony Scully - Manchester C. to Stoke C.; Bryan Small - Bolton W. to Bury; Bob Taylor - WBA to Bolton W.; Michall Vlachos - AEK Athens to Portsmouth; Neill Woods - Grimsby T. to Scunthorpe U.

February 1998

Nathanial Abbey - Luton T. to Woking; Martin Aldridge - Oxford U. to Southend U.; Steve Basham - Southampton to Wrexham; Peter Beardsley - Bolton W. to Manchester C.; Danny Boxall - C. Palace to Oldham A.; Steven Boyack - Rangers to Hull C.; Guy Branston - Leicester C. to Colchester U.; Lee Briscoe - Sheffield U. to Manchester C.; Lee Charles - QPR to Cambridge U.; Nick Colgan - Chelsea to Reading; Barry Conlan - Manchester C. to Plymouth Ar.; Paul Connor - Middlesbrough to Hartlepool U.; Jon Conforth - Wycombe W. to Peterborough U.; Mark Crossley - N. Forest to Millwall; Steve Davis - Barnsley to Oxford U.; Mark Dempsey - Dover A. to Shrewsbury T.; Ryan Denys - Brentford to Yeovil T.; Ian Duerden - Burnley to Telford U.; Stuart Elliot - Newcastle U. to Swindon T.; Phil Eastwood - Burnley to Telford U.; Dominic Foley - Wolverhampton W. to Watford; Nigel Gleghorn - Burnley to Northampton T.; Kim Helselberg - Sunderland to Sebgerg; Laurens Ten Heuvel - Barnsley to Northampton T.; Danny Hill Tottenham H. to Cardiff C.; Richard Huxford - Burnley to Dunfirmline; Stig Johansen - Southampton to Bristol C.; Richard Landon - Macclesfield T. to Hednesford; Craig Liddle - Middlesbrough to Darlington; Michael Mahoney Johnson - QPR to Brighton & HA; Tony Lormor - Preston NE to Notts Co.; Andrew Melville - Sunderland to Bradford C.; John Mullin - Sunderland to Preston NE; Robert Murray - AFC Bournemouth to Dorchester T.; John O'Connor -

Everton to Sheffield U.; Tony Parks - Burnley to Doncaster R.; Graham Paxton - Newcastle U. to Millwall; Mark Perry - Walsall to Stafford R.; Tony Philliskirk - Cardiff C. to Macclesfield T.; Wayne Phillips - Wrexham to Stockport Co.; Michael Pollitt - Notts Co. to Sunderland; Darren Roberts - Darlington to Peterborough U.; Zeke Rowe - Peterborough U. to Doncaster R.; Ian Rush - Newcastle U. to Sheffield U.; Neville Southall - Everton to Stoke C.; Michael Thomas - Liverpool to Middlesbrough; Bill Turley - Northampton T. to L. Orient; Stephen Tutill - York C. to Darlington; Mark Walton - Fulham to Gillingham; Julian Watts - Leicester C. to Huddersfield T.; Tony Williams - Blackburn R. to QPR; Mark Wilson - Manchester Co. to Wrexham; Neil Woods - Grimsby T. to Mansfield T.

March 1998

Rory Allen - Tottenham H. to Luton T.; Peter Beardsley - Bolton W. to Fulham; Gijsbert Bos - Rotherham to Walsall; David Brown - Manchester U. to Hull C.; Jonathan Cross - Wrexham to Tranmere R.; Neil Cutler - Crewe Alex. to Stalybridge Ce.; Julian Darby - Preston NE to Rotherham; Neale Fenn - Tottenham H. to Norwich C.; Ashley Fickling - Grimsby T. to Darlington; John Finnigan - N. Forest to Lincoln C.; Mark Gayle - Crewe Alex. to Luton T.; Steve Heath - Rotherham to Stalybridge Ce.; Paddy Kelly - Newcastle U. to Reading; Steve McAnespie - Fulham to Bradford C.; Sean McCarthy - Oldham A. to Bristol C.; Eddie McGoldrick - Manchester C. to Stockport Co.; John Mullin - Sunderland to Burnley; Rob Newman - Norwich C. to Wigan A.; David Nurse - Millwall to Brentford; Jason Roberts - Wolverhampton W. to Bristol C.; Neil Ruddock - Liverpool to QPR; Matthew Russell - Scarborough to Doncaster R.; Les Sealey - West Ham U. to Bury; Craig Shakespeare - Grimsby T. to Telford U.; Lee Sinnott - Oldham A. to Bradford C.; Bob Taylor - WBA to Bolton W.; Scott Taylor - Bolton W. to Blackpool; Graeme Tomlinson - Manchester U. to Millwall; Mark Walton - Fulham to Norwich C.; Stephen Woods - Stoke C. to Plymouth Ar.; David Barnett - Dunfermline to Port Vale; Paul Beesley - Manchester C. to WBA; Matt Boswell - Port Vale to Barnet; Chris Greenacre - Manchester C. to Blackpool; Stephen Guinan - N. Forest to Crewe Alex.; Neil Heaney - Manchester C. to Charlton A.; Robert Hughes - Aston Villa to Carlisle U.; Robin Hulbert - Swindon T. to Newcastle U.; Rae Ingram - Manchester C. to Macclesfield T.; Richard Leadbeater - Wolverhampton W. to Hereford U.; Ray Kelly - Manchester C. to Wrexham; Dariusz Kubicki - Wolverhampton W. to Tranmere R.; Steve Nicol - Sheffield W. to WBA; Michael O'Neill - Coventry C. to Reading; Rodney McAree - Fulham to Woking; Martin Phillips - Manchester C. to Exeter C.; Chris Greenacre - Manchester C. to Blackpool; Mark Stein - Chelsea to AFC Bournemouth; John Spencer - QPR to Everton; Scott Thomas - Manchester C. to Brighton & HA; Neil Thompson - Barnsley to York C.; Gavin Tipple - Norwich C. to Wisbech T.; David Morley - Manchester C. to Ayr U.; Ronald Wallwork - Manchester U. to Stockport Co.; Stephen Wright - Rangers to Wolverhampton W.

RECORD SEQUENCES

Longest Winning Runs

Team	No	Start	End
Bristol City	14	09-Sep-05	02-Dec-05
Manchester United	14	15-Oct-04	03-Jan-05
Preston NE	14	25-Dec-50	27-Mar-51
Birmingham City	13	17-Dec-1892	16-Sep-1893
Newcastle United	13	25-Apr-92	18-Oct-92
Reading	13	17-Aug-85	19-Oct-85
Sunderland	13	14-Nov-1891	02-Apr-1892
Tottenham Hotspur	13	23-Apr-60	01-Oct-60
Bristol Rovers	12	18-Oct-52	17-Jan-53
Everton	12	24-Mar-1894	13-Oct-1894
Liverpool	12	21-Apr-90	06-Oct-90
Bolton Wanderers	11	05-Nov-04	02-Jan-05
Grimsby Town	11	19-Jan-52	29-Mar-52
Huddersfield Town	11	05-Apr-20	04-Sep-20
West Bromwich Albion	11	05-Apr-30	08-Sep-30
Arsenal	10	12-Sep-87	14-Nov-87
Barnsley	10	05-Mar-55	23-Apr-55
Bradford City	10	26-Nov-83	03-Feb-84
Burnley	10	16-Nov-12	18-Jan-13
Chesterfield	10	06-Sep-33	04-Nov-33
Doncaster Rovers	10	22-Jan-47	04-Apr-47
Hull City	10	01-May-48	28-Sep-48
Hull City	10	23-Feb-66	20-Apr-66
Leyton Orient	10	21-Jan-56	30-Mar-56
Lincoln City	10	01-Sep-30	18-Oct-30
Millwall	10	10-Mar-28	25-Apr-28
Norwich City	10	23-Nov-85	25-Jan-86
Notts County	10	03-Dec-97	31-Jan-98
Oldham Athletic	10	12-Jan-74	12-Mar-74

Longest Undefeated Runs

Team	No	Start	End
Nottingham Forest	42	26-Nov-77	25-Nov-78
Leeds United	34	26-Oct-68	26-Aug-69
Bristol Rovers	32	07-Apr-73	27-Jan-74
Liverpool	31	04-May-87	16-Mar-88
Burnley	30	06-Sep-20	25-Mar-21
Chelsea	27	29-Oct-88	08-Apr-89
Huddersfield Town	27	24-Jan-25	17-Oct-25
West Ham United	27	27-Dec-80	10-Oct-81
Arsenal	26	28-Apr-90	19-Jan-91
Manchester United	26	04-Feb-56	13-Oct-56

Coventry City	25	26-Nov-66	13-May-67
Stoke City	25	05-Sep-92	20-Feb-93
Bristol City	24	09-Sep-05	10-Feb-06
Middlesbrough	24	08-Sep-73	19-Jan-74
Blackburn Rovers	23	30-Sep-87	27-Feb-88
Bolton Wanderers	23	13-Oct-90	09-Mar-91
Ipswich Town	23	08-Dec-79	26-Apr-80
Derby County	22	08-Mar-69	20-Sep-69
Manchester City	22	26-Dec-36	01-May-37
Manchester City	22	16-Nov-46	19-Apr-47
Plymouth Argyle	22	20-Apr-29	21-Dec-29
Sheffield United	22	2-Sep-1899	13-Jan-1900
Swindon Town	22	12-Jan-86	23-Aug-86
Tottenham Hotspur	22	31-Aug-49	31-Dec-49
Watford	22	01-Oct-96	01-Mar-97
Wimbledon	22	15-Jan-83	14-May-83

Most Games Without a Win

Cambridge United	31	08-Oct-83	23-Apr-84
Crewe Alexandra	30	22-Sep-56	06-Apr-57
Rochdale	28	14-Nov-31	29-Aug-32
Hull City	27	27-Mar-89	04-Nov-89
Oxford United	27	14-Nov-87	27-Aug-88
Barnsley	26	13-Dec-52	26-Aug-53
Bolton Wanderers	26	07-Apr-02	10-Jan-03
Chester City	25	19-Sep-61	03-Mar-62
Norwich City	25	22-Sep-56	23-Feb-57
Portsmouth	25	29-Nov-58	22-Aug-59
Burnley	24	16-Apr-79	17-Nov-79
Arsenal	23	28-Sep-12	01-Mar-13
Leyton Orient	23	06-Oct-62	13-Apr-63
Halifax Town	22	26-Aug-78	10-Feb-79
Huddersfield	22	04-Dec-71	29-Apr-72
Chelsea	21	03-Nov-87	02-Apr-88
Ipswich Town	21	28-Aug-63	14-Dec-63
Newcastle United	21	14-Jan-78	23-Aug-78
Bristol Rovers	20	05-Apr-80	01-Nov-80
Colchester United	20	02-Mar-68	31-Aug-68
Crystal Palace	20	03-Mar-62	08-Sep-62
Derby County	20	15-Dec-90	23-Apr-91
Doncaster Rovers	20	09-Aug-97	29-Nov-97
Millwall	20	26-Dec-89	05-May-90
Notts County	20	03-Dec-96	31-Mar-97
QPR	20	07-Dec-68	07-Apr-69
Sheffield Wednesday	20	23-Oct-54	12-Mar-55
Sheffield Wednesday	20	11-Jan-75	30-Aug-75
Southampton	20	30-Aug-69	27-Dec-69

Most Successive Drawn Games

Birmingham City	8	18-Sep-90	23-Oct-90
Middlesbrough	8	03-Apr-71	01-May-71
Peterborough United	8	18-Dec-71	12-Feb-72
Torquay United	8	25-Oct-69	13-Dec-69
Barnsley	7	28-Mar-11	22-Apr-11
Halifax Town	7	22-Jan-82	20-Feb-82
Ipswich Town	7	10-Nov-90	21-Dec-90
Norwich City	7	09-Dec-78	10-Feb-79
Norwich City	7	15-Jan-94	26-Feb-94
Nottingham Forest	7	29-Apr-78	02-Sep-78
Southampton	7	28-Dec-94	11-Feb-95
Stockport County	7	04-May-73	19-Sep-73
Stockport County	7	17-Mar-89	14-Apr-89
Watford	7	30-Nov-96	27-Jan-97

Most Successive Games Without a Draw

Aston Villa	51	1-Jan-1891	17-Dec-1892
Stoke City	46	30-Mar-1895	14-Nov-1896
Sunderland	46	26-Dec-07	13-Mar-09
Leicester City	44	30-Jan-09	26-Mar-10
Walsall	44	6-Jan-1894	7-Sep-1896
Birmingham City	43	10-Dec-1892	22-Sep-1894
Portsmouth	38	17-Mar-28	09-Feb-29
Sheffield Utd.	38	22-Oct-04	18-Nov-05
Bristol Rovers	37	15-Nov-47	02-Oct-48
Wolverhampton W.	37	03-May-30	04-Apr-31
Lincoln City	36	23-Mar-1894	7-Sep-1895
Stockport County	36	12-Oct-46	25-Aug-47
Bristol City	35	30-Jan-04	31-Dec-04
West Bromwich Albion	35	03-Apr-15	25-Feb-20
Doncaster Rovers	34	01-Dec-34	21-Sep-35
Newcastle United	34	16-Nov-1895	5-Dec-1896
Middlesbrough	33	02-May-25	27-Feb-26
Reading	33	31-Aug-35	18-Mar-36
Rochdale	33	26-Dec-25	09-Oct-26
Plymouth Argyle	31	23-Nov-46	30-Aug-47
Tranmere Rovers	31	21-Jan-53	26-Sep-53
Blackburn Rovers	30	13-Nov-65	27-Aug-66
Burnley	30	18-Jan-08	21-Nov-08
Grimsby Town	30	29-Apr-33	10-Feb-34

Longest Losing Run

Rochdale	17	14-Nov-31	12-Mar-32
Walsall	15	29-Oct-88	04-Feb-89
Manchester United	14	26-Apr-30	25-Oct-30

Nottingham Forest	14	21-Mar-13	27-Sep-13
Brighton & HA	12	11-Nov-72	27-Jan-73
Lincoln City	12	21-Sep-1896	9-Jan-1897
Aston Villa	11	23-Mar-63	04-May-63
Barnet	11	08-May-93	02-Oct-93
Bolton Wanderers	11	07-Apr-02	18-Oct-02
Fulham	11	02-Dec-61	24-Feb-62
Millwall	11	10-Apr-29	16-Sep-29
Stoke City	11	06-Apr-85	17-Aug-85
West Brom	11	28-Oct-95	26-Dec-95
Charlton Athletic	10	11-Apr-90	15-Sep-90
Crewe Alexandra	10	29-Sep-23	15-Dec-23
Crewe Alexandra	10	26-Dec-57	01-Mar-58
Crewe Alexandra	10	16-Apr-79	22-Aug-79
Gillingham	10	20-Sep-88	05-Nov-88
Ipswich Town	10	04-Sep-54	16-Oct-54
Newcastle United	10	23-Aug-77	15-Oct-77

Successive Number of Clean Sheets

Millwall	11	27-Feb-26	10-Apr-26
Reading	11	28-Mar-79	05-May-79
York City	11	01-Oct-73	08-Dec-73
Chelsea	9	04-Nov-05	25-Dec-05
Leeds United	9	03-Mar-28	14-Apr-28
Arsenal	8	10-Apr-03	03-Oct-03
Barnsley	8	05-Mar-55	12-Apr-55
Bury	8	09-Feb-24	22-Mar-24
Grimsby Town	8	02-Apr-56	30-Apr-56
Huddersfield	8	13-Mar-65	19-Apr-65
Liverpool	8	30-Dec-22	03-Mar-23
Portsmouth	8	26-Aug-22	30-Sep-22
Southampton	8	17-Apr-22	26-Aug-22
Stockport County	8	02-May-21	01-Oct-21
Watford	8	24-Sep-49	12-Nov-49
Wolverhampton W.	8	31-Aug-82	09-Oct-82

Successive Number of Games in which Scored a Goal

Chesterfield	46	25-Dec-29	26-Dec-30
Barnsley	44	02-Oct-26	08-Oct-27
Manchester City	44	03-Oct-36	09-Oct-37
Wolverhampton W.	41	20-Dec-58	05-Dec-59
Everton	40	15-Mar-30	07-Mar-31
Sheffield Wednesday	40	14-Nov-59	29-Oct-60
Plymouth Argyle	39	15-Apr-39	07-Apr-47
Lincoln City	37	01-Mar-30	15-Jan-31
West Bromwich Albion	36	26-Apr-58	31-Mar-59
Aston Villa	35	10-Nov-1894	12-Dec-1895

Notts County	35	26-Apr-30	21-Mar-31
Notts County	35	10-Oct-59	27-Aug-60
Sheffield United	34	30-Mar-56	01-Jan-57
Blackpool	33	23-Feb-29	25-Dec-29
Grimsby Town	33	06-Oct-28	27-Apr-29
Grimsby Town	33	31-Jan-33	25-Nov-33
Peterborough United	33	20-Sep-60	18-Apr-61
QPR	33	09-Dec-61	08-Sep-62
Blackburn Rovers	32	24-Apr-54	26-Feb-55
Reading	32	01-Oct-32	26-Apr-33
Tottenham Hotspur	32	09-Apr-49	31-Dec-49
Tottenham Hotspur	32	24-Feb-62	24-Nov-62
Tranmere Rovers	32	24-Feb-34	15-Dec-34
Arsenal	31	03-May-30	28-Feb-31
Brighton & HA	31	04-Feb-56	06-Oct-56
Leicester City	31	12-Nov-32	28-Aug-33
Swindon Town	31	17-Apr-26	05-Feb-27
Bradford City	30	26-Dec-61	15-Sep-62
Leeds United	30	27-Aug-27	25-Feb-28
Preston NE	30	15-Nov-52	26-Aug-53
Rotherham United	30	03-Apr-54	27-Dec-54

Successive Number of Games Not Scored a Goal

Coventry City	11	11-Oct-19	20-Dec-19
Hartlepool United	11	09-Jan-93	02-Mar-93
Sunderland	10	27-Nov-76	05-Feb-77
Chelsea	9	14-Mar-81	02-May-81
Crewe Alexandra	9	06-Nov-74	28-Dec-74
Crystal Palace	9	19-Nov-94	02-Jan-95
Rochdale	9	14-Mar-80	26-Apr-80
Cardiff City	8	20-Dec-52	14-Feb-53
Derby County	8	30-Oct-20	18-Dec-20
Halifax Town	8	25-Aug-90	06-Oct-90
Leyton Orient	8	19-Nov-94	07-Jan-95
Sheffield Wednesday	8	08-Mar-75	12-Apr-75
Stoke City	8	29-Dec-84	16-Mar-85
Bradford City	7	18-Apr-25	05-Sep-25
Chesterfield	7	23-Sep-77	22-Oct-77
Darlington	7	05-Sep-75	11-Oct-75
Darlington	7	25-Feb-95	25-Mar-95
Doncaster Rovers	7	27-Sep-47	08-Nov-47
Huddersfield	7	22-Jan-72	21-Mar-72
Ipswich Town	7	28-Feb-95	11-Apr-95
Leicester City	7	21-Nov-87	01-Jan-88
Northampton	7	07-Apr-39	06-May-39
Scunthorpe United	7	19-Apr-75	06-Sep-75
Stockport County	7	10-Mar-23	07-Apr-23
Torquay United	7	08-Jan-72	04-Mar-72

Tranmere Rovers	7	20-Dec-97	04-Feb-98
Watford	7	18-Dec-71	12-Feb-72
Wolverhampton W.	7	02-Feb-85	16-Mar-85
York City	7	28-Aug-72	26-Sep-72

Start of Season: Most Games Undefeated

Leeds United	29	1973-74
Liverpool	29	1987-88
Bristol Rovers	27	1973-74
Arsenal	23	1990-91
Preston NE	22	1888-89
Sheffield United	22	1899-00
West Ham United	21	1990-91
Everton	19	1978-79
Millwall	19	1959-60
Notts County	18	1930-31
Plymouth Argyle	18	1929-30
Port Vale	18	1969-70
Burnley	16	1972-73
Derby County	16	1948-49
Nottingham Forest	16	1978-79
Oldham Athletic	16	1990-91
Tottenham Hotspur	16	1960-61
Birmingham City	15	1900-01
Coventry City	15	1937-38
Manchester United	15	1985-86
Sheffield Wednesday	15	1983-84
Southend United	15	1931-32
Bournemouth	14	1961-62
Brentford	14	1932-33
Chelsea	14	1925-26
Darlington	14	1968-69
Ipswich Town	14	1980-81
Reading	14	1973-74
Reading	14	1985-86
Sunderland	14	1910-11
Torquay United	14	1990-91

Start of Season: Most Games No Win

Barnsley	23	1952-53
Bolton Wanderers	22	1902-03
Rochdale	22	1973-74
Doncaster Rovers	20	1997-98
Coventry City	19	1919-20
Burnley	17	1889-90
Sheffield Wednesday	17	1974-75
Hull City	16	1989-90
Sheffield United	16	1990-91
Crystal Palace	15	1973-74
Darlington	15	1988-89
Leicester City	15	1975-76
Portsmouth	15	1937-38
Swindon Town	15	1993-94
York City	15	1987-88
Bristol Rovers	14	1980-81
Huddersfield Town	14	1997-98
Huddersfield Town	14	1987-88
Wolverhampton W.	14	1983-84
Birmingham City	13	1978-79
Bristol City	13	1933-34
Bury	13	1905-06
Bury	13	1911-12
Northampton Town	13	1965-66
Norwich City	13	1920-21
Walsall	13	1938-39

DIVISION 1 WINNING RECORDS

NEW DIVISION 1

Season	Champions	P	W	D	L	F	A	Pts
1997-98	Nottingham Forest	46	28	10	8	82	42	94
1996-97	Bolton Wanderers	46	28	14	4	100	53	98
1995-96	Sunderland	46	22	17	7	59	33	83
1994-95	Middlesbrough	46	23	13	10	67	40	82
1993-94	Crystal Palace	46	27	9	10	73	46	90
1992-93	Newcastle United	46	29	9	8	92	38	96

ORIGINAL DIVISION 1

Season	Champions	P	W	D	L	F	A	Pts
1991-92	Leeds United	42	22	16	4	74	37	82
1990-91	Arsenal +	38	24	13	1	74	18	83
1989-90	Liverpool	38	23	10	5	78	37	79
1988-89	Arsenal †	38	22	10	6	73	36	76
1987-88	Liverpool	40	26	12	2	87	24	90
1986-87	Everton	42	26	8	8	76	31	86
1985-86	Liverpool	42	26	10	6	89	37	88
1984-85	Everton	42	28	6	8	88	43	90
1983-84	Liverpool	42	22	14	6	73	32	80
1982-83	Liverpool	42	24	10	8	87	37	82
1981-82	Liverpool	42	26	9	7	80	32	87
1980-81	Aston Villa	42	26	8	8	72	40	60
1979-80	Liverpool	42	25	10	7	81	30	60
1978-79	Liverpool	42	30	8	4	85	16	68
1977-78	Nottingham Forest	42	25	14	3	69	24	64
1976-77	Liverpool	42	23	11	8	62	33	57
1975-76	Liverpool	42	23	14	5	66	31	60
1974-75	Derby County	42	21	11	10	67	49	53
1973-74	Leeds United	42	24	14	4	66	31	62
1972-73	Liverpool	42	25	10	7	72	42	60
1971-72	Derby County	42	24	10	8	69	33	58
1970-71	Arsenal	42	29	7	6	71	29	65
1969-70	Everton	42	29	8	5	72	34	66
1968-69	Leeds United	42	27	13	2	66	26	67
1967-68	Manchester City	42	26	6	10	86	43	58
1966-67	Manchester United	42	24	12	6	84	45	60

Season	Champions	P	W	D	L	F	A	Pts
1965-66	Liverpool	42	26	9	7	79	34	61
1964-65	Manchester United *	42	26	9	7	89	39	61
1963-64	Liverpool	42	26	5	11	92	45	57
1962-63	Everton	42	25	11	6	84	42	61
1961-62	Ipswich Town	42	24	8	10	93	67	56
1960-61	Tottenham Hotspur	42	31	4	7	115	55	66
1959-60	Burnley	42	24	7	11	85	61	55
1958-59	Wolverhampton W.	42	28	5	9	110	49	61
1957-58	Wolverhampton W.	42	28	8	6	103	47	64
1956-57	Manchester United	42	28	8	6	103	54	64
1955-56	Manchester United	42	25	10	7	83	51	60
1954-55	Chelsea	42	20	12	10	81	57	52
1953-54	Wolverhampton W.	42	25	7	10	96	56	57
1952-53	Arsenal *	42	21	12	9	97	64	54
1951-52	Manchester United	42	23	11	8	95	52	57
1950-51	Tottenham Hotspur	42	25	10	7	82	44	60
1949-50	Portsmouth *	42	22	9	11	74	38	53
1948-49	Portsmouth	42	25	8	9	84	42	58
1947-48	Arsenal	42	23	13	6	81	32	59
1946-47	Liverpool	42	25	7	10	84	52	57
	World War II							
1938-39	Everton	42	27	5	10	88	52	59
1937-38	Arsenal	42	21	10	11	77	44	52
1936-37	Manchester City	42	22	13	7	107	61	57
1935-36	Sunderland	42	25	6	11	109	74	56
1934-35	Arsenal	42	23	12	7	115	46	58
1933-34	Arsenal	42	25	9	8	75	47	59
1932-33	Arsenal	42	25	8	9	118	61	58
1931-32	Everton	42	26	4	12	116	64	56
1930-31	Arsenal	42	28	10	4	127	59	66
1929-30	Sheffield Wednesday	42	26	8	8	105	57	60
1928-29	Sheffield Wednesday	42	21	10	11	86	62	52
1927-28	Everton	42	20	13	9	102	66	53
1926-27	Newcastle United	42	25	6	11	96	58	56
1925-26	Huddersfield Town	42	23	11	8	92	60	57
1924-25	Huddersfield Town	42	21	16	5	69	28	58
1923-24	Huddersfield Town *	42	23	11	8	60	33	57
1922-23	Liverpool	42	26	8	8	70	31	60
1921-22	Liverpool	42	22	13	7	63	36	57
1920-21	Burnley	42	23	13	6	79	36	59
1919-20	West Bromwich Albion	42	28	4	10	104	47	60
	World War I							
1914-15	Everton	38	19	8	11	76	47	46

Season	Champions	P	W	D	L	F	A	Pts
1913-14	Blackburn Rovers	38	20	11	7	78	42	51
1912-13	Sunderland	38	25	4	9	86	43	54
1911-12	Blackburn Rovers	38	20	9	9	60	43	49
1910-11	Manchester United	38	22	8	8	72	40	52
1909-10	Aston Villa	38	23	7	8	84	42	53
1908-09	Newcastle United	38	24	5	9	65	41	53
1907-08	Manchester United	38	23	6	9	81	48	52
1906-07	Newcastle United	38	22	7	9	74	46	51
1905-06	Liverpool	38	23	5	10	79	46	51
1904-05	Newcastle United	34	23	2	9	72	33	48
1903-04	Sheffield Wednesday	34	20	7	7	48	28	47
1902-03	Sheffield Wednesday	34	19	4	11	54	36	42
1901-02	Sunderland	34	19	6	9	50	35	44
1900-01	Liverpool	34	19	7	8	59	35	45
1899-00	Aston Villa	34	22	6	6	77	35	50
1898-99	Aston Villa	34	19	7	8	76	40	45
1897-98	Sheffield United	30	17	8	5	56	31	42
1896-97	Aston Villa	30	21	5	4	73	38	47
1895-96	Aston Villa	30	20	5	5	78	45	45
1894-95	Sunderland	30	21	5	4	80	37	47
1893-94	Aston Villa	30	19	6	5	84	42	44
1892-93	Sunderland	30	22	4	4	100	36	48

FOOTBALL LEAGUE

Season	Champions	P	W	D	L	F	A	Pts
1891-92	Sunderland	26	21	0	5	93	36	42
1890-91	Everton	22	14	1	7	63	29	29
1889-90	Preston North End	22	15	3	4	71	30	33
1888-89	Preston North End	22	18	4	0	74	15	40

* won on goal average/goal difference
† won on goals scored
+ 2 points deducted

PROMOTIONS

Clubs listed in brackets were not promoted – all other listed clubs promoted. In the case of play-off winners the number after their final points (Pts) tally is the position they finished in the division. Note: for ease of reference current club names are used.

NEW DIVISION 1 TO PREMIER LEAGUE

Season	Champions	Pts	Runners-up	Pts	Play-off	Pts	Pn
97-98	N. Forest	94	Middlesbrough	91	Charlton A.	88	4
96-97	Bolton W.	98	Barnsley	80	C. Palace	71	6
95-96	Sunderland	83	Derby Co.	79	Leicester C.	71	5
94-95	Middlesbro	82	(Reading	79)			
93-94	C. Palace	90	N. Forest	83	Leicester C.	73	4
92-93	Newcastle U.	96	West Ham U.	88	Swindon T.	76	5

NEW DIVISION 2 TO NEW DIVISION 1

Season	Champions	Pts	Runners-up	Pts	Play-off	Pts	Pn
97-98	Watford	88	Bristol C.	85	Grimsby T.	72	3
96-97	Bury	84	Stockport Co.	82	Crewe Alex.	73	6
95-96	Swindon T.	92	Oxford U.	83	Bradford C.	73	6
94-95	Birmingham C.	89					
93-94	Reading	89	Port Vale	88	Burnley	73	6
92-93	Stoke C.	93	Bolton W.	90	West Brom	85	4

NEW DIVISION 3 TO NEW DIVISION 2

Season	Champions	Pts	Runners-up	Pts	Third	Pts	Play-off	Pts	Pn
97-98	Notts Co.	99	Macces'd	82	Lincoln C.	75	Colchester U.	74	4
96-97	Wigan Ath.	87	Fulham	87	Carlisle U.	84	Northampton	72	4
95-96	Preston NE	86	Gillingham	83	Bury	79	Plymouth	78	4
94-95	Carlisle U.	91							
93-94	Shrewsbury	79	Chester C.	74					
92-93	Cardiff C.	83	Wrexham	80	Barnet	79	York C.	75	4

DIVISION 2 TO DIVISION 1

Season	Champions	Pts	Runners-up	Pts	Third/Play-off	Pts	Pn
91-92	Ipswich T.	84	Middlesbro	80	Blackburn R	74	6
90-91	Oldham Ath.	88	West Ham U.	87	Sheffield Wed.	82	
	Notts Co.	80 – 4th					
89-90	Leeds U.	85	Sheffield U.	85	Sunderland	74	6
88-89	Chelsea	99	Manchester C.	82	C. Palace	81	
87-88	Millwall	82	Aston Villa	78	Middlesbro	78	
86-87	Derby Co.	84	Portsmouth	78			
85-86	Norwich C.	84	Charlton Ath.	77	Wimbledon	76	
84-85	Oxford U.	84	Birmingham C.	82	Manchester C.	74	
83-84	Chelsea	88	Sheffield Wed.	88	Newcastle U.	80	
82-83	QPR	85	Wolves	75	Leicester C.	70	
81-82	Luton T.	88	Watford	80	Norwich C.	71	
80-81	West Ham U.	66	Notts Co.	53	Swansea	50	
79-80	Leicester C.	55	Sunderland	54	Birmingham C.	53	
78-79	C. Palace	57	Brighton & HA	56	Stoke C.	56	
77-78	Bolton W.	58	Southampton	57	Tottenham H	56	

Season	Team	Pts	Team	Pts	Team	Pts
76-77	Wolves	57	Chelsea	55	N. Forest	52
75-76	Sunderland	56	Bristol C.	53	West Brom	53
74-75	Manchester U.	61	Aston Villa	58	Norwich C.	53
73-74	Middlesbro	65	Luton T.	50	Carlisle U.	49
72-73	Burnley	62	QPR	61		
71-72	Norwich C.	57	Birmingham C.	56		
70-71	Leicester C.	59	Sheffield U.	56		
69-70	Huddersfield	60	Blackpool	53		
68-69	Derby Co.	63	C. Palace	56		
67-68	Ipswich T.	59	QPR	58		
66-67	Coventry C.	59	Wolves	58		
65-66	Manchester C.	59	Southampton	54		
64-65	Newcastle U.	57	Northampton	56		
63-64	Leeds U.	63	Sunderland	61		
62-63	Stoke C.	53	Chelsea	52		
61-62	Liverpool	62	Leyton Orient	54		
60-61	Ipswich T.	59	Sheffield U.	58		
59-60	Aston Villa	59	Cardiff C.	58		
58-59	Sheffield Wed.	62	Fulham	60		
57-58	West Ham U.	57	Blackburn R.	56		
56-57	Leicester C.	61	N. Forest	54		
55-56	Sheffield Wed.	55	Leeds U.	52		
54-55	Birmingham C.	54	Luton T.	54		
53-54	Leicester C.	56	Everton	56		
52-53	Sheffield U.	60	Huddersfield	58		
51-52	Sheffield Wed.	53	Cardiff C.	51		
50-51	Preston NE	57	Manchester C.	52		
49-50	Tottenham H	61	Sheffield Wed.	52		
48-49	Fulham	57	West Brom	56		
47-48	Birmingham C.	59	Newcastle U.	56		
46-47	Manchester C.	62	Burnley	58		
38-39	Blackburn R.	55	Sheffield U.	54		
37-38	Aston Villa	57	Manchester U.	53		
36-37	Leicester C.	56	Blackpool	55		
35-36	Manchester U.	56	Charlton Ath.	55		
34-35	Brentford	61	Bolton W.	56		
33-34	Grimsby T.	59	Preston NE	52		
32-33	Stoke C.	56	Tottenham H	55		
31-32	Wolves	56	Leeds U.	54		
30-31	Everton	61	West Brom	54		
29-30	Blackpool	58	Chelsea	55		
28-29	Middlesbro	55	Grimsby T.	53		
27-28	Manchester C.	59	Leeds U.	57		
26-27	Middlesbro	62	Portsmouth	54		
25-26	Sheffield Wed.	60	Derby Co.	57		
24-25	Leicester C.	59	Manchester U.	57		
23-24	Leeds U.	54	Bury	51		
22-23	Notts Co.	53	West Ham U.	51		
21-22	N. Forest	56	Stoke C.	52		
20-21	Birmingham C.	58				
19-20	Tottenham H	70	Huddersfield	64		
14-15	Derby Co.	53	Preston NE	50	Arsenal	43 5

294

Season	Champions	Pts	Runners-up	Pts
13-14	Notts Co.	53	Bradford PA	49
12-13	Preston NE	53	Burnley	50
11-12	Derby Co.	54	Chelsea	54
10-11	West Brom	53	Bolton W.	51
09-10	Manchester C.	54	Oldham Ath.	53
08-09	Bolton W.	52		
07-08	Bradford C.	54	Leicester C.	52
06-07	N. Forest	60	Chelsea	57
05-06	Bristol C.	66	Manchester U.	62
04-05	Liverpool	58	Bolton W.	56
03-04	Preston NE	50	Arsenal	49
02-03	Manchester C.	54	Birmingham C.	51
01-02	West Brom	55	Middlesbro	51
00-01	Grimsby T.	49	Birmingham C.	48
99-00	Sheffield Wed.	54	Bolton W.	52
98-99	Manchester C.	52		
97-98	Burnley	48	Newcastle U.	45
96-97	Notts Co.	42		1
95-96	Liverpool	46		1
93-94	Birmingham C.	42		2
92-93	Darwen	30		3

DIVISION 3 TO DIVISION 2

Season	Champions	Pts	Runners-up	Pts	Third/Play-off	Pts	Pn
91-92	Brentford	82	Birmingham C.	81	Peterborough	74	6
90-91	Cambridge U.	86	Southend U.	85	Grimsby T.	83	
					Tranmere R.	78	5
89-90	Bristol R.	93	Bristol C.	91	Notts Co.	87	
88-89	Wolves	92	Sheffield U.	84	Port Vale	84	
87-88	Sunderland	93	Brighton & HA	84	Walsall	82	
86-87	Bournemouth	97	Middlesbro	94	Swindon T.	87	
85-86	Reading	94	Plymouth Arg	87	Derby Co.	84	
84-85	Bradford C.	94	Millwall	90	Hull C.	87	
83-84	Oxford U.	95	Wimbledon	87	Sheffield U.	83	
82-83	Portsmouth	91	Cardiff C.	86	Huddersfield	82	
81-82	Burnley	80	Carlisle U.	80	Fulham	78	
80-81	Rotherham U.	61	Barnsley	59	Charlton Ath.	59	
79-80	Grimsby T.	62	Blackburn R.	59	Sheffield Wed.	58	
78-79	Shrewsbury T.	61	Watford	60	Swansea	60	
77-78	Wrexham	61	Cambridge U.	58	Preston NE	56	
76-77	Mansfield T.	64	Brighton & HA	61	C. Palace	59	
75-76	Hereford U.	63	Cardiff C.	57	Millwall	56	
74-75	Blackburn R.	60	Plymouth Arg	59	Charlton Ath.	55	
73-74	Oldham Ath.	62	Bristol R.	61	York C.	61	
72-73	Bolton W.	61	Notts Co.	57			
71-72	Aston Villa	70	Brighton & HA	65			
70-71	Preston NE	61	Fulham	60			
69-70	Leyton Orient	62	Luton T.	60			
68-69	Watford	64	Swindon T.	64			
67-68	Oxford U.	57	Bury	56			
66-67	QPR	67	Middlesbro	55			
65-66	Hull C.	69	Millwall	65			

Season			Runners-up	Pts	Third		
64-65	Carlisle U.	60	Bristol C.	59			
63-64	Coventry C.	60	C. Palace	60			
62-63	Northampton	62	Swindon T.	58			
61-62	Portsmouth	65	Grimsby T.	62			
60-61	Bury	68	Walsall	62			
59-60	Southampton	61	Norwich C.	59			
58-59	Plymouth Arg	62	Hull C.	61			

DIVISION 4 TO DIVISION 3

Season	Champions	Pts	Runners-up	Pts	Third	Pts	4th/Play-off	Pt P
58-59	Port Vale	64	Coventry C.	60	York C.	60	Shrewsbury T.	58
59-60	Walsall	65	Notts Co.	60	Torquay U.	60	Watford	57
60-61	Peterborough	66	C. Palace	64	Northamp'n	60	Bradford PA	60
61-62	Millwall	56	Colchester U.	55	Wrexham	53	Carlisle U.	52
62-63	Brentford	62	Oldham Ath.	59	Crewe Alex.	59	Mansfield T.	57
63-64	Gillingham	60	Carlisle U.	60	Workington	59	Exeter C.	58
64-65	Brighton & HA	63	Millwall	62	York C.	62	Oxford U.	61
65-66	Doncaster R.	59	Darlington	59	Torquay U.	58	Colchester U.	56
66-67	Stockport Co.	64	Southport	59	Barrow	59	Tranmere R.	58
67-68	Luton T.	66	Barnsley	61	Hartlepool	60	Crewe Alex.	58
68-69	Doncaster R.	59	Halifax T.	57	Rochdale	56	Bradford C.	56
69-70	Chesterfield	64	Wrexham	61	Swansea	60	Port Vale	59
70-71	Notts Co.	69	Bournemouth	60	Oldham A.	59	York C.	56
71-72	Grimsby T.	63	Southend U.	60	Brentford	59	Scunthorpe U.	57
72-73	Southport	62	Hereford U.	58	Cambridge	57	Aldershot	56
73-74	Peterborough	65	Gillingham	62	Colchester	60	Bury	59
74-75	Mansfield T.	68	Shrewsbury	62	Rotherham	59	Chester C.	57
75-76	Lincoln C.	74	Northampton	68	Reading	60	Tranmere R.	58
76-77	Cambridge U.	65	Exeter C.	62	Colchester	59	Bradford C.	59
77-78	Watford	71	Southend U.	60	Swansea	56	Brentford	59
78-79	Reading	65	Grimsby T.	61	Wimbledon	61	Barnsley	61
79-80	Huddersfield	66	Walsall	64	Newport Co.	61	Portsmouth	60
80-81	Southend U.	67	Lincoln C.	65	Doncaster R.	56	Wimbledon	55
81-82	Sheffield U.	96	Bradford C.	91	Wigan Ath.	91	Bournemouth	88
82-83	Wimbledon	98	Hull C.	90	Port Vale	88	Scunthorpe U.	83
83-84	York C.	101	Doncaster R.	85	Reading	82	Bristol C.	82
84-85	Chesterfield	91	Blackpool	86	Darlington	85	Bury	84
85-86	Swindon T.	102	Chester C.	84	Mansfield T.	81	Port Vale	79
86-87	Northampton	99	Preston NE	90	Southend U.	80	Aldershot	70 6
87-88	Wolves	90	Cardiff C.	85	Bolton W.	78	Swansea	70 6
88-89	Rotherham U.	82	Tranmere R.	80	Crewe Alex.	78	Leyton Orient	75 6
89-90	Exeter C.	89	Grimsby T.	79	Southend U.	75	Cambridge U.	73 6
90-91	Darlington	83	Stockport Co.	82	Hartlepool	82	Peterborough	80
							Torquay U.	72 7
91-92	Burnley	83	Rotherham U.	77	Mansfield T.	77	Blackpool	76

PROMOTED/ELECTED TO FOOTBALL LEAGUE

Season	Team	
59-60	Peterborough	Elected in place of Gateshead
69-70	Cambridge U.	Elected in place of Bradford PA
61-62	Oxford U.	Elected after Accrington Stanley resigned
71-72	Hereford U.	Elected in place of Barrow

76-77	Wimbledon	Elected in place of Workington
77-78	Wigan A.	Elected in place of Southport
86-87	Scarborough	Promoted from Conference
87-88	Lincoln C.	Promoted from Conference
88-89	Maidstone U.	Promoted from Conference
89-90	Darlington	Promoted from Conference
90-91	Barnet	Promoted from Conference
91-92	Colchester U.	Promoted from Conference
92-93	Wycombe W.	Promoted from Conference
96-97	Macclesfield T.	Promoted from Conference
97-98	Halifax T.	Promoted from Conference

RELEGATIONS

PREMIER LEAGUE TO NEW DIVISION 1

Season	Team	Pts/Pn	Team	Pts/Pn	Team	Pts/Pn
97-98	Bolton W.	33/18	Barnsley	35/19	C. Palace	33/20
96-97	Sunderland	40/18	Middlesbrough	39/19	N. Forest	34/20
95-96	Manchester C.	38/18	QPR	33/19	Bolton W.	29/20
	Ipswich T.	27/22				
94-95	C. Palace	45/19	Norwich C.	43/20	Leicester C.	29/21
93-94	Sheffield U.	42/20	Oldham Ath.	40/21	Swindon T.	30/22
92-93	C. Palace	49/20	Middlesbro	44/21	N. Forest	40/22

NEW DIVISION 1 TO NEW DIVISION 2

Season	Team	Pts/Pn	Team	Pts/Pn	Team	Pts/Pn
97-98	Manchester C.	48/22	Stoke C.	46/23	Reading	42/24
96-97	Grimsby T.	46/22	Oldham Ath.	43/23	Southend U.	39/24
95-96	Millwall	52/22	Watford	48/23	Luton T.	45/24
94-95	Swindon T.	48/21	Burnley	46/22	Bristol C.	45/23
	Notts Co.	40/24				
93-94	Birmingham C.	51/22	Oxford U.	49/23	Peterborough	37/24
92-93	Brentford	49/22	Cambridge U.	49/23	Bristol R.	41/24

NEW DIVISION 2 TO NEW DIVISION 3

Season	Team	Pts/Pn	Team	Pts/Pn	Team	Pts/Pn
97-98	Brentford	50/21	Plymouth Ar.	49/22	Carlisle U.	44/23
	Southend U.	43/24				
96-97	Peterborough	47/21	Shrewsbury T.	46/22	Rotherham U.	35/23
	Notts Co.	35/24				
95-96	Carlisle U.	49/21	Swansea C.	47/22	Brighton & HA	40/23
	Hull C.	31/24				
94-95	Cambridge U.	48/20	Plymouth Arg	46/21	Cardiff C.	38/22
	Chester C.	29/23	Leyton Orient	26/24		
93-94	Fulham	52/21	Exeter C.	45/22	Hartlepool U.	36/23
	Barnet	28/24				
92-93	Preston NE	47/21	Mansfield T.	44/22	Wigan Ath.	41/23
	Chester C.	29/24				

DIVISION 1 TO DIVISION 2

Season	Team	Pts/Pn	Team	Pts/Pn	Team	Pts/Pn

Season	Team	Score	Team	Score	Team	Score
91-92	Luton T.	42/20	Notts Co.	40/21	West Ham U.	38/22
90-91	Sunderland	34/19	Derby Co.	24/20		
89-90	Sheffield Wed.	43/18	Charlton Ath.	30/19	Millwall	26/20
88-89	Middlesbro	39/18	West Ham U.	38/19	Newcastle U.	31/20
87-88	Chelsea	42/18 †	Portsmouth	35/19	Watford	32/20
	Oxford U.	31/21				
86-87	Leicester C.	42/20	Manchester C.	39/21	Aston Villa	36/22
85-86	Ipswich T.	41/20	Birmingham C.	29/21	West Brom	24/22
84-85	Norwich C.	49/20	Sunderland	40/21	Stoke C.	17/22
83-84	Birmingham C.	48/20	Notts Co.	41/21	Wolves	29/22
82-83	Manchester C.	47/20	Swansea	41/21	Brighton & HA	40/22
81-82	Leeds U.	42/20	Wolves	40/21	Middlesbro	39/22
80-81	Norwich C.	33/20	Leicester C.	32/21	C. Palace	19/22
79-80	Bristol C.	31/20	Derby Co.	30/21	Bolton W.	25/22
78-79	QPR	25/20	Birmingham C.	22/21	Chelsea	20/22
77-78	West Ham U.	32/20	Newcastle U.	22/21	Leicester C.	22/22
76-77	Sunderland	34/20	Stoke C.	34/21	Tottenham H	33/22
75-76	Wolves	30/20	Burnley	28/21	Sheffield U.	22/22
74-75	Luton T.	33/20	Chelsea	33/21	Carlisle U.	29/22
73-74	Southampton	36/20	Manchester U.	32/21	Norwich C.	29/22
72-73	C. Palace	30/21	West Brom	28/22		
71-72	N. Forest	25/21	Huddersfield	25/22		
70-71	Burnley	27/21	Blackpool	23/22		
69-70	Sunderland	26/21	Sheffield Wed.	25/22		
68-69	Leicester C.	30/21	QPR	18/22		
67-68	Sheffield U.	32/21	Fulham	27/22		
66-67	Aston Villa	29/21	Blackpool	21/22		
65-66	Northampton	33/21	Blackburn R.	20/22		
64-65	Wolves	30/21	Birmingham C.	27/22		
63-64	Bolton W.	28/21	Ipswich T.	25/22		
62-63	Manchester C.	31/21	Leyton Orient	21/22		
61-62	Cardiff C.	32/21	Chelsea	28/22		
60-61	Newcastle U.	32/21	Preston NE	30/22		
59-60	Leeds U.	34/21	Luton T.	30/22		
58-59	Aston Villa	30/21	Portsmouth	21/22		
57-58	Sunderland	32/21	Sheffield Wed.	31/22		
56-57	Cardiff C.	29/21	Charlton Ath.	22/22		
55-56	Huddersfield	35/21	Sheffield U.	33/22		
54-55	Leicester C.	35/21	Sheffield Wed.	26/22		
53-54	Middlesbro	30/21	Liverpool	28/22		
52-53	Stoke C.	34/21	Derby Co.	32/22		
51-52	Huddersfield	28/21	Fulham	27/22		
50-51	Sheffield Wed.	32/21	Everton	32/22		
49-50	Manchester C.	29/21	Birmingham C.	28/22		
48-49	Preston NE	33/21	Sheffield U.	33/22		
47-48	Blackburn R.	32/21	Grimsby T.	22/22		
46-47	Brentford	25/21	Leeds U.	18/22		
38-39	Birmingham C.	32/21	Leicester C.	29/22		
37-38	Manchester C.	36/21	West Brom	36/22		
36-37	Manchester U.	32/21	Sheffield Wed.	30/22		
35-36	Aston Villa	35/21	Blackburn R.	33/22		
34-35	Leicester C.	33/21	Tottenham H	30/22		

33-34	Newcastle U.	34/21	Sheffield U.	31/22		
32-33	Bolton W.	33/21	Blackpool	33/22		
31-32	Grimsby T.	32/21	West Ham U.	31/22		
30-31	Leeds U.	31/21	Manchester U.	22/22		
29-30	Burnley	36/21	Everton	35/22		
28-29	Bury	31/21	Cardiff C.	29/22		
27-28	Tottenham H	38/21	Middlesbro	37/22		
26-27	Leeds U.	30/21	West Brom	30/22		
25-26	Manchester C.	35/21	Notts Co.	33/22		
24-25	Preston NE	26/21	N. Forest	24/22		
23-24	Chelsea	32/21	Middlesbro	22/22		
22-23	Stoke C.	30/21	Oldham Ath.	30/22		
21-22	Bradford C.	32/21	Manchester U.	28/22		
20-21	Derby Co.	26/21	Bradford PA	24/22		
19-20	Notts Co.	36/21	Sheffield Wed.	23/22		
14-15	Tottenham H	28/20				
13-14	Preston NE	30/19	Derby Co.	27/20		
12-13	Notts Co.	23/19	Arsenal	18/20		
11-12	Preston NE	33/19	Bury	21/20		
10-11	Bristol C.	27/19	N. Forest	25/20		
09-10	Chelsea	29/19	Bolton W.	24/20		
08-09	Manchester C.	34/19	Leicester C.	25/20		
07-08	Bolton W.	33/19	Birmingham C.	30/20		
06-07	Derby Co.	27/19	Stoke C.	26/20		
05-06	N. Forest	31/19	Wolves	23/20		
03-04	Liverpool	26/17	West Brom	24/18		
02-03	Grimsby T.	25/17	Bolton W.	19/18		
1899-00	Burnley	27/17	Glossop	18/18		
98-99	Bolton W.	25/17	Sheffield Wed.	24/18		
96-97	Burnley	19/16				
95-96	Birmingham C.	20/15				
94-95	Liverpool	22/16				
93-94	Darwen	19/15	Manchester U.	14/16		
92-93	Notts Co.	24/14				

† *Chelsea relegated after play-off*

DIVISION 2 TO DIVISION 3

Season	Team	Pts/Pn	Team	Pts/Pn	Team	Pts/Pn
91-92	Plymouth Arg	48/22	Brighton & HA	47/23	Port Vale	45/24
90-91	West Brom	48/23	Hull C.	45/24		
89-90	Bournemouth	48/22	Bradford C.	41/23	Stoke C.	37/24
88-89	Shrewsbury T.	42/22	Birmingham C.	35/23	Walsall	31/24
87-88	Sheffield U.	46/21	Reading	42/22	Huddersfield	28/23
86-87	Sunderland	48/20	Grimsby T.	44/21	Brighton & HA	39/22
85-86	Carlisle U.	46/20	Middlesbro	45/21	Fulham	36/22
84-85	Notts Co.	37/20	Cardiff C.	35/21	Wolves	33/22
83-84	Derby Co.	42/20	Swansea	29/21	Cambridge U.	24/22
82-83	Rotherham U.	45/20	Burnley	44/21	Bolton W.	44/22
81-82	Cardiff C.	44/20	Wrexham	44/21	Leyton Orient	39/22
80-81	Preston NE	36/20	Bristol C.	30/21	Bristol R.	23/22
79-80	Fulham	29/20	Burnley	27/21	Charlton Ath.	22/22
78-79	Sheffield U.	34/20	Millwall	32/21	Blackburn R.	30/22

77-78	Blackpool	37/20	Mansfield T.	31/21	Hull C.	28/22
76-77	Carlisle U.	34/20	Plymouth Arg	32/21	Hereford U.	31/22
75-76	Oxford U.	33/20	York C.	28/21	Portsmouth	25/22
74-75	Millwall	32/20	Cardiff C.	32/21	Sheffield Wed.	21/22
73-74	C. Palace	34/20	Swindon T.	25/22		
72-73	Huddersfield	33/21	Brighton & HA	29/22		
71-72	Charlton Ath.	33/21	Watford	19/22		
70-71	Blackburn R.	27/21	Bolton W.	24/22		
69-70	Aston Villa	29/21	Preston NE	28/22		
68-69	Bury	30/21	Fulham	25/22		
67-68	Rotherham U.	31/21	Plymouth Arg	27/22		
66-67	Northampton	30/21	Bury	28/22		
65-66	Middlesbro	33/21	Leyton Orient	23/22		
64-65	Swindon T.	33/21	Swansea	32/22		
63-64	Grimsby T.	32/21	Scunthorpe U.	30/22		
62-63	Walsall	31/21	Luton T.	29/22		
61-62	Bristol R.	33/21	Brighton & HA	31/22		
60-61	Portsmouth	33/21	Lincoln C.	24/22		
59-60	Hull C.	30/21	Bristol C.	27/22		
58-59	Grimsby T.	28/21	Barnsley	27/22		
57-58	Notts Co.	30/21	Doncaster R.	27/22		
56-57	Bury	25/21	Port Vale	22/22		
55-56	Plymouth Arg	28/21	Hull C.	26/22		
54-55	Ipswich T.	28/21	Derby Co.	23/22		
53-54	Brentford	31/21	Oldham Ath.	25/22		
52-53	Southampton	33/21	Barnsley	18/22		
51-52	Coventry C.	34/21	QPR	34/22		
50-51	Chesterfield	30/21	Grimsby T.	28/22		
49-50	Plymouth Arg	32/21	Bradford PA	31/22		
48-49	N. Forest	35/21	Lincoln C.	28/22		
47-48	Doncaster R.	29/21	Millwall	29/22		
46-47	Swansea	29/21	Newport Co.	23/22		
38-39	Norwich C.	31/21	Tranmere R.	17/22		
37-38	Barnsley	36/21	Stockport Co.	31/22		
36-37	Bradford C.	30/21	Doncaster R.	24/22		
35-36	Port Vale	32/21	Hull C.	20/22		
34-35	Oldham Ath.	26/21	Notts Co.	25/22		
33-34	Millwall	33/21	Lincoln C.	26/22		
32-33	Chesterfield	34/21	Charlton Ath.	31/22		
31-32	Barnsley	33/21	Bristol C.	23/22		
30-31	Reading	30/21	Cardiff C.	25/22		
29-30	Hull C.	35/21	Notts Co.	33/22		
28-29	Port Vale	34/21	Leyton Orient	32/22		
27-28	Fulham	33/21	Gateshead	23/22		
26-27	Darlington	30/21	Bradford C.	23/22		
25-26	Stoke C.	32/21	Stockport Co.	25/22		
24-25	C. Palace	34/21	Coventry C.	31/22		
23-24	Nelson	30/21	Bristol C.	29/22		
22-23	Rotherham U.	35/21	Wolves	27/22		
21-22	Bradford PA	33/21	Bristol C.	33/22		
20-21	Stockport Co.	30/22				
19-20	Grimsby T.	25/22				

DIVISION 3 TO DIVISION 4

Season	Team	Pt/Pn	Team	Pt/Pn	Team	Pt/Pn	Team	Pt/Pn
91-92	Bury	51/21	Shrewsbury T.	47/22	Torquay U.	47/23	Darlington	37/24
90-91	Crewe Alex.	44/22	Rotherham U.	42/23	Mansfield T.	38/24		
89-90	Cardiff C.	50/21	Northampton	47/22	Blackpool	46/23	Walsall	41/24
88-89	Southend U.	54/21	Chesterfield	49/22	Gillingham	40/23	Aldershot	37/24
87-88	Rotherham U.	52/21	Grimsby T.	50/22	York C.	33/23	Doncaster R.	33/24
86-87	Bolton W.	45/21	Carlisle U.	38/22	Darlington	37/23	Newport Co.	37/24
85-86	Lincoln C.	46/21	Cardiff C.	45/22	Wolves	43/23	Swansea	43/24
84-85	Burnley	46/21	Leyton Orient	46/22	Preston NE	46/23	Cambridge U.	21/24
83-84	Scunthorpe U.	46/21	Southend U.	43/22	Port Vale	43/23	Exeter C.	33/24
82-83	Reading	53/21	Wrexham	51/22	Doncaster R.	38/23	Chesterfield	37/24
81-82	Wimbledon	53/21	Swindon T.	52/22	Bristol C.	46/23	Chester C.	32/24
80-81	Sheffield U.	40/21	Colchester U.	39/22	Blackpool	32/23	Hull C.	32/24
79-80	Bury	39/21	Southend U.	38/22	Mansfield T.	36/23	Wimbledon	34/24
78-79	Peterborough	36/21	Walsall	32/22	Tranmere R.	32/23	Lincoln C.	25/24
77-78	Port Vale	36/21	Bradford C.	34/22	Hereford U.	32/23	Portsmouth	31/24
76-77	Reading	35/21	Northampton	34/22	Grimsby T.	33/23	York C.	32/24
75-76	Aldershot	39/21	Colchester U.	38/22	Southend U.	37/23	Halifax T.	35/24
74-75	Bournemouth	38/21	Tranmere R.	37/22	Watford	37/23	Huddersfield	32/24
73-74	Cambridge U.	35/21	Shrewsbury T.	31/22	Southport	28/23	Rochdale	21/24
72-73	Rotherham U.	41/21	Brentford	37/22	Swansea	37/23	Scunthorpe	30/24
71-72	Mansfield T.	36/21	Barnsley	36/22	Torquay U.	32/23	Bradford C.	32/24
70-71	Reading	39/21	Bury	38/22	Doncaster R.	35/23	Gillingham	35/24
69-70	Bournemouth	39/21	Southport	38/22	Barrow	30/23	Stockport Co.	23/24
68-69	Northampton	40/21	Hartlepool U.	39/22	Crewe Alex.	35/23	Oldham Ath.	35/24
67-68	Peterborough	50/9*	Grimsby T.	37/22	Colchester U.	33/23	Scunthorpe	32/24
66-67	Swansea	39/21	Darlington	37/22	Doncaster R.	34/23	Workington	31/24
65-66	Southend U.	36/21	Exeter C.	35/22	Brentford	32/23	York C.	27/24
64-65	Luton T.	33/21	Port Vale	32/22	Colchester U.	30/23	Barnsley	29/24
63-64	Millwall	38/21	Crewe Alex.	34/22	Wrexham	32/23	Notts Co.	32/24
62-63	Bradford PA	40/21	Brighton & HA	36/22	Carlisle U.	35/23	Halifax T.	30/24
61-62	Torquay U.	36/21	Lincoln C.	35/22	Brentford	34/23	Newport Co.	22/24
60-61	Tranmere R.	38/21	Bradford C.	36/22	Colchester U.	33/23	Chesterfield	32/24
59-60	York C.	38/21	Mansfield T.	36/22	Wrexham	36/23	Accrington S.	27/24
58-59	Stockport Co.	36/21	Doncaster R.	33/22	Notts Co.	29/23	Rochdale	28/24

*Peterborough United demoted

RELEGATED TO CONFERENCE

Season	Team	Pts/Pn
59-60	Gateshead	22/23
61-62	Accrington S.	Resigned
69-70	Bradford PA	24/20
71-72	Barrow	22/37
76-77	Workington	24/19
77-78	Southport	23/31
86-87	Lincoln C.	24/48
87-88	Newport Co.	24/25
88-89	Darlington	24/42
89-90	Colchester	24/43
91/92	Aldershot	Expelled
91/92	Maidstone U.	18/42
92/93	Halifax T.	22/36
96-97	Hereford U.	47/24
97-98	Doncaster R.	24/24

Form 'n' Encounter Guide

Our unique *Form 'n' Encounter Guide* will allow you to plan your season's Nationwide League schedule by providing you with a form guide which helps you to predict what are likely to be the most exciting games to attend on a day-by-day basis. Listed are the results from the previous two encounters for the matches (divisions permitting of course). Please do check that the game you are looking to attend is on before you set out. Match dates and kick-off times are all subject to change to cope with TV schedules and the like.

Encounter 96-97 97-98

8th August 1998

Match	96-97	97-98
1 Barnsley v WBA	2-0	-
1 Bradford C. v Stockport Co.	-	2-1
1 Bristol C. v Oxford U.	-	-
1 Bury v Huddersfield T.	-	2-2
1 C. Palace v Bolton W.	1-1	2-2
1 Grimsby T. v Ipswich T.	-	2-1
1 Norwich C. v Crewe Alex.	-	0-2
1 Port Vale v Birmingham C.	3-0	0-1
1 Portsmouth v Watford	-	-
1 Sheffield U. v Swindon T.	2-0	2-1
1 Sunderland v QPR	-	2-2
1 Wolverhampton W. v Tranmere R.	3-2	2-1
2 Bournemouth v Lincoln C.	-	-
2 Burnley v Bristol R.	2-2	0-0
2 Colchester U. v Chesterfield	-	-
2 Gillingham v Walsall	2-0	2-1
2 Macclesfield T. v Fulham	-	-
2 Manchester C. v Blackpool	-	-
2 Northampton T. v Stoke C.	-	-
2 Oldham Ath. v Notts County	-	-
2 Preston NE v York C.	1-0	3-2
2 Reading v Wrexham	-	-
2 Wigan v Millwall	-	0-0
2 Wycombe W. v Luton T.	0-1	2-2
3 Brentford v Mansfield T.	-	-
3 Carlisle U. v Brighton & HA	2-1	-
3 Chester C. v Leyton O.	0-1	1-1
3 Darlington v Barnet	0-1	2-3
3 Hartlepool U. v Cardiff C.	2-3	2-0
3 Peterborough U. v Halifax T.	-	-
3 Plymouth Ar. v Rochdale	-	-
3 Rotherham U. v Hull C.	-	5-4
3 Scarborough v Southend U.	-	-
3 Shrewsbury T. v Scunthorpe U.	-	0-2
3 Swansea C. v Exeter C.	3-1	2-1
3 Torquay U. v Cambridge U.	0-1	0-3

15th August 1998

Match	96-97	97-98
1 Birmingham C. v Crystal P.	1-0	-
1 Bolton W. v Grimsby T.	6-1	-
1 Crewe Alex. v Barnsley	-	-
1 Huddersfield T. v Port Vale	0-1	0-4
1 Ipswich T. v Bury	-	2-0
1 Oxford U. v Wolverhampton W.	1-1	3-0
1 QPR v Bristol C.	-	-
1 Stockport Co. v Norwich C.	-	2-2
1 Swindon T. v Sunderland	-	1-2
1 Tranmere R. v Portsmouth	4-3	2-2
1 Watford v Bradford C.	-	-
1 WBA v Sheffield U.	-	1-2	2-0
2 Blackpool v Oldham Ath.	-	2-2
2 Bristol R. v Reading	-	-
2 Chesterfield v Burnley	0-0	1-0
2 Fulham v Manchester C.	-	-
2 Lincoln C. v Wigan	-	1-3
2 Luton T. v Preston NE	5-1	1-3
2 Millwall v Wycombe W.	2-1	1-0
2 Notts County v Bournemouth	0-2	-
2 Stoke C. v Macclesfield T.	-	-
2 Walsall v Northampton T.	-	0-2
2 Wrexham v Colchester U.	-	-
2 York C. v Gillingham	2-3	2-1
3 Barnet v Hartlepool U.	1-0	1-1
3 Brighton & HA v Chester C.	2-1	3-2
3 Cambridge U. v Swansea C.	2-1	4-1
3 Cardiff C. v Peterborough U.	-	0-0
3 Exeter C. v Scarborough	2-2	1-1

Encounter	96-97	97-98
3 Halifax T. v Brentford	-	
3 Hull C. v Darlington	3-2	1-1
3 Leyton O. v Rotherham U.	-	1-1
3 Mansfield T. v Plymouth Ar.	-	
3 Rochdale v Torquay U.	2-1	0-1
3 Scunthorpe U. v Carlisle U.	0-0	
3 Southend U. v Shrewsbury T.	-	

19th August 1998

Encounter	96-97	97-98
1 Birmingham C. v Grimsby T.	0-0	

22nd August 1998

Encounter	96-97	97-98
1 Barnsley v Stockport Co.	-	
1 Bradford C. v Bolton W.	2-4	
1 Bristol C. v Watford	-	1-1
1 Bury v Crewe Alex.	1-0	1-1
1 C. Palace v Oxford U.	-	
1 Grimsby T. v Huddersfield T.	2-2	
1 Norwich C. v QPR	1-1	0-0
1 Port Vale v WBA	2-2	1-2
1 Portsmouth v Ipswich T.	0-1	0-1
1 Sheffield U. v Birmingham C.	4-4	0-0
1 Sunderland v Tranmere R.	-	3-0
1 Wolverhampton W. v Swindon T.	1-0	3-1
2 Bournemouth v Millwall	1-1	0-0
2 Burnley v York C.	1-2	7-2
2 Colchester U. v Fulham	2-1	
2 Gillingham v Bristol R.	2-1	1-1
2 Macclesfield T. v Lincoln C.	-	1-0
2 Manchester C. v Wrexham	-	
2 Northampton T. v Notts County	-	
2 Oldham Ath. v Chesterfield	-	2-0
2 Preston NE v Stoke C.	-	
2 Reading v Luton T.	-	
2 Wigan v Blackpool	-	3-0
2 Wycombe W. v Walsall	0-2	4-2
3 Brentford v Brighton & HA	-	
3 Carlisle U. v Rochdale	3-2	
3 Chester C. v Hull C.	0-0	1-0
3 Darlington v Halifax T.	-	
3 Hartlepool U. v Scunthorpe U.	0-1	0-1
3 Peterborough U. v Southend U.	-	
3 Plymouth Ar. v Barnet	-	
3 Rotherham U. v Cambridge U.	-	2-2
3 Scarborough v Mansfield T.	2-1	2-2
3 Shrewsbury T. v Cardiff C.	-	3-2
3 Swansea C. v Leyton O.	1-0	1-1
3 Torquay U. v Exeter C.	2-0	1-2

29th August 1998

Encounter	96-97	97-98
1 Birmingham C. v Barnsley	0-0	
1 Bolton W. v Sheffield U.	2-2	
1 Crewe Alex. v Bradford C.	-	5-0
1 Huddersfield T. v Portsmouth	1-3	1-1
1 Ipswich T. v Sunderland	-	2-0
1 Oxford U. v Grimsby T.	3-2	
1 QPR v Bury	-	0-1
1 Stockport Co. v Crystal P.	-	-
1 Swindon T. v Port Vale	1-1	4-2
1 Tranmere R. v Bristol C.	-	
1 Watford v Wolverhampton W.	-	
1 WBA v Norwich C.	5-1	1-0
2 Blackpool v Gillingham	-	2-1
2 Bristol R. v Wigan	-	5-0
2 Chesterfield v Reading	-	
2 Fulham v Bournemouth	-	0-1
2 Lincoln C. v Preston NE	-	
2 Luton T. v Colchester U.	-	
2 Millwall v Macclesfield T.	-	
2 Notts County v Manchester C.	-	
2 Stoke C. v Oldham Ath.	2-1	
2 Walsall v Burnley	1-3	0-0
2 Wrexham v Northampton T.	-	
2 York C. v Wycombe W.	2-0	2-0
3 Barnet v Brentford	-	
3 Brighton & HA v Torquay U.	2-2	1-4
3 Cambridge U. v Hartlepool U.	1-0	2-0
3 Cardiff C. v Rotherham U.	-	2-2
3 Exeter C. v Carlisle U.	2-1	
3 Halifax T. v Shrewsbury T.	-	
3 Hull C. v Peterborough U.	-	3-1
3 Leyton O. v Scarborough	0-1	3-1
3 Mansfield T. v Swansea C.	0-0	1-0
3 Rochdale v Darlington	-	5-0
3 Scunthorpe U. v Plymouth Ar.	-	
3 Southend U. v Chester C.	-	

31st August 1998

Encounter	96-97	97-98
1 Barnsley v Oxford U.	0-0	
1 Bradford C. v Birmingham C.	0-2	0-0
1 Bristol C. v Huddersfield T.	-	
1 Bury v Swindon T.	-	1-0
1 C. Palace v Tranmere R.	0-1	
1 Grimsby T. v WBA	1-1	
1 Norwich C. v Bolton W.	1-1	
1 Port Vale v Ipswich T.	2-2	1-3
1 Portsmouth v QPR	1-2	3-1

Encounter 96-97 97-98

Encounter	96-97	97-98
1 Sheffield U. v Crewe Alex.	1-0	-
1 Sunderland v Watford	-	-
1 Wolverhampton W. v Stockport Co.	-	3-4
2 Bournemouth v Blackpool	0-0	2-0
2 Burnley v Millwall	0-2	1-2
2 Colchester U. v Stoke C.	-	-
2 Gillingham v Wrexham	1-2	1-1
2 Macclesfield T. v Notts County	-	2-0
2 Manchester C. v Walsall	-	-
2 Oldham Ath. v Fulham	-	1-0
2 Preston NE v Chesterfield	0-1	0-0
2 Reading v York C.	-	-
2 Wigan v Luton T.	-	1-1
2 Wycombe W. v Bristol R.	2-0	1-0
3 Brentford v Rochdale	-	-
3 Carlisle U. v Southend U.	-	5-0
3 Chester C. v Cambridge U.	1-1	1-1
3 Darlington v Cardiff C.	2-1	0-0
3 Hartlepool U. v Hull C.	1-1	2-2
3 Peterborough U. v Exeter C.	-	1-1
3 Plymouth Ar. v Halifax T.	-	-
3 Rotherham U. v Mansfield T.	-	2-2
3 Scarborough v Brighton & HA	1-1	2-1
3 Shrewsbury T. v Barnet	-	2-0
3 Swansea C. v Scunthorpe U.	1-2	2-0
3 Torquay U. v Leyton O.	0-0	1-1

1st September 1998

Encounter	96-97	97-98
2 Northampton T. v Lincoln C.	1-1	-

5th September 1998

Encounter	96-97	97-98
1 Birmingham C. v Bury	-	1-3
1 Bolton W. v Port Vale	4-2	-
1 Crewe Alex. v Sunderland	-	0-3
1 Huddersfield T. v Sheffield U.	2-1	0-0
1 Ipswich T. v Wolverhampton W.	0-0	3-0
1 Oxford U. v Portsmouth	2-0	1-0
1 QPR v Barnsley	3-1	-
1 Stockport Co. v Grimsby T.	-	-
1 Swindon T. v Bristol C.	-	-
1 Tranmere R. v Bradford C.	3-0	3-1
1 Watford v Norwich C.	-	-
1 WBA v Crystal P.	1-0	-
2 Blackpool v Northampton C.	-	1-1
2 Bristol R. v Preston NE	1-0	2-2
2 Chesterfield v Gillingham	2-2	1-1
2 Fulham v Wycombe W.	-	0-0
2 Lincoln C. v Oldham Ath.	-	-

Encounter	96-97	97-98
2 Luton T. v Burnley	1-2	2-3
2 Millwall v Manchester C.	-	-
2 Notts County v Wigan	-	-
2 Stoke C. v Bournemouth	-	-
2 Walsall v Reading	-	-
2 Wrexham v Macclesfield T.	-	-
2 York C. v Colchester U.	-	-
3 Barnet v Peterborough U.	-	2-0
3 Brighton & HA v Swansea C.	3-2	0-1
3 Cambridge U. v Scarborough	2-1	2-3
3 Cardiff C. v Plymouth Ar.	-	-
3 Exeter C. v Chester C.	1-5	5-0
3 Halifax T. v Hartlepool U.	-	-
3 Hull C. v Brentford	-	-
3 Leyton O. v Carlisle U.	2-1	-
3 Mansfield T. v Darlington	2-1	4-0
3 Rochdale v Shrewsbury T.	-	3-1
3 Scunthorpe U. v Torquay U.	1-0	2-0
3 Southend U. v Rotherham U.	-	-

8th September 1998

Encounter	96-97	97-98
1 Barnsley v Norwich C.	3-1	-
1 Birmingham C. v Stockport Co.	-	4-1
1 Bury v Portsmouth	-	0-2
1 Crewe Alex. v Crystal P.	-	-
1 Huddersfield T. v Watford	-	-
1 Ipswich T. v Bradford C.	3-2	2-1
1 Port Vale v Wolverhampton W.	1-2	0-2
1 Sheffield U. v Grimsby T.	3-1	-
1 Sunderland v Bristol C.	-	-
1 WBA v Bolton W.	2-2	-
2 Blackpool v Notts County	-	1-0
2 Bristol R. v Chesterfield	2-0	3-1
2 Fulham v Stoke C.	-	-
2 Gillingham v Northampton T.	-	1-0
2 Oldham Ath. v Macclesfield T.	-	-
2 Walsall v York C.	1-1	2-0
2 Wigan v Colchester U.	1-0	-
2 Wrexham v Luton T.	2-1	2-1
2 Wycombe W. v Preston NE	0-1	0-0
3 Cardiff C. v Barnet	1-2	1-1
3 Carlisle U. v Swansea C.	4-1	-
3 Darlington v Hartlepool U.	1-2	1-1
3 Exeter C. v Brighton & HA	2-1	2-1
3 Hull C. v Rochdale	1-1	0-2
3 Leyton O. v Mansfield U.	2-1	2-2
3 Peterborough v Chester C.	-	2-1
3 Rotherham U. v Plymouth Ar.	1-2	-

Encounter 96-97 97-98

3 Scunthorpe U. v Cambridge U. 3-2   3-3
3 Southend U. v Halifax T. ... ... -   -
3 Torquay U. v Brentford ... ... -   -

9th September 1998
1 QPR v Tranmere R. 2-0   0-0
1 Swindon U. v Oxford U. ... 1-0   4-1

2 Manchester C. v Bournemouth ... -
2 Millwall v Lincoln C. ... ... -
2 Reading v Burnley ... ... -

3 Scarborough v Shrewsbury T. ... -   0-0

12th September 1998
1 Bolton W. v Birmingham C. ... 2-1
1 Bradford C. v Sheffield U. 1-2   1-1
1 Bristol C. v WBA ... ... -
1 C. Palace v Port Vale 1-1   -
1 Grimsby T. v Barnsley 2-3   -
1 Norwich C. v Bury ... ... -   2-2
1 Oxford U. v Ipswich T. 3-1   1-0
1 Portsmouth v Swindon T. ... 0-1   0-1
1 Stockport Co. v Crewe Alex. ... 1-0   0-1
1 Tranmere R. v Huddersfield T. 1-1   1-1
1 Watford v QPR ... ... -
1 Wolverhampton W. v Sunderland -   0-1

2 Bournemouth v Wigan ... ... -   1-0
2 Burnley v Wycombe W. 2-1   2-2
2 Chesterfield v Walsall 1-0   3-1
2 Colchester U. v Gillingham ... -
2 Lincoln C. v Blackpool ... ... -
2 Luton T. v Bristol R. 2-1   2-4
2 Macclesfield v Manchester C. ... -
2 Northampton T. v Oldham Ath. ...   0-0
2 Notts County v Fulham ... ... -
2 Preston NE v Reading ... ... -
2 Stoke C. v Millwall ... ... -
2 York C. v Wrexham 1-0   1-0

3 Barnet v Hull C. 1-0   2-0
3 Brentford v Rotherham U. ... 4-2
3 Brighton & HA v Southend U. ... -
3 Cambridge U. v Leyton O. ... 2-0   1-0
3 Chester C. v Torquay U. ... 0-0   1-3
3 Halifax T. v Cardiff C. ... ... -
3 Hartlepool U. v Exeter C. ... 1-1   1-1
3 Mansfield T. v Carlisle U. ... 0-0
3 Plymouth Ar. v Darlington ... -
3 Rochdale v Scunthorpe U. ... 1-2   2-0

Encounter 96-97 97-98

3 Shrewsbury T. v Peterborough U.2-2   4-1
3 Swansea C. v Scarborough 1-2   0-0

19th September 1998
1 Barnsley v C. Palace 0-0   1-0
1 Birmingham v Grimsby 0-0   -
1 Bury v Tranmere R. ... ... -   1-0
1 Crewe Alex. v Bolton W. ... ... -
1 Huddersfield v W'hampton W. 0-2   1-0
1 Ipswich T. v Bristol C. ... ... -
1 Port Vale v Portsmouth 0-2   2-1
1 QPR v Stockport Co. ... ... -   2-1
1 Sheffield U. v Norwich C. ... 2-3   2-2
1 Sunderland v Oxford U. ... ... -   3-1
1 Swindon T. v Watford ... ... -
1 WBA v Bradford C. 0-0   1-1

2 Blackpool v Luton T. 0-0   1-0
2 Bristol R. v Lincoln C. ... ... -
2 Fulham v York C. ... ... -   1-1
2 Gillingham v Burnley 1-0   2-0
2 Manchester C. v Chesterfield ... -
2 Millwall v Northampton T. ... -   0-0
2 Oldham Ath. v Preston NE ... -   1-0
2 Reading v Colchester U. ... ... -
2 Walsall v Notts County ... 3-1
2 Wigan v Macclesfield T. ... ... -
2 Wrexham v Stoke C. ... ... -
2 Wycombe W. v Bournemouth ... 1-1   1-1

3 Cardiff C. v Rochdale 2-1   2-1
3 Carlisle U. v Chester C. 3-1   -
3 Darlington v Shrewsbury T. ... -   3-1
3 Exeter C. v Barnet 1-1   0-0
3 Hull C. v Halifax T. ... ... -
3 Leyton O. v Brighton & HA ... 2-0   3-1
3 Peterborough U. v Plymouth Ar. 0-0
3 Rotherham U. v Hartlepool U. ... -   2-1
3 Scarborough v Brentford ... ... -
3 Scunthorpe U. v Mansfield T. ... 0-2   1-0
3 Southend U. v Cambridge U. ... -
3 Torquay U. v Swansea C. ... 2-0   2-0

26th September 1998
1 Bolton W. v Huddersfield T. ... 2-0
1 Bradford C. v Barnsley 2-2
1 Bristol C. v Crewe Alex. 3-0
1 C. Palace v Sheffield U. 0-1
1 Grimsby T. v Port Vale 1-1   -
1 Norwich C. v Birmingham C. ... 0-1   3-3

Encounter 96-97 97-98

Encounter	96-97	97-98
1 Oxford U. v QPR	2-3	3-1
1 Portsmouth v Sunderland	-	1-4
1 Stockport Co. v WBA	-	2-1
1 Tranmere R. v Swindon T. ...	2-1	3-0
1 Watford v Ipswich T.	-	-
1 Wolverhampton W. v Bury ...	-	4-2
2 Bournemouth v Oldham Ath.	-	0-0
2 Burnley v Wigan	-	0-2
2 Chesterfield v Wrexham	0-0	3-1
2 Colchester U. v Wycombe W. ...	-	-
2 Lincoln C. v Fulham	2-0	-
2 Luton T. v Walsall	3-1	0-1
2 Macclesfield T. v Reading	-	-
2 Northampton T. v Manchester C.	-	-
2 Notts County v Millwall ...	1-2	-
2 Preston NE v Gillingham ...	1-0	1-3
2 Stoke C. v Blackpool	-	-
2 York C. v Bristol R.	2-2	0-1
3 Barnet v Rotherham U.	-	0-0
3 Brentford v Darlington	-	-
3 Brighton & HA v Scunthorpe U.	1.01	2-1
3 Cambridge U. v Exeter C. ...	3-2	2-1
3 Chester C. v Cardiff C.	0-1	0-0
3 Halifax T. v Torquay U.	-	-
3 Hartlepool U. v Peterborough U.	-	2-1
3 Mansfield T. v Hull C.	1-0	2-0
3 Plymouth Ar. v Scarborough ...	-	-
3 Rochdale v Leyton O.	1-0	0-2
3 Shrewsbury T. v Carlisle U. ...	-	-
3 Swansea C. v Southend U.	-	-

29th September 1998

Encounter	96-97	97-98
1 Bolton W. v Swindon T.	-	-
1 Bradford C. v Port Vale	1-0	2-1
1 Bristol C. v Barnsley	-	-
1 C. Palace v Bury	-	-
1 Grimsby T. v Crewe Alex.	-	-
1 Norwich C. v Sunderland	-	2-1
1 Oxford U. v WBA	1-0	2-1
1 Portsmouth v Birmingham C. ...	1-1	1-1
1 Stockport Co. v Huddersfield T. ...	-	3-0
1 Tranmere R. v Ipswich T. ...	3-0	1-1
1 Watford v Sheffield U.	-	-
1 Wolverhampton W. v QPR ...	1-1	3-2

3rd October 1998

Encounter	96-97	97-98
1 Barnsley v Bolton W.	0-0	-
1 Birmingham C. v Tranmere R.	0-0	0-0

Encounter	96-97	97-98
1 Bury v Bristol C.	4-0	-
1 Crewe Alex. v Wolverhampton W.	-	0-0
1 Huddersfield T. v Oxford U. ...	1-0	5-1
1 Ipswich T. v Crystal P.	3-1	-
1 Port Vale v Norwich C.	6-1	2-2
1 QPR v Grimsby T.	3-0	-
1 Sheffield U. v Portsmouth	1-0	2-1
1 Sunderland v Bradford C.	-	2-0
1 Swindon T. v Stockport Co.	-	1-1
1 WBA v Watford	-	-
2 Blackpool v York C.	3-0	1-0
2 Bristol R. v Bournemouth	3-2	5-3
2 Fulham v Luton T.	-	0-0
2 Gillingham v Macclesfield T. ...	-	-
2 Manchester C. v Burnley	-	-
2 Millwall v Chesterfield	2-1	1-1
2 Oldham Ath. v Colchester U. ...	-	-
2 Reading v Stoke C.	2-2	2-0
2 Walsall v Preston NE	1-0	1-1
2 Wigan v Northampton T.	-	1-1
2 Wrexham v Lincoln C.	-	-
2 Wycombe W. v Notts County ...	1-0	-
3 Cardiff C. v Brighton & HA ...	1-0	0-0
3 Carlisle U. v Barnet	-	-
3 Darlington v Swansea C.	4-1	3-2
3 Exeter C. v Mansfield T.	0-0	1-0
3 Hull C. v Cambridge U.	1-3	1-0
3 Leyton O. v Hartlepool U.	1-2	2-1
3 Peterborough U. v Brentford ...	0-1	-
3 Rotherham U. v Shrewsbury T.	1-2	0-1
3 Scarborough v Chester C.	-	4-1
3 Scunthorpe U. v Halifax T.	-	-
3 Southend U. v Rochdale	-	-
3 Torquay U. v Plymouth Ar.	-	-

10th October 1998

Encounter	96-97	97-98
1 Barnsley v Port Vale	1-0	-
1 Bradford C. v Bury	-	1-0
1 Bristol C. v Portsmouth	-	-
1 Crewe Alex. v WBA	-	2-3
1 Norwich C. v Grimsby T.	2-1	-
1 Oxford U. v Tranmere R. ...	2-1	1-1
1 QPR v Ipswich T.	0-1	0-0
1 Stockport Co. v Bolton W.	-	-
1 Sunderland v Crystal P.	-	-
1 Swindon T. v Huddersfield T. ...	6-0	1-1
1 Watford v Birmingham C.	-	-
1 Wolverhampton W. v Sheffield U.	1-2	-

Encounter … … … … … … … 96-97 97-98

	96-97	97-98
2 Blackpool v Millwall ………	3-0	3-0
2 Colchester U. v Burnley ………	-	
2 Fulham v Reading ………	-	
2 Gillingham v Wycombe W. ……	1-0	1-0
2 Macclesfield v Bournemouth ……	-	
2 Manchester C. v Preston NE ……	-	
2 Northampton T. v Bristol R. ……	-	1-1
2 Notts County v Lincoln C. ……	-	
2 Oldham Ath. v Wigan ………	-	3-1
2 Stoke C. v Chesterfield ………	-	
2 Wrexham v Walsall ………	1-2	2-1
2 York C. v Luton T. ………	1-1	1-2
3 Barnet v Chester C. ………	1-2	2-1
3 Cambridge U. v Brighton & HA	1-1	1-1
3 Carlisle U. v Scarborough ……	1-0	
3 Darlington v Peterborough U…	-	3-1
3 Hartlepool U. v Shrewsbury T.	-	2-1
3 Hull C. v Cardiff C. ………	-	0-1
3 Leyton O. v Exeter C. ………	1-1	1-0
3 Mansfield T. v Torquay U. ……	1-2	2-2
3 Plymouth Ar. v Brentford ……	1-4	0-0
3 Rochdale v Halifax T. ………	-	
3 Scunthorpe U. v Southend U. …	-	
3 Swansea C. v Rotherham U. ……	-	1-1

17th October 1998

	96-97	97-98
1 Birmingham C. v Crewe Alex. …	-	0-1
1 Bolton W. v Oxford U. ………	4-0	-
1 Bury v Stockport Co. ………	0-0	0-1
1 C. Palace v Norwich C. ………	2-0	-
1 Grimsby T. v Bradford C. ……	1-1	-
1 Huddersfield T. v QPR ………	1-2	1-1
1 Ipswich T. v Swindon T. ……	2-0	2-1
1 Port Vale v Bristol C. ………	-	
1 Portsmouth v Wolverhampton W.	0-2	3-2
1 Sheffield U. v Barnsley ………	1-2	-
1 Tranmere R. v Watford ………	-	
1 WBA v Sunderland ………	-	3-3
2 Bournemouth v Northampton T. …	-	3-0
2 Bristol R. v Wrexham ………	2-0	1-0
2 Burnley v Notts County ……	1-0	-
2 Chesterfield v York C. ………	2-0	1-1
2 Lincoln C. v Stoke C. ………	-	
2 Luton T. v Oldham Ath. ………	-	1-1
2 Millwall v Fulham ………	-	1-1
2 Preston NE v Colchester U. ……	-	
2 Reading v Gillingham ………	-	
2 Walsall v Blackpool ………	1-1	2-1

Encounter … … … … … … … 96-97 97-98

	96-97	97-98
2 Wigan v Manchester C. ………	-	
2 Wycombe W. v Macclesfield T. …	-	
3 Brentford v Hartlepool U. ……	-	
3 Brighton & HA v Mansfield T.	1-1	1-1
3 Cardiff C. v Cambridge U. ……	0-0	0-0
3 Chester C. v Swansea C. ……	2-0	2-0
3 Exeter C. v Scunthorpe U. ……	0-1	2-3
3 Halifax T. v Barnet ………	-	
3 Peterborough U. v Rochdale ……	-	3-1
3 Rotherham U. v Darlington ……	-	3-0
3 Scarborough v Hull C. ………	3-2	2-1
3 Shrewsbury T. v Plymouth Ar.	2-3	
3 Southend U. v Leyton O. ……	-	
3 Torquay U. v Carlisle U. ……	-	1-2

20th October 1998

	96-97	97-98
1 Birmingham C. v Swindon T. …	1-0	3-0
1 Bolton W. v Watford ………	-	
1 Bury v Oxford U. ………	-	1-0
1 C. Palace v Wolverhampton W.	2-3	-
1 Grimsby T. v Bristol C. ……	-	1-1
1 Huddersfield T. v Sunderland …	-	2-3
1 Ipswich T. v Norwich C. ……	2-0	5-0
1 Port Vale v Crewe Alex. ………	-	2-3
1 Portsmouth v Bradford C. ……	3-1	1-1
1 Sheffield U. v Stockport Co. …	-	5-1
1 Tranmere R. v Barnsley ………	1-1	-
1 WBA v QPR ………	4-1	1-1
2 Bournemouth v Gillingham ……	2-2	4-0
2 Bristol R. v Stoke C. ………	-	
2 Burnley v Oldham Ath. ………	-	0-0
2 Chesterfield v Notts County …	1-0	-
2 Lincoln C. v Manchester C. ……	-	
2 Luton T. v Northampton T. ……	-	2-2
2 Preston NE v Macclesfield T. …	-	
2 Walsall v Colchester U. ………	-	
2 Wigan v Fulham ………	1-1	2-1
2 Wycombe W. v Wrexham ……	0-0	0-0
3 Brentford v Scunthorpe U. ……	-	
3 Brighton & HA v Plymouth Ar. …	-	
3 Cardiff C. v Leyton O. ………	0-0	1-0
3 Chester C. v Hartlepool U. ……	0-0	3-1
3 Exeter C. v Hull C. ………	0-0	3-0
3 Halifax T. v Cambridge U. ……	-	
3 Peterborough U. v Carlisle U. ……	-	
3 Rotherham U. v Rochdale ……	-	2-2
3 Shrewsbury T. v Swansea C. …	-	1-0
3 Southend U. v Mansfield T. ……	-	

Encounter	96-97	97-98
3 Torquay U. v Darlington	1-1	2-1

21st October 1998

2 Millwall v York C.	1-1	2-3
2 Reading v Blackpool	-	
3 Scarborough v Barnet	1-1	1-0

24th October 1998

1 Barnsley v Portsmouth	3-2	
1 Bradford C. v C. Palace	0-4	-
1 Bristol C. v Bolton W.	-	
1 Crewe Alex. v Tranmere R.	-	2-1
1 Norwich C. v Huddersfield T.	2-0	5-0
1 Oxford U. v Sheffield U.	4-1	2-3
1 QPR v Birmingham C.	1-1	1-1
1 Stockport Co. v Ipswich T.	-	0-1
1 Sunderland v Bury	-	2-1
1 Swindon T. v WBA	2-3	0-2
1 Watford v Port Vale	-	
1 Wolverhampton W. v Grimsby T.	1-1	
2 Blackpool v Chesterfield	0-1	2-1
2 Colchester U. v Bournemouth	-	
2 Fulham v Walsall	-	1-1
2 Gillingham v Luton T.	1-2	2-1
2 Macclesfield T. v Burnley	-	
2 Manchester C. v Reading	-	0-0
2 Northampton T. v Preston NE	-	2-2
2 Notts County v Bristol R.	1-1	
2 Oldham Ath. v Wycombe W.	-	0-1
2 Stoke C. v Wigan	-	
2 Wrexham v Millwall	3-3	1-0
2 York C. v Lincoln C.	-	
3 Barnet v Brighton & HA	3-0	2-0
3 Cambridge U. v Shrewsbury T.	-	4-3
3 Carlisle U. v Cardiff C.	0-2	-
3 Darlington v Exeter C.	0-1	3-2
3 Hartlepool U. v Torquay U.	1-1	3-0
3 Hull C. v Southend U.	-	
3 Leyton O. v Halifax T.	-	
3 Mansfield T. v Peterborough U.	-	2-0
3 Plymouth Ar. v Chester C.	-	
3 Rochdale v Scarborough	3-3	4-0
3 Scunthorpe U. v Rotherham U.	-	1-1
3 Swansea C. v Brentford	-	

31st October 1998

1 Birmingham C. v Huddersfield T.	1-0	0-0

Encounter	96-97	97-98
1 Bolton W. v Sunderland	-	-
1 Bradford C. v Bristol C.	-	-
1 Bury v Watford	-	-
1 Grimsby T. v Crystal P.	2-1	-
1 Ipswich T. v WBA	5-0	1-1
1 Oxford U. v Crewe Alex.	-	0-0
1 Port Vale v Sheffield U.	-	0-1
1 Portsmouth v Norwich C.	0-1	1-1
1 Swindon T. v QPR	1-1	3-1
1 Tranmere R. v Stockport Co.	-	3-0
1 Wolverhampton W. v Barnsley	3-3	
2 Blackpool v Fulham	-	2-1
2 Bournemouth v Preston NE	2-0	0-2
2 Bristol R. v Walsall	0-1	2-0
2 Burnley v Wrexham	2-0	1-2
2 Lincoln C. v Gillingham	-	
2 Luton T. v Chesterfield	0-1	3-0
2 Macclesfield T. v Northampton T.	-	
2 Manchester C. v Colchester U.	-	-
2 Millwall v Oldham Ath.	-	2-1
2 Notts County v Stoke C.	-	
2 Wigan v York	-	1-1
2 Wycombe W. v Reading	-	
3 Barnet v Rochdale	3-2	3-1
3 Brentford v Carlisle U.	-	0-1
3 Brighton & HA v Hartlepool U.	5-0	0-0
3 Cardiff C. v Exeter C.	2-1	1-1
3 Chester C. v Shrewsbury T.	-	2-0
3 Halifax T. v Swansea C.	-	
3 Leyton O. v Scunthorpe U.	0-1	1-0
3 Mansfield T. v Cambridge U.	1-0	3-2
3 Peterborough U. v Rotherham U.	6-2	1-0
3 Plymouth Ar. v Hull C.	-	
3 Scarborough v Torquay U.	3-1	4-1
3 Southend U. v Darlington	-	

7th November 1998

1 Barnsley v Bury	-	
1 Bristol C. v Wolverhampton W.	-	
1 Crewe Alex. v Swindon T.	-	2-0
1 C. Palace v Portsmouth	1-2	
1 Huddersfield T. v Ipswich T.	2-0	2-2
1 Norwich C. v Bradford C.	2-0	2-3
1 QPR v Bolton W.	1-2	
1 Sheffield U. v Tranmere R.	0-0	2-1
1 Stockport Co. v Port Vale	-	3-0
1 Sunderland v Grimsby T.	-	
1 Watford v Oxford U.	-	

308

Encounter	96-97	97-98
1 WBA v Birmingham C.	2-0	1-0
2 Chesterfield v Lincoln C.	-	-
2 Colchester U. v Macclesfield T.	-	-
2 Fulham v Bristol R.	-	1-0
2 Gillingham v Wigan	-	0-0
2 Northampton T. v Wycombe W.	-	2-0
2 Oldham Ath. v Manchester C.	1-0	-
2 Preston NE v Burnley	1-1	2-3
2 Reading v Bournemouth	-	-
2 Stoke C. v Luton T.	-	-
2 Walsall v Millwall	2-1	2-0
2 Wrexham v Blackpool	2-1	3-4
2 York C. v Notts County	1-2	-
3 Cambridge U. v Barnet	1-0	1-3
3 Carlisle U. v Halifax T.	-	-
3 Darlington v Brighton & HA	2-0	1-0
3 Exeter C. v Southend U.	-	-
3 Hartlepool U. v Plymouth Ar.	-	-
3 Hull C. v Leyton O.	3-1	3-2
3 Rochdale v Mansfield T.	0-1	2-0
3 Rotherham U. v Scarborough	-	0-0
3 Scunthorpe U. v Chester C.	0-2	2-1
3 Shrewsbury T. v Brentford	0-3	-
3 Swansea C. v Peterborough U.	-	0-1
3 Torquay U. v Cardiff C.	2-0	1-0

10th November 1998

Encounter	96-97	97-98
2 Bristol R. v Blackpool	0-0	0-3
2 Burnley v Stoke C.	-	-
2 Chesterfield v Bournemouth	1-1	1-1
2 Colchester U. v Northampton T.	0-0	-
2 Gillingham v Oldham Ath.	-	2-1
2 Luton T. v Notts County	2-0	-
2 Preston NE v Millwall	2-1	2-1
2 Walsall v Lincoln C.	-	-
2 Wrexham v Fulham	-	0-3
2 Wycombe W. v Manchester C.	-	-
2 York C. v Macclesfield T.	-	-
3 Barnet v Scunthorpe U.	1-1	0-1
3 Brentford v Southend U.	-	1-1
3 Cardiff C. v Scarborough	1-1	1-1
3 Darlington v Carlisle U.	2-1	-
3 Halifax T. v Chester C.	-	-
3 Hartlepool v Mansfield T.	2-2	2-2
3 Hull C. v Brighton & HA	3-0	0-0
3 Peterborough U. v Cambridge U.	-	1-0
3 Plymouth Ar. v Swansea C.	-	-
3 Rochdale v Exeter C.	2-0	3-0

Encounter	96-97	97-98
3 Rotherham U. v Torquay U.	-	0-1
3 Shrewsbury T. v Leyton O.	-	1-2

11th November 1998

Encounter	96-97	97-98
2 Reading v Wigan	-	-

14th November 1998

Encounter	96-97	97-98
1 Barnsley v Ipswich T.	1-2	-
1 Birmingham C. v Oxford U.	2-0	0-0
1 Bolton W. v Tranmere R.	1-0	-
1 Bradford C. v Swindon T.	2-1	1-1
1 Crewe Alex. v QPR	-	2-3
1 C. Palace v Bristol C.	-	-
1 Grimsby T. v Portsmouth	0-1	-
1 Norwich C. v Wolverhampton W.	1-0	0-2
1 Port Vale v Sunderland	-	3-1
1 Sheffield U. v Bury	-	3-0
1 Stockport Co. v Watford	1-0	-
1 WBA v Huddersfield T.	1-1	0-2

21st November 1998

Encounter	96-97	97-98
1 Bristol C. v Stockport Co.	1-1	-
1 Bury v Grimsby T.	-	-
1 Huddersfield T. v Bradford C.	3-3	1-2
1 Ipswich T. v Bolton W.	0-1	-
1 Oxford U. v Port Vale	0-2	2-0
1 Portsmouth v WBA	4-0	2-3
1 QPR v Sheffield U.	1-0	2-2
1 Sunderland v Barnsley	-	-
1 Swindon T. v C. Palace	0-2	-
1 Tranmere R. v Norwich C.	3-1	2-0
1 Watford v Crewe Alex.	0-1	-
1 W'hampton W. v Birmingham C.	1-2	1-3
2 Blackpool v Preston NE	2-1	2-1
2 Bournemouth v Burnley	0-0	2-1
2 Fulham v Chesterfield	-	1-1
2 Lincoln C. v Luton T.	-	-
2 Macclesfield U. v Walsall	-	-
2 Manchester C. v Gillingham	-	-
2 Millwall v Bristol R.	2-0	1-1
2 Northampton T. v Reading	-	-
2 Notts County v Colchester U.	-	-
2 Oldham Ath. v Wrexham	-	3-0
2 Stoke C. v York C.	-	-
2 Wigan v Wycombe W.	-	5-2
3 Brighton & HA v Halifax T.	-	-
3 Cambridge U. v Darlington	5-2	1-0
3 Carlisle U. v Rotherham U.	-	-

Encounter	96-97	97-98
3 Chester C. v Rochdale 0-0		4-0
3 Exeter C. v Shrewsbury T. .... -		2-2
3 Leyton O. v Brentford		
3 Mansfield T. v Barnet 0-0		1-1
3 Scarborough v Hartlepool U. ... 2-4		1-1
3 Scunthorpe U. v Hull C........... 2-2		2-0
3 Southend U. v Plymouth Ar. ... -		3-0
3 Swansea C. v Cardiff C........... 0-1		1-1
3 Torquay U. v Peterborough U. ... -		3-1

28th November 1998

Encounter	96-97	97-98
1 Barnsley v Huddersfield T...... 3-1		-
1 Birmingham C. v Bristol C.		-
1 Bolton W. v Bury		-
1 Bradford C. v QPR 3-0		1-1
1 Crewe Alex. v Ipswich T.		0-0
1 C. Palace v Watford		-
1 Grimsby T. v Swindon T.		-
1 Norwich C. v Oxford U. 1-1		2-1
1 Port Vale v Tranmere R. 2-1		0-1
1 Sheffield U. v Sunderland		2-0
1 Stockport Co. v Portsmouth		3-1
1 WBA v Wolverhampton W. ... 2-4		1-0
2 Bristol R. v Oldham Ath.		3-1
2 Burnley v Blackpool 2-0		1-2
2 Chesterfield v Macclesfield T. ... -		
2 Colchester U. v Millwall		-
2 Gillingham v Fulham		2-0
2 Luton T. v Manchester C.		-
2 Preston NE v Wigan...............		1-1
2 Reading v Lincoln C.		-
2 Walsall v Bournemouth 2-1		2-1
2 Wrexham v Notts County 3-3		-
2 Wycombe W. v Stoke C.		-
2 York C. v Northampton T.......		0-0
3 Barnet v Torquay U. 0-0		3-3
3 Brentford v Chester C.............		-
3 Cardiff C. v Southend C.		-
3 Darlington v Scarborough 1-1		1-2
3 Halifax T. v Mansfield T.		-
3 Hartlepool U. v Swansea C. ... 1-1		4-2
3 Hull C. v Carlisle U. 0-1		-
3 Peterborough U. v Scunthorpe U. ... -		0-1
3 Plymouth Ar. v Leyton O. .... -		
3 Rochdale v Cambridge U. 3-0		2-0
3 Rotherham U. v Exeter C.		1-0
3 Shrewsbury T. v Brighton & HA ... -		2-1

5th December 1998

Encounter	96-97	97-98
1 Bristol C. v Sheffield U.		-
1 Bury v WBA		1-3
1 Huddersfield T. v C. Palace ... 1-1		-
1 Ipswich T. v Birmingham C. ... 1-1		0-1
1 Oxford U. v Bradford C. 2-0		0-0
1 Portsmouth v Crewe Alex.......		-
1 QPR v Port Vale 1-2		0-1
1 Sunderland v Stockport Co. ...		4-1
1 Swindon T. v Norwich C. 0-3		1-0
1 Tranmere R. v Grimsby T. 3-2		-
1 Watford v Barnsley		-
1 Wolverhampton W. v Bolton W. 1-2		1-3

12th December 1998

Encounter	96-97	97-98
1 Bristol C. v C. Palace		-
1 Bury v Sheffield U.		1-1
1 Huddersfield T. v WBA......... 0-0		1-0
1 Ipswich T. v Barnsley 1-1		-
1 Oxford U. v Birmingham C. ... 0-0		0-2
1 Portsmouth v Grimsby T. 1-0		-
1 QPR v Crewe Alex.		3-2
1 Sunderland v Port Vale		4-2
1 Swindon T. v Bradford C. 2-2		-
1 Tranmere R. v Bolton W. 2-2		-
1 Watford v Stockport Co. 1-0		-
1 Wolverhampton W. v Norwich C. 3-2		5-0
2 Blackpool v Wycombe W. 0-0		2-4
2 Bournemouth v York C.......... 1-1		0-0
2 Fulham v Burnley		1-0
2 Lincoln C. v Colchester U. 3-2		-
2 Macclesfield T. v Luton T.		-
2 Manchester C. v Bristol R.......		-
2 Millwall v Reading		-
2 Northampton T. v Chesterfield ... -		0-0
2 Notts County v Preston NE.....		2-1
2 Oldham Ath. v Walsall		0-0
2 Stoke C. v Gillingham		-
2 Wigan v Wrexham		3-2
3 Brighton & HA v Rotherham U. ... -		1-2
3 Cambridge U. v Plymouth Ar. ... -		-
3 Carlisle U. v Hartlepool U. 1-0		-
3 Chester C. v Darlington 2-1		2-1
3 Exeter C. v Brentford		-
3 Leyton O. v Peterborough U. ... -		1-0
3 Mansfield T. v Shrewsbury T. ... -		1-1
3 Scarborough v Halifax T.		-
3 Scunthorpe U. v Cardiff C. 0-1		3-3

Encounter 96-97 97-98

3 Southend U. v Barnet ... ... - -
3 Swansea C. v Rochdale 2-1 3-0
3 Torquay U. v Hull C. 1-1 5-1

19th December 1998
1 Barnsley v Swindon T. ... ... 1-1 -
1 Birmingham C. v Sunderland ... ... - 0-1
1 Bolton W. v Portsmouth ... ... 2-0 -
1 Bradford C. v Wolverhampton W. 2-1 2-0
1 Crewe Alex. v Huddersfield T. ... - 2-5
1 C. Palace v QPR ... ... 3-0 -
1 Grimsby T. v Watford ... ... - 0-1
1 Norwich C. v Bristol C. ... ... - -
1 Port Vale v Bury ... ... - -
1 Sheffield U. v Ipswich T. 1-3 0-1
1 Stockport Co. v Oxford U. ... ... - 3-2
1 WBA v Tranmere R. 1-2 2-1

2 Bristol R. v Macclesfield T. ... ... - -
2 Burnley v Northampton T. ... ... - 2-1
2 Chesterfield v Wigan ... ... - 2-3
2 Colchester U. v Blackpool ... ... - -
2 Gillingham v Notts County ... ... 1-0 -
2 Luton T. v Millwall 0-2 0-2
2 Preston NE v Fulham ... ... - 3-1
2 Reading v Oldham Ath. ... ... 2-1 -
2 Walsall v Stoke C. ... ... - -
2 Wrexham v Bournemouth 2-0 2-1
2 Wycombe W. v Lincoln C. ... ... - -
2 York C. v Manchester C. ... ... - -

3 Barnet v Leyton O. 3-0 1-2
3 Brentford v Cambridge U. ... ... - -
3 Cardiff C. v Mansfield T. 1-2 4-1
3 Darlington v Scunthorpe U. 2-0 1-0
3 Halifax T. v Exeter C. ... ... - -
3 Hartlepool U. v Southend U. ... ... - -
3 Hull C. v Swansea C. 1-1 7-4
3 Peterborough U. v Scarborough ... - 0-0
3 Plymouth Ar. v Carlisle U. ... ... - 2-1
3 Rochdale v Brighton & HA ... 3-0 2-0
3 Rotherham U. v Chester C. ... ... - 4-2
3 Shrewsbury T. v Torquay U. ... ... - 1-2

26th December 1998
1 Birmingham C. v Sheffield U. ... 1-1 2-0
1 Bolton W. v Bradford C. ... ... 2-1 -
1 Crewe Alex. v Bury ... ... - 1-2
1 Huddersfield T. v Grimsby T. ... 2-0 -
1 Ipswich T. v Portsmouth 1-1 2-0

Encounter 96-97 97-98

1 Oxford U. v C. Palace ... ... 1-4 -
1 QPR v Norwich C. 3-2 1-1
1 Stockport Co. v Barnsley ... ... - -
1 Swindon T. v Wolverhampton W. 1-2 0-0
1 Tranmere R. v Sunderland ... ... - 0-2
1 Watford v Bristol C. ... ... - 1-1
1 WBA v Port Vale 1-1 2-2

2 Blackpool v Wigan ... ... - 0-2
2 Bristol R. v Gillingham 0-0 2-1
2 Chesterfield v Oldham Ath. ... ... - 2-1
2 Fulham v Colchester U. ... ... 3-1 -
2 Lincoln C. v Macclesfield T. ... ... - -
2 Lincoln C. v Macclesfield T. ... ... - -
2 Luton T. v Reading ... ... - -
2 Millwall v Bournemouth 0-1 1-2
2 Notts County v Northampton T. ... - -
2 Stoke C. v Preston NE ... ... - -
2 Walsall v Wycombe W. 2-2 0-1
2 Wrexham v Manchester C. ... ... - -
2 York C. v Burnley 1-0 3-1

3 Barnet v Plymouth Ar. ... ... - -
3 Brighton & HA v Brentford ... ... - -
3 Cambridge U. v Rotherham U. ... - 2-1
3 Cardiff C. v Shrewsbury T. ... ... - 2-2
3 Exeter C. v Torquay U. 1-1 1-1
3 Halifax T. v Darlington ... ... - -
3 Hull C. v Chester C. 1-0 1-0
3 Leyton O. v Swansea C. 1-0 2-2
3 Mansfield T. v Scarborough ... 2-0 3-2
3 Rochdale v Carlisle U. ... ... 2-2 -
3 Scunthorpe U. v Hartlepool U. ... 2-1 1-1
3 Southend U. v Peterborough U. ... - -

28th December 1998
1 Barnsley v QPR ... ... 1-3 -
1 Bradford C. v Tranmere R. 1-0 0-1
1 Bristol C. v Swindon T. ... ... - -
1 Bury v Birmingham C. ... ... - 2-1
1 C. Palace v WBA ... ... 0-0 -
1 Grimsby T. v Stockport Co. ... ... - -
1 Norwich C. v Watford ... ... - -
1 Port Vale v Bolton W. ... ... 1-1 -
1 Portsmouth v Oxford U. 2-1 2-1
1 Sheffield U. v Huddersfield T. ... 3-1 1-1
1 Sunderland v Crewe Alex. ... ... - 2-1
1 Wolverhampton W. v Ipswich T. 0-0 1-1

2 Bournemouth v Luton T. 3-2 1-1
2 Burnley v Lincoln C. ... ... - -

Encounter	96-97	97-98
2 Colchester U. v Bristol R.	-	-
2 Gillingham v Millwall	2-3	1-3
2 Macclesfield T. v Blackpool	-	-
2 Manchester C. v Stoke C.	-	0-1
2 Northampton T. v Fulham	0-1	1-0
2 Oldham Ath. v York C.	-	3-1
2 Preston NE v Wrexham	2-1	0-1
2 Reading v Notts County	-	-
2 Wigan v Walsall	-	2-0
2 Wycombe W. v Chesterfield	1-0	1-1
3 Brentford v Cardiff C.	-	-
3 Carlisle U. v Cambridge U.	3-0	-
3 Chester C. v Mansfield T.	1-0	0-1
3 Darlington v Leyton O.	1-1	1-0
3 Hartlepool U. v Rochdale	1-2	2-0
3 Peterborough U. v Brighton & HA	-	1-2
3 Plymouth Ar. v Exeter C.	-	-
3 Rotherham U. v Halifax T.	-	-
3 Scarborough v Scunthorpe U.	3-2	0-0
3 Shrewsbury T. v Hull C.	-	2-0
3 Swansea C. v Barnet	3-0	0-2
3 Torquay U. v Southend U.	-	-

2nd January 1999

	96-97	97-98
2 Bournemouth v Fulham	-	2-1
2 Burnley v Walsall	2-1	2-1
2 Colchester U. v Luton T.	-	-
2 Gillingham v Blackpool	2-3	1-1
2 Macclesfield T. v Millwall	-	-
2 Manchester C. v Notts County	-	-
2 Northampton T. v Wrexham	-	0-1
2 Oldham Ath. v Stoke C.	1-2	-
2 Preston NE v Lincoln C.	-	-
2 Reading v Chesterfield	-	-
2 Wigan v Bristol R.	-	3-0
2 Wycombe W. v York C.	3-1	1-0
3 Brentford v Barnet	-	-
3 Carlisle U. v Exeter C.	2-0	-
3 Chester C. v Southend U.	-	-
3 Darlington v Rochdale	-	1-0
3 Hartlepool U. v Cambridge U.	0-2	3-3
3 Peterborough U. v Hull C.	-	2-0
3 Plymouth Ar. v Scunthorpe U.	-	-
3 Rotherham U. v Cardiff C.	-	1-1
3 Scarborough v Leyton O.	2-1	2-0
3 Shrewsbury T. v Halifax T.	-	-
3 Swansea C. v Mansfield T.	3-2	0-1
3 Torquay U. v Brighton & HA	2-1	3-0

9th January 1999

	96-97	97-98
1 Birmingham C. v Port Vale	1-2	1-1
1 Bolton W. v C. Palace	2-2	5-2
1 Crewe Alex. v Norwich C.	-	1-0
1 Huddersfield T. v Bury	-	2-0
1 Ipswich T. v Grimsby T.	1-1	-
1 Oxford U. v Bristol C.	-	-
1 QPR v Sunderland	-	0-1
1 Stockport Co. v Bradford C.	-	1-2
1 Swindon T. v Sheffield U.	2-1	1-0
1 Tranmere R. v Wolverhampton W.	0-2	2-1
1 Watford v Portsmouth	-	-
1 WBA v Barnsley	1-2	-
2 Blackpool v Manchester C.	-	-
2 Bristol R. v Burnley	1-2	1-0
2 Chesterfield v Colchester U.	-	-
2 Fulham v Macclesfield T.	-	-
2 Lincoln C. v Bournemouth	-	-
2 Luton T. v Wycombe W.	0-0	0-0
2 Millwall v Wigan	-	1-1
2 Notts County v Oldham Ath.	-	-
2 Stoke C. v Northampton T.	-	-
2 Walsall v Gillingham	1-0	1-0
2 Wrexham v Reading	-	-
2 York C. v Preston NE	3-1	1-0
3 Barnet v Darlington	0-0	2-0
3 Brighton & HA v Carlisle U.	1-3	-
3 Cambridge U. v Torquay U.	2-0	1-1
3 Cardiff C. v Hartlepool U.	2-0	1-1
3 Exeter C. v Swansea C.	1-2	1-0
3 Halifax T. v Peterborough U.	-	-
3 Hull C. v Rotherham U.	-	0-0
3 Leyton O. v Chester C.	0-0	1-0
3 Mansfield T. v Brentford	-	-
3 Rochdale v Plymouth Ar.	-	-
3 Scunthorpe U. v Shrewsbury T.	-	1-1
3 Southend U. v Scarborough	-	-

16th January 1999

	96-97	97-98
1 Barnsley v Birmingham C.	0-1	-
1 Bradford C. v Crewe Alex.	-	1-0
1 Bristol C. v Tranmere R.	-	-
1 Bury v QPR	-	1-1
1 C. Palace v Stockport Co.	-	-
1 Grimsby T. v Oxford U.	0-2	-
1 Norwich C. v WBA	2-4	1-1
1 Port Vale v Swindon T.	1-0	0-1
1 Portsmouth v Huddersfield T.	3-1	3-0

Encounter 96-97 97-98

1 Sheffield U. v Bolton W. ...... 1-1 -
1 Sunderland v Ipswich T. .... - 2-2
1 Wolverhampton W. v Watford ... - -

2 Bournemouth v Notts County ... 0-1 -
2 Burnley v Chesterfield 0-0 0-0
2 Colchester U. v Wrexham ...... - -
2 Gillingham v York C. 0-1 0-0
2 Macclesfield T. v Stoke C. ...... - -
2 Manchester C. v Fulham ...... - -
2 Northampton T. v Walsall ...... - 3-2
2 Oldham Ath. v Blackpool ...... - 0-1
2 Preston NE v Luton T. 3-2 1-0
2 Reading v Bristol R. .... - -
2 Wigan v Lincoln C. .... 1-0 -
2 Wycombe W. v Millwall 1-0 0-0

3 Brentford v Halifax T. .... - -
3 Carlisle U. v Scunthorpe U. ...... 3-2 -
3 Chester C. v Brighton & HA 2-1 2-0
3 Darlington v Hull C. 1-0 4-3
3 Hartlepool U. v Barnet .... 4-0 -
3 Peterborough U. v Cardiff C. ...... - 2-0
3 Plymouth Ar. v Mansfield T. ...... - -
3 Rotherham U. v Leyton O. ...... - 2-1
3 Scarborough v Exeter C. 3-4 4-1
3 Shrewsbury T. v Southend U. ...... - -
3 Swansea C. v Cambridge U. 3-1 1-1
3 Torquay U. v Rochdale 0-1 0-0

23rd January 1999

2 Blackpool v Bournemouth 1-1 1-0
2 Bristol R. v Wycombe W. 3-4 3-1
2 Chesterfield v Preston NE 2-1 3-2
2 Fulham v Oldham Ath. .... - 3-1
2 Lincoln C. v Northampton T. ...... 1-1 -
2 Luton T. v Wigan .... - 1-1
2 Millwall v Burnley 2-1 1-0
2 Notts County v Macclesfield T. ... - -
2 Stoke C. v Colchester U. ...... - -
2 Walsall v Manchester C. ...... - -
2 Wrexham v Gillingham 1-1 0-0
2 York C. v Reading .... - -

3 Barnet v Shrewsbury T. .... - 1-1
3 Brighton & HA v Scarborough ... - 1-1
3 Cambridge U. v Chester C. 2-2 1-2
3 Cardiff C. v Darlington 2-0 0-0
3 Exeter C. v Peterborough U. ...... - 0-0
3 Halifax T. v Plymouth Ar. ...... - -
3 Hull C. v Hartlepool U. 1-0 2-1

Encounter 96-97 97-98

3 Leyton O. v Torquay U. 1-0 2-1
3 Mansfield T. v Rotherham U. ...... - 3-3
3 Rochdale v Brentford .... - -
3 Scunthorpe U. v Swansea C. 1-0 1-0
3 Southend U. v Carlisle U. ...... - 1-1

27th January 1999
1 Bolton W. v Crewe Alex. .... - -

30th January 1999
1 Birmingham C. v Bradford C. ... 3-0 0-0
1 Bolton W. v Norwich C. .... 3-1 -
1 Crewe Alex. v Sheffield U. ...... - 2-1
1 Huddersfield T. v Bristol C. ...... - -
1 Ipswich T. v Port Vale 2-1 5-1
1 Oxford U. v Barnsley .... 5-1 -
1 QPR v Portsmouth 2-1 1-0
1 Stockport Co. v Wolverhampton W. - -
1 Swindon T. v Bury .... - 3-1
1 Tranmere R. v C. Palace ...... - 1-3
1 Watford v Sunderland .... - -
1 WBA v Grimsby T. .... 2-0 -

2 Blackpool v Macclesfield T. ...... - -
2 Bristol R. v Colchester U. ...... - -
2 Chesterfield v Wycombe W. 4-2 1-0
2 Fulham v Northampton T. 0-1 1-1
2 Lincoln C. v Burnley .... - -
2 Luton T. v Bournemouth 2-0 1-2
2 Millwall v Gillingham 0-2 1-0
2 Notts County v Reading ...... - -
2 Stoke C. v Manchester C. 2-1 2-5
2 Walsall v Wigan .... - 1-0
2 Wrexham v Preston NE 1-0 0-0
2 York C. v Oldham Ath. .... - 0-0

3 Barnet v Swansea C. 1-0 2-0
3 Brighton & HA v Peterborough U. - 2-2
3 Cambridge U. v Carlisle U. ...... 1-3 -
3 Cardiff C. v Brentford .... - -
3 Exeter C. v Plymouth Ar. ...... - -
3 Halifax T. v Rotherham U. ...... - -
3 Hull C. v Shrewsbury T. .... - 1-4
3 Leyton O. v Darlington 0-0 2-0
3 Mansfield T. v Chester C. 0-2 4-1
3 Rochdale v Hartlepool U. 1-3 2-1
3 Scunthorpe U. v Scarborough ... 0-2 1-3
3 Southend U. v Torquay U. ...... - -

6th February 1999
1 Barnsley v Crewe Alex. .... - -

Encounter	96-97	97-98
1 Bradford C. v Watford	-	-
1 Bristol C. v QPR	-	-
1 Bury v Ipswich T.	-	0-1
1 C. Palace v Birmingham C.	0-1	-
1 Grimsby T. v Bolton W.	1-2	-
1 Norwich C. v Stockport Co.	-	1-1
1 Port Vale v Huddersfield T.	0-0	4-1
1 Portsmouth v Tranmere R.	1-3	1-0
1 Sheffield U. v WBA	1-2	2-4
1 Sunderland v Swindon T.	-	0-0
1 Wolverhampton W. v Oxford U.	3-1	1-0
2 Bournemouth v Stoke C.	-	-
2 Burnley v Luton T.	0-2	1-1
2 Colchester U. v York C.	-	-
2 Gillingham v Chesterfield	0-1	1-0
2 Macclesfield T. v Wrexham	-	-
2 Manchester C. v Millwall	-	-
2 Northampton T. v Blackpool	-	2-0
2 Oldham Ath. v Lincoln C.	-	-
2 Preston NE v Bristol R.	0-0	1-2
2 Reading v Walsall	-	-
2 Wigan v Notts County	-	-
2 Wycombe W. v Fulham	-	2-0
3 Brentford v Hull C.	-	-
3 Carlisle U. v Leyton O.	1-0	-
3 Chester C. v Exeter C.	2-1	1-1
3 Darlington v Mansfield T.	2-4	0-0
3 Hartlepool U. v Halifax T.	-	-
3 Peterborough U. v Barnet	-	5-1
3 Plymouth Ar. v Cardiff C.	-	-
3 Rotherham U. v Southend U.	-	-
3 Scarborough v Cambridge U.	1-0	1-0
3 Shrewsbury T. v Rochdale	-	1-0
3 Swansea C. v Brighton & HA	1-0	1-0
3 Torquay U. v Scunthorpe U.	1-2	2-4

13th February 1999

Encounter	96-97	97-98
1 Bolton W. v WBA	1-0	-
1 Bradford C. v Ipswich T.	2-1	2-1
1 Bristol C. v Sunderland	-	-
1 C. Palace v Crewe Alex.	-	-
1 Grimsby T. v Sheffield U.	2-4	-
1 Norwich C. v Barnsley	1-1	-
1 Oxford U. v Swindon T.	2-0	2-1
1 Portsmouth v Bury	-	1-1
1 Stockport Co. v Birmingham C.	-	2-2
1 Tranmere R. v QPR	2-3	2-1
1 Watford v Huddersfield T.	-	-

Encounter	96-97	97-98
1 Wolverhampton W. v Port Vale	0-1	1-1
2 Bournemouth v Manchester C.	-	-
2 Burnley v Reading	-	-
2 Chesterfield v Bristol R.	1-0	0-0
2 Colchester U. v Wigan	3-1	-
2 Lincoln C. v Millwall	-	-
2 Luton T. v Wrexham	0-0	2-5
2 Macclesfield T. v Oldham Ath.	-	-
2 Northampton T. v Gillingham	-	2-1
2 Notts County v Blackpool	1-1	-
2 Preston NE v Wycombe W.	2-1	1-1
2 Stoke C. v Fulham	-	-
2 York C. v Walsall	0-2	1-0
3 Barnet v Cardiff C.	3-1	2-2
3 Brentford v Torquay U.	-	-
3 Brighton & HA v Exeter C.	1-0	1-3
3 Cambridge U. v Scunthorpe U.	0-2	2-2
3 Chester C. v Peterborough U.	-	0-0
3 Halifax T. v Southend U.	-	-
3 Hartlepool U. v Darlington	1-2	2-2
3 Mansfield T. v Leyton O.	0-2	0-0
3 Plymouth Ar. v Rotherham U.	1-0	-
3 Rochdale v Hull C.	1-2	2-1
3 Shrewsbury T. v Scarborough	-	0-1
3 Swansea C. v Carlisle U.	0-1	-

20th February 1999

Encounter	96-97	97-98
1 Barnsley v Grimsby T.	1-3	-
1 Birmingham C. v Bolton W.	3-1	-
1 Bury v Norwich C.	-	1-0
1 Crewe Alex. v Stockport Co.	1-0	0-1
1 Huddersfield T. v Tranmere R.	0-1	3-0
1 Ipswich T. v Oxford U.	1-1	5-2
1 Port Vale v C. Palace	0-2	-
1 QPR v Watford	-	-
1 Sheffield U. v Bradford C.	3-0	2-1
1 Sunderland v Wolverhampton W.	-	1-1
1 Swindon T. v Portsmouth	0-1	0-1
1 WBA v Bristol C.	-	-
2 Blackpool v Lincoln C.	-	-
2 Bristol R. v Luton T.	3-2	2-1
2 Fulham v Notts County	-	-
2 Gillingham v Colchester U.	-	-
2 Manchester C. v Macclesfield T.	-	-
2 Millwall v Stoke C.	-	-
2 Oldham Ath. v Northampton T.	-	2-2
2 Reading v Preston NE	-	-
2 Walsall v Chesterfield	1-1	3-2

Encounter	96-97	97-98
2 Wigan v Bournemouth … … … -		1-0
2 Wrexham v York C. … … … 0-0		1-2
2 Wycombe W. v Burnley	5-0	2-1
3 Cardiff C. v Halifax T. … … … -		
3 Carlisle U. v Mansfield T. … … 1-1		
3 Darlington v Plymouth Ar. … … -		
3 Exeter C. v Hartlepool U.	2-0	1-1
3 Hull C. v Barnet … … … … 0-0		0-2
3 Leyton O. v Cambridge U. … … -		0-2
3 Peterborough U. v Shrewsbury T. 1-1		
3 Rotherham v Brentford … … 0-1		
3 Scarborough v Swansea C. … … 0-1		3-2
3 Scunthorpe U. v Rochdale … … 2-2		2-0
3 Southend U. v Brighton & HA … -		
3 Torquay U. v Chester C. … 0-0		3-1

27th February 1999

1 Bradford C. v WBA … … 1-1		0-0
1 Bristol C. v Ipswich T. … … … -		
1 C. Palace v Barnsley … … … 1-0		0-1
1 Grimsby T. v Birmingham C. … 1-2		
1 Norwich C. v Sheffield U. … 1-1		2-1
1 Oxford U. v Sunderland … … … -		1-1
1 Portsmouth v Port Vale … … 1-1		3-1
1 Stockport Co. v QPR … … … -		2-0
1 Tranmere R. v Bury … … … -		0-0
1 Watford v Swindon T. … … … -		
1 Wolverhampton W. v Huddersfield 0-0		1-1
1 Bournemouth v Wycombe W. … 2-1		0-0
1 Burnley v Gillingham … … 5-1		
2 Chesterfield v Manchester C. … -		
2 Colchester U. v Reading … … -		
2 Lincoln C. v Bristol R. … … … -		
2 Luton T. v Blackpool	1-0	3-0
2 Macclesfield v Wigan … … … -		
2 Northampton T. v Millwall … -		2-0
2 Notts County v Walsall … … 2-0		
2 Preston NE v Oldham Ath. … 1-1		
2 Stoke C. v Wrexham … … … -		
2 York C. v Fulham … … … -		0-1
3 Barnet v Exeter C. … … 3-0		1-2
3 Brentford v Scarborough … … -		
3 Brighton & HA v Leyton O. … 4-4		0-1
3 Cambridge U. v Southend U. … -		
3 Chester C. v Carlisle U. … … 1-1		
3 Halifax T. v Hull C. … … … -		
3 Hartlepool U. v Rotherham U. … -		0-0
3 Mansfield T. v Scunthorpe U. … 2-0		1-0

Encounter	96-97	97-98
3 Plymouth Ar. v Peterborough U. 1-1		-
3 Rochdale v Cardiff C. … … 1-0		0-0
3 Shrewsbury T. v Darlington … -		3-0
3 Swansea C. v Torquay U. … … 2-0		2-0

2nd March 1999

1 Barnsley v Bradford C. … … 2-0		
1 Birmingham C. v Norwich C. … 2-3		1-2
1 Bury v Wolverhampton W. … -		1-3
1 Crewe Alex. v Bristol C. … … 1-2		
1 Huddersfield T. v Bolton W. … 1-2		
1 Ipswich T. v Watford … … … -		
1 Port Vale v Grimsby T. … … 1-1		
1 Sheffield U. v C. Palace … … 3-0		
1 Sunderland v Portsmouth … … -		2-1
1 WBA v Stockport Co. … … … -		3-2

3rd March 1999

| 1 QPR v Oxford U. … … … 2-1 | | 1-1 |
| 1 Swindon T. v Tranmere R. … 2-1 | | 2-1 |

6th March 1999

1 Barnsley v Bristol C. … … … -		
1 Birmingham C. v Portsmouth … 0-3		2-1
1 Bury v C. Palace … … … -		
1 Crewe Alex. v Grimsby T. … … -		
1 Huddersfield T. v Stockport Co. … -		1-0
1 Ipswich T. v Tranmere R. … 0-2		0-0
1 Port Vale v Bradford C. … 1-1		0-0
1 QPR v Wolverhampton W. … 2-2		0-0
1 Sheffield U. v Watford … … … -		
1 Sunderland v Norwich C. … … -		0-1
1 Swindon T. v Bolton W. … … -		
1 WBA v Oxford U. … … 3-3		1-2
2 Blackpool v Stoke C. … … … -		
2 Bristol R. v York C. … … 1-1		1-2
2 Fulham v Lincoln C. … … 1-2		
2 Gillingham v Preston NE … 1-1		0-0
2 Manchester C. v Northampton T. … -		
2 Millwall v Notts County … 1-0		
2 Oldham Ath. v Bournemouth … -		2-1
2 Reading v Macclesfield T. … … -		
2 Walsall v Luton T. … … 3-2		2-3
2 Wigan v Burnley … … … -		5-1
2 Wrexham v Chesterfield … 3-2		0-0
2 Wycombe W. v Colchester U. … -		
3 Cardiff C. v Chester C. … … 1-0		0-2
3 Carlisle U. v Shrewsbury T. … -		

Encounter	96-97	97-98
3 Darlington v Brentford ... ... -		
3 Exeter C. v Cambridge U. ... 0-1		1-0
3 Hull C. v Mansfield T. 1-1		0-0
3 Leyton O. v Rochdale 2-1		2-0
3 Peterborough U. v Hartlepool U. ... -		0-0
3 Rotherham U. v Barnet ... ... -		2-3
3 Scarborough v Plymouth Ar. ... ... -		-
3 Scunthorpe U. v Brighton & HA 1-0		0-2
3 Southend U. v Swansea C. ... ... -		-
3 Torquay U. v Halifax T. ... ... -		-

9th March 1999

1 Bolton W. v Barnsley 2-2		1-1
1 Bradford C. v Sunderland ... ... -		0-4
1 Bristol C. v Bury 1-0		-
1 C. Palace v Ipswich T. 0-0		-
1 Grimsby T. v QPR 2-0		-
1 Norwich C. v Port Vale ... 1-1		1-0
1 Oxford U. v Huddersfield T. ... 1-0		2-0
1 Portsmouth v Sheffield U. ... 1-1		1-1
1 Stockport Co. v Swindon T. ... -		4-2
1 Tranmere R. v Birmingham C. 1-0		0-3
1 Watford v WBA ... ... -		-
1 Wolverhampton W. v Crewe Alex. -		1-0

2 Bournemouth v Bristol R. 1-0		1-1
2 Burnley v Manchester C. ... ... -		-
2 Chesterfield v Millwall 1-0		3-1
2 Colchester U. v Oldham Ath. ... ... -		-
2 Lincoln v Wrexham ... ... -		-
2 Luton T. v Fulham ... ... -		1-4
2 Macclesfield T. v Gillingham ... ... -		-
2 Northampton T. v Wigan ... 0-1		1-0
2 Notts County v Wycombe W. ... 1-2		-
2 Preston NE v Walsall 2-0		0-0
2 York C. v Blackpool 1-0		1-1
2 Barnet v Carlisle U. 0-0		-

3 Brentford v Peterborough U. ... ... -		0-1
3 Brighton & HA v Cardiff C. ... 2-0		0-1
3 Cambridge U. v Hull C. 1-0		0-1
3 Chester C. v Scarborough 1-0		1-1
3 Halifax T. v Scunthorpe U. ... ... -		-
3 Hartlepool U. v Leyton O. ... 3-1		2-2
3 Mansfield T. v Exeter C. 0-1		3-2
3 Plymouth Ar. v Torquay U. ... ... -		-
3 Rochdale v Southend U. ... ... -		-
3 Shrewsbury T. v Rotherham U. 0-2		2-1
3 Swansea C. v Darlington 1-1		4-0

Encounter	96-97	97-98

10th March 1999

1 Bradford C. v Portsmouth 3-1		1-3
2 Stoke C. v Reading 1-1		1-2

13th March 1999

1 Birmingham C. v WBA 2-3		1-0
1 Bolton W. v QPR 2-1		-
1 Bradford C. v Norwich C. ... 0-2		2-1
1 Bury v Barnsley ... ... -		-
1 Grimsby T. v Sunderland ... ... -		-
1 Ipswich T. v Huddersfield T. ... 1-3		5-1
1 Oxford U. v Watford ... ... -		-
1 Port Vale v Stockport Co. ... ... -		2-1
1 Portsmouth v C. Palace 2-2		-
1 Swindon T. v Crewe Alex. ... ... -		2-0
1 Tranmere R. v Sheffield U. ... 1-1		3-3
1 Wolverhampton W. v Bristol C. ... -		-

2 Blackpool v Wrexham 3-3		1-2
2 Bournemouth v Reading ... ... -		-
2 Bristol R. v Fulham ... ... -		2-3
2 Burnley v Preston NE ... 1-2		1-1
2 Lincoln v Chesterfield ... ... -		-
2 Luton T. v Stoke C. ... ... -		-
2 Macclesfield T. v Colchester U. ... -		0-0
2 Manchester C. v Oldham Ath. ... ... -		-
2 Millwall v Walsall 1-0		0-1
2 Notts County v York C. 0-1		-
2 Wigan v Gillingham ... ... -		1-4
2 Wycombe W. v Northampton T. ... -		0-0

3 Barnet v Cambridge U. 2-1		2-0
3 Brentford v Shrewsbury T. 0-0		-
3 Brighton & HA v Darlington ... 2-3		0-0
3 Cardiff C. v Torquay U. 2-0		1-1
3 Chester C. v Scunthorpe U. ... 1-0		1-0
3 Halifax T. v Carlisle U. ... ... -		-
3 Leyton O. v Hull C. 1-1		2-1
3 Mansfield T. v Rochdale 0-0		3-0
3 Peterborough U. v Swansea C. ... -		3-1
3 Plymouth Ar. v Hartlepool U. ... -		-
3 Scarborough v Rotherham U. ... -		1-2
3 Southend U. v Exeter C.		

20th March 1999

1 Barnsley v Wolverhampton W. 1-3		-
1 Bristol C. v Bradford C. ... ... -		-
1 Crewe Alex. v Oxford U. ... ... -		2-1
1 C. Palace v Grimsby T. 3-0		-
1 Huddersfield T. v Birmingham C. 3-0		0-1

Encounter	96-97	97-98
1 Norwich C. v Portsmouth	1-0	2-0
1 QPR v Swindon T.	1-1	1-2
1 Sheffield U. v Port Vale	3-0	2-1
1 Stockport Co. v Tranmere R.		3-1
1 Sunderland v Bolton W.		1-1
1 Watford v Bury	0-0	-
1 WBA v Ipswich T.	0-0	2-3
2 Chesterfield v Luton T.	1-1	0-0
2 Colchester U. v Manchester C.	-	
2 Fulham v Blackpool		1-0
2 Gillingham v Lincoln C.		
2 Northampton T. v Macclesfield T.	-	
2 Oldham Ath. v Millwall		1-1
2 Preston NE v Bournemouth	0-1	0-1
2 Reading v Wycombe W.		
2 Stoke C. v Notts County		
2 Walsall v Bristol R.	1-0	0-1
2 Wrexham v Burnley	0-0	0-0
2 York C. v Wigan		2-2
3 Cambridge U. v Mansfield T.	2-1	2-0
3 Carlisle U. v Brentford		1-2
3 Darlington v Southend U.		
3 Exeter C. v Cardiff C.	2-0	1-1
3 Hartlepool U. v Brighton & HA	2-3	0-0
3 Hull C. v Plymouth Ar.		
3 Rochdale v Barnet	1-1	2-1
3 Rotherham U. v Peterborough U.	2-0	2-2
3 Scunthorpe U. v Leyton O.	1-0	1-0
3 Shrewsbury T. v Chester C.		1-1
3 Swansea C. v Halifax T.		
3 Torquay U. v Scarborough	1-0	1-0

27th March 1999

Encounter	96-97	97-98
1 Birmingham C. v QPR	0-0	1-0
1 Bolton W. v Bristol C.		
1 Bury v Sunderland		1-1
1 C. Palace v Bradford C.	3-1	
1 Grimsby T. v Wolverhampton W.	1-3	
1 Huddersfield T. v Norwich C.	2-0	1-3
1 Ipswich T. v Stockport Co.		0-2
1 Port Vale v Watford		
1 Portsmouth v Barnsley	4-2	
1 Sheffield U. v Oxford U.	3-1	1-0
1 Tranmere R. v Crewe Alex.		0-3
1 WBA v Swindon T.	1-2	0-0
2 Bournemouth v Colchester U.	-	
2 Bristol R. v Notts County	1-0	
2 Burnley v Macclesfield T.	-	
2 Chesterfield v Blackpool	0-0	1-1
2 Lincoln C. v York C.		
2 Luton T. v Gillingham	2-1	2-2
2 Millwall v Wrexham	1-1	0-1
2 Preston NE v Northampton T.		1-0
2 Reading v Manchester C.	2-1	3-0
2 Walsall v Fulham		1-1
2 Wigan v Stoke C.		
2 Wycombe W. v Oldham Ath.	-	2-1
3 Brentford v Swansea C.		
3 Brighton & HA v Barnet	1-0	0-3
3 Cardiff C. v Carlisle U.	2-0	
3 Chester C. v Plymouth Ar.	-	
3 Exeter C. v Darlington	3-2	1-0
3 Halifax T. v Leyton O.		
3 Peterborough U. v Mansfield T.		1-1
3 Rotherham U. v Scunthorpe U.		1-3
3 Scarborough v Rochdale	2-2	1-0
3 Shrewsbury T. v Cambridge U.		1-1
3 Southend U. v Hull C.		
3 Torquay U. v Hartlepool U.	0-1	1-0

3rd April 1999

Encounter	96-97	97-98
1 Barnsley v Sheffield U.	2-0	
1 Bradford C. v Grimsby T.	3-4	
1 Bristol C. v Port Vale		
1 Crewe Alex. v Birmingham C.		0-2
1 Norwich C. v C. Palace	1-1	
1 Oxford U. v Bolton W.	0-0	
1 QPR v Huddersfield T.	2-0	2-1
1 Stockport Co. v Bury	2-1	0-0
1 Sunderland v WBA		2-0
1 Swindon T. v Ipswich T.	0-4	0-2
1 Watford v Tranmere R.		
1 Wolverhampton W. v Portsmouth	0-1	2-0
2 Blackpool v Walsall	2-1	1-0
2 Colchester U. v Preston NE	-	
2 Fulham v Millwall		1-2
2 Gillingham v Reading		
2 Macclesfield T. v Wycombe W.	-	
2 Manchester C. v Wigan		
2 Northampton T. v Bournemouth	-	0-2
2 Notts County v Burnley	1-1	
2 Oldham Ath. v Luton T.		2-1
2 Stoke C. v Lincoln C.		
2 Wrexham v Bristol R.	1-0	1-0
2 York C. v Chesterfield	0-0	0-1

Encounter	96-97	97-98
3 Barnet v Halifax T.	-	-
3 Cambridge U. v Cardiff C.	0-2	2-2
3 Carlisle U. v Torquay U.	5-1	-
3 Darlington v Rotherham U.	-	1-1
3 Hartlepool U. v Brentford	-	-
3 Hull C. v Scarborough	0-2	3-0
3 Leyton O. v Southend U.	-	-
3 Mansfield T. v Brighton & HA	1-1	1-1
3 Plymouth Ar. v Shrewsbury T.	-	-
3 Rochdale v Peterborough U.	-	1-2
3 Scunthorpe U. v Exeter C.	4-1	2-1
3 Swansea C. v Chester C.	2-1	2-0

5th April 1999

Encounter	96-97	97-98
1 Birmingham v Watford	-	-
1 Bolton W. v Stockport Co.	-	-
1 Bury v Bradford C.	-	2-0
1 C. Palace v Sunderland	-	-
1 Grimsby T. v Norwich C.	1-4	-
1 Huddersfield T. v Swindon T.	-	0-0
1 Ipswich T. v QPR	2-0	0-0
1 Port Vale v Barnsley	-	1-3
1 Portsmouth v Bristol C.	-	-
1 Sheffield U. v Wolverhampton W.	2-3	1-0
1 Tranmere R. v Oxford U.	0-0	0-1
1 WBA v Crewe Alex.	-	0-1
2 Bournemouth v Macclesfield T.	-	-
2 Bristol R. v Northampton T.	-	0-2
2 Burnley v Colchester U.	-	-
2 Chesterfield v Stoke C.	-	-
2 Lincoln C. v Notts County	-	-
2 Luton T. v York C.	2-0	3-0
2 Millwall v Blackpool	2-1	2-1
2 Preston NE v Manchester C.	-	-
2 Reading v Fulham	-	-
2 Walsall v Wrexham	0-1	3-0
2 Wigan v Oldham Ath.	-	1-0
2 Wycombe W. v Gillingham	1-1	1-1
3 Brentford v Plymouth Ar.	-	3-1
3 Brighton & HA v Cambridge U.	1-2	0-2
3 Cardiff C. v Hull C.	2-0	2-1
3 Chester C. v Barnet	1-0	0-1
3 Exeter C. v Leyton O.	3-2	2-2
3 Halifax T. v Rochdale	-	-
3 Peterborough U. v Darlington	-	1-1
3 Rotherham U. v Swansea C.	-	1-1
3 Scarborough v Carlisle U.	1-1	-
3 Shrewsbury T. v Hartlepool U.	-	1-0

Encounter	96-97	97-98
3 Southend U. v Scunthorpe U.	-	-
3 Torquay U. v Mansfield T.	1-2	2-1

10th April 1999

Encounter	96-97	97-98
1 Barnsley v Tranmere R.	3-0	-
1 Bradford v Portsmouth	3-1	1-3
1 Bristol C. v Grimsby T.	-	4-1
1 Crewe Alex. v Port Vale	-	0-1
1 Norwich C. v Ipswich T.	3-1	2-1
1 Oxford U. v Bury	-	1-1
1 QPR v WBA	0-2	2-0
1 Stockport Co. v Sheffield U.	-	1-0
1 Sunderland v Huddersfield T.	-	3-1
1 Swindon T. v Birmingham C.	3-1	1-1
1 Watford v Bolton W.	-	-
1 Wolverhampton W. v C. Palace	0-3	-
2 Blackpool v Reading	-	-
2 Colchester U. v Walsall	-	-
2 Fulham v Wigan	1-1	2-0
2 Gillingham v Bournemouth	1-1	2-1
2 Macclesfield T. v Preston NE	-	-
2 Manchester C. v Lincoln C.	-	-
2 Northampton T. v Luton T.	-	1-0
2 Notts County v Chesterfield	0-0	-
2 Oldham Ath. v Burnley	-	3-3
2 Stoke C. v Bristol R.	-	-
2 Wrexham v Wycombe W.	2-0	2-0
2 York C. v Millwall	3-2	2-3
3 Barnet v Scarborough	1-3	1-1
3 Cambridge U. v Halifax T.	-	-
3 Carlisle U. v Peterborough U.	-	-
3 Darlington v Torquay U.	2-3	1-2
3 Hartlepool U. v Chester C.	-	0-0
3 Hull C. v Exeter C.	2-0	3-2
3 Leyton O. v Cardiff C.	3-0	0-1
3 Mansfield T. v Southend U.	-	-
3 Plymouth Ar. v Brighton & HA	-	-
3 Rochdale v Rotherham U.	-	0-1
3 Scunthorpe U. v Brentford	-	-
3 Swansea C. v Shrewsbury T.	-	0-1

13th April 1999

Encounter	96-97	97-98
2 Blackpool v Burnley	1-3	2-1
2 Bournemouth v Walsall	0-1	1-0
2 Fulham v Gillingham	-	3-0
2 Lincoln C. v Reading	-	-
2 Macclesfield T. v Chesterfield	-	-
2 Northampton T. v York C.	-	1-1

Encounter	96-97	97-98
2 Notts County v Wrexham	0-0	-
2 Oldham Ath. v Bristol R.	-	4-4
2 Wigan v Preston NE	-	1-4
3 Brighton & HA v Shrewsbury T.	-	0-0
3 Cambridge U. v Rochdale	2-2	1-1
3 Carlisle U. v Hull C.	0-0	-
3 Chester C. v Brentford	-	-
3 Exeter C. v Rotherham U.	3-1	-
3 Leyton O. v Plymouth Ar.	-	-
3 Mansfield T. v Halifax T.	-	-
3 Scunthorpe U. v Peterborough U.	-	1-3
3 Southend U. v Cardiff C.	-	-
3 Swansea C. v Hartlepool U.	2-2	0-2
3 Torquay U. v Barnet	1-2	0-0

14th April 1999

2 Manchester C. v Luton T.	-	-
2 Millwall v Colchester U.	-	-
2 Stoke C. v Wycombe W.	-	-
3 Scarborough v Darlington	4-1	2-1

17th April 1999

1 Barnsley v Sunderland	-	-
1 Birmingham v Wolverhampton W.	1-2	1-0
1 Bolton W. v Ipswich T.	1-2	-
1 Bradford C. v Huddersfield T.	1-1	1-1
1 Crewe Alex. v Watford	-	-
1 C. Palace v Swindon T.	1-2	-
1 Grimsby T. v Bury	-	-
1 Norwich C. v Tranmere R.	1-1	0-2
1 Port Vale v Oxford U.	2-0	3-0
1 Sheffield U. v QPR	1-1	2-2
1 Stockport Co. v Bristol C.	1-1	-
1 WBA v Portsmouth	0-2	0-3
2 Bristol R. v Millwall	1-0	2-1
2 Burnley v Bournemouth	1-0	2-2
2 Chesterfield v Fulham	-	0-2
2 Colchester U. v Notts County	-	-
2 Gillingham v Manchester C.	-	-
2 Luton T. v Lincoln C.	-	-
2 Preston NE v Blackpool	3-0	3-3
2 Reading v Northampton T.	-	-
2 Walsall v Macclesfield T.	-	-
2 Wrexham v Oldham Ath.	-	3-1
2 Wycombe W. v Wigan	-	1-2
2 York C. v Stoke C.	-	-

Encounter	96-97	97-98
3 Barnet v Mansfield T.	1-1	0-1
3 Brentford v Leyton O.	-	-
3 Cardiff C. v Swansea C.	1-3	0-1
3 Darlington v Cambridge U.	2-0	1-1
3 Halifax T. v Brighton & HA	-	-
3 Hartlepool U. v Scarborough	1-0	3-0
3 Hull C. v Scunthorpe U.	0-2	2-1
3 Peterborough U. v Torquay U.	-	2-0
3 Plymouth Ar. v Southend U.	-	-
3 Rochdale v Chester C.	0-1	1-1
3 Rotherham U. v Carlisle U.	-	-
3 Shrewsbury T. v Exeter C.	-	1-1

24th April 1999

1 Bristol C. v Birmingham C.	-	-
1 Bury v Bolton W.	-	-
1 Huddersfield T. v Barnsley	0-0	-
1 Ipswich T. v Crewe Alex.	-	3-2
1 Oxford U. v Norwich C.	0-1	2-0
1 Portsmouth v Stockport Co.	-	1-0
1 QPR v Bradford C.	1-0	1-0
1 Sunderland v Sheffield U.	-	4-2
1 Swindon T. v Grimsby T.	3-3	-
1 Tranmere R. v Port Vale	2-0	1-2
1 Watford v C. Palace	-	-
1 Wolverhampton W. v WBA	2-0	0-1
2 Blackpool v Bristol R.	3-2	1-0
2 Bournemouth v Chesterfield	3-0	-
2 Fulham v Wrexham	-	1-0
2 Lincoln C. v Walsall	-	-
2 Macclesfield T. v York C.	-	-
2 Manchester C. v Wycombe W.	-	-
2 Millwall v Preston NE	3-2	0-1
2 Northampton T. v Colchester U.	2-1	-
2 Notts County v Luton T.	1-2	-
2 Oldham Ath. v Gillingham	-	3-1
2 Stoke C. v Burnley	-	-
2 Wigan v Reading	-	-
3 Brighton & HA v Hull C.	3-0	2-2
3 Cambridge U. v Peterborough U.	-	1-0
3 Carlisle U. v Darlington	1-0	-
3 Chester C. v Halifax T.	-	-
3 Exeter C. v Rochdale	0-0	3-0
3 Leyton O. v Shrewsbury T.	-	2-3
3 Mansfield T. v Hartlepool U.	1-0	2-2
3 Scarborough v Cardiff C.	0-0	3-1
3 Scunthorpe U. v Barnet	1-2	1-1
3 Southend U. v Brentford	-	3-1

Encounter	96-97	97-98
3 Swansea C. v Plymouth Ar.	-	-
3 Torquay U. v Rotherham U.	-	1-2

1st May 1999

Encounter	96-97	97-98
1 Barnsley v Watford	-	
1 Birmingham C. v Ipswich T.	1-0	1-1
1 Bolton W. v Wolverhampton W.	3-0	
1 Bradford C. v Oxford U.	2-0	0-0
1 Crewe Alex. v Portsmouth	-	3-1
1 C. Palace v Huddersfield T.	1-1	
1 Grimsby T. v Tranmere R.	0-0	
1 Norwich C. v Swindon T.	2-0	5-0
1 Port Vale v QPR	4-4	2-0
1 Sheffield U. v Bristol C.	-	
1 Stockport Co. v Sunderland	-	1-1
1 WBA v Bury	-	1-1
2 Bristol R. v Manchester C.	-	-
2 Burnley v Fulham	-	2-1
2 Chesterfield v Northampton T.	-	2-1
2 Colchester U. v Lincoln C.	7-1	-
2 Gillingham v Stoke C.	-	-
2 Luton T. v Macclesfield T.	-	-
2 Preston NE v Notts County	2-0	-
2 Reading v Millwall	-	-
2 Walsall v Oldham Ath.	-	0-0
2 Wrexham v Wigan	-	2-2
2 Wycombe W. v Blackpool	1-0	2-1
2 York C. v Bournemouth	1-2	0-1
3 Barnet v Southend U.	-	-
3 Brentford v Exeter C.	-	-
3 Cardiff C. v Scunthorpe U.	0-0	0-0
3 Darlington v Chester C.	1-1	1-0
3 Halifax T. v Scarborough	-	-
3 Hartlepool U. v Carlisle U.	1-2	-
3 Hull C. v Torquay U.	2-0	3-3
3 Peterborough U. v Leyton O.	-	2-0
3 Plymouth Ar. v Cambridge U.	-	
3 Rochdale v Swansea C.	2-2	3-0
3 Rotherham U. v Brighton & HA	-	0-0
3 Shrewsbury T. v Mansfield T.	-	3-2

8th May 1999

Encounter	96-97	97-98
2 Blackpool v Colchester U.	-	-
2 Bournemouth v Wrexham	2-1	0-1
2 Fulham v Preston NE	-	2-1
2 Lincoln C. v Wycombe W.	-	-
2 Macclesfield T. v Bristol R.	-	-
2 Manchester C. v York C.	-	-
2 Millwall v Luton T.	0-1	0-2
2 Northampton T. v Burnley	-	0-1
2 Notts County v Gillingham	1-1	-
2 Oldham Ath. v Reading	1-1	-
2 Stoke C. v Walsall	-	-
2 Wigan v Chesterfield	-	2-1
3 Brighton & HA v Rochdale	3-0	2-1
3 Cambridge U. v Brentford	-	-
3 Carlisle U. v Plymouth Ar.	-	2-2
3 Chester C. v Rotherham U.	-	4-0
3 Exeter C. v Halifax T.	-	-
3 Leyton O. v Barnet	0-1	2-0
3 Mansfield T. v Cardiff C.	1-3	1-2
3 Scarborough v Peterborough U.	-	1-3
3 Scunthorpe U. v Darlington	3-2	1-0
3 Southend U. v Hartlepool U.	-	-
3 Swansea C. v Hull C.	0-0	2-0
3 Torquay U. v Shrewsbury T.	-	3-0

9th May 1999

Encounter	96-97	97-98
1 Bristol C. v Norwich C.	-	
1 Bury v Port Vale	-	2-2
1 Huddersfield T. v Crewe Alex.	-	2-0
1 Ipswich T. v Sheffield U.	3-1	2-2
1 Oxford U. v Stockport Co.	-	3-0
1 Portsmouth v Bolton W.	0-3	
1 QPR v C. Palace	0-1	
1 Sunderland v Birmingham C.	-	1-1
1 Swindon T. v Barnsley	3-0	
1 Tranmere R. v WBA	2-3	0-0
1 Watford v Grimsby T.	-	0-0
1 Wolverhampton W. v Bradford C.	1-0	2-1